EMOTIONAL GROWTH AND LEARNING

An appreciation of the processes in social interactions and relationships which influence emotional growth and learning is important for work with all children, and especially those who are troubled.

A timely contribution to the debate on work with children experiencing emotional and behavioural difficulties, *Emotional Growth and Learning* clarifies these processes and serves as a practical and theoretical resource for the training of teachers and other professionals. Paul Greenhalgh illustrates the relevant concepts with case studies drawn from his own experience. He also provides individual and group exercises which help adults to explore the nature of their own participation in facilitating emotional growth and learning.

The book's multi-disciplinary approach and accessible style will appeal to teachers in mainstream and special schools, researchers and professionals in the related fields of educational psychology, counselling and social work, as well as to parents.

Paul Greenhalgh is an adviser with responsibility for Personal and Social Education in the London Borough of Merton, where he was previously Advisory Teacher for Special Educational Needs. He has taught in mainstream schools and in support services for children with emotional/behavioural difficulties. He has provided training in association with the University of London, and was a tutor on Westminster Pastoral Foundation's Counselling Course.

EMOTIONAL GROWTH AND LEARNING

Paul Greenhalgh

London and New York

First published 1994
by Routledge
11 New Fetter Lane, London EC4P 4EE

Simultaneously published in the USA and Canada
by Routledge
29 West 35th Street, New York, NY 10001

© 1994 Paul Greenhalgh

Typeset in Baskerville by LaserScript, Mitcham, Surrey
Printed and bound in Great Britain by
Biddles Ltd, Guildford and King's Lynn

British Library Cataloguing in Publication Data
A catalogue record for this book is available from the British Library.

Library of Congress Cataloging in Publication Data
Greenhalgh, Paul.
Emotional growth and learning / Paul Greenhalgh.
p. cm.
Includes bibliographical references (p.   ) and index.
1. Emotions and cognition.   2. Affective education.
3. Child development.   4. Learning, Psychology of.
5. Problem children–Education–Great Britain.
I. Title.
LB1073.G74   1994
370.15'3—dc20   93-24329
                                                            CIP

ISBN 0–415–10133–6 (hbk)
ISBN 0–415–10134–4 (pbk)

For troubled children
who are waiting
to see the start of spring

CONTENTS

CONTENTS

Part II Facilitating emotional growth and learning

CONTENTS

FIGURES

EXERCISES

Key: *   Most suitable for individual work.
         **   Most suitable for work in pairs.
         ***   Most suitable for work in groups.

ACKNOWLEDGEMENTS

I wish to thank the editors of journals who have given permission for material, mostly in reworked form, to be republished. Chapter Five is a reworking and extension of 'The Discovery of Learning through Involvement with the Imaginal', *The Journal of Educational Therapy*, 2, 2. The first part of Chapter Seven is based on 'Working with Groups: The Function of the Group in work with Children with Emotional and Behavioural Difficulties', *Maladjustment and Therapeutic Education*, 9, 1. Some of the case material was previously published in 'The Holding/Letting Go Dialectic as a Factor in the Recovery of Learning', *Maladjustment and Therapeutic Education*, 5, 3, and in 'The Creative Tension of Separation and Integration: Processes in Support Provision for Children with Emotional and Behavioural Difficulties', *European Journal of Special Needs Education*, 6, 3.

I am grateful to Bruce Reed and the Grubb Institute for permission to quote extensively from *An Introduction to Organisational Behaviour* (1972), a new edition of which is being submitted for publication. I acknowledge with thanks permission from *Special Children* to print diagrams by Janet Spillman (as Figures 27 and 28), and to Alfred A. Knopf Inc. and Faber and Faber for permission to reprint part of 'Prologues to What is Possible', from *Collected Poems* by Wallace Stevens (Copyright 1952 by Wallace Stevens).

My thanks also go to Mary Brown and Linda Murgatroyd for permission to make use of material from their professional practice.

The encouragement, support and detailed editorial comments of Stephen Jusypiw have been of considerable value, and for this I would like to express my gratitude. Finally, I would like to thank Philip Maggs, Bani Shorter and Peter Masani for their inspiration, insights and support some years ago in my attempts to realise and to put into practice many of the ideas which became the foundation for this book.

INTRODUCTION

... he knew that likeness of him extended
Only a little way, and not beyond, unless between himself
And things beyond resemblance there was this and that intended to
be recognised,
. . .

What self, for example, did he contain that had not yet been loosed,
Snarling in him for discovery as his attentions spread,
As if all his hereditary lights were suddenly increased
. . .

The way the earliest single light in the evening sky, in spring,
Creates a fresh universe out of nothingness by adding itself,
The way a look or a touch reveals its unexpected magnitudes.
        'Prologues to What is Possible', Wallace Stevens, 1952

Children and young people who are troubled and suffering emotional
distress not only trouble others with whom they come into contact, but find
it difficult to be available for learning, and often give the impression of
being stuck, somehow frozen, in their difficulties. The frozen landscape
can be a very painful one, and very often the children and those who work
with them, as well as their family and friends, strive for distraction from the
pain. Those who work with distressed children naturally become drawn into
making responses which help one to feel that one has 'tried to do
something', sometimes at the expense of approaching and responding to
the children's disturbing feelings, and therefore appropriately meeting
their needs. Troubled children present themselves within all educational
and social service settings. This book is about working and relating with
such children to help them to come to terms with their difficulties, and to
help strengthen their inner resources so that they may become more
self-aware, autonomous and open to learning. This process is symbolised in

1

the start of spring, a time when natural, organic processes take over, nourish growth, and provide the resources necessary to cope with the next winter. This book is not concerned, metaphorically, with the garden planted with annuals, but with gardens of perennials cared for with respect for their own organic life.

Awkward, irritating and painful feelings can play a powerful role in getting in the way of learning. The realm of feelings, of our subjective experiences, can indeed both facilitate and inhibit growth, development and learning. In the sometimes troubling experience of working with children in distress, difficult feelings can be aroused in teachers and other workers, as well as in other children, and the adult's capacity for reflection upon his/her work can be hampered. Yet the capacity to provide for the needs of disturbing children is powerfully enhanced when the adult is able to reflect upon, and respond to, what is happening in relationships with the child – in other words, when the adult consciously works from an understanding of the processes of development and interaction. This is the field of enquiry of this book. The core of the discussion is the processes of taking account of emotional aspects of experience, to facilitate emotional growth and to enable children to become more autonomous learners, able to take more effective responsibility for themselves.

This book speaks to the developmental needs of all children. It is where things go wrong in interaction and emotional experience that we are obliged to pay more attention to these realms, and so it relates particularly to the needs of children experiencing emotional/behavioural difficulties. The writing has emerged from the experiences of working with troubled and troublesome children, of trying to understand both their experiences and my own. I taught children experiencing emotional and behavioural difficulties in mainstream schools, a unit for 'disruptive' 14–16 year olds, and a tutorial unit. The last of these was part of a support service for students aged 5–16 with emotional difficulties, and for their teachers and parents (and is described more fully in Appendix One). The writing of this book has also been informed by working with teachers consultatively and as a trainer (in an advisory teacher capacity), and working with multi-professional groups as a teacher of counselling skills.

By way of introduction, a historical perspective on perceptions of work with children with emotional/behavioural difficulties leads to the assertion that we are at a point in time when we need to rethink our work in this field. I argue that such a rethink is necessary because of a crisis in the public services in work with troubled children, and also because of the need to re-examine our conceptual frameworks. I argue for the importance of an approach based on an understanding and awareness of *how* things are done, of the processes of interaction. Finally, in this introduction, I make some comments about using this book.

2

HISTORICAL PERSPECTIVES

Perceptions of special educational needs and of troubled and troublesome children have varied in relation to changing attitudes in society and government legislation. In the period immediately after the Second World War, the prevailing perception of children thought of then as 'maladjusted' was that they were ill. This was largely due to the prevalence of the medically oriented model and medical terminology. Although the Underwood Report of the Committee on Maladjusted Children (1955) acknowledged some difficulties in relation to the 1944 Education Act, the tenor of the report reflected prevailing attitudes and the continuing predominance of the medical model. Laslett (1983: 11) argues that from 1945 to 1970, the tendency to regard 'maladjusted' children as being ill or sick was greater than was legitimate. Some headteachers in this period did acknowledge that some children who showed signs of emotional disturbance and who were difficult to manage were probably reacting in a healthy way to environmental factors, but most maladjusted children were perceived as suffering from neurotic illnesses of childhood; the model was based on illness rather than reaction to the environment. In the model of 'illness', individuals are considered to be ill, irrespective of their environment, and this perception reinforced notions of the children's passivity and dependence (Laslett 1983).

In the 1960s, perspectives began to change. For example, Becker (1963) argued that deviance does not lie in behaviour but in the interaction between the person who commits an act and those who respond to it. Similarly, Ullman and Krasner (1965) made the case that so-called 'abnormal' behaviour is an interaction of the behaviour itself, its social context, and an observer who is in a position of power. It was beginning to be more widely recognised that 'so much maladjustment is interactional and may well be context-bound' (Laslett 1983: 21). During the 1970s there was a resurgence of the behaviourist school, which, with its emphasis on learned behaviour, helped to challenge the long-held belief in the difference between the handicapped and the non-handicapped, between the perception of what is normal and what is abnormal.

The Warnock Report (DES 1978) took the view that one in five pupils have special educational needs at some time in their school career, and recommended the abolition of the statutory categorisation of pupils by type of disability or disorder, ending the rigid distinction between the handicapped and the non-handicapped. A broader concept of special educational needs was recognised, relating to the child's individual needs, as distinct from his/her disability. Rather than being called 'maladjusted', children were seen to have 'emotional and behavioural difficulties'. Perceptions of the child as having a deficit were giving way to the idea of the child having special educational needs. Under the 1981 Education Act, which incorporated many of the recommendations of the Warnock Report, a child is defined as needing special educational provision (which can be made in many ways) if s/he has a disability which interferes with her/his education, or if s/he has a significantly greater difficulty in learning than the majority of children of her/his age. Whilst the 1981 Education Act has the overt intention of more effectively meeting individual needs which arise from learning difficulties, its focus on the individual learner serves to perpetuate the idea that factors which may inhibit learning are located in the individual rather than in the learning environment (Cline 1990).

The report chaired by Fish, *Educational Opportunities for All?* (ILEA 1985), did much to influence the perception of the importance of context in defining special educational needs. The report emphasised the dynamic and relative aspects of development and viewed special educational needs as a function more of context than of factors in the child:

> Special educational needs arise from learning difficulties and limitations of access to the educational provision made for all. Most can only be defined precisely by individual schools in terms of the flexibility of their approach to individual differences. . . . Our definition of handicap is a dynamic and relative one. Disabilities and difficulties become more or less handicapping depending on the expectations of others and on social contexts. Handicaps thus arise from the mismatch between the intellectual, physical, emotional and social behaviour and aspirations of the individual and the expectations, or otherwise, of the community and society at large. Individuals with disabilities or significant difficulties may be handicapped by their own attitude to them and by the attitudes of others. Of equal significance, the degree to which the individual is handicapped is determined by the educational, social, physical and emotional situations which he or she encounters. Handicapping effects will vary from situation to situation and may change over time.
>
> (ILEA 1985: 3–4)

With regard to emotional and behavioural difficulties, the dynamic and relative definition of special educational need reinforced the notion of 'disturbing' children, rather than 'disturbed' children, implying the significance of the interactive and contextual dimensions.

Today, pupils with special educational needs continue to be seen not as a fixed group, but as individuals whose needs vary over time and in response to school policies and teaching (National Curriculum Council 1989a). A special educational need is not a static thing. Rather than clear and discrete categories of need, there is a continuum of need, and individuals may occupy a different place on the continuum at different times. This is the case in the area of emotional and behavioural difficulties more than any other. No sharp boundary can be drawn between 'pupils

4

who are "dissatisfied" or who become unco-operative, and those deemed "maladjusted" and therefore in need of special educational provision' (ILEA 1984: 1).

In general terms, schools have been able to consider their practices in response to these changing notions of special educational needs relating to context. Her Majesty's Inspectorate comment that it is generally agreed that 'the main features of practice which resulted in work of at least satisfactory standard among pupils with special educational needs also constituted good practice for all pupils' (DES 1989b: 2). This principle relates also to work with children with emotional and behavioural difficulties. Galloway and Goodwin (1987) show that, in general, schools which cater successfully for their most disturbing pupils also cater successfully for the rest of their pupils. Some years ago, a study by Kounin *et al.* (1966), investigating the effect of teaching styles on the progress and behaviour of 'maladjusted' children in American primary schools, concluded that the approaches which are most effective in responding to 'disturbed' behaviour are not special or different, but are those which are most effective with all pupils.

Schools did address themselves to the implications of the changes in perception in the relationship between special educational needs and social context. These changes were reflected in the changing attitudes and practices of schools. It became widely recognised that the school has a major impact upon the perception of needs, and upon the way in which they are created or met. This was reflected in the wealth of evidence submitted to the Elton Committee (Galloway 1990).

These changes in perception and practice resulted in widespread consideration and active work upon a range of issues: the interaction between teachers and learners having an impact on the creation and meeting of special educational needs; curriculum modification being targeted at teaching methods and materials in general rather than exclusively at the lower attainers; the curriculum being viewed as ripe for differentiation and a source of new learning and solutions found within the classroom; the importance of whole-school approaches, and of collaborative and team work; perceptions and attitudes needing to be understood as much as practical stategies; and the possibility that training for co-operative teaching, and consultancy between staff, might include an emphasis on communication skills. Such issues have been an integral part of the thinking of advances in practice introduced through initiatives such as GCSE, Records of Achievement, the Technical and Vocational Educational Initiative, etc. (e.g. Gleeson 1987, Hitchcock 1988).

The 1988 Education Reform Act, providing the legal framework for an entitlement to a broad and balanced curriculum, could benefit children with special educational needs if implemented sensitively, so that special educational needs issues are perceived as an integral part of improving access to the curriculum for all. Within such a framework, assessment and record keeping are perceived as improving diagnosis for the benefit of all, and children with special educational needs will not be marginalised.

However, the government has very much shifted priorities away from special educational needs, and, in relation to such needs, gains made through the Warnock Report and the 1981 Act are at risk. Teaching in relation to attainment targets and standard tests of a limited nature increases pressure to teach to targets and subject-matter at the expense of responding to needs, and gives an impetus to bald, undifferentiated teaching, aimed at the middle ground. Testing (through which some children may be more likely to perceive themselves as failures), and the option for schools to exclude special needs in their published Standard Assessment Test results, produce further marginalisation. There is evidence to show that local management of schools (LMS) tempts heads and governors to target resources to pupils who they think will gain the most favourable test and exam results (e.g. Channel 4, *Class Action*, 28 January 1992). The policy of open enrolment, within an LMS climate, poses difficult questions for schools about what priorities a school will adopt in relation to its ethos and special educational needs, and how to develop an acceptable public relations and marketing stance in relation to this area of work. Governors are overwhelmed by the extent of their new duties (NUT 1990a). There is a danger that the special needs of those children without statutory statements of special educational needs (under the 1981 act) will be overlooked, and that, for the newly powerful governors, special educational needs will become associated with negative tasks such as procedures for disapplication from the National Curriculum, and parental appeals. 'There is a need for vigilance in case governing bodies are refusing to admit pupils with special educational needs because of lack of finance or fear about the school's image in relation to competitive test results' (NUT 1990b: 3).

The 1988 Education Reform Act heralded the enterprise culture in education: 'the day of the consumer and the market has arrived' (Shipman 1990: 47). This supposedly gives the consumer a wider range of choice and enables schools specialising in particular curricular areas to emerge, providing a greater range of learning opportunities through the resultant diversity. However, in the context of local financial management, league tables, open enrolment and governmental encouragement of grant maintained status, schools' survival or growth is related to being seen to perform well within a narrowly focused definition of education based upon accredited attainments.

There is already evidence that, rather than pupils and parents having greater choice of school, schools are choosing their children: nearly a third of opted out comprehensive schools have used interviews and exam results to select pupils for over-subscribed places (*Times Educational Supplement*, 10

April 1992). The 'emerging stratification of schools not only rests upon a competition between schools, it also creates the basis for a large-scale return to competition for places between pupils' (Ball 1990: 93). Thompson and Barton (1992: 13) take up the theme: 'The real worry is that winners in such a context will be at the expense of others. Family background and geographical location, for example, will influence the nature and extent of the benefits pupils receive in a diverse system of school provision.' So in the wake of the Education Reform Act learners with special educational needs are particularly vulnerable, and if many such pupils are to be found in the least successful schools they could become the educational underclass of the future (Witty and Menter 1991).

In this climate, when children with special educational needs have become so vulnerable, those with emotional and behavioural difficulties are potentially at the most risk, not only since these children can be difficult to work with, but because of the potential negative impact upon perceptions of the school and its public persona.

THE NEED FOR A RETHINK

Crisis in the public services

Today there is a crisis in the services offered by the helping professions – in schools and in social service departments – to children experiencing emotional/behavioural difficulties.

In schools, this crisis was heralded by Her Majesty's Inspectorate, who concluded that 'Schooling for pupils with emotional and behavioural difficulties gives particular cause for concern' (DES 1990: viii). A slightly earlier survey specifically on provision for children with emotional and behavioural difficulties found that:

> All the schools placed a high priority on promoting the personal and social development of their pupils. While personal and social relationships were generally good and pupils were treated with care and consideration, it was unusual to find carefully planned arrangements or well thought out policies for meeting their personal and social needs on a systematic and developmental basis.
>
> (DES 1989a: 14)

These concerns were present before the impact of the Education Reform Act had time to take hold.

More recently we are witnessing some of the more 'raw' effects of the ERA. There is a growing mass of evidence (e.g. Association of Educational Psychologists 1992) that the rate of expulsions for children with emotional/behavioural difficulties is increasing dramatically. In open competition for survival in the market place, the Education Reform Act has had the effect of making schools much less willing to spend time and resources on needy and demanding children. With public image at the forefront of schools' minds, children with emotional and behavioural difficulties do not appear 'market friendly'. With the limits imposed by the Education Reform Act and subsequent legislation to the proportion of education spending decided by LEAs, LEA special educational needs support services are not only endangered (e.g. NUT 1990a), but undergoing severe cuts. Educational psychologists are burdened by the statutory requirements imposed by the 1981 Act, and have less and less time to work consultatively with schools on issues which go beyond the individual child. Many child guidance services have been abolished or cut severely (Bennathan 1992). The current trend of closures of residential schools for children with emotional and behavioural difficulties (e.g. in 1992 Red Hill, Chalvington and St Francis schools) is evidence of the decline in local authority funding of placements in residential schools. LEAs no longer have the power or the resources to soften blows imposed upon mainstream schools and to offer supportive consultation. The challenge and the onus are directly upon schools to find more creative ways of engaging and working positively with troubled children and young people.

Within the social service sector concern has become acute about some practices in residential child care in particular, and about the poor level of training of staff working in the field. The Levy-Kahan Report into the 'pin-down' scandals in Staffordshire spoke to the need for improvements in residential treatment. The report, *Children in the Public Care* (Department of Health 1991), by Sir William Utting, Chief Social Services Inspector, points out that hitherto, in spite of the best intentions, children whose families cannot care for them adequately have often been disadvantaged and stigmatised, and that the rapid decline over the last decade in the number of children in residential care has resulted in 'a loss of purpose and direction, deficiencies in policy and management, a largely unqualified and inexperienced staff, and problems of control' (Department of Health 1991, quoted in Bennathan 1992: 46).

This crisis has grave implications. For those providing educational services which involve encouraging emotional growth, the external pressures are immense. The exertion associated with the amount of change required in our schools, along with the unfamiliar pressures of the market system, have a significant impact on the levels of staff anxiety and morale. This, in turn, detrimentally affects capacities for patience and tolerance. 'The widely held opinion is that the level of tolerance in schools for difficult and disturbed children has dropped sharply' (Bennathan 1992: 39). Such a climate is the antithesis of an environment which facilitates emotional development.

Moreover, there are growing numbers of young people who, excluded from school, face increasing alienation and despair. Bennathan speaks eloquently of the implications:

> It also needs to be widely recognised that the problems of disturbed or disruptive children inadequately helped quickly become the problems of society. Some of them become the psychopaths, the criminals, the thugs, the hooligans that lower the quality of life in many of our towns. They also become a serious burden on services for adults, in prisons, in hospitals, and in the trail of social disaster they leave behind them in their family lives. Many mildly disturbed young people who are excluded from school could with adequate support be helped through their difficulties. Instead they are left rejected and turn in despair to the only social groups that will give them some self-esteem. There is at present great public concern about drug and substance abuse, about vandalism, joyriding, public disorder, burglaries, homelessness, prostitution and alcoholism in the young. These are not disconnected phenomena. They are the end result of systems which have failed to protect properly, to nurture, to educate.
>
> (Bennathan 1992: 48–9)

Changing language and concepts

Ever since the needs of troubled children and young people have been recognised in educational circles, there have been different views about the place of the curriculum, therapeutic approaches and behaviour management in meeting their needs. Reinert (1976) suggested a plethora of approaches to these issues, which included the biophysical, psychodynamic, behavioural and socio-ecological perspectives. A time of crisis in service delivery prompts a questionning of the very language and conceptual frameworks upon which the work rests. 'The vocabulary of special needs has become threadbare and deficient and has tended to reduce all problems to a learning and behavioural perspective and to ignore the individual weaknesses and strengths of children and their families' (Rimmer 1992: 58). This situation has its impact on practice. Norwich (1990) notes that school-based experiences which have rehabilitative or restorative goals are often viewed as the prerogative of the specialist, not part of the ordinary school programme. Yet, if such work is to be possible in today's climate, it needs to be accommodated within the broad curricular framework.

In examining recent developments Mongan and Hart explain them in terms of changes in the underlying paradigm:

> The shift of emphasis towards a whole-school policy is sometimes described in terms of a move away from the deficit or medical model of special education towards a more environmental or ecological

9

model. . . . The ecological model starts from the position that the growth and development of children can be understood only in relation to the nature of their interactions with the various environments which impinge on them and with which they are constantly interacting.

(Mongan and Hart 1989: xi)

Others are beginning to see the value of the combination of an 'ecological' and systems approach in this field (e.g. Upton and Cooper 1990). Feiler and Thomas (1992) argue the need for an ecological model in relation to a range of special educational needs.

Potentially, an ecological approach seeks to integrate an understanding of inner experience and its relationships with the world at intra-personal, inter-personal, group and institutional levels. This reflects a growing concern for more holistic approaches: 'The new vision of reality . . . is based on awareness of the essential interrelatedness and interdependence of all phenomena – physical, biological, psychological, social and cultural' (Capra 1982: 285). From the perspective of individual development, an ecological approach is similar to Bowlby's idea of developmental pathways, which 'regards an infant at birth as having an array of pathways potentially open to him, the one along which he will in fact proceed being determined at every moment by the interaction of the individual as he now is with the environment in which he happens then to be' (Bowlby 1988: 136). Norwich (1990) argues that the dichotomy between interactive and within-child models of special educational needs is false. The search for a more holistic conceptualisation carries with it an increasing recognition of the importance not of cause and effect, but of process, or the impact of interaction. 'The dynamics of life are such that every experience and attitude and thought of every individual is constantly changing in relation to the interplay of psychological and environmental forces upon each and every individual' (Axline 1989: 10).

This debate takes place at a time of increasing publicity and concern, not only over public service provision, but over various forms of child abuse. It seems as if the pain of those children in our societies who are experiencing emotional distress is demanding to be heard and given adequate response; as if service providers are being challenged to struggle with their language, concepts and understanding. We are summoned towards renewal, towards a more holistic pattern of connections in helping us to make sense of emotional growth and learning. The challenge lies in developing our language and understanding in ways which acknowledge and reflect the meaning of children's dilemmas; which help us return the humanity to our thinking and practice; which enable us to make effective use of our relationships and the curriculum; and which help us to provide responsive yet flexible services in a rapidly changing environment.

'PROCESS' THINKING

Our capacities to be effective in promoting the emotional development of children depend on our understanding and our deployment of understanding in the way we manage relationships, classrooms and the wider school or other organisation. When children's learning is impeded by distress or intense feelings, teachers' attitudes towards, and skills in, interactive processes are a significant factor in meeting (or creating additional) special educational needs. 'Process' understanding is concerned with the impact of interaction. The importance of interaction for the proactive work of the teacher is well recognised. For example Jordan (1974, quoted in Mongan and Hart 1989) distinguishes two types of teacher: the 'deviance-provocative' teacher, and the 'deviance-insulative' teacher whose handling of problem behaviour serves to inhibit it. But if we are to make the most effective use of thinking about interactive processes, then we must be prepared to consider honestly our own individual impact upon interaction. 'Alongside extending our knowledge and skills we must develop an ever more conscious use and presentation of self. . . . developing essential insight [is] born of bringing oneself more centrally into the frame of reference' (Rollinson 1992: 16–17). Then we must look at the way we relate, the communications we make about all the various factors which influence the capacity for learning for each child. We must be as conscious as we can, in order to minimise any detrimental unconscious communications which may inhibit development. So taking due account of process requires reflective consideration of our attitudes, approaches and the way in which communications are made, rather than the easy application of 'techniques picked from a shelf'. That is why some of the exercises in this book are concerned with aspects of self-awareness important in helping troubled children. (The exercises are discussed further later in this introduction.)

The capacity a person has for learning, at any one time, is a function of the sense s/he makes of the experiences of interaction both in the here and now and in events in the past. This includes all experiences of interaction, with individuals and groups, family and friends, and in institutions, for example with teachers. Inevitably some of the interaction in these environments is affected by the wider social, political, cultural and economic environment. What each of us makes of all these experiences depends partly on the way in which they reflect and confirm our inner world (or intra-personal experience). There is a dynamic relationship between the way we relate inter-personally, and our intra-personal experience. The troubles of disturbed and disturbing children present themselves in relationships, and also in their inner worlds (see Figure 1).

Developing understanding of the multi-faceted nature of processes involved in influencing the capacity for learning enables and enhances the

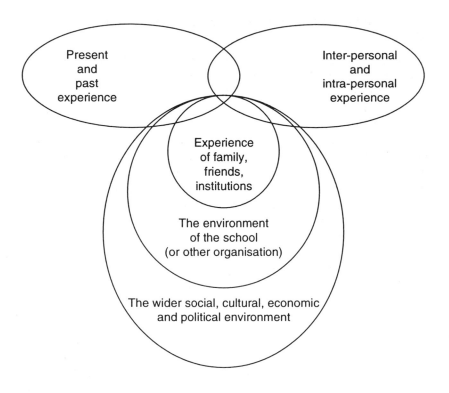

Figure 1 Factors influencing the capacity for learning

teachers' abilities to work with these processes in order to improve access to learning. Interaction has a powerful effect upon development. How any of us experiences interaction can make a difference to our subjective experience of the world, and hence the ways in which we relate to the world. Helping damaged children to change their experience of the world requires us to increase our understanding of process, and put our understanding into effect through relationship. If we take a 'process' view of interaction then we recognise that:

- Human conditions are never static, but change in relation to factors in the outer environment and in our inner worlds.
- Our experience of relationship affects us both consciously and unconsciously.
- Our experience of relationship affects our capacities to overcome our difficulties and to be in touch with, and show, our potentials.
- Work takes place through a process of interventions – a whole series of actions – at various levels.

12

- *How* something is done can have as much effect as, or more than, *what* is done.

The last of these features of 'process' thinking and relating is amplified by the words of the popular song about it not being *what* you say or do, but the *way* that you say/do it which gets results. Zinkin (1991: 60–1) suggests that, for prose purposes, the lyrics could be amended to 'It's not so much what you do – the most important thing is the way you do it. That's what gets results.' In thinking about facilitating emotional growth and learning, this book is less concerned with *what* one might do than with one's *awareness* of how one intervenes. Reflection and understanding are the bases for doing.

Rogers (1961: 122) argues that individuals who become themselves seem 'to be more content to be a *process* rather than a *product*'. In educational circles there is a habit of valuing 'process' less than 'content'. The Education Reform Act's introduction of the National Curriculum could be interpreted as reinforcing this situation. In secondary schools in particular, the prevailing culture has reinforced the notion of teaching subjects – i.e. content – rather than young people – i.e. process. The emphasis on content, to the detriment of process, is also the case in relation to initial teacher training:

> It would seem sensible that the main thrust of teacher training should be divided between contents which involves the organisation of the material to be taught and the process, which refers to the set of relationships within which the learning takes place. Historically, however, this has never been the case and the power in teacher training has always been in the hands of educators largely concerned with content.

> (Hall and Hall 1988: 1)

One of the more unfortunate effects of the introduction of the National Curriculum is to reinforce the domination, in Britain's education system, of left-hand side of the brain thinking. It can be said (e.g. George 1991) that 70 per cent of the National Curriculum, with its emphasis on the cognitive and the rational, is concerned with left-brained thinking. 'Process' thinking involves the left and the right sides of the brain functions, a way of thinking which promotes synthesis, 'ecological' thought, and the perception of all phenomena as intrinsically dynamically interrelated. Change, in this view, does not occur as a consequence of some force, but in relationship to all things and situations.

Exploring the effect of the various dimensions of relating and feeling upon development and learning is the major theme of this book. Particularly in the case of children with emotional and behavioural difficulties, the factors affecting the capacity for learning are related to the capacity for relationship. In order to enable such children to improve

13

access to learning, one has to pay particular attention to processes of relationship. A major aim of this book is to consider how to facilitate the learning of pupils – particularly those with emotional and behavioural difficulties – through setting out principles of emotional process, and demonstrating the practical value of 'process' thinking and relating. An understanding of processes of relationship, as this applies to the teaching and learning of children with emotional and behavioural difficulties, is the most fundamental factor in enhancing the capacity of teachers to facilitate the learning of disturbing children. The processes of emotional development and learning are considered in relation to the child's inner world, the child's experience of key relationships, the child's experience of groups, and the experience of the classroom and the wider school (or other organisation).

USING THIS BOOK

The process approach of this book relates to practice in a range of schools – from the 'EBD' boarding school to the local mainstream school – and other organisations working with children. Whilst focusing on emotional growth and learning, and thus of specific importance to schools, the book is also relevant to social workers, including those involved in residential social work. The processes have implications for teachers and other educationalists, counsellors, educational psychologists, social workers, administrators, managers and trainers. The book is a synthesis of experience and theory. The aim throughout is to consider how process helps practice, and to encourage reflective teaching, in which practice is informed by understanding. Discussion, examples and suggested exercises are used. Below I give an overview of the content of the book, and then discuss the features of the way in which the book is organised, particularly in relation to case examples and exercises.

In Part One the factors which help and hinder emotional development and learning are explored. Chapter One explores the relationship between feelings or affect and learning, and then goes on to consider the emotional or affective needs for learning to take place. Chapter Two continues the consideration of the links between affect and learning, and focuses upon those processes which inhibit development. Here the emphasis is on understanding and making sense of behaviours and feelings which can seem confusing, perplexing and irritating. Empirical examples are linked to the relevant theoretical insights. These chapters explore the issues which need to be taken into account in order to understand what might affect the child's developmental processes. Particular significance is given to the child's experience of the *qualities* of relationship. The issues explored in Chapters One and Two clarify the conditions which foster and inhibit emotional development and learning, a necessary basis for the subsequent formulation of the processes of facilitating emotional development and learning.

Part Two focuses upon the processes of working to facilitate emotional development and learning. Chapter Three explores the significance of attitudes to difficult behaviours and feelings, and presents the attitudes for facilitating the processes of emotional development and learning. Issues involved in observing and assessing children's emotional and developmental needs within a 'process' perspective are highlighted. In Chapter Four appropriate responses to children's needs are considered. The chapter focuses upon the qualities of experience necessary to facilitate development. The provision of emotional holding is considered to be the essential ingredient in helping children to feel safe. Where a child's sense of safety is particularly insecure, there may be a need to provide what is referred to as 'emotional holding' over an exended period. This is an area of work in which the positive image of the 'container' plays a vital role. Chapter Four emphasises the processes of helping children to develop the rudiments of inner strength necessary for learning, and the related affective dimensions in the relationship between child and adult, teacher and pupil.

However, emotional change cannot merely be willed to happen. Development is helped by providing appropriate opportunities to work on issues at an inner level and to find personally meaningful resolutions. Chapter Five explores the role of image and metaphor in communication and development. The chapter explores first of all what the use of imagery and metaphor can do in this regard. The question of how to facilitate such work is then examined.

Even where present in a rudimentary form, inner strengths and self-esteem need to be nurtured if they are to continue to develop and support the child's growing potential. Chapter Six explores ways of supporting children to enhance their inner strengths and their sense of esteem, of empowering children, through using words to foster related-ness. Issues in talking and counselling are considered. Ways of supporting children to make better relationships with peers are discussed. In the notion of supporting children through the stages of emotional holding, strengthening and using image and metaphor, progress does not take place neatly from one stage to another, but through work at multiple levels simultaneously. The processes involved in these 'stages' are in dynamic relationship with each other. Change is brought about not by single actions or events, but by a whole series of multi-dimensional processes.

Chapter Seven goes on to consider working with the group dimension. In what ways can an understanding of group processes be useful in educational settings? The opportunities provided by the group context are first of all considered, followed by a discussion of group phenomena which inhibit development. The implications for facilitating groups are then examined.

All the processes considered thus far are vital in helping children with emotional/behavioural difficulties to have access to the curriculum. Chapter Eight looks at the ways in which the teacher should take into account these process factors in mediating the curriculum so that troubled children may relate more readily with it. The first part of the chapter focuses on current tensions in curriculum planning to meet individual needs. The second part is a more practical look at emotional factors in providing a differentiated curriculum.

Chapter Nine moves to the dimension of the school/organisation as a system. The processes which inhibit the effective functioning of an organisation are first considered. Then the implications for providing an effective organisational base for meeting the needs of emotional development and learning are examined.

The layout of the text is designed to facilitate access to the various components of the book according to personal taste and need. The case examples and the exercises are presented in a distinctive way to enable the book to be used flexibly, and to facilitate the readers' choices about concentration upon theory, practice demonstrated through examples, or exercises.

The case examples are used to illustrate and amplify the discussion, and are given a distinctive appearance. They speak their own stories without the need for over-interpretation. All the examples of work with children took place in group contexts, many of which are taken from work in a tutorial class (see Appendix 1). In cases of reference to particular children, the name of the child has been changed in order to protect confidentiality. Examples taken from the practice of making sandworlds (conducted in a small-group, support-service setting) are given to illustrate symbolic and metaphorical processes. Whilst it is not suggested that the sandworld technique *per se* is applicable to regular classroom situations, the principles are highly relevant to other sorts of work providing opportunities for imaginative free association, such as drawing, painting, clay-work, sculpting, etc. (Appendix 2 gives a summary of sandplay therapy.) More general examples relating to work with teachers are taken from a variety of in-service training and consultation work, in a number of different education authorities.

The exercises are also presented so that they are distinctive. I have developed and used these exercises in initial and in-service training contexts with teachers, and in training inter-professional groups in using counselling skills. The aim of them is to foster personal explorations and awareness of affective realms, and the emphasis is upon the 'how' of managing process factors. As discussed earlier in the introduction, practitioners are very much part of the equation, making a difference to children's lives. Effective work with disturbing children demands considerable awareness of the varied elements of personal involvement in the process of facilitating emotional development and learning. Practitioners are most effective when they manage process consciously, not only from a 'technique' point of view, but from the point of view of being aware of the ways in which personal experience and understanding are used, and the exercises are designed to facilitate this. They are planned to enable staff to develop reflective capacities, resourcefulness and effectiveness, to become better able to respond to situations encountered with troubled children and young people. It is not the intention here to provide exercises which themselves may be undertaken with children/young people.

The exercises may be undertaken individually, or in group training contexts. The symbols */**/*** indicate whether each exercise might most effectively be used as an individual/paired/group exploration, respectively. Cold on the page, some might seem to have little potency; they need involvement to fulfil their intention as insight- and skill-generators on the ways in which we each relate to inter-personal and interactive dimensions, in the interests of the children we serve. Some of the exercises are easier to engage with than others: used in a training context, some require trust to have developed between group members. The appropriate use of the exercises for training purposes requires careful consideration and management. This is not only the case for group exercises, but also where exercises designed for individuals and pairs or small groups are used in a large-group context.

Part I

EMOTIONAL GROWTH AND LEARNING – AND THEIR ENEMIES!

1

EMOTIONAL GROWTH AND LEARNING

INTRODUCTION

Bennathan (1992) makes the point that the importance of the overall ethos of a school for the progress of its pupils has been well recognised – for example in the classic Rutter *et al.*'s *Fifteen Thousand Hours* (1979) – but that teacher training has presented an over-simplified model of the child. This model is one which moves, with the help of a well-presented curriculum, through the Piagetian stages of cognitive development:

> It is a model which lacks the understanding of the emotional causes of learning failure that have to do with the child's early development, its home circumstances, its social experience, all factors which may have been so damaging that learning can hardly take place. This inadequacy was recognised by almost every enquiry into the good management of children in school from the Warnock Report in 1979 to the Elton Report in 1989. The call was always for more emphasis on understanding the emotional realities for many children. Children do not come to school with uniformly good experiences and attitudes. The good teacher knows this and both understands the subject to be taught and the nature of the child who is to be taught. It would be a most retrograde step to encourage teachers to think that understanding the curriculum is more important than understanding the child.
>
> (Bennathan 1992: 41)

Effective learning is dependent upon emotional growth. If we are to facilitate better the learning of those whose learning and emotional growth has become stuck, i.e. those children with emotional and behavioural difficulties, then we need to understand better the relationship between affect and learning. This calls first for a theoretical consideration. We will then look at those experiences which are necessary for emotional growth and learning to proceed.

AFFECT AND LEARNING

This discussion begins from a theoretical perspective, and then considers the stance taken by recent major reports upon work with affect and learning.

Affect is defined by *Chambers's Twentieth Century Dictionary* as 'the emotion that lies behind action'. Affect is not static, neither is the capacity for learning, nor is a special educational need. So the way in which adults engage in affective processes has an impact on the child's capacity for learning. Estrada *et al.* (1987) conclude, in their study of children at 4, 5, 6 and 12 years of age, that 'the affective relationship (i.e. mother/child) continues to make a unique contribution to cognitive functioning beyond its influence in the early years' (in Barrett and Trevitt 1991: 10).

At a very general level, Capra (1982: 324) argues that 'human evolution . . . progresses through an interplay of inner and outer worlds, individuals and societies, nature and culture'. Capra's comment applies equally to individual and collective processes of 'evolution'. Something of the nature of this evolution is explained by 'personal construct' theory, developed by Kelly (1955). From the point of view of this theory, each of us is said to construct our own reality, coming to know the world only through personal interpretations, or the constructions that we make of it. Writing from the point of view of personal construct theory, Salmon explains that:

> as members of a society, each of us has to achieve a workable understanding of our social world. It is the psychology we construct which allows us to define ourselves in relation to others, which underlies our moment-to-moment dealings, our social transactions, and governs the stances we take up, the projects we launch in the course of our lives.
>
> (Salmon 1988: 92)

Salmon argues that our 'personal constucts' develop when:

> from the very beginning of life, interpretations – the meanings to be accorded to things – are offered and exchanged between infants and their care-givers. . . . A personal system of meaning has to be forged which is viable, liveable, yet which remains open rather than closed. Education, in this psychology, is the systematic interface between personal construct systems. This view of formal learning puts as much emphasis on teachers' personal meanings as on those of learners. . . . Our personal construct systems carry what, in the broadest possible sense, each of us knows. . . . They represent the possibilities of action, the choices we can make. They embody the dimensions of meaning which give form to our experience, the kind of interpretation which we cast upon events. Since none of us can know anything of the world,

except through the meanings we have available to us, the dimensions we have constructed – our constructs – are crucially important.

(Salmon 1988: 22–3)

This has implications for the way we conceive of learning and of the function of the curriculum. Salmon argues that in the traditional mode of education, which assumes the transmission of ready-made understanding, validational outcomes are implicitly defined in terms of right and wrong. If knowledge is absolute, pupils either possess it or they do not. In a model based on personal constructs, validation has a different character, since knowledge, in whatever sphere, is never final.

> What essentially matters is its *viability* in practical, personal and social terms. No formulation has sole rights. There are always many possible ways of defining things. Helpful validation then becomes, not a matter of final arbitration, but of simultaneously affirming and challenging existing constructions of meaning. . . . Whereas the traditional trans- mission model can insist on a single formulation of understanding, within a constructivist view, many viewpoints are possible.
>
> (Salmon 1988: 79, 83)

This formulation is important, given that each of us constructs our own meanings based on individual experience, since it allows for the possibility that, ultimately, children need to construct their understanding of the curriculum out of their own real experience. From this perspective, under- standing does not proceed quantitatively, by a series of additive steps, but 'by significant changes of position, of angle of approach, changes in the whole perspective from which things are viewed. It is, as Kelly saw it, a matter of imaginative reconstruction' (Salmon 1988: 72). This formulation parallels Dewey's conception of education as the reconstruction of experi- ence (Rogers 1961).

As Marris argues (1986), we grow up as adaptable beings, able to handle a wide variety of circumstances, only because our sense of meaning of life becomes more consolidated. Marris suggests that meanings are learned in the context of specific relationships and circumstances and we may not readily see how to translate them to an apparently different context.

> Both learning theories and theories of personality focus attention on self-development as a process, which can be blocked or distorted, or assisted, but not replaced. . . . [a person] construes his experience and therefore helps to determine what his experience shall be and what he will learn from it.
>
> (Blackham 1978: 30–1)

Piaget developed the notion that in order for a child to understand some- thing, s/he must construct it for himself, must reinvent it. The evolution of each individual's learning is dependent upon the capacity to symbolise – the basis of understanding language and number – and upon the development of sufficient autonomy to take the exploratory, inventive risks necessary for one's own thinking. The level of functioning of the capacities for symbolisation and autonomy is related to emotional development. Piaget conceives intellectual development as evolving by the interplay of assimilation and accommodation. Assimilation depends on an internal organising structure sufficiently developed, both cognitively and emotionally, to incorporate experience. Dockar-Drysdale (1990) distinguishes between the realisation, symbolisation and conceptualisation of experience, referring respectively to the capacities to experience inside oneself, to store the good inside oneself, and to use words to understand experience. 'Experience must be realized and symbolized before it can be conceptualized' (Dockar-Drysdale 1990: 162).

Learning is a process of continual reordering of perceptions and knowledge in order to refine the sense one makes of one's experiences. The qualities which we experience in others, and which we 'take in', consciously and unconsciously, have a significant impact upon our capacities as learners. A person's inner capacities develop through a process of largely unconscious exploration of her/his relationship with the external world, as represented by significant other people. Theorists of the psychodynamic school have made the major contributions to our understanding of the emotional aspects of the processes involved in the construction of our experience. The notion of 'object relations' has made a significant contribution to psychodynamic thinking. Object relations theories are useful here since they help our understanding of the way in which we relate to parts of – or 'objects' in – our internal world, and the impact of these objects upon our experience of others. Individuals may unconsciously push out or 'project' parts of themselves onto other people, and experience this unwanted aspect of themselves in the other person. The projecting person may become identified with the person upon whom s/he is projecting, or the subject may identify him/herself with the projected material – the process known as 'projective identification'. In this process the 'content' attributed with the other person (external object) may be reintrojected, or taken back inside by the projecting person. Whilst this mechanism may be used defensively (see Chapter Two), it is also important for growth. Responses related to such contents are the foundations for the capacity for empathy and become the prototype for more advanced forms of empathy. Empathy is an important basis for relationship, and it is through relationship that our sense of meanings develop.

The processes of projection and introjection take place unconsciously in early childhood. Through them we establish our subjective meanings and develop our sense of identity, increasingly learning to differentiate between what is 'me' and what is 'not me' (see the section below on

24

'Emotional needs and learning'). A sense of security in one's own identity is required to face the possibility of the unknown, the yet-to-be-invented. Without some security in our identity, we may experience such a task as a threat to our very sense of ourselves. This is particularly the case when we are vulnerable and without much ego strength, i.e. capacity to manage our feelings and to mediate between our inner and outer worlds. When we feel vulnerable, we are more likely to lose our capacity for imagination, the basis of the process of invention, so necessary for learning. In such situations it is as if the person has become – at least temporarily – frozen, emotionally stuck, as if unavailable for learning.

Given that the individual construction of meaning is so vital to the capacity for learning, it is not surprising that humanistic psychologist Carl Rogers, who also views the personality as a 'process of becoming' (1951), makes the following statements about teaching and learning. First, we cannot teach another person directly, we can but facilitate his/her learning. Second, significant learning takes place only of those things which the person perceives as being involved in the maintenance of, or enhancement of, the structure of the self. Third, significant learning is resisted, since the personality protects itself. If the person sees that the learning is going to require a reorganisation of self, s/he will not open up the boundaries of the personality to include new behaviours until the person feels that it is safe to do so and that the new behaviours are in his/her self-interest. Fourth, Rogers views the situation which most effectively promotes effective learning as one in which any threat to the self of the learner is reduced to a minimum, and in which learning is facilitated.

It is interesting to compare the developmental issues involved in a child's construction of his/her experience with Maslow's hierarchy of human needs (see Figure 2). Maslow suggests that only when one's needs have been met at a particular point on the hierarchy is one able to 'progress' to fulfilling one's needs at a higher level in the hierarchy. People achieve their potential when they are able to fulfil the characteristics shown at the top of his hierarchy.

Yet many children who experience emotional difficulties are struggling to establish their sense of basic safety, and to manage the anxiety which ensues from a lack of safety. Similarly, Erikson's (1977) notion of developmental tasks begins with the concept of needing to resolve the conflict of basic trust versus mistrust. Children need to develop a sense of emotional safety and trust in others for development and learning to proceed. If we do not sufficiently establish personal constructs which provide nourishing forms of meaning and identity, then we will find little meaning in learning, and we will resist it. If part of the teachers' role is to enhance access to learning for those who find it difficult, then this role also demands work to be undertaken on developing creatively meaningful personal constructs and identities. How do schools, our institutions responsible for fostering

Self-actualisation needs

- developing talents
- personal fulfilment
- gaining recognition and respect
- benefiting others

Self-esteem needs

- self-respect
- self-confidence
- autonomy
- knowing one's talents

Social/affiliation/belongingness needs

- friendship/companionship
- group identity
- expressing oneself
- being understood
- caring

Safety needs

- security
- predictability
- safety against danger or threat

Physiological needs

- food
- shelter
- warmth
- sleep

Figure 2 Maslow's hierarchy of human needs
(adapted from Maslow 1943, 1954)

learning, relate to such tasks, and, more precisely, what sorts of encouragement have recent major reports given in this regard?

Traditionally schools have perceived themselves to have a legitimate and necessary concern to foster 'personal', or social and emotional, development. Her Majesty's Inspectorate's recent interpretation of the National Curriculum takes this into account when making the point that the Education Reform Act 'includes the requirement that every pupil of school age has access to a balanced and broadly based curriculum, promoting personal development, and preparing that pupil for adult life' (DES 1990: 29). Hall and Hall (1988) state that there is convincing evidence to show that improving the quality of human relations in an institution also improves the quality and amount of academic work produced and the attendance of the students.

Where learning is impeded by distress or intense feelings, the child's relationships with teachers, peers and family are often tense. It is particularly noteworthy that the National Curriculum Council (1989a: 35) recognises these implications for the teacher's role: 'For pupils with emotional/behavioural difficulties, there are dangers in over-emphasis on "managing" the behaviour without attempts to understand the child's feelings.' The teachers' attitudes towards, and skills in, interactive processes go a considerable way to either meeting, or negatively reinforcing, the special educational needs. Yet the social and interactive skills required of pupils by the National Curriculum are, from an early age, demanding. For example, to take the risks necessary to formulate and test hypotheses, and to operate as a member of a group comparing results with other groups (as demanded in the early stages of the science syllabus), demands a considerable degree of autonomy. The teacher is asked not only to be sophisticated in interactive skills, but to facilitate the development of such skills in pupils struggling in this area themselves. The importance of the teacher's role in this regard has been recognised and acknowledged by the Elton Report, *Discipline in Schools*:

> We are convinced that there are skills, which all teachers need, involved in listening to young people and encouraging them to talk about their hopes and concerns before coming to a judgement about their behaviour. We consider that these basic counselling skills are particularly valuable for creating a supportive school atmosphere. The skills needed to work effectively with adults, whether teachers or parents, are equally crucial. We therefore recommend that initial teacher-training establishments should introduce all their students to basic counselling skills and their value. We regard such skills as particularly important for all senior pastoral staff (deputy heads, heads of year and heads). We recommend that LEAs provide in-service training in basic counselling skills for senior pastoral staff at least.
>
> (DES 1989c: 114–15)

Understanding feelings, and taking the consequent responsibilities, requires that teachers take account of subjective experience and synthesise their understanding within teaching practice. If teachers are to do this, then what emotional experiences are necessary to help development?

EMOTIONAL NEEDS AND LEARNING

The above discussion has highlighted the significance of the development of personal constructions of meaning and identity in relation to the capacity for learning. In order to develop a structure of personal meanings which sustain development we need an environment of emotional safety and trust. In particular, in order for learning to proceed effectively, we need to feel safe and accepted, to develop internal strength and the capacity to symbolise, to feel secure and be able to explore, and to have a sense of individual identity. In the rest of this chapter each of these is discussed in turn.

First, what sort of general developments might be expected at various stages in childhood? A Kleinian-influenced view of the construction of experience and the development of emotional life and learning is summarised in Figure 3.

Figure 3 gives an overview of expectations about development. Yet development is highly individual, and it does not always proceed in line with general expectations. The following discussion selects some key areas of emotional experience, without which it is difficult for development to proceed. The more schools are able to provide these emotional experiences, the more learning will be facilitated. To experience these qualities in school is particularly important for troubled children, who may have only limited experience of them elsewhere in their lives. Whatever the external reality of each child's life, we must remember that each individual will subjectively make his/her own meanings. However we have constructed our own meanings, the following experiences are vital for further development. Development is able to proceed naturally when we have had sufficient of these sorts of experience to have internalised their helpful qualities.

Feeling safe and accepted

To experience the feeling of safety and acceptance, we have to allow ourselves to feel in some ways dependent upon significant other people in our lives. We cannot risk trust if we cannot risk some form of dependence on another person. At first the child is in almost absolute dependence on the support of the mother-figure, followed by her careful and incremental actions to withdraw her support for the infant's total dependency (Winnicott 1984). The way in which the adult manages the child's conflicting needs for dependency and independence has an impact on the child's ego development. The ego is the conscious part of the personality, relating and mediating between inner and outer realities. Having a weak ego might be compared to being like a learner driver; a strong ego to being like a strong, competent driver.

Dependency is the pre-condition for independence, but too much dependence is emotionally depleting. From a state of absolute dependence, the person moves towards independence through a stage which Winnicott (1984) describes as relative dependency. This is significant for the teacher, since there are times when it is necessary to support relative dependency, in order to help a child to feel safe and accepted, but not to

Infancy, 0–6 months:
> The stage of infancy is characterised by the split between love and hate, the former being associated with joy and pleasure and the latter with anger, destructiveness, fear of annihilation or disintegration, and envy.

6 months to 1 year:
> At this time the capacity to love and hate the same person, associated with the depressive position (see the section on 'Anxiety and depression', in Chapter Two), potentially begins. Transitional objects begin to have a role, providing a place to play, think, reflect, have fun. The wish to make reparation emerges, along with separation anxiety. The core of the self begins to develop, along with the beginnings of psychological separation and individuation.

1–3 years:
> Between the ages of 1 and 3 years, continuing individuation and separation provide further developments in autonomy. During this time there are intense sexual feelings for both parents. Girls feel rivalrous of the mother: at this stage girls are said to feel the mother's envy. There is a danger of omnipotent fantasies and behaviour, flight into 'I can do it all myself.' This is associated with temper tantrums and fear of abandonment.

4–6 years:
> This is said to be the age when differences, for example of race and gender, can be acknowledged with awareness and acceptance. Sibling rivalry intensifies. Thinking is concrete, magical, timeless, animistic. Feelings are related to concrete thoughts through symbols.

6–10 years:
> The 6–10 age-group has traditionally been termed the latency phase. Here there is increasing autonomy and socialisation, a rapid acquisition of skills, the relinquishment of omnipotence, opening to vulnerability and a sense of inferiority. Thinking remains concrete. Potential problems associated with this stage include isolation, depression, and a retreat into a fantasy world.

10–14/15 years:
> Early adolescence is said to be characterised by a re-emergence of the qualities of early sexuality and of the love/hate phenomenon. There is alternating rivalry and identification with both parents. Omnipotence re-emerges and oscillates with despair. There is experimentation in relationships and activities, but confusion over identity, particularly sexual identity.

15 years onwards:
> The late adolescent phase is characterised by a movement towards physical separation and independence. Identity consolidates and real intimacy and a sense of responsibility emerge. There is an increase in energy. The capacity to think in abstract terms relates to the growing capacity to develop creative ideas.

Figure 3 A Kleinian-influenced view of the developmental stages of childhood
(adapted from Trowell 1990)

do so at the expense of the child's need to move towards independence. A measure of relative dependency can thus be helpful for learning. This is particularly the case in relation to children whose ego strength is limited or fragile.

Hirschhorn (1988) explains the function which relative dependency fulfils for the process of learning. Discussing a company training programme in which adult trainees adopted a dependent role, Hirschhorn comments that the trainees liked the programme, since they could sit in awe of the experts who protected them, and so did not feel frustrated at their own incompetencies. However, the trainees felt that they had to grab all they could get so that they could walk away with at least some of the expertise displayed before them: greedy people feel empty and angry at those who deny them 'food'. '[I]nsofar as they become dependent on the instructors and on the program, they believed that they had no inner resources' (Hirschhorn 1988: 128). Generalising from such evidence, Hirschhorn describes two models of a training situation, and shows how some degree of dependency for a learner is appropriate. In learning, one experiences one's ignorance, one's lack of skills. If learners develop a secure relationship with their teacher, they may feel protected from the consequences of their own ignorance. The trainer stands between them and the inner, judgemental voices (of the super-ego – see Chapter Two, section on 'Self-Judgement') that admonish them for their stupidity. In short, they regress, and an appropriate relationship of dependency emerges between the two. However, if for some reason they fail to develop this relationship, they can be overwhelmed by the experience of their own helplessness and consequently transform their self-punishing impulse into attacks on the teacher. The relationship between the teacher and the learner is thus central to the learner's experience.

Exercise: The link between feeling safe and being able to reflect

*/**

1 Think of a time when you felt unsafe. Try to remember how this impeded your capacity for reflection.
2 Think of a time when you worked particularly reflectively. In what ways did you feel safe at that time?

Developing internal strengths and the capacity to symbolise

Much of our capacity for internal strength derives from the ego's mediation of inner and outer realities. The ego's mediation helps us to manage difficult feelings such as loss, frustration, greed and envy. The ego also defines the boundary between 'me' and 'not me'. Winnicott's work has aided understanding of how the emotionally available adult can help mediate forces in the child's experience – those psychologically unintegrated affects – which may hamper the development of the ego, and thus help the psychic negotiation required for ego development. These processes are dependent upon trust. In the context of a trusting relationship, the child feels safe enough to 'let in' – to feel and to think about – a greater range of experience, which in turn facilitates the child's growing capacities for differentiation of both affect and thought. In contrast, where the child experiences a lack of empathetic 'holding' (see Chapter Four) by the adult, feelings of disintegration can be produced. In such situations the personality 'closes in' to protect itself, and there is little capacity to undertake the risks involved in learning. The level of a child's ego functioning can be assessed (Dockar-Drysdale 1990) in relation to such factors as the child's dependency, his/her management of difficult feelings, the capacity for empathy, stress, aggression, communication, and modelling upon those admired (where the last of these is accompanied by a retention of individual identity).

How does the development proceed of the capacity to understand 'me/not me', to perceive oneself as a separate person, and to develop and make use of ego strength? A key feature of these developments was identified by Winnicott as the young child's capacity to make use of what he 'termed transitional objects'. Transitional objects refer to the soft toys or rags to which the young child becomes attached. The child's use of a transitional object represents the first indication of symbolisation, and belongs to the stage in a child's development when s/he is beginning to separate from the mother. The transitional object bridges the gap between mother and child. 'The object represents the infant's transition from a state of being merged with the mother to a state of being in relation to the mother as something outside and separate' (Winnicott 1974: 17). The transitional object is also symptomatic of the beginnings of the child's ego development. For Winnicott the transitional object was one indication that a relationship to the outside world, acceptable to the self, had begun (Davies and Wallbridge 1990). Transitional objects act as a sort of bridge to the handling of 'not me' objects, forming the first possession recognised as 'not me'.

Through the infant's affectionate fondling activity with the transitional object, this object may become very important to the infant. There is a sense in which this is the first possession which affectively belongs to the infant, and yet which is not part of the infant, like the thumb or fingers. The infant needs this object to be available, needs it to be returned when thrown away, over and over again. 'From the infant's point of view this first object was indeed created out of his or her imagination. It was the beginning of the infant's creation of the world' (Winnicott 1964: 167).

31

Winnicott argued that an object such as a child's teddy-bear actively helps the child separate from his/her mother. The object stands both *for* the mother and *between* the child and the mother. The child projects onto the teddy-bear the good relationship s/he has with mother and so feels protected by the teddy-bear in his/her mother's absence. As the child develops, s/he then takes back inside those images and good feelings associated with the mother. S/he no longer places them in the teddy-bear but rather contains them wholly in her/his own mind. The teddy-bear thus helps the child make the transition from dependency to independence.

Rollinson (1992) describes the field of the transitional object as a 'neutral area of illusion' which will not be challenged:

> Once experienced sufficiently mothers can introduce disillusion-ment, the introduction of object reality as part of the gradual change to independence which is operating naturally in the infant, vital to prevent illusion from becoming disillusion. However, the experience of the areas of overlap enables continued use of objects to help with the development of 'me' and its differentiation from 'not me'. Now this intermediate area between subjective inner reality and objective external reality, where both can interplay, protects the child from serious trauma of disillusionment. It provides a safe place for it to continue in a way that need not negatively affect functioning in the shared world. With trust in the environment established, playing occurs which helps develop a whole human being, who can experi-ence intensely, be creative, act spontaneously and enrich the self while discovering 'meaning in the world of seen things'.
>
> (Rollinson 1992: 9)

Once trust in the environment happens there can be what Winnicott refers to as a psychological 'potential space', a third area beyond the I/thou dichotomy, a space in which creativity can take place.

> A baby can be *fed* without love, but loveless and impersonal *manage-ment* cannot succeed in producing a new autonomous human child ... Here where there is trust and reliability is potential space, one that can become an infinite area of separation, which the baby, child, adolescent, adult may creatively fill with playing, which in time becomes the enjoyment of the cultural heritage.
>
> (Winnicott 1974: 127)

Through cultural experiences 'each human being as a unique individual can form a bridge leading from the past to the future' (Davies and Wallbridge 1990: 170).

How do learners need transitional objects to secure their potential for learning? Hirschhorn (1988) suggests that if the learner were to be totally dependent on the teacher, s/he would not learn, and if the learner were to have no experience of psychological support, s/he would be overwhelmed. Teachers have the task of incorporating psychologically acceptable forms of transitional objects into their practice for those children who have need of them, whatever their age. Hirschhorn argues that techniques themselves can function as transitional objects: they help learners make the transition from feelngs of incompetence to feelings of competence. As learners feel competent, they depend less on the technique and more on their own situational judgements and intuitions. Also, Hirschhorn maintains, a working alliance between the teacher and the learner can create a transitional relationship: learners can depend on the teacher to protect and help them as they develop their competence. But learners can learn and teachers can facilitate their learning only if the teachers develop a working alliance with the learners in which teachers become, in terms of psychoanalytic theory, an 'object' onto which learners can assign complex feelings.

Learners experience the teacher as a source of frustration, but also as someone who can stand to one side of their experience and understand it. The learners feel dependent and look to the teacher for guidance, but the teacher can also become their collaborator, as learners pass through a stage of frustration and discover their own expertise and capacity to learn. Learners must identify with the teacher's observing and interpreting stance so that they can learn to deploy their own 'observing ego', i.e. their capacity to observe themselves and use these observations to make judgements about managing themselves in relation to other people or a task.

Exercise: Relating with transitional objects

*

This exercise is designed to encourage you to consider transitional objects from the perspective of your own experience.

Think of a transitional object which you had as a child. Write a letter to your transitional object, or make a poem about it.

Feeling secure and able to explore

Bowlby's work on attachment made a major contribution to our under-standing of the issues involved in feeling secure, and being able to undertake the exploring which is necessary for learning. 'All of us, from the cradle to the grave, are happiest when life is organised as a series of excursions, long or short, from the secure base provided by our attachment figure(s)' (Bowlby 1988: 62). Bowlby argues that human infants are programmed to develop in a socially co-operative way, and that whether they do so or not depends largely on how they are treated. 'Children who have not participated in a "good enough" relationship with an "attachment figure" are less likely to learn effectively in school' (Barrett and Trevitt 1991: 4). Attachment is the condition from which emotions and purposes arise.

> The organisation of meaning depends on a maturing power to conceptualise the relationship between feelings, purposes and actions. Attachment influences this development, not only as our first and for a long time most crucial experience of security and danger, order and predictability, but as the guarantor of all other learning. . . . growth rests on the durability of the expectations we have already learned to trust.
>
> (Marris 1986: ix, 104)

The more secure we feel, the more open we are to experience, so long as we believe it will enlarge rather than undermine our sense of self.

Ainsworth's (1967) study of mothers and infants in Uganda showed how infants, once mobile, commonly use their mother as a base from which to explore. When conditions are favourable an infant moves away from mother on exploratory excursions and returns to her again from time to time. By 8 months of age almost every infant observed who had had a stable mother-figure to whom to become attached showed this behaviour, but when the mother was absent, such organised excursions became much less evident or ceased. Similarly, according to a study conducted in a London park, a healthy 2 year old child whose mother is resting on a garden seat will make a series of excursions away from her, each time returning to her before making the next excursion. On some occasions, when returning, the child simply smiles; on others s/he leans against the parent's knee; on yet others s/he wants to climb on the parent's lap. In this situation the child stays for a long period only when s/he is frightened or tired or thinks the parent is about to leave.

Bowlby (1988: 26–7) defines attachment behaviour as 'any form of behaviour that results in a person attaining or maintaining proximity to some other clearly identified individual who is conceived as better able to cope with the world'. He formulated three patterns of attachment. The first he terms *secure attachment.* This pattern develops where the individual is confident that the parent figure will be available, responsive and helpful should s/he encounter adverse or frightening situations. With this assurance, s/he feels bold in explorations of the world. When there is assurance that primitive wants will be satisfied, confidence to confront the uncertainties of growth is renewed (Marris 1986).

> those [children] who are most stable emotionally and make the most of their opportunities are those who have [parent figures] who, whilst

always encouraging their children's autonomy, are none the less available and responsive when called upon. . . . for a person to know that an attachment figure is available and responsive gives him a strong and pervasive feeling of security, and so encourages him to value and continue the relationship.

(Bowlby 1988: 12, 27)

This sense of security is related to the development of confidence, because of the qualities of relationship which the child internalises. 'The confident child becomes increasingly adventurous and can tolerate brief separations, because he can carry a picture of himself interacting with his mother [or significant parental figure] inside his head' (Barrett and Trevitt 1991: 9). Barrett and Trevitt speak of how the child builds up a picture of him/herself as a worthwhile individual interacting with a preferred attachment figure by being validated through numerous gestures, tone of voice, and eye contact, as well as concrete provision.

It is unlikely that these feelings are consciously recognised by an infant until later in his first year of life, but these two important aspects of an internal working model – the infant's active seeking of attention from his mother and mother's active response to this – affirm a secure base. Then, if all goes well, the infant can extend his goal-seeking beyond the immediate presence of his mother; he has built up an internal picture or memory of his attachment figure, which he can retain even when she is not close-by. This is a gradual process; in the early months eye contact will suffice as re-assurance, but later it becomes possible to tolerate actual short separations, safe in the knowlege that this figure will return.

(Barrett and Trevitt 1991: 29–30)

So, as long as the attachment figure remains accessible and responsive, the attachment behaviour – which confirms the internal memory of attachment – may consist of little more than checking by eye or ear on the whereabouts of the figure and exchanging occasional glances and greetings.

Example: Attachment behaviour with a school special educational needs co-ordinator

Barrett and Trevitt (1991) give an example of four boys, newly transferred to a secondary school, who had severe reading problems and who were provided English support lessons with the teacher in charge of special educational needs. The boys each found various reasons for returning to her room on a daily basis, outside the times scheduled for their extra English lessons. They needed just to say 'Hi Miss', or to eat their sandwiches in her room at lunchtime, and so on. Two of the boys seemed to need to engage the teacher in conversation beyond the ostensible reason for the visit, whilst brief acknowledgement of the other two was enough to reassure them.

This behaviour is similar to a younger child's ability to function within the sound of mother but only with occasional sight of her, for example when playing in another room. The 'idea' of themselves and a caring figure had become part of a growing memory which allowed the boys to move towards behaving more age-appropriately in school.

(Barrett and Trevitt 1991: 19)

So long as the attachment bond endures, the various forms of attachment behaviour which contribute to it are active only when required. The systems mediating attachment are triggered by a sense of strangeness or fear, and come to an end if a familiar environment or the ready availability and responsiveness of an attachment figure is lost (Bowlby 1980).

Bowlby termed his second mode of attachment *anxious resistant attachment*. This occurs when the child is uncertain whether the adult will be available or responsive when called upon. The child becomes prone to separation anxiety, tends to be clingy, and is anxious about exploring the world. 'When an individual (of any age) is feeling secure he is likely to explore away from his attachment figure. When alarmed, anxious, tired, or unwell he feels an urge towards proximity' (Bowlby 1988: 121).

Bowlby's third mode of attachment is *anxious avoidant attachment*. With this type of attachment the individual expects to be rebuffed when seeking care, and tries to become emotionally self-sufficient, developing a narcissistic, or, in Winnicott's terms, a false, self.

Who better to summarise the concept of attachment than Bowlby:

> it seems clear that sensitive loving care results in a child developing confidence that others will be helpful when appealed to, becoming increasingly self-reliant and bold in his explorations of the world, co-operative with others, and also . . . sympathetic and helpful to others in distress. Conversely, when a child's attachment behaviour is responded to tardily and unwillingly and is regarded as a nuisance, he is likely to become anxiously attached, that is, apprehensive lest his caregiver be missing or unhelpful when he needs her and therefore reluctant to leave her side, unwillingly and anxiously obedient, and unconcerned about the troubles of others. Should his caregivers, in addition, actively reject him, he is likely to develop a pattern of behaviour in which avoidance of them competes with his desire for proximity and care, and in which angry behaviour is apt to become prominent.

(Bowlby 1988: 82)

One of the key questions for people working with children is 'How can we help the children to feel safe?' Bowlby's work has helped the recognition that, to feel safe, pupils need to feel secure in their attachment to the teacher, and to feel that their autonomy is respected and appropriately encouraged. Where an adult displays the qualities of sensitivity, responsiveness and emotional involvement, the child is encouraged to make an emotional attachment to the relationship (Schaffer 1977). The significance of attachment and separation in education was also recognised by Winnicott (1964: 203): 'The more we look, the more we see that if teachers and pupils are living healthily they are engaged in a mutual sacrifice of spontaneity and independence, and that is almost as important a part of education as teaching and learning in the set subjects.'

Exercise: Our own experience of attachment

*/**

Reflect upon the nature of the attachments to key adults which you made as a child. How did your childhood experiences of attachment affect your capacity for attachment as an adult?

Exercise: Using attachment theory to help understand individual children

*/**

By way of example, choose a particular child with whom you work. Reflect upon the nature of the attachment which the child makes with you. How does attachment theory inform your understanding of the child and his/her needs?

Individual identity

An emerging ego strength and a sense of inner security facilitate the risk-taking necessary for learning. A sense of personal identity, as it relates to purpose in the world, is necessary to enable a person to learn in relation to wider contexts of meaning. Learning, and its meaning, become related to the wider social and cultural sphere.

Winnicott argues that it is first through the development of inner reality that the infant becomes recognisable as an individual. 'Of every individual who has reached the state of being a unit with a limited membrane and an outside and an inside, it can be said that there is an inner reality to that individual, an inner world which can be rich or poor and can be at peace or in a state of war' (Winnicott 1975, quoted in Davies and Wallbridge 1990: 29–30). The concept of 'personal psychic reality' comes into being, according to Winnicott, as part of the self, as soon as the infant has reached:

the state of being a unit with a limiting membrane and an inside and outside. . . . The establishment of this state of affairs roughly corresponds to, or is soon followed by, the beginnings of self-consciousness, so that it becomes possible to talk about an individual with the connotation of personal identity.

(Davies and Wallbridge 1990: 54)

Jung's concept of the self is helpful in thinking about the process of finding one's own meaning in relation to the wider world. Jung (1971: 460–1) defined the self as expressing 'the unity of the personality as a whole. . . . it encompasses both the experienceable and the inexperienceable (or the not yet experienced)'. Jung extended psychological work beyond the confines of work with ego consciousness. He viewed the ego and the self as being in dynamic relation to each other. Relatedness between ego and self brings balance, and the capacity for emotional regeneration – psychological homeostasis. Where ego development is inhibited, the self of the child is unable to manifest as an independent entity. For a time after birth, the self is preserved within the self of the mother. Following Jung's work, analytical psychologists such as Neumann (1973) and Kalff (1983) have postulated that, after approximately one year, the self of the child separates from that of the mother, and most often between the second and third years of life establishes itself in the unconscious of the child. Once this has happened, the child can begin the process of individuation, that is, a person's becoming himself or herself. The process of individuation in children was first recognised and identified by Fordham (1969).

As one gains identity in relation to inner and outer worlds, one is increasingly able to engage in open-ended learning explorations, with the complexity of potential connections these entail. The development of identity is closely linked with the development of autonomy.

In our plural society, personal autonomy is an avowed educational aim . . . When the behaviour is autonomous the agent feels that he is acting on his own, not as the agent of another who is primarily responsible. . . . personal autonomy implies a coming to terms with oneself, one's society, the cosmos. It is a settlement, not a posture. Mere rebellion, willful self-assertion, the rejection or usurpation of authority, defiant doing of one's own thing, does not amount to autonomy, although it may be a necessary negative moment in the achievement of autonomy.

(Blackham 1978: 27–9)

Let us further explore the development of individual identity through the example of a particular child.

Example: Kelvin

Kelvin had been somewhat dominated at home, and his case provides an example of a boy who struggled to achieve autonomy and a more rounded identity.

Kelvin's situation was referred to tutorial class in his third year of junior school because of significant underachievement and concern about his passivity in relationships. The educational psychologist reported that Kelvin was anxious and had such poor self-confidence that he was reluctant to make guesses or commit himself to paper, even when copying. He often sat doing nothing. Kelvin was described as a gentle and sensitive boy at school, 'retiring' in his relationships with other children. Kelvin was originally referred to the Schools' Psychological Service two years earlier because of his mother's concern that he was 'backward'. When he was assessed at the time of his referral to tutorial class, he was functioning at a slightly below average level. The educational psychologist noted his mother's reports of several 'minor' ailments, e.g. bad nosebleeds, recurrent vomiting, hayfever: she said he had a sensitive digestive system and had to be careful what he ate.

In my first meeting with Kelvin's mother and father, with Kelvin also present, his parents described him as affectionate, loving, considerate and helpful. He has two older sisters. Whilst mother and father said that they welcomed Kelvin's friends to their house, they were both reluctant to encourage Kelvin to join his friends in their houses. Mother remarked that Kelvin was beginning to go to the local shops and to school on his own, and commented, 'I never thought he would.' In this initial meeting, Kelvin's parents were asked to tell his story from the time he was in gestation. Mother described her labour as a long one, saying that she felt that Kelvin 'did not seem to want to help himself come out'. A current concern in the household was the way in which Kelvin's sisters would regularly gang up on him, denying him access to toys, and physically abusing him.

Later in the meeting, I reflected back some of the patterns that I had observed during the meeting, and I suggested that Kelvin might be given more of an opportunity by his parents to give his own answers. (It was mum, in particular, who had dominated this interview.) Kelvin's father responded by sharing his own childhood experience of not being able to say what he needed and wanted to say. I suggested that this might be an area in which Kelvin had something to learn from his father. It had been felt by mum that Kelvin would not ever be able to act independently. We discussed the importance of communicating to Kelvin that he might sometimes be able to be more independent.

Kelvin began to attend a tutorial class group for two half-days each week, the rest of the time continuing in his regular school. One year later, during a meeting between myself and Kelvin's mother, she reported that his sisters were no longer 'ganging up' on him, that he socialised in the homes of his friends, that he was reading well, and that his self-confidence had shown a marked improvement. The mother's comments reflected my own observations of Kelvin in the tutorial class group, and the reports given by his regular school. What had happened in the intervening period?

I would like to illustrate this by referring to Kelvin's work with image during his sessions in a tutorial class group. This work enabled him to make more significant contact with his own inner needs, and to explore in a non-threatening way the issues which were facing him, and to make sustaining links between his inner development and outer strengths and skills. The importance of work with imagery is explored more fully in Chapter Five. I would like to use as examples some of Kelvin's images constructed in sand – sandworlds. A sandworld is a world constructed with miniature models in a sandtray. The technique is explained in more detail in Appendix 2. Here suffice it to say that in the tutorial class groups the sandtray was sometimes used for shared play, but all the children knew that it was available for individual work to make a sandworld, and that such work was to be given respect by everyone and not intruded upon. The invitation to make sandworlds was put in terms of an invitation to the children to make a world in the sand, using any of the miniatures on the surrounding shelves, and with an assurance that their world would be no better or worse than anyone else's world: it would be a picture of their world on that session. When sandworlds were completed I would ask the child concerned if I could take a photograph of it, and the photographs were kept in a folder in the room, to which the children had access. (Whilst the making of sandworlds is not a technique which can be used in large groups of children, these pictures – Figures 4–6 are used here as an example of the way in which working through image can help the development of individual identity, and the understanding of an individual child.)

Kelvin's sandworlds help to tell his story. In his first sandworld, in February (shown in Figure 4), two motorised dinghies, each driven by a diver, are going into a tunnel. A dark, unknown part of a journey is being embarked upon, a journey associated with divers, with the depths of the water – feelings. His second sandworld, a few weeks later in March (Figure 5), shows some half-buried animals, being looked after by humans, in one half of the world, and the 'appropriately functioning' lions and cheetahs in the other half. The two groups are separated by a line of fences. This image speaks of a split, a lack of meeting, between the animal instincts of aggression and ferocity and those instincts which are submerged, half buried, in the context of being looked after by humans. (The mechanism of splitting is explained in Chapter Two, section on 'Defences against development'.) At the time of this sandworld Kelvin was talking of confusion about the reasons why he was not let out to play football, reporting that his mum would hit him if he said he was going out to play football.

Speaking of a sandworld of some months later – September (not illustrated) – Kelvin reported that the cheetah wanted to join the other cats, to be accepted into the group. To do so the cheetah had to fight the tiger. The split nature of the previous sandworld was changing here. To gain entry into the group an initiation is necessary, which requires the ability to risk and to access one's own potency, that is, the availability of psychic energy. Shortly after this sandworld Kelvin's class teacher in school made a comparison between Kelvin in his second year of junior school, when he spent long periods doing nothing, and the pattern of his then fourth year, when he was task-focused and a popular member of the class.

There was then a period of consolidation. This was expressed in a sandworld of November (Figure 6) in which those people journeying home have come through the tunnel, emerging with bags of goods and with weapons of aggression, should they be necessary. A jeep and a van are now the modes of transport, journeying upon socially constructed paths. They emerge from the tunnel towards, in sandworld terms, the side of consciousness. Kelvin's final sandworld – the following February (not illustrated) – showed a scientist looking for gold. Kelvin commented that the scientist knew how to tell if the gold was real. The scientist

Figure 4 Kelvin's sandworld: February

Figure 5 Kelvin's sandworld: March

Figure 6 Kelvin's sandworld: November

has the means of access to research, analysis and thinking. This scientist knows how to discern the real value of the treasure he is looking for.

Kelvin had developed a considerable degree of autonomy, and found an identity which was meaningful to him psychologically, for his relationships at home, at school and in his social world. He was engaging in learning activities and functioning at a level above average for his age.

SUMMARY

- Feelings have a vital role in the development of learning, since it is through our subjective, emotional world that we develop our personal constructs and meanings of outer reality, and make sense of our relationships and, eventually, of our place in the wider world.
- To be open to learning and to be able to learn effectively we need:
    - to feel safe and accepted – which requires a measure of 'relative dependency' upon the teacher or other key adult. We can allow some form of dependency to take place in relationships and settings where we experience trust. Dependency is a pre-condition for independence.
    - to be able to symbolise.
    - to have a well-enough functioning ego to mediate the experiences of our inner world and outer experience.

- Transitional objects are an aid to establishing our psychological separation as an individual person, and to symbol formation and ego development.
- In order to be able to make the explorations involved in autonomous learning, we need to feel secure in our attachment to significant adults.
- The development of personal identity is necessary for learning to develop in relation to the wider world of meaning.

2

ENEMIES OF EMOTIONAL
GROWTH AND LEARNING

INTRODUCTION

In this chapter I explore the processes which get in the way of growth and learning. It focuses on what can happen to inhibit learning, on making sense of what can go wrong. The better we are able to understand what is getting in the way of learning for children with emotional/behavioural difficulties, the more we are able to provide effectively for their needs in a way which helps them to participate in the learning process. So what we might call 'process-blockers' are examined in this chapter. Manifestations of process-blockers in the interaction between teachers and pupils are identified. Phenomena which seem to affect communication are related to the experience of key relationships, in both the present and the past, and to the pictures of reality, personal constructs or emotional frames of reference which are developed to make sense of relationships. The way in which adults relate to children in the present is very important in providing opportunities for children to restructure their emotional constructs, or frames of reference.

Working with children experiencing emotional and behavioural difficulties can bring joy in seeing change and growth in the child's capacities for relationships and learning. But such change rarely comes about without much hard work, testing-out or anxiety about whether positive change seems at all possible. One might attend to such children with care and devotion, and at times feel oneself impoverished and exhausted by the scale of the demands. Working with such children brings a lot of stress. Their behaviour challenges us professionally, and also challenges much about our personal selves, our tolerances, and our values and ethics. Understanding our own relationships with processes which inhibit learning requires an awareness of all aspects of the communications which we make, as well as the multi-faceted factors which create defences against development and learning.

Working with disturbed and disturbing children presents many potential difficulties. For example, how often do we find it difficult to try to understand the meaning of the behaviour as a way of informing our interventions, and instead get stuck on the 'symptoms', and what to 'do' in reaction to a particular presenting problem? As Dockar-Drysdale (1990: 3) says, 'we are accustomed to regressive behaviour, but not to understanding its meaning so that we can provide what is needed'. Understanding something of the meaning of behaviour is an important step in being able to facilitate not only personal development, but effective learning. We may also get stuck in the intensity of feelings – our own or those of the child(ren) – which can be generated in work with troubled children. 'In general, regressive behaviour arouses anxiety in adults, who cannot imagine recovery from such a state' (Dockar-Drysdale 1990: 70). In addition, there are dangers for the adults themselves: danger, for example, of over-identifying with the children, of psychologically merging with them, of the vicarious enjoyment of experiencing one's own unresolved emotional issues through the children, and of the power of the pull of regression. There is the danger that 'primitive' material can pick up wavelengths in the unconscious of the workers, leading to collusive pairings, and inhibiting the capacity for further development.

Let us begin by looking at some of the symptoms of blocked communication, which may well be an indication that something is getting in the way of development and learning. We will then explore some of the underlying defences against development.

SYMPTOMS OF BLOCKED COMMUNICATION

The consideration of process-blockers begins with the surface manifestations of blocked communication. We all face pressures (internal and external) which make us prone to communication-blocking, and we may often engage in communication-blocking unconsciously. Carl Rogers argues (1961: 331) that 'the major barrier to mutual interpersonal communication is our very natural tendency to judge, to evaluate, to approve or disapprove, the statement of the other person, or the other group'. The stronger our feelings the more likely it is that mutual elements in communication become difficult. Some of the symptoms of blocked communication are shown in Figure 7.

In the next exercise I invite you to consider your own experiences in thinking about the issue of blocked communication.

'Not-managing-oneself' listening
- On and off:

  Spending part of the listening time thinking of other things.
- Jumping to conclusions:

  Assuming we know what the other person is going to say and then not really listening.
- It is OK as long as it is what one wants to hear:

  Ceasing to listen when one's own opinions or judgements are challenged.
- Own agenda:

  Denying the other person the necessary space for communication.
- Being caught up in distractions:

  Pretending to listen when other distractions clamour for attention.
- Dominating or overcontrolling:

  'I'm going to get my way.'
- Competing:

  'I must score all the points.'
- Self-confessing.
- Withdrawing.

'Getting-lost-in-the-feelings' listening
- Red flag to a bull:

  Reacting unconsciously rather than consciously to communications which arouse strong feelings.
- Focus on the symptoms:

  Getting stuck, annoyed or irritated with the 'symptoms' of behaviour, rather than relating to the symptoms as communications about personal meaning.
- Wallowing in feeling:

  Getting stuck in the feelings associated with the other person.
- Repressing:

  Concentrating on repressing the behaviour 'symptoms', and forcing communication into the shadows.
- Not trusting.

'Losing-the-story' listening
- Facts not experience:

  Concentrating too much on the details of the facts and losing what the other person is really saying.
- Losing the symbolic:

  Not seeing the multiple levels of communication (e.g. body language, communication through behaviour, etc.).

Figure 7 Symptoms of blocked communication

Exercise: Symptoms of blocked communication

*

Use the list in Figure 7, showing symptoms of blocked communication, to help observe yourself:

1 Note the symptom which, when encountered in other people, irritates you the most. Note how you respond.
2 Note the two most frequent symptoms which you use as blocking mechanisms.

You might consider your responses in relation to children you work with, their parents, and other staff.

The sort of process-blockers shown in Figure 7 and which you may have considered in the exercise on symptoms of blocked communication become manifest in teaching and learning situations, as they do in many forms of interaction. Hall and Hall (1988) considered process-blockers in relation to classrooms and have identified blocks to communication which can be found in educational settings (see Figure 8).

Teachers' interaction with children can positively reinforce children's emotional needs for acceptance, security, respect for identity, and so on, or negatively reinforce other aspects of experience which might serve to inhibit learning. Teachers might justifiably feel that the experience of children with emotional/behavioural difficulties makes it difficult always to be the sort of teacher one would like to be, and to sustain the patterns of communication and interaction that one would like to. One might find oneself, as a result of pressure, reacting in ways which surprise one, shouting when one did not intend to, or saying something unintended which just seemed to 'pop out'. In response to the significant pressures of working with troubled and troubling children, teachers might develop defensive patterns of communication (such as those listed above), possibly as a method of self-protection, a strategy which children with emotional/behavioural difficulties themselves use.

To work in the service of the children's development, and to understand what might be getting in the way of growth and learning, requires reflection upon the symptoms of blocked communication in order to try to understand something of their meaning. For example, what might the form a blockage takes be saying about the dilemma underlying the blockage?

The emotionally maladjusted person . . . is in difficulty first, because communication within himself has broken down, and second because, as a result of this, his communication with others has been

Threatening:

'If you talk once more, I'm going to send you to the head.'

Moralising:

'A boy of your age should be able to behave in a more mature manner.'

Giving advice:

'If I were you, I'd keep away from those girls in 5c, they will only lead you into trouble.'

Lecturing:

'That sounds reasonable, but let's look at the way it should be. It's important to get it right.'

Judging:

'This is the worst class I have ever had to teach.'

Labelling:

'He has always been a backward reader, I don't think there is much we can do for him.'

Interpreting:

'I can tell you're not telling the truth because you can't look me in the eye.'

Using sympathy in a way which does not show empathy for the young person's frame of reference:

'I can understand that you feel bad about not getting into college, but you'll feel differently once you've been working for a few weeks.'

Interrogating:

'What on earth do you think you're doing? Why haven't you done your homework?'

Distracting and using sarcasm:

'I don't think we want to hear about that.' 'It's nice to see that you've honoured us with your presence today.'

Figure 8 Blocks to communication in educational settings
(adapted from Hall and Hall 1988)

damaged. . . . In the 'neurotic' individual, parts of himself which have been termed unconscious, or repressed, or denied to awareness, become blocked off so that they no longer communicate themselves to the conscious or managing part of himself. As long as this remains true, there are distortions in the way he communicates himself to others, and so he suffers both within himself and in his interpersonal communications.

(Rogers 1961: 330)

The more we can engage in reflective practice, particularly in relation to times when things go wrong, the better we will be able to understand the child and to meet his/her need. 'Real communication occurs, and this evaluative [i.e. judgemental] tendency is avoided, when we listen with understanding' (Rogers 1961: 331). To develop this sort of 'process thinking' approach, we must now move beyond the symptom into a consideration of the idea of defences.

DEFENCES AGAINST DEVELOPMENT

A defence is a psychological barrier which functions to protect the personality from the fear of threat or anxiety, and to keep the conflict which it masks out of consciousness. Emotional defences manifest themselves as various forms of behaviour which serve to keep the child at an emotional distance from other people. It is not surprising that teachers, hard-pressed and working to multiple agendas, are often confounded by children's negative behaviours which sometimes seem to erupt without apparent reason. Striving to come to an understanding of such events is important, since teachers contribute to the process of enabling children to come to terms with the underlying affect or feeling, and so to attain greater availability for the business of learning.

Let us begin to look at the dynamics of defences by using the following quotation by Maggs:

> Freud alleged that 'acting out is in place of remembering'. . . . The forgetting that has had to take place, which might also be called denial, is of . . . incidents in . . . earlier life that have been extremely painful and distressing. In the same way that, mercifully, we generally become unconscious when physical pain is too much for us to endure, so when psychic or psychological pain has become too much to bear then forgetting takes place. Sometimes, through lack of loving support from parenting or loving people around us (perhaps on account of their painful preoccupations at the time), the pain is repressed. . . . the hope could be that the sympathetic teacher could possibly have time to listen to expressions of the pain of recent events, so that it can be acknowledged, fully owned and does not have to be acted out, for example, through delinquent acts often perpetrating the violence which had caused the pain.
>
> (Maggs 1987: 4)

Acting out is different from wilful naughtiness. What is being excluded in defensive, acting-out behaviour is the signals which would activate attachment and enable the child both to love and to experience being loved. The child becomes:

> afraid to allow himself to become attached to anyone for fear of a further rejection with all the agony, anxiety, and the anger to which that would lead. As a result there is a massive block against his

expressing or even feeling his natural desire for a close trusting relationship, for care, comfort, and love.

(Bowlby 1988: 55)

A child who has been rejected, overprotected or abused may find it difficult to accept even a positive expression of worth: in such circumstances, to consider oneself worthy of being liked may arouse conflicting feelings (Rogers 1961). Defences are about the protection of psychic space, and the delineation of boundaries against intrusion. They appear in interactions when we feel emotionally unsafe. The employment of defences aims to make an emotionally unsafe experience feel safer.

Defences, though, do not only keep development static, they hinder the capacity for imagination and change. Psychologically, this might be described as militating against 'psychic fluidity', or the capacity for the component parts of the inner world to communicate with each other unhindered. It is as if the component parts of the inner world become isolated in boxes, rather than being able to make the sorts of connection with each other which are associated with flexibility and creativity. Defences operate in the *inter-personal* and *intra-personal* realms – both between people and within the individual. In the discussion below, examples of each are given. (The way in which institutions develop social defences is considered in Chapter Nine.) Since we all prefer to sit upon threatening feelings, we all to some extent make unconscious use of defences. It is important for teachers and others to approach defences without the need to apportion blame. In an in-service training series on counselling, a group of teachers wanted to know how to 'get past defences'. Perhaps the issue is more about how to *enable the child to lower* his/her defences. On account of the emotional pain which was behind the reason for the defence, the undoing of a defence is always associated with resistance (Matte Blanco 1975). Defences require non-collusive acceptance before the interactive dynamic can shift.

Defences, paradoxically, both constitute a logical, protective adaptation to emotional experience, and also inhibit further development. Without defences the conflicts between impulses and the demands of reality or conscience generate such a degree of anxiety that the child may break down (Laslett 1983). But defences also:

prevent our reaching our own cherished goals and our 'self-realization'. For what is being kept out and being defended against is a needy, invasive, hostile or deprived self who can never break through to what it wants (being prevented from doing so by these very defences). . . . The defences of the self and the need for security are the basis both of the quest of self-fulfilment and for the obstacles in its own path.

(Redfearn 1985: xii)

Emotionally detached children who continue to depend upon defences may develop what Winnicott calls a 'false self' and what Kohut refers to as a 'narcissistic self', which is similar to Jung's 'pathological persona'. In Winnicott's notion, the false self sets up as a 'real self', and observers tend to think that this is the real self, but in relationship the false self begins to fail. It cannot provide adequate protection, and it is as if the pain breaks through the cracks. When defences become actively acute, neurotic and psychotic conditions may develop. The neurotic, sometimes described as 'nervy' and sad, is troubled by anxiety states. In a neurotic condition, only quantitatively different from 'normal' experience, the capacity for insight remains available. Psychotic experience, colloquially described as 'mad', is on the other hand qualitatively different from 'normal' experience, and insight is less available. Psychotic experience may arise from both functional/affective conditions, and organic conditions.

Whilst various traditions and schools of thought categorise differing defences, the two main types can be said to be unconscious blocking and distortion. The typology of defences which follows is given as a tool to aid understanding. In reality defences do not present themselves as if they come from neat boxes: 'in practice defences ofen overlap and defy categorization' (Jacobs 1982: 94). First to be considered are blocking defences, which might include splitting, denial, projection and repression. When these mechanisms operate it is as if parts of ourselves freeze or get buried to prevent us having an intolerable feeling.

Splitting

The splitting mechanism makes it difficult to be able to acknowledge both the good and the bad in a situation, and a 'Jekyll-and-Hyde' dynamic develops, in which one side of a situation is seen as all good, and the other as all bad. So where it is difficult to acknowledge the pain in a situation, the pain or the blame or the badness will be attributed to others. Before considering some examples, I must repeat that the mechanism will mostly be made use of unconsciously, so when it is encountered, it is important for no blame to be attributed, since this might reinforce the defence.

Examples

It is sometimes hard for parents to acknowledge that they are in difficulty with their child. Such circumstances might be dealt with through splitting, saying for example, 'Oh we don't have any problems with him at home – the difficulties are all at school.'

Sometimes we split off parts of ourselves which are difficult to face, pretending that the split-off parts do not really exist, and that we do not have to own or live with them. Such a child is described in Chapter Five (in the section on 'The role of image and metaphor in helping emotional growth'), under the name of Richard. He often presented as 'angelic', yet at other times was a thief and compulsive liar. It was as if he was trying to say to himself and others, 'If I'm such a nice and helpful boy, I can't possibly be doing the sorts of things I'm sometimes accused of.' Other examples of work with children which demonstrates the splitting mechanism are found in Jason's sandworld in Chapter Five (Figure 21), and Kelvin's second sandworld (Figure 5), described in Chapter One, in the section on 'Individual identity'.

The process of splitting can happen intra-psychically, inter-personally and in a social or organisational system. If one person or a group of people in an organisation are made to carry the badness or the blame, it is possible that splitting is at work as a way of avoiding something painful. Examples of splitting in social defence systems are given in Chapter Nine.

Denial

When we deny something we are unable to acknowledge it. Denial involves the avoidance of acceptance of painful feelings, often at an unconscious level. That denial is a fairly common human experience is reflected in phrases such as 'having one's head in the sand', 'whistling past the graveyard' and 'if you ignore it, it'll go away' (Cox and Theilgaard 1987).

Meeting this sort of defence can sometimes make one feel exasperated, particularly when there appears to be so much evidence which is counter to the denial. This can be the case in the classroom when a child denies a wrongdoing which was blatant to a number of other people. In such circumstances it can be tempting to ask the perpetrator, 'Why did you do it?' But if the acting out and the denial arise from defence mechanisms which are unconscious, then the child is most likely *not* to know why s/he has committed the offence. From a 'process-thinking' point of view, we might reflect upon the meaning of the action – for example, what might the child be defending against? – and store up these reflections to help gain greater understanding of the child. The immediate situation might be dealt with through a communication which reinforces boundaries, or provides an opportunity for reparation (see Chapter Three); and one might then look for a situation in which the child might be more receptive, and less defensive, to take up some of the underlying issues, for example by considering what sorts of feeling might be around for the child.

Projection

I invite you to begin this section with an exercise.

> **Exercise: How does working with children experiencing emotional and behavioural difficulties make you feel?**
>
> */**/***
>
> Brainstorm the feelings that are aroused in you by working with children with emotional/behavioural difficulties.

When asking teachers to do this exercise, of those feelings acknowledged positive ones are usually in the minority. Mostly acknowledged are feelings such as frustration, attacks on self-worth, anger, resentment, betrayal, etc. I suggest that we can understand these feelings in a way which helps us to understand the children better, and therefore to be able to meet their needs better. That is the aim of this section.

One of the most difficult aspects of working with children with emotional and behavioural difficulties is the problem of what one is made to feel. It is not just a question of feeling drained each day – the feelings are often much more precise and intense than that. It probably will not be difficult for anyone working with children to call to mind a time when a child 'got under the skin', provoking difficult and intense feelings. When working with disturbing children one might find oneself feeling hurt, abused, angry, frustrated, intolerant, anxious, de-skilled and even frightened. One of the reasons that working with children experiencing emotional and behavioural difficulties is so disturbing is that such intense and painful feelings are somehow pushed into the staff (as well as the other children). Sometimes it might feel as if it is difficult to know where the feelings are coming from, and the intensity of them might lead one to question one's own competence and professional worth. The task is to look in detail at behaviour as a form of communication and as an expression of feelings.

When we have difficult feelings, a psychologically logical but often unconscious response is to try to get rid of them. Freud's work helps here. Through his psychoanalytic work, it was he who first recognised and named the unconscious processes by which feelings get pushed out and onto other things. The idea was expanded by Ferenczi (1916: 32), who showed that such processes relate to everyday living: 'The daily occurrence of a simple civic life offers the neurotic the richest opportunity for displacement on to permissible fields of impulses that are capable of being conscious'. The theory is one of Freud's discoveries which has since been actively taken up by all the major schools of psychology.

Projection is the term given to the unconscious pushing out of a part of the personality onto other people or things. By pushing out the difficult feeling, the problematic content is controlled and the individual feels a – temporary – sense of release. It may happen in the classroom when a child faces a learning task which makes him/her feel threatened or anxious. Perhaps through a piece of irritating behaviour, the child's peers or the teachers are made to have the intolerable feeling which really belongs to the child in difficulty. Most often, negative projections will be experienced by teachers as niggling remarks or irritating bits of behaviour. Projection can also involve 'good' parts of the personality which have not yet been integrated or owned. This happens in those feelings of, 'Oh, I can't do it – (s)he's the one who's good at that!'

We all project onto many people we meet and know. Jung emphasised that, as long as psychic contents remain unconscious, they generally manifest themselves first in the form of projections. The task for each of us is to become aware of when we are projecting, and to learn to 'withdraw' or not make the projection. For children with emotional and behavioural difficulties, this is a process full of pain, since it involves not using this mechanism as a defence against the emotional pain, taking off the mask, owning the pain as one's own, and coming to terms with it. It is not surprising that some of the strongest projections come from children or young people with behavioural difficulties. A child without the inner resources to tolerate a difficult feeling, a capacity for reflection, and language to communicate, is likely to express the difficult feeling through unconsciously 'acting it out' thus making others have the feeling associated with the difficulty. In doing this, the projecting person genuinely believes that the difficulty is located in the other person. 'Mistakes are blamed upon someone else's malign influence; "look what you made me do". Self-hatred is turned into hatred of oneself by someone else' (Reed and Palmer 1972: 8). Whilst projecting a difficulty may provide a temporary sense of release for the person doing the projecting, this in itself does not enable the person to become more aware of the difficulty.

> The effectiveness of the individual lies in knowing the boundary between the self and the outside world and perceiving what is inside and what is outside. Projection blurs this boundary and distorts reality by making what is inside . . . appear to be outside. As long as this happens, not only is energy wasted but the internal state of the individual remains unaffected. Action is based on unreality and the facts are distorted.
>
> (De Board 1978: 116)

'Transference' is a particular form of projection which takes place when feelings from the past, or emotions one has about someone significant, are unconsciously transferred onto another person. When feelings are unconsciously transferred to teachers, it is as if the teacher catches the flak originally associated with someone else, most often the child's parents. Transferring feelings to another person serves the function of making something easier, providing an illusory sense of security, rather than confronting a difficulty. The transference of feelings unconsciously sets up a situation which somehow challenges the teacher to collude in some way and reinforce, or change, the expected pattern of behaviour and the pupil's part in it. Casement (1990: 7) speaks of transference as 'an expression of "unconscious hope" by which the [person] signals to the external world that there is a conflict needing attention'.

In work with troubled and troubling children, I place a high value on the notion of projection. It can be a very significant tool in helping to understand what is happening when difficult feelings are aroused in ourselves, and to make *hypotheses* about what might be affectively happening for the child. Let me quote a somewhat extreme example to make the point.

Example: John

The situation of 8 year old John was referred to the tutorial class service during his second year of junior school. He was described as unable to concentrate, using displacement and attention-seeking activities, and seriously underachieving. Attempts at improving the situation through management strategies had not been successful. John had no friends, provoked other children, was the victim of bullying, and was nicknamed 'Flea-bag'. His father had left the family home when his mother was pregnant with John. Mother found it difficult to set and consistently use appropriate limits and controls; corporal punishment, sometimes using a horsewhip, was inflicted erratically. It was at home that John's wilfulness was most noticeable.

During his first few months of twice-weekly attendance in a tutorial class group, John had a series of temper tantrums in which his anger and hatred were intense. During these tantrums he not only abused me, but screamed that he was not going back to 'that shit school', and, on one occasion, that he wanted to put himself under a car. In the projection I was made to feel as if I was in turmoil, not knowing what was happening to me, wondering if I could cope, and wishing I could give up and put an end to the suffering. I was made to feel something akin to what John was feeling. One of my readings of these events was that John had 'found' this way of communicating his feelings and that, at this point, he had at his disposal few other means of making such communication. Examples of further work with John are given in later chapters.

Where disturbing children are not able to articulate or communicate their difficulties in any other way than through the mechanism of projection, identifying those feelings which are projected onto us provides an opportunity to learn something about the child's experience. This is a difficult task; being able to distinguish one's own feelings from those received through projection is demanding of self-knowledge. Where adults are able to identify the projected feelings of a child, this information may be used to help assess his/her emotional needs. To some extent all humans struggle with inner issues of strength and self-esteem, and learning can feel like a very risky business. In relation to work with disturbing children, the adult has the task of enabling them to feel safer, become less projecting, and thereby recognise and own more of their own feelings.

The notion of projection might be used to understand group phenomena. For example, in the case of a group where there is some collective communication of difficulty, the children may at some level be communicating that 'we don't feel safe enough yet'. Such a communication may demand improved classroom management strategies, which will fulfil the function of helping the group to feel safer. (Group phenomena are considered in more detail in Chapter Seven.)

Projection and transference are mechanisms which allow us to cope temporarily with intolerable situations, but, if not recognised and worked with, these unconscious processes may also serve as mechanisms to block out the further experiences or relationships which might help to develop a greater capacity for tolerating risk and anxiety. In other words, projections serve to defend against development. Whilst projections operate, they beg the question, 'In what way is this an opportunity for the child to experience other ways of relating, which help to develop alternative internal structures of meaning?'

Responses to projections are considered in the next chapter.

Exercise: Recognising projections 1

*

Observe yourself in interactions with another person in which there is some issue which is difficult for the other person to talk about. Note the feelings which are aroused in yourself. Reflect upon the extent to which the feelings aroused in you reflect the feelings of the other person. You may wish to choose a situation in your professional or your personal life for this exercise.

Exercise: Recognising projections 2

*

Over the next week, watch out for situations in which you are made to have a feeling which you think might belong to the person with whom you are interacting. Consider the various situations in which you might meet this phenomenon – at work with children, at work with other staff, or in your personal or social life.

Exercise: Recognising projections 3

**

In pairs, role-play a situation in which a pupil is presenting some sort of difficulty to a teacher. The pupil is not able to be very articulate about the difficulty, and the teacher perceives the pupil as being obtuse. At the end of the role-play, acknowledge to each other the feelings which were aroused during the exercise. Note in particular the way in which the feelings aroused in the person playing the teacher may reflect those of the person playing the pupil.

Repression

Repression is a defence mechanism by which an impulse or idea unacceptable to the ego is rendered unconscious (Appignanesi 1979). Impulses, memories and painful emotions arising from conflicts are thrust into the unconscious, remain active, and indirectly influence experience and behaviour.

Example: Darren

The case of Darren illustrates how repressive defences may be related to the world of secrets. Darren's situation was referred to the tutorial class service after prolonged difficulty settling in class. He was described by the school educational psychologist as very restless, reluctant to try work, abusive of other children and feeling victimised by them, and often appearing moody and unhappy. The educational psychologist reported that, in testing, Darren performed at a good average/slightly above average level in his ability to make generalisations, arithmetic skills and visual skimming, with a slightly below average score on the picture arrangement subtest. He showed good verbal ability but was a virtual non-reader, recognising one or two sight words only.

Prior to tutorial class placement, Darren's mainstream headteacher described Darren as a cardboard cut-out figure, saying, 'I don't feel I know him.' He appeared to the headteacher to have the 'detachment of a deaf child', and to get into a lot of trouble without her being able to put her finger on exactly what it was. This head experienced the family as floating around her, and mum as 'slipping between the woodwork'. I first met Darren as a 7 year old, on his own in school. He said very little, made little eye contact, maintained that he liked learning, and acknowledged only that he was picked on, and got into fights.

My next meeting was with Darren and his mother, who spoke of Darren's circumstances somewhat passively and resignedly. She reported that Darren was an only child who lived with herself and other relatives on the maternal side. Mother had become pregnant with Darren when she was 14 years old, and his father was younger than this at conception. Father 'left mother' when she was pregnant, his attitude to the pregnancy being, 'It's up to you, it's your life.' Mother said she 'wasn't bothered' by this as she did not really like dad being around. She 'didn't like the thought of breast feeding' and so bottle-fed Darren. When Darren was five days old, father arrived back 'on the scene', and since has visited mother and Darren at his own convenience. Mum herself had to spend time in hospital during Darren's early months. In his early years Darren was diagnosed as having asthma. Because of mother's need for a break from Darren's boisterousness, he attended nursery. At first he did not want to stay, and used to scream and shout. When transferring to infant school he did not settle well, and soon became involved in fights. At the time of this meeting his contact with children out of school was mainly with older children of between 14 and 17 years old, with whom he went bike-riding. Mum did not seem very thoughtful about this pattern of peer contact. Neither did she seem able to think very much about her own relationship with Darren. She did note his tendency, when reading to her, of memorising rather than really understanding. Father was said to call in most days. Darren made one of his few acknowledgements at this point, in response to a question from me: he liked it when his dad came to play with him. Mum added, 'But dad plays when dad feels like it.'

Darren began twice-weekly attendance in a tutorial class group. It was through symbolic communication that he was able to begin to explore, and to indicate further, the nature of his defences. Darren's first sandworld – Figure 9 – showed a variety of sea-craft interspersed with sea monsters, a bicycle, a hiker, two bagpipe players and a fireman holding a lamp. Darren described the water monsters, the bike, the man with the bagpipes, and spoke of the man holding a light in a shelter. Here Darren's world is mainly on, and in, water, in the presence of widely distributed water monsters. It is as if, in this realm of water, of feeling, he faces monsters, and this watery realm just about takes over the whole world. Un-differentiated feeling in the unconscious overwhelms, submerges. The fireman holding a light is in a shelter within banks, protected from the water.

Figure 9 Darren's first sandworld

Figure 10 Darren's second sandworld

Darren's second sandworld – Figure 10 – came a month later. A formation of boats, an aeroplane and a horse face the right side of the tray where there is a sort of podium upon which three figures face the line of movement. Darren commented that 'the horse is the policeman's horse, and that if you learn the secret police will take you to prison'. This sandworld indicates that for Darren, the issues inhibiting his learning are related to secrets and the inner policeman.

The task with Darren involved furthering the exploration of issues of knowing what one is not supposed to know, learning what one is not supposed to learn, feeling what one is not supposed to feel, and fear of retribution if one tells a secret. Where there are defences related to such issues as secrets, knowing what one is not supposed to know, this may be related to the experience of abuse (Bowlby 1988).

Distortion

An individual may sometimes distort his/her view of experience to fit with a particular internal frame of reference. To some extent we all do this – a common example might be the various constructions of a road accident from the point of view of the parties involved. Where experience is systematically distorted to comply with an inner frame of reference, difficulties in relating to the shared world present themselves. Psychological distortion is said to take place through the processes of identification with an aggressor, through regression, or through introjection – feeling and acting as though an outer goodness has become an inner certainty. By means of the operation of introjection, the individual takes attributes of external persons and objects into himself and installs them in his own inner world. This is a mechanism of defence, in that in fantasy the individual meets his need to control and keep someone on whom he depends, by setting up inside an image of him or her, which then becomes part of himself.

(Reed and Palmer 1972: 10)

(Note that the mechanism of introjection is also important for growth, since it is through introjecting good objects, and in particular, in infancy, a loving relationship with the key parent, that the individual develops a basic sense of being a lovable and loving person.)

Another form of distortion can take the form of obsessiveness, for example guarding oneself from the experience of annihilation by endless warding-off rituals. Organisations as well as individuals may develop distorting defences: these are considered in Chapter Nine.

Example: Joshua

Joshua seemed to distort things. Things he said were often not perceived to be 'logical' by his teacher, and what seemed to be his version of reality sometimes included apparently fantastic situations. Joshua was referred to tutorial class when he was aged 7. In my initial discussions with his mainstream class teacher, he was described as someone who rarely expressed apparently logical connections between things. The class teacher spoke of how difficult it seemed to be to get through to Joshua. He was said to be isolated and aggressive and to feel picked upon. The class teacher commented that the boy's defences seemed to lock him into his own world, yet by her tone she seemed to show quite a dismissive attitude to these defences. I commented that if he felt picked upon a lot of the time, and everything 'out there' felt so terrible, then Joshua's current defences made good sense. They inhibited further development, but they also protected him. Helping someone out of this sort of situation first requires an acknowledgement and an acceptance of the situation as it is, from the child's point of view, without colluding with the regressive pulls. My hope was that this teacher would be able to respect Joshua in his current state of development, and then, together, they might be able to find a way forward.

I next met Joshua with his father. The father reported how, when Joshua was 6, the family had left home in another continent to come to live in England. In response to my question about what might have been left behind in the original country, and what might be missed, Joshua referred to his older sisters and brothers. Joshua seemed convinced about what he said. Father looked perplexed and quietly said, 'There are no older brothers or sisters.'

The evidence suggested that Joshua was using some form of distorting defence. When Joshua began to attend a tutorial class group, my sense that he had very little available ego with which to differentiate inner and outer experience was confirmed. For example, in the early days of his placement, when reporting to the group traumatic incidents in the playground at school, he would sometimes get totally carried away in the flow of his story, speaking and breathing more and more quickly, without pause or reflection, and apparently losing all capacity to manage

60

his increasingly unconnected flow of speech. Here, the distorting defence seemed related to a lack of ego and an undifferentiated emotional state.

Although defences protect and delineate, and are psychically logical responses to the way experiences are interpreted, they serve to maintain a psychic status quo, rather than to encourage facing and working on a difficulty.

If an individual's tolerance of frustration is so low he may fall back on these defences so frequently and compulsively that his capacity to maintain relationships may be seriously impaired. On the other hand the capacity to use the same mechanisms in a sophisticated way is essential for normal life. Splitting is the basis of the faculty of discrimination, and of a sense of right and wrong. Without projection and introjection it would be impossible to appreciate other people's feelings, to put oneself in their shoes. We should probably say, therefore, that these mechanisms are part of the standard equipment of the ego.

(Reed and Palmer 1972: 10)

In defensive activity these mechanisms are used to avoid confronting what are felt to be the intolerable demands of the external world. In facilitating a child's development, the task is to create other ways of feeling safe, so that the adverse impact of defences upon growth and change is reduced; and to enable the child to use such mechanisms to develop an appreciation of the external world upon which realistic courses of action can be based.

Exercise: Recognising defensive processes

Think about a particular child whom you know or with whom you work.

*

Imagine the child's dilemma in metaphorical language, in terms of a story. Make a drawing or a piece of writing about this child's story. This method can be used to clarify the issues a person is struggling with.

*/**

What underlies the child's difficulties? How is the child's self- esteem under attack at home/school? What are the child's defences?

> ## Exercise: Behaviours and attitudes which might inhibit the development of others
>
> *
>
> Look back at your own experience as a child and think of times when the attitudes of adults or their behaviour towards you subjectively seemed somehow to get in the way of your development.
>
> ***
>
> If you are in a group situation you could write anonymously each experience on a separate piece of paper, and then pool the papers for discussion.

You may wish to compare what emerged in your exercises with the results of a group of teachers who did this exercise, and produced the following memories from their own childhoods:

> When she was wide-eyed, very hurt and angry, and clearly not in control of herself.
> 'You are *trusted* to do this.'
> 'You're behaving like a prima donna!'
> 'It'll kill me if you . . . '
> The expectation that I should be a 'tomboy' *and* 'feminine'.
> Mum was really worried.
> Arguing is wrong; showing anger is wrong.
> Flying through the room in a rage and then mockingly saying, 'Well, you would say that wouldn't you.'
> Friends leaving without saying goodbye.
> A teacher telling my mum, who then told me, that another teacher in the school (who had been my teacher the whole of the previous year) wasn't respected by the staff.
> Not having an interest valued – somehow getting the feeling that it wouldn't be good enough as a career.
> 'As long as you do your best, nobody's going to be cross' – i.e. low expectations of academic work.

The group categorised the above memories as follows: mockery and sarcasm; mixed messages; lack of expectations and adult collaboration; goodbyes and leavings; emotional blackmail, burdening, guilt; judgement; adult losing control; and not acknowledging, validating, showing feelings.

This sample response of one group to the above exercise demonstrates some of the feelings and experiences which can get in the way of growth, and which may encourage the development of defences. The factors which contribute negatively towards, or reinforce, defences, are considered in the next section.

ANXIETY AND SEPARATION

Holt describes how, despite the kindliest of intentions on the part of teachers, fear is a debilitating characteristic of many pupils' experience of school.

> They . . . all said the same thing, that when the teacher asked them a question and they didn't know the answer they were scared half to death. I was flabbergasted – to find this in a school which people think of as progressive. . . . Even in the kindest and gentlest of schools children are afraid, many of them a great deal of the time, some of them almost all the time.
>
> (Holt 1965: 50)

That children might be fearful or anxious in school because of difficulties in relationships with peers is often acknowledged. Holt's observation suggests that anxiety in school-children is often much more common than is realised. Anxieties may of course also arise because of difficulties in relationships with teachers or family members, and due to factors in the school's organisation. Learning itself can feel like a risky business.

> New understanding is, potentially, threatening. . . . To be confronted with an unfamiliar curriculum can result in a feeling of complete bewilderment. You feel totally at sea, lost, without anchors of any kind, unable to relate what is being offered to personally meaningful interpretations. This is the experience of being unable to engage with learning because it is impossible even to formulate a question. In Kelly's terms, anxiety means a lack of implication. Where what is presented seems to bear no relation to any of one's ways of making sense of things, there is no possibility of grasping it, no sense of its connotations.
>
> (Salmon 1988: 27)

The work of child psychoanalyst Melanie Klein is helpful in understanding the mechanisms and dynamics which generate anxiety. Based upon substantial observation of infants and mothers, her work focused on the emergence of fear and anxiety in processes of separation between infant and mother. In Klein's terms, where the child has the experience of early anxiety being insufficiently considered and understood, fear and intolerance inhibit movement from what Klein calls the 'paranoid-schizoid' position to a more related state which she terms the 'depressive' position. The way in which the child negotiates the psychological passage between these two states is of crucial concern in development. Whilst the significant first moves towards the depressive position typically occur in early child-hood, we all continue to face, at least to some extent, the challenge of mediating experience in a depressive rather than in a paranoid-schizoid manner. So there is a sense in which we do not completely make this passage in infancy or even the rest of childhood, and feelings associated with the paranoid-schizoid state continue to erupt. It is important for teachers and other adults to understand how their interventions can help or hinder children's psychological movement towards the depressive position.

Paranoid-schizoid experience

I have found Klein's concept of the paranoid-schizoid position helpful particularly in understanding and working with children and young people with omnipotent, wilful behaviours, and with issues concerning the development of trust and dependency/independence. A key feature of the paranoid-schizoid position is omnipotence, having to have things one's own way. Omnipotence is partly related to the 'defensive use of such operations as splitting and projection to cope with powerful feelings of frustration, rage and terror which [the very young infant] experiences when its bodily needs for food and care are not met sufficiently quickly' (Reed and Palmer 1972: 12). Omnipotence is also related to the fear that getting one's own way is the only way of preserving the experience of things being good. Feelings of inferiority are sometimes related to the unconscious workings of a part of the personality which has become grandiose.

> It is as if the grandiose self was sending the following message: 'If you are not able to satisfy my demands for absolute perfection, you are absolutely worthless'. These attacks from within are normally feared by the individual who experiences them as threatening to his feeling of self-worth; they may be provoked by the slightest event.
>
> (Jacoby 1990: 87)

In the paranoid-schizoid state, which is viewed as the state prior to psychological separation from the mother, the infant wishes to remain in control of experience and there is a lack of capacity to tolerate fear, or anything bad, independently. These emotions are split off and are seen as belonging to someone else and so the child feels his/her rage to be justified. In infancy that 'someone else' might well be the mother; where this mechanism is active in school-children, that 'someone else' might be the teacher. The child perceives him/herself as totally good, and so it is as if the mother/teacher, in relation to this aspect of the personality, is thought of as a sort of slave. It is this dynamic of omnipotent behaviour which can underlie battles of wills between child and adult. The splitting of good and bad is a displacement of painful feelings which arises out of the difficulty of being able to acknowledge that one can love and hate the same person. From the perspective of paranoid-schizoid experience, others are blamed for everything. When a child is operating from within this sort of experience, his/her ability to make links is attacked, and curiosity and the foundations of learning are inhibited.

The paranoid-schizoid experience is demonstrated in an extreme but realistic way in the film *Whatever Happened to Baby Jane?*. Jane is not only subject to, but overwhelmed by, her impulses to make external reality fit to the framework of her subjective experience. Jane is totally unable to tolerate the perceptions of other people (in the film, her sister and the maid), and she seeks to obliterate these other frameworks and to construct a reality based only upon her own terms. In doing this she projects all the pain which she is unable to tolerate herself into her sister. She attempts to 'relate' to only those experiences which fit her own framework of what is good – demonstrated in the film by the relationship with her musical accompanyist, who is willing to collude. With the startling revelation, at the end of the film, that both sisters have been living with a false view of a major incident, Jane's experience of this is simply that her relationship with her sister could have been on her own terms all the time: 'So we could have been friends all along!' Where the paranoid-schizoid experience is un-restrained, a false personality develops due to a difficulty in integrating and acknowledging good and bad within oneself.

Klein linked the experience of the paranoid-schizoid state to the mechanisms of projection and introjection. These mechanisms are used to explain how the infant identifies these feelings of persecutory anxiety with the only object present in its world, namely the mother's breast, and projects these unpleasant feelings into it. Thus, Klein argued, the breast is experienced as persecutory, an external, uncontrollable object. This is then introjected into the rudimentary ego, where it becomes an internal per-secutor, 'reinforcing the fear of the destructive impulse within' (Klein 1946: 100). However, in reality the breast provides the infant with intense feelings of bliss and satisfaction during feeding. Klein supposed that the infant experiences the breast as providing two completely different kinds of feeling, and consequently relates this to two completely different objects, 'the good breast' and 'the bad breast'. This is achieved by the process of splitting. Alongside this process are the related ones of idealisation and denial. The more persecutory anxiety is experienced, the more the good aspects of the breast are exaggerated, resulting in an idealised breast, capable of inexhaustible gratification. With this goes the complementary process of denying the bad breast and the painful feelings experienced in frustration (De Board 1978).

Whilst these processes begin in the psychological negotiations of early infancy, to some extent they remain as forces with which children and adults have to struggle. In a sense, we all have our inner 'Baby Janes' with which we have to contend. These processes are associated with the foundations of defences, so an understanding of them can help in comprehending the way in which defences operate later in life. The continuing regressive pull of paranoid-schizoid experience faces us all at times and in relation to parts of our personalities. For example:

> fear of loss of control may lead an individual to attempt to dissociate himself from his inner world all together. He adopts rigid patterns of behaviour which exclude all contact with his inner world. When this happens spontaneity is lost. The individual goes through the motions of work, but there is no creative activity to understand and modify and adapt to his environment.
>
> (Reed and Palmer 1972: 14)

The task is to be able to relate to more of our experiences in what Klein refers to as a 'depressive' way.

Depressive experience

'When the infant develops to the point of being able to perceive his mother, other people, and himself as whole, separate persons, he reaches what Klein calls the "depressive position"' (Reed and Palmer 1972: 12). In this position one can tolerate acceptance, loss and limitations and one is more open to relationship. In the depressive position, separation and loss are experienced with less anxiety, and ego development can proceed. Understanding the crucial step between the two states is very important. In the paranoid-schizoid state we believe that we remain in control, but if we are really to relate to the other person we have to give up control, and so become in some way dependent upon him/her, in order to experience trust in the relationship. This movement is a constant quest with which, to some extent, we all have to struggle. The move from the idealised paranoid-schizoid state to the ordinary depressive state engenders great fear because we have to accept dependency. This is a particular difficulty for some children with emotional and behavioural difficulties, for whom dependency might be associated with rejection or active abuse. Hence it is as if such children are in a Catch 22 situation with regard to moving 'across the bridge' towards the depressive position, and establishing the capacity to trust, a pre-condition of independence. In terms of Winnicott's work, this development of maturity 'involves acceptance of a "not-me" world and a relationship to it; only in this way can autonomy and viability be achieved' (Davies and Wallbridge 1990: 55). As this development is so crucial, it is worth further exploration from the point of view of Klein's theory.

In the depressive position the child begins to relate to the mother as a whole object – as distinct from part objects, such as the breast, the face. The child also begins to recognise that the good and bad experiences do not emanate from two separate sources – a good mother and a bad mother –

but from one person who is the source of both. As this recognition develops, so the ego develops as an integrated whole, with a diminution of splitting and projection (De Board 1978). This leads to 'an increased understanding of psychic reality and better perception of the external world, as well as greater synthesis between inner and external situations' (Klein 1946: 105).

As the infant begins to realise that the source of both frustration and gratification is the same, s/he also realises that s/he can love and hate the same person – for example, the most available parent. The characteristic feelings in this position are depression, despair and guilt due to the infant's believing that s/he has damaged or may damage, has destroyed or may destroy, his/her loved object. Hence the name 'depressive' position. How are this depression and guilt helpful for further development? This set of theories explains their value as follows:

> As the infant works through this position, with the increasing integration of the ego and the establishment of a whole object relationship, there arises the drive for reparation, the wish to restore and repair what was felt to be destroyed by his own sadistic impulses. Just as the infant believed he had destroyed, so he now believes he can restore and make well and this results in a constant struggle between destructiveness and loving reparative impulses. If the loving impulses are successful and the mother's love strengthens, confirms, and returns these impulses, then the infant will experience renewed hope. This will lead to a further diminution of projection and splitting and the firm establishment of a super-ego, experienced as a source of love rather than as a severely persecuting object.
>
> (De Board 1978: 32)

The transition from the state of absolute dependence to that of relative dependence corresponds in many ways to Freud's idea of the transition from the pleasure principle to the reality principle (Davies and Wallbridge 1990). If development from the paranoid-schizoid to the depressive position is to proceed, rapid and effective help must be available to the child in replacing the anxiety state with a more tolerable state of mind. Menzies Lyth (1988) articulates what the key adult provides in this regard. Her description, which follows, highlights what may also be provided, in appropriate circumstances, by a sensitive teacher.

> Very important in these interactions is the mother's capacity to feel what the baby feels and respond appropriately. This implies that she should have enough capacity to take in the baby's massive projections of intense feelings and phantasies, to accept them without undue diminishment through denials or other defences, and not be physically overhelmed by them as the baby fears he will be. The 'good

enough' mother values and respects the reality of his feelings while making a more reality-based assessment of their phantasy content. By her reactions she conveys back to him an appropriately modified version of what he has projected. . . . Bion's formulations of these processes [are] useful: the mother is seen as a 'container' who can contain what the baby projects and work with it, her capacity for reverie being crucial. Bion also discusses the role of the mother in helping the baby develop his own capacity for thinking and so become more able to deal with himself in these situations. . . . The baby comes to be and to know himself as he is known and reflected back to himself by others, both the quality of the other's response and its consistency being important. . . . [The baby] needs a consistent picture of himself as reflected by the other if he is to build an integrated identity.

(Menzies Lyth 1988: 213–15)

The provision of these qualities of experience forms the basis of what I refer to as 'emotional holding', discussed in further detail in Chapter Four.

The gaining of maturity enables us to engage in the struggle with ambivalent feelings, and to accept, relate to and manage tensions within our personalities. 'The truly responsible people of the world are those who accept the fate of their own hate, nastiness and cruelty, things which co-exist with their capacity to love and to construct. Sometimes their sense of their own awfulness gets them down' (Winnicott 1965, quoted in Davies and Wallbridge 1990: 150). The way in which children negotiate the shift from the paranoid-schizoid state to the depressive position has significant implications for the toleration and negotiation of further anxieties, separations and losses. Issues of loss, separation and anxiety can be particularly pertinent for children experiencing emotional difficulties. Klein's work shows that early separations – and later separations experienced in daily life – may be experienced as losses which elicit anxiety. In school the child may try to renegotiate some of those separation anxieties. Challenging behaviour challenges teachers to make responses which can help the child gradually to internalise other possibilities.

Example: John

The background to John's situation is described earlier as an example of projection. During the early period of John's part-time placement in the small group of a tutorial class, he would disintegrate into rage when apparently small things went wrong. His rigid attempts to control situations were, I feel, about a fear of dependency, which may have been experienced by him as making him open to insult and violation. At this point, John seemed to me to be stuck in a world of inner omnipotence, related to Klein's paranoid-schizoid position. It was intensely painful for John to open up to trust, but if he was to extend his ability to symbolise, and to learn to differentiate experience, then he had to let in more experience. Paradoxically, the temper tantrums were a beginning for this. On some occasions he would break down and weep over the bullying and name-calling in school. The one occasion in which something was broken during a tantrum presented an opportunity for reparation. This is discussed in the next chapter.

Example: Carrie

The example of Carrie demonstrates something of the difficulty of moving beyond the dichotomised love–hate experiences of the paranoid-schizoid state towards being able to live with ambivalence – as in the depressive position.

Carrie's situation was referred to the tutorial class service when she was aged 9. A younger sibling had been in the care of the local authority, and then had gone to live with the father. In school Carrie was thought of as an unhappy child who had made very little progress with basic attainments. The class teacher wrote that Carrie seemed 'to be finding classroom life very difficult . . . She is late most days which starts a day off badly. She can arrive very angry and extremely rude. She seems to want to read and write well but is often not stable enough to cope with working.' Carrie's moodiness and unpredictable aggression alienated her from other children, and she would often destroy her own work. The educational psychologist found that Carrie did not acknowledge her father and had only irregular contact with him. Mother felt that Carrie would prefer to see her as both mother and father. At the time there was the expectation of a court case to re-examine care arrangements for Carrie and another sibling, with the possibility that father might press for custody.

In my first meeting with Carrie and her mother, mother was able to acknowledge that difficult feelings might get in the way of learning. However, when I tried to open this discussion further, she became agitated and defensive at my attempt to explore what sort of feelings might be around in relation to father. I had the impression that father was portrayed as the 'baddy', the scapegoat for the family's ills.

Carrie began her part-time placement in a tutorial class group, and it was noticeable how much of a struggle it was for her to think about difficult feelings. For example, when she returned after a period of absence, she did not want to acknowledge that she had been ill. When, as part of a wider exercise, she faced the completion of the sentence 'I feel sad when. . . . ', she wrote 'I dot feel sad.' Yet on the other hand Carrie seemed alert when she acknowledged that she knew what I was talking about when I said that sometimes strong feelings can get in the way of our learning.

Soon after her start at tutorial class, the new educational year began, and Carrie had a new class teacher. The class teacher and headteacher told me how Carrie apparently liked her new teacher, and would, on occasion, verbally acknowledge this. However, at times, she also sought out the headteacher to say how much she hated her class teacher, and to request a change of classes. On one occasion, Carrie shocked herself and the school staff by hitting her class teacher. I considered that circumstances were conspiring to make it very difficult for Carrie to move beyond a love–hate set of experiences, to be able to live with ambivalence. As part of my regular liaison with the school, I met with Carrie and her class teacher and we explored the issue of mixed feelings. We talked about all of us having mixed feelings about people in our lives, sometimes liking them, sometimes feeling angry with them, and sometimes thinking that we hate them. This meeting was one of a variety of means of demonstrating to Carrie that having mixed feelings is acceptable, and that one can learn to live with them.

These examples bring us to the wider discussion of being influenced by parental difficulties.

THE INFLUENCE OF PARENTAL DIFFICULTIES

The Croll and Moses survey of junior school practice (1985) confirms that teachers still tend to attribute many children's difficulties to adverse home circumstances. This prevailing assumption is still often expressed through expressions such as, 'What can you expect from a child from that kind of family?' The danger in such attitudes is that they may assume that the parents do not care about the child's education, that the child's development is a static, given phenomenon and that the interventions by teachers do not make sufficient difference to a child's capacity to learn. Where teachers collude with such attitudes, it is as if they wish to avoid the guilt of underachievement in their pupils. If sustained, such attitudes serve to distance the teacher from the responsibilities of the situation, and expectations conspire to reinforce negatively the child's capacity for learning and development. Not only does teacher–pupil interaction have a major impact on the capacity for learning, but Paul Widlake's recent books give the lie to the often expressed view that some parents are 'not interested in their child's education' (Mongan and Hart 1989: xvi). There is also a wealth of evidence which shows that the nature of the partnership between school and home, as advocated in and since the Warnock Report, makes a positive and significant difference. The impact of such partnership is enhanced where teachers are able to take account of the dynamic of interaction between pupils and their parents.

Productive work with children who bring a painful experience of parenting to the educational setting is helped by an understanding of the issues the child faces.

> Children will bring to the school situation doubts and suspicions that belong to their own characters and experiences, that are part and parcel of their own emotional development distortions; also children will always be liable to distort what they find at school, because they will be expecting to find their home environment either reproduced there or else represented by its opposite.
>
> (Winnicott 1964: 203)

Barrett and Trevitt (1991) suggest three common ways in which children may be negatively influenced by parental affect. The first is rejection:

> When a mother is unable to tolerate the infant within her space, this may result in her rejection of him. . . . This mother is unable to be emotionally available for her child, and he is unable to gain the reassurance, support and encouragement that are essential to him. His basic needs are met without reference to his feelings and he is therefore deprived of meaningful interactions. All the energy of such a child may be directed towards trying to attract his mother's attention, though if this fails he may develop his own rejecting responses. . . . If he adopts attention-seeking strategies to ensure that he is noticed (particularly if these demands become excessive) his mother's rejecting behaviour may be exacerbated. Alternatively, the child may withdraw, making fewer and fewer demands.
>
> (Barrett and Trevitt 1991: 11–12)

The second is overprotection:

> When a mother is unable to allow her infant to explore independently, he has few opportunities to learn that he and she can survive separately. The resulting relationship is sometimes referred to as symbiotic or 'smothering mothering'. . . . A child with an over-protective mother is rarely allowed to experience frustration. . . . He has therefore had no chance to develop problem-solving strategies nor to discover that frustration and anger can be survived. This can result in omnipotent behaviour with the child never discovering that his wishes are not commands.
>
> (Barrett and Trevitt 1991: 12–13)

The third is confusion:

> Where neither mother nor infant discover a shared, fixed point of reference they give the impression of spinning within an uncontained space. No contact seems possible. There is no apparent opportunity for the formation of any attachment since the mother's emotional availability is inconsistent. The infant's behaviour appears to be excessively anxious. Because he receives few responses, he is unable to learn any meaningful strategies for interacting with others. He may be offered tantalising glimpses of closeness by his mother only to have them instantly withdrawn. Both mother and infant seem to alternate between perpetual motion, often frantically searching for each other, or sinking into despair. While excessive activity can defend against feelings of depression for some children, others may attempt to take control for themselves by adopting a parental role.
>
> (Barrett and Trevitt 1991: 13)

From a slightly different perspective, the theories of transactional analysis suggest that we learn 'scripts' – or particular roles – which we internalise and live out in our daily lives. The way a child lives in and experiences the world reflects the way s/he has learned to see it in the family. Our personal constructs are influenced by our position in the family, the number of siblings, the gender balance, and so on. The family dynamic is a powerful one in which we may learn to play particular roles. Behaviour may be more comprehensible if it is related to messages carried from the family – the script. Similarly, attachment theory (see Chapter One, section on 'Emotional needs and learning') suggests that what children explore in the world is powerfully influenced by what their attachment figures, either consciously or unconsciously, want them to discover. So these scripts or experiences affect the inner unconscious life of the child. Jungian analyst Francis Wickes (1977: 39) writes, 'Children gather from us the atmosphere of all that we most carefully ignore in ourselves.' Wickes (1977: 41) describes the analysis of several children and shows how 'in each one the unsolved problem of the parent was intuited by the unconscious of the child'. Horney (1951, in Bowlby 1988: 78) argues that adverse influences 'boil down to the fact that the people in the environment are too wrapped up in their own neuroses to be able to love the child, or even to conceive of him as the particular individual he is'. Bowlby speaks of mothers who have themselves been abused being prone to periods of intense anxiety punctuated by outbursts of anger. They are distrustful, extremely sensitive to any type of separation situation, even the most everyday and commonplace, with responses of high levels of anxiety or anger. He argues that where the parent–child relationship becomes inverted, the child may appear to be overindulged, often expected to be grateful for care s/he receives and not to notice the demands being made. In such situations the child may be under pressure to conform to seeing the parent in the light which the parent requires.

We are all influenced to some extent by parental difficulties. Where difficulties with parental experience become particularly entrenched for the school-child, the role of the teacher is significant in giving the child the opportunity to experience the hope of other possibilities. Through a process-related approach, we become more aware of those signals which help our understanding, and of the ways in which we can be more effective in helping emotional growth and access to learning. However, we should not think that teachers are omnipotent, able to solve the problems of all those who come before us. For some children, the script implied by the parent–child dynamic may be too strong in relation to the development thus far of the child's inner resources. This was the case at the time of my work with Mary.

Example: Mary

Mary was referred to the tutorial class service when she was aged 7. The referring educational psychologist described Mary as presenting the behaviour of a younger child, reporting that she did not mix well with other children, being often on her own and sometimes aggressive towards them. She was said to be uninterested in many class activities and often unco-operative. With the educational psychologist, she was very talkative, but avoided any eye contact. Mary was described as having many mannerisms or affectations of a younger child, for example her walk, the babyish sound of her voice, and her facial expressions. But other aspects of her behaviour, for example the structure and content of her language, were more age-appropriate. Her scores on the tests which were administered varied between the average range and the well-below-average range. At this point she could count 1–10, but had not firmly established 1:1 correspondence. She was at a pre-reading stage, but understood concepts of print and would hold a book and 'read' a made up story making use of clues from the pictures.

Mary was the only child in a single-parent family. Father was occasionally seen by mother and daughter, but had never lived with them. Mother seemed to find it difficult to hold a notion of her own authority in relation to Mary's difficult behaviour at home, and to set appropriate structures and limits. At the point of the referral to tutorial class, mother readily acknowledged that she herself had been to a special school for children with moderate learning difficulties, and that she would be willing for Mary to go to a special school if Mary did not make progress as a result of her tutorial class placement. There were reports that, when Mary had attended the local nursery, mother herself had maladroitly tried to join in the activities in a way which appeared to be for her own enjoyment rather than to support Mary. Mary's mainstream primary school reported that mother made great demands for time. When the school later imposed more boundaries on this, mother would sometimes swear and spit at teachers, and on one occasion threw a chair. There had already been a long history of social service involvement with the family. A few years earlier, when mother feared that Mary might be taken away from her, she had thrown herself out of a window and broken her leg.

Over the first year of Mary's part-time tutorial class placement there were considerable areas of improvement. She became able to sustain concentration and try hard in activities involving literacy and numeracy, such as making her own books with pictures. She participated in group discussions, demonstrating a wide vocabulary, listened to and enjoyed stories, and took a delight in craft work. On the journeys with her escort to and from the class, she had initially habitually rolled her head around and bumped into things, and had to have her hand held at the kerb edges. During her first year in placement, she learned to manage the journey to and from the class appropriately and independently. By the end of her first year in placement, Mary had a part-time general assistant assigned to her in school (the same person who escorted her to and from tutorial class). (It was in the second half of this first year at tutorial class that the experiences described in Chapter Five, section on 'The role of image and metaphor in helping emotional growth', took place.)

The school staff and I became concerned, however, that Mary, despite progress, also continued to present the image of a little girl who did not feel it was her place to develop and eventually grow up. Those working with Mary were careful to maintain for her the expectations of the peer group. Over the next year

73

Mary's development continued. There was a concerted effort to enable Mary to travel independently the quarter-mile or so between home and school, to enable mother to allow this to be possible, and to support Mary in this venture. Mary seemed to be making great strides in her self-confidence. Previously she had often described herself as 'stupid', and would almost always say 'I can't . . .' at the beginning of any activity. Now a more alert, direct child was developing, who believed in herself as someone who could learn and be independent. She told her peers that she wanted to become a teacher when she grew up, and this communication was taken seriously by them.

Mother had considerable social worker support for her parenting skills. It was evident that mother was also changing in some ways. For example, she bought a series of puzzle books which she worked on with Mary. However, it was also apparent that Mary's experience of success met with erratic reactions at home. It seemed that mother still found it difficult to value the work, pictures, models and cookery which Mary took home. It was as if some fundamental attitude in mother was not ready to shift. At this point, Mary's literacy and numeracy skills were, at an estimate, approaching mother's skills in these areas.

As we went into the third year of Mary's part-time placement, her educational attainments regressed. In school she was again crying with regularity, and there was a worsening in her relationships with her peers, in her academic work and in her general behaviour. On her journeys to and from tutorial class she once again began to roll her head around and not look where she was going. Mother had been suggesting that Mary might need a special school, and Mary was already talking of her expectation that that was where she was going. The difference between Mary's attainments and those of her peers was becoming more and more marked. A statutory review of Mary's Statement (under the 1981 Education Act), involving all those working with the family, led to the conclusion that the LEA should offer Mary a place at a day school for students with moderate learning difficulties. Mother and Mary accepted the offer.

It was as if the taste of success set up too many conflicts for Mary, as if the script with which she was presented by her mother was too strong, and she defended against these conflicts by regressing. It was as if her functioning as a pupil with moderate learning difficulties was an unconscious collusion with the expectations of her mother.

Inevitably those working with troubled children sometimes face disappointments. However, what matters is that the child senses that one tried one's best, that, in Bettelheim's terms, one tried to do the right thing: one never knows at what point in the future the child is going to be able to make use of the experience of a relationship to help towards growth. Indeed, Quinton's (1987) research showed that ex-secondary school-girls who had had problems in school were as likely to report positive experiences retrospectively as those who had not, and that positive memories of school were strongly related to whether the girls planned for work or marriage:

it may be that the girls acquired a sense of their own worth and their ability to control their destinies as a result of their pleasure, success, and accomplishments in a few specific areas of their childhood lives. . . . Our findings suggest that the experience of some form of success, accomplishment or even just pleasure in activities at school may be important, not because it dilutes the impact of stressful happenings, but because it serves to enhance confidence and competence in dealing with the hazards and dilemmas of life.

(Quinton 1987: 27)

It was the perception of a number of those working with Mary's case that she had been emotionally abused. It is appropriate here to mention the influence of active physical or sexual abuse.

Active abuse raises questions of knowing what you are not supposed to know and feeling what you are not supposed to feel. Physical or sexual abuse leads to a pressure to shut away information related to events in the outside world. 'Threats to abandon a child make her (or him) intensely anxious about separation, however routine it might appear to others' (Bowlby 1988: 86). Bowlby describes abused children as exhibiting malicious behaviour which appears to have the sole intent of making the victim show distress. 'Almost always it occurs suddenly without any evident cause. Such attacks, coming suddenly, are frightening and seem to invite retaliation; clinical studies report them to be directed especially towards an adult to whom the child is becoming attached' (Bowlby 1988: 91).

The anxiety which children who have been sexually abused are likely to have felt is described by Wilson (in Maggs 1989a) in terms of four areas of fear. First are fears of annihilation, of violence, of being killed. Second are fears of arousal, of lack of control, of bewildering excitement and of traumatic sexualisation. Third are fears of disapproval, stigmatisation, moral judgement, a sense of disorder, potential catastrophe and family disintegration. Wilson's fourth area of fear is that of intolerable betrayal, being let down, deceit, trickery, with no place for safety. Here the experience is of outrageous intrusion, enforced intimacy, being put down, stolen from; here it is possible to develop a state of impossible comprehension, knowing it not to be right.

Miller (1985) suggests that the experience of sexual abuse by family members may result in an interlinkage of love and hate. The abused person may not be able to express his/her anger towards the loved person for fear of losing that person. It may become difficult for the abused person to imagine that love is possible without suffering and sacrifice, without fear of being abused, without being hurt and intimidated. Miller suggests that where the fact of the abuse is repressed in order for the person to 'survive', knowledge which threatens to undo this repression is warded off, and that repressing a trauma reinforces it, by heightening its unconscious power. Where this happens, the adult who has been abused as a child may abuse his/her own children for his/her own unconscious needs, which are the more urgent and uncontrollable the more deeply repressed the original trauma.

75

Physical attraction and affection are always part of love, and this has nothing to do with abuse. But parents who have had to repress the fact of having been abused and who have never consciously relived it can become very confused in this regard where their children are concerned. They will either suppress their genuine feelings of affection for fear of seducing their child or they will unconsciously do the same to their child as was done to them, without having any idea of how much harm they are causing, since they themselves always had to distance themselves from their suffering.

(Miller 1985: 163)

Even where a child has not been actively physically or sexually abused, the child's experience of the parents has a profound affect upon development. For example, when difficulties with parents are associated with the parents being experienced as critical in a way which seems to negate acceptance, these critical voices become internalised. The resulting self-criticism may then get in the way of further development. I now explore this phenomenon more fully.

SELF-JUDGEMENT

Punitive self-judgement, another potential inhibiting factor in development and learning, is a common characteristic of children with emotional and behavioural difficulties, who often feel themselves to be worthless, to be unable to complete learning tasks, or who destroy their own work. The concept of the super-ego, originally developed by Freud, helps in understanding this phenomenon.

The super-ego relates to inner, unconscious self-judgement which reflects difficulties experienced in the outer world. The super-ego manifests through, for example, those voices within us which evoke the early reprimands of our parents, upbraiding us for our failings, for 'being bad'. Such voices can be frightening because they reside within us. They can spy on us and hold us accountable for failings we hide from everyone else.

Psychological violence frequently forges the links in the anxiety chain as a result of the interplay between anxiety created by real uncertainty and anxiety created by threatening voices within. The super-ego voices are mobilized when the real uncertainty evokes memories of having been 'bad' children, of having failed in the eyes of our parents. Unconsciously we link the threat from without with a feeling of our worthlessness, as though 'good' people would or should never face such a threat.

(Hirschhorn 1988: 49)

The super-ego relates not just to unconscious conscience. Bowlby asserts that the beginnings of the development of the super-ego are through the baby's first fears of abandonment by her/his mother, or close parenting figure. If sudden or permanent losses are experienced at this point in development then the chances are that a rather fierce super-ego, or 'inner police officer', is born. Freud sees the super-ego as heir to the Oedipus complex. The infant feels deep hostility towards its parents, which it cannot express, partly because of love, partly from fear. So the infant projects its aggression onto them, which seems reflected back as exaggerated strictness. The super-ego is introjected parental authority. In Freudian terms, it is the result of a defensive effort which prohibits the expression of Oedipal wishes.

The super-ego can become so persecuting that it can be too difficult for the child to begin to own his/her guilt, and thereby become what might be regarded as psychopathic, i.e. apparently without a conscience. It can lead to lying of the kind where the child is completely unconscious of telling a lie. Maggs makes connections between the operation of the super-ego and dynamics experienced in school situations:

> It is a paradox, then, that it is the super-ego, the determinant of morality, which can also be the determinant of immorality. . . . for children so afflicted in this way the use of punishment is likely to be of little effect and could even be counterproductive. Yet it is lying, probably more than any other form of misbehaviour, which can 'wind us up': we often feel insulted by it, can be filled with moral rectitude and it stirs up in us the worst possibilities of retaliation. This is . . . where the infliction of punishment . . . may be a certain inhibitor of growth. One could well ask whether punishment, inflicting pain, actually heightens consciousness (I think it can with those people who are quite secure) or whether it prevents the individual from taking greater responsibility for her/his behaviour.
>
> (Maggs 1987: 3)

Exercise: Yourself as a child

*

In reflecting upon the issues discussed in Chapters One and Two, think of yourself as a child. Express the memories of yourself as a child in the form of a drawing.

SUMMARY

- Symptoms of blocked interaction and communication indicate those areas which may generate further understanding of a situation.

- Emotional defences are brought into operation for the purpose of protection and safety, yet they also serve to inhibit development.
- Emotional defences may block experience (through splitting, denial, projection, repression) or distort experience.
- Anxiety is generated in the experience of negotiating a separate sense of identity in relation to key adults.
- The desire to remain in control of experience (as in Klein's paranoid-schizoid state) inhibits the capacity for curiosity, for making links and for more related relationships (Klein's depressive position).
- Aspects of the 'scripts' provided by parents may have to be struggled with in order to proceed with development and learning.
- Inner, unconscious, self-judgement (associated with the super-ego) may reflect difficulties experienced in the outer world, and internalised aspects of parental judgement.
- Processes which inhibit emotional development and learning are not static, but are a function of the experience of interaction with key people in our lives.

Part II

FACILITATING EMOTIONAL GROWTH AND LEARNING

3

ATTITUDES AND
OBSERVATIONS

INTRODUCTION

In Part One I examined the links between emotions, or affect, and learning, the qualities of emotional experience helpful to stimulate learning, and emotional experiences which inhibit learning. Part Two is much more concerned with 'doing', with how to facilitate emotional development and learning. I begin, in this chapter, by considering the role of attitudes and approaches to difficult behaviours and feelings, and issues concerning the observation and assessment of needs.

Strong opinions and attitudes can be aroused by working with troubled and troubling children, partly because of the intensity of feeling aroused, and partly because of the practical difficulties encountered in trying to help such children engage with learning. Some of the difficulties relate to the children's capacities for managing learning, such as coping with difficulties without becoming unduly upset, having an adequate concentration span, and being able to accept help and sustain interest in an activity until completion. Many of the difficulties are associated with the capacity of the children to relate with others in the learning environment: for example, the capacity to wait, to take turns, to accept being a loser in a game, to share attention or resources, to make and keep friends, to negotiate independently with peers and take responsibility for the consequences. Being able to relate better with others in the learning environment can require some children to develop the capacities to manage difficult feelings, such as greed, envy, and the desire to 'act out' difficulties through dominating group situations, bullying, 'over-reacting' to provocation, needing to have one's own way, and so on. In contrast to seemingly 'overcontrolling' children, there is also the range of difficulties experienced by apparently 'over-controlled' children. For the latter it is a struggle to express their own identity, to become appropriately assertive, or to avoid being a victim. Maggs cogently expresses the nature of some of the difficulties in working with troubled and troublesome children:

These children are those who have suffered such emotional, physical or sexual abuse so that they carry baggage and preoccupations that prevent them from getting on with learning. They have generally suffered the most appalling separations and losses of significant loved persons which have not been mourned. They are tormented from within and their anxieties and persecutions are acted out, in spite of themselves. They are at the mercy of their most infantile desires. Such is the enormity of the internalising or external expression of their pain, often shown in aggression and pure anger, that it makes it extremely difficult for adults, teachers, parents and other caregivers to stay with their pain and not retaliate and/or opt out. [Such children] have lost confidence in themselves, their self-esteem is very low and they find it difficult to make the emotional investment and take the risks needed in order to learn. They have suffered from over-positive or over-negative mothering and fathering. They may have had inconsistent care so that parental neglect may have been followed by parental zeal, and parental disappointment, and parental punishment and parental guilt and parental over-indulgence and parental disappointment – a vicious circle. So unhappy may have been their relationships with parents and transitory parenting figures that they find it difficult to trust adults, and authority figures in particular. They can be defiant or over-compliant or vacillate between omnipotence and impotence.

(Maggs 1989b: 5–6)

Winnicott suggests some of the school-based needs that such children and young people may have. He argues that those whose homes are not secure come to school, partly, to:

find a home from home. This means that they seek an emotional situation in which they can exercise their own emotional lability, a group of which they can gradually become a part, a group that can be tested out as to its ability to withstand aggression and tolerate aggressive ideas.

(Winnicott 1964, quoted in Davies and Wallbridge 1990: 149)

For teachers to maintain the capacity to continue sensitively to assess and meet the educational needs of children with such emotional difficulties is an inordinately arduous task. Part One of this book focused on *understanding* the issues involved in emotional growth and learning. It is also our *attitudes* towards working with such children and young people which have a profound influence upon our actions and our capacity to facilitate emotional growth and learning effectively. In order to explore the issue of attitudes and approaches, I consider in this chapter those attitudes which have a facilitating effect on emotional growth and learning in direct work with children. One's attitudes towards such work are significant for the learning and development of all children. In particular, the significance of one's attitude towards work with troubled and troubling children is explored, as are the core attitudes necessary for effective work.

One's attitude affects the way one approaches the task of observing a child. It is through careful observation that we come to appreciate the links between the child's behaviour, interactions and feelings, and to a better understanding of the child's needs. These issues are explored in the second half of the chapter. In subsequent chapters the focus on understanding and attitude is widened to embrace *skills* used in facilitating emotional growth and learning.

ATTITUDES FACILITATING EMOTIONAL GROWTH AND LEARNING

One's attitude represents the starting point for facilitating emotional growth and learning. From the point of view of the processes of interaction, *how* something is done can be as or more important than *what* is done. (This argument is made in more detail in the introductory chapter.) How something is done depends upon one's attitude towards it. This section speaks of attitudes necessary to facilitate the emotional growth and learning of all children. These issues are particularly pertinent for work with troubled and troublesome children. The nature of one's attitude towards, and one's relationship with, children with emotional and behavioural difficulties has a large part to play in one's effectiveness in facilitating their emotional growth and learning. One's attitude and interaction has an impact on the child's engagement and response. Troubled children, whose experience of relationship has been in some way traumatic, seek to protect themselves from further trauma, and are alert to discover one's attitude towards them. And what they find will have a significant impact on whether their protective screens are reinforced, or whether they might be open to new possibilities in relationship.

How might the worker conceive of the difficulties which the child brings to the relationship? To what extent is s/he able to reflect upon the meaning of particular forms of behaviour by the child, and view the overt behaviour as a symptom of an underlying issue? The 'symptoms' a child brings to relationships in educational settings can be seen to express and communicate something of the child's dilemma. The notion of symptoms is not here used derogatorily, or from the perspective of a medical model, but from the perspective of being manifestations or symptomatic of some psychological necessity.

The feelings teachers receive from children can often tell them something about how the child is feeling (see Chapter Two, section on 'Projection'). The capacity to receive and assess such communication requires workers not to 'get stuck' in the associated difficulties. For example, the mainstream class teacher of Richard, described in Chapter Five, was able, although he felt and recognised his frustration, to offer the observation that Richard's name-calling and stealing were communications about needs. When a child communicates something through a piece of difficult behaviour in which others might be made to carry the bad feeling, this action by the child may be the best possible adaptation the child currently has available. The symptoms brought by a child can be seen as responses which are psychologically logical – the best possible adaptation of the child to the particular experience and circumstances. From the perspective of the psychology of Jung, we can say that symptoms have an intentionality, in that, at some level, they represent an urge towards meaning. Every symptom offers both a challenge and an opportunity – the opportunity, that is, to discover and grasp the problem that underlies it. Since 'symptoms' are a necessary communication of the child's experience, they need to be taken seriously, related to non-judgementally and with empathy. In 'process' terms one *relates* to the child's difficulty or depression, rather than trying to *do* something *to* the child.

Real change can only come from within the child. When children have experienced emotional or physical abuse, mistrust or neglect, they will only allow themselves to be open to change if they are able to experience acceptance and trust. Where the child experiences threats in relation to symptoms, his/her defences are reinforced. The paradoxical nature of defences has already been mentioned (Chapter Two, section on 'Defences against development'). Paradox is also present where defences are lowered or given up. This is illustrated by an example from the story of *I Never Promised You a Rose Garden*. The following comment shows that the heroine was able to give up her defences and be available for other experience: 'And at the instant she discovered emptiness, she discovered hunger' (Green 1964: 234).

The attitude of a teacher or other worker towards difficult feelings and behaviours has a considerable impact upon a group dynamic and the potential of the individuals concerned to make creative use of the environment. The importance of attitude in educational settings is well documented. For example, Nash (1973) shows how children modify their behaviour for better or worse in response to the way they *feel* themselves to be perceived by their teachers. The idea that the 'climate' of the classroom has an important effect on pupils' achievements and behaviour is now widely acknowledged. There is a substantial literature which suggests that whether the classroom climate is positive or negative is, to a considerable extent, under the teacher's control (Mongan and Hart 1989). Galloway (1990) suggested that training for teachers in the area of special educational needs could best focus as much on attitudes as on skills.

Rogers presents an important argument:

The attitudes that make for change and growth and improved relationships are not mysterious, even though they may be difficult to attain. One is the willingness to 'indwell' in the perceived world of the other; a willingness to step into his or her private world and perceive it as if it were one's own. The more such profound understanding occurs, the more tensions relax, fresh insights occur, and communication becomes possible. Another facilitative attitude is the valuing and respecting and caring for the other person. The more this exists, the more the individual gains in self-esteem, and hence in a more responsible and responsive stance toward others. Finally, realness and absence of facade in one party draws out realness in the other, and genuine meeting (to use Buber's term) becomes possible.

(Rogers 1978: 139)

So what are the key features of a facilitating attitude? Rogers' comments above link to the three core attitudes or conditions which he suggests (1961) are nececessary for development to take place. These are realness or genuineness; prizing, acceptance and trust; and empathic understanding. Rogers argues that if a certain type of relationship, based on such conditions, can be created, 'the other person will discover within himself the capacity to use that relationship for growth, and change and personal development will occur' (1961: 33). Rogers argues that it is the attitudinal elements in therapeutic relationships, such as feeling trusted and being understood, which account for changes. Of clients in a therapeutic relationship, 'it is the way in which [the therapist's] attitudes and procedures are *perceived* which makes a difference to the client, and . . . it is this perception which is crucial' (Rogers 1961: 44). Rogers argues that to the extent to which a teacher establishes a 'therapeutic relationship' with his/her class, based upon such principles, learners are enabled potentially to become more self-initiated, more original, more self-disciplined and less anxious (1961).

Rogers' 'core conditions' are used as a framework for the following discussion. Then I consider the importance of communicating a sense of belief in children, and in being open towards reparative possibilities.

Realness or genuineness

For Rogers, the notion of realness or genuineness implied relating without facade (1961). Dockar-Drysdale (1990) calls those children with such poor ego development that the various aspects of themselves remain unintegrated within the personality 'unintegrated' children. These children need ego-provision, or help with developing a functioning ego, and depend upon what is nascent and newly emerging in themselves to find meaning through relating to another. Dockar-Drysdale points out that in order to protect the attempt to build a creative relationship with this 'other' we have to be careful that children find *us* when they reach out, and that they do not again find defences, or flat personas instead of people prepared to relate. In enabling children to become persons, the children need the experience of the fullness of the adult worker as a person in his/her own right. This involves being able to listen to a child's communication with the whole of oneself, to the exclusion of all else. This fullness of presence occurs where the person is without front or facade, is in contact with his/her own feelings, and is able to communicate those feelings, when appropriate, honestly and sensitively.

Realness or genuineness implies being personally involved in the relationship with the child, whilst also being able to observe the relationship with detachment. Dockar-Drysdale (1990) refers to the quality of involvement necessary as 'conscious involvement with concern'. Involvement implies leaving one's own defences behind, as it were, there to return to, but not to use in a situation where they would be inappropriate. 'The adult *must* be involved, but never at the expense of his boundaries, which need to be maintained. The delinquent must be able to feel that the adult is deeply concerned, but *never* collusive' (Dockar-Drysdale 1990: 144). Involvement with unintegrated children has its dangers. 'There is a very great difference between the integrated [person] who becomes consciously involved with a regressed child and the unintegrated person who for his or her own instinctual satisfaction becomes involved without concern for the child who needs to regress' (Dockar-Drysdale 1990: 15).

A further example of 'realness' is where children in emotional difficulty are enabled to experience the availability of the caring adult's fullness of presence and concern, in a variety of manifestations, for example the teacher's capacity to join in play.

Prizing, acceptance, trust

'Prizing' refers to treating the other person as if they were a prize: accepting implies showing positive regard for the other as a person of unconditional self-worth (Rogers 1961). Prizing and accepting do not mean approving of all the other person's behaviours, but they do mean appreciating and accepting him/her as a person. This involves accepting how the other person perceives experience, that their experience is different from one's own, yet valid.

Dockar-Drysdale (1990: 105) describes the perception of a boy at the Mulberry Bush Therapeutic Community, who said, 'At the Bush they let you start all over again in all sorts of ways.' Prizing, accepting and trusting involve caring for the other person and non-judgementally accepting her/him in her/his own right. Some would refer to this quality as unconditional love. Redfearn (1985) explains the importance of this, commenting that it seems to be a fundamental law of human relationships that the individual can only yield up his/her pertinent part of unconsciousness when that part is given, or maybe feels it is given, enough recognition, value and sympathy by a key caring adult. A non-judgemental attitude involves accepting the child and his/her emotional state of being, without colluding or being permissive with the child.

When one prizes a child, one should never promise anything one cannot be sure to provide, since such failure can have disastrous effects on an emotionally deprived child. It is important that the grown-up should not consent to make an adaptation which cannot be sustained for a period, because reliability is a fundamental ingredient in facilitating emotional development and learning (Dockar-Drysdale 1990). Dockar-Drysdale makes the point that failure to meet needs is different to letting a child down, since an adult is not going to be able to give a child everything s/he needs all the time.

Empathic understanding

Empathy is the function by which we attempt to perceive and understand what is happening in other people. Empathic understanding concerns being able to appreciate what life is like for the other person, understanding the other person's frame of reference, how the other person sees situations, relationships and the world in which s/he lives. It involves being figuratively able to stand in his/her shoes whilst remaining in one's own. In *To Kill a Mockingbird*, lawyer Atticus Finch says to his daughter, Scout, 'You never really understand a person until . . . you climb into his skin and walk around in it' (Lee 1963: 35). To relate empathically to other people usually involves a certain effort, as empathy is an attitude that requires one to set aside one's own feelings and needs and to step *partially* outside oneself. In relation to children with emotional and behavioural difficulties, one seeks to empathise with the contents of the child's unconscious, the motivations of which s/he will not be aware. Empathy implies 'affective resonance and a partial, temporary fusion of perspectival worlds' (Cox and Theilgaard 1987: 87). Being heard with empathy has significant implications for emotional change: as the other person 'finds someone else listening acceptantly to his feelings, he little by little becomes able to listen to himself. He begins to receive communications from within himself' (Rogers 1961: 63).

Empathy is different from sympathy. Sympathy is concerned with appreciating how someone else feels because that is the way one would feel in that situation oneself. We can never know this precisely. If there is what might be called 'too much empathy', too much accent on feeling and compassion, there is a danger that one might lose understanding; one needs to combine empathy with abstraction and reflection (Dreifuss 1988). 'Too much empathy' might involve overidentifying with the child. If one loses one's perspective in this way one loses one's capacity to help the child. A symptom of this might be wanting to do 'too much' for the child. Paradoxically, as Hillman says (1967: 28, 34), 'the first block to knowing another is wanting to know another. . . . Active love cannot redeem from fear since the deepest cause of fear is the fear of love itself.' There is always the question of whether one is grasping something in the other person through empathy, or whether one is projecting one's own feelings or fantasies onto him/her (Jacoby 1990). Part of this involves trying to understand how the child experiences events differently from oneself.

Teachers may find it relatively easy to empathise with children who appear similar to the way they were themselves as children. Salmon (1988) suggests that for such children it may be relatively easy to know what sort of involvement in the curriculum they could develop, and the teacher might have a particular feeling for introducing the material to these pupils in their own terms, in forms they can grasp and engage with. 'But for other children in the class, who seem very unlike the children we were ourselves, whose personal lives are mysterious, even alien – what does this curriculum mean to them, what could it mean?' (Salmon 1988: 44).

Permitting oneself to understand another person carries some risks. Rogers comments, 'If I let myself really understand another person, I might be changed by that understanding' (1961: 18). When thinking particularly of work with unintegrated children, empathic understanding demands well-developed capacities for tolerating frightening feelings. Bettelheim speaks of being able to see through the eyes of the child and to experience the degree of terror in one's own imagination. Dockar-Drysdale cites a child who said to her, 'The reason why you are the only person who has been able to help me is that you are *the only person prepared to be terrified with me*' (1990: 17, my emphasis). Bettelheim and Dockar-Drysdale argue that what the adult has to show, above all, is that s/he is prepared to take the same risk as the child is asked to take. The risk for the adult is the risk of empathy, which is a risk that children sense one's capacity to take.

This has implications for the way in which adults who work with disturbing children relate to their own emotional experience and sources of fear, and what each individual adult has made of these experiences. What the adults as individuals have become, emotionally, is part of the equation of interaction, making a difference, consciously or unconsciously. The more that adults who work with disturbing children can be conscious of the part played by their own emotional history, the more valuable they can be in helping such children. Being alongside people in pain can be frightening, so people who are trying to meet the needs of emotionally deprived children should, for their own emotional safety, seek to be extremely conscious of what they are doing. When someone else's pain triggers one's own it is not uncommon to want to run away. 'People working with deprived children have to learn a lot of painful things about themselves, if they are to be of use to children: for example, to become aware of the violence in themselves' (Dockar-Drysdale 1990: 129).

In the range of impulses and desires among which we live there is considerable communality. All along Freud's continuum between the normal and abnormal personality the same principles are involved. 'Pathology, by making things larger and coarser, can draw our attention to normal conditions which would otherwise have escaped us' (Freud 1933: 58). This is echoed by Graham and Rutter's comment (1970) that it seems highly probable that, with some exceptions, 'disorders' of behaviour in childhood do not constitute 'diseases' or 'illnesses' which are qualitatively different from the normal. The dilemma of the other person is not significantly different from those which one has, or could have, faced oneself. The vital element of bearing witness through empathy is the capacity to understand, in relation to the other person, that 'there but for the grace of God go I'. One's capacity for empathy is affected by one's capacity to relate to the disturbing parts of oneself, and to one's understanding of one's own history.

Rogers summarises the value of relating genuinely, with acceptance and empathy, in the quotation which follows. Although he speaks of the relationship between therapist and client, these processes are pertinent to relationships in the 'helping professions'.

> As the client finds the therapist listening acceptantly to her feelings, she becomes able to listen acceptantly to herself – to hear and accept the anger, the fear, the tenderness, the courage that is being experienced. As the client finds the therapist prizing and valuing even the hidden and awful aspects which have been expressed, she experiences a prizing and liking of herself. As the therapist is experienced as being real, the client is able to drop facades, to more openly *be* the experiencing within.
>
> (Rogers 1978: 11–12)

The helper's capacity to be genuine, be accepting and relate empathetically depends on the extent to which s/he has been able to be genuine, accepting and empathetic towards *him/herself*, i.e. his/her own internal world. This brings us to a discussion of the importance of self-awareness.

Self-awareness

Rogers writes, 'the more I am simply willing to be myself . . . and the more I am willing to understand and accept the realities in myself and the other person, the more change seems to be stirred up' (1961: 22). Self-awareness is fundamental to building helping relationships with others. 'If I can be sensitively aware of and acceptant towards my own feelings – then the likelihood is great that I can form a helping relationship toward another'

(Rogers 1961: 51). Moreover, the more self-awareness one has of oneself, the more one is able to help others develop self-awareness. Rogers says of himself, 'the degree to which I can create relationships which facilitate the growth of others as separate persons is a measure of the growth I have achieved in myself' (1961: 56).

In seeking to meet the needs of children with emotional and behavioural difficulties, there is the danger of seeking quick solutions, which may serve to allay the anxiety aroused in those taking quick actions, rather than provide effective ways of meeting developmental needs. Self-awareness is a vital component of being able to reflect upon anxiety-provoking situations, of containing one's own anxiety, and of being able to think genuinely and creatively about the issues at hand. Rogers says, 'the more I am open to realities in me and in the other person, the less do I find myself wishing to rush in and to "fix things"' (1961: 21).

Self-awareness of the impact of one's own feelings upon the dynamics of a situation is of fundamental importance. Given the potency of some of the projections experienced when working with children experiencing emotional and behavioural difficulties, the adult needs to be keenly aware of the feelings aroused in him/herself, and what happens to those feelings. To what extent are we able to observe ourselves and recognise feelings being aroused by others? To what extent can we manage those feelings? To what extent do such feelings become unconsciously part of our interaction? Where the last of these happens, we lose the capacity to relate to the other person from the perspective of his/her own experience. Something as simple as an unconscious sigh may be experienced by the child as a further rejection, as further evidence of his/her hopelessness.

> For change to occur, people have to become aware of their own authentic feelings, and of the effect these feelings are having on their own EBD [emotional/behavioural difficulties]. In psychotherapy, such awareness is called countertransference and it is recognised as one of the most powerful means the therapist has for reaching out towards the nub of any situation. There is no reason why its use has to be confined to psychotherapy.
>
> (Higgins 1990: 13)

The sort of dynamic that we find ourselves getting drawn into through countertransference is a significant indication of the nature of the conflict with which the other person is presented. Where the adult can muster self-awareness s/he is more able to manage the countertransference and use it to help the child to experience other perspectives on his/her inner conflicts. This process gradually enables the child to make use of a wider and more flexible range of assumptions and responses in his/her relationships.

The following exercises are designed to explore issues of self-awareness.

Exercise: Self-awareness – capacities for empathy

*/***

Make two masks. One is to represent the childish, unsure, uneasy, shadowy or disturbing parts of yourself. The other is to represent how you have healed, your strengths or your creativity. Quietly centre yourself and put each of the masks to your face, in turn. Note your feelings as you look through and empathetically take on the qualities of each of the masks. Put the two masks to your face, the first nearest your skin, the second on the outside. Look through the two masks together. Note to yourself how it feels.

Exercise: One's own self-esteem

*/**

Reflect upon the following questions:

1 What did you think of yourself in your early life? What were your bruises? How did you learn to live with them? How did the bruises enrich your emotional life?
2 How have you become healed? What have you discovered of the well-springs of your own creativity and healing?
3 How have your hurts and healings increased your sensitivity to others, improved your caring skills, enlarged your capacity for holding pain? Make a statement of your strengths.
4 How can you use your own experience, knowledge of your bruises and life awareness to help the growth of self-esteem of the children trusted to you?

(adapted from an idea by Michael Brown)

Communicating a sense of belief in the child

Hope is a passion for what is possible.

Kierkegaard

It has long been recognised that the beliefs or expectations which teachers hold of their pupils tend to become self-fulfilling prophecies. Rosenthal and Jacobson (1968) report an experiment in which teachers in the first five grades were given false information indicating that a small number of students were likely to make considerable academic gains in the coming

91

year. A significant proportion did make such gains. Surveying the wealth of writing in this field, Hamacheck (1978) suggests that on balance research confirms the hypothesis that teacher expectations make a difference to pupil achievements.

With regard to children troubled by disturbing feelings, who remain unintegrated in terms of the development of an ego effective in mediating the feelings and the influences of the outside world, communicating a sense of belief in the child is necessary to enable the development and internalisation of ego strength. It is not unusual for children with entrenched emotional and behavioural difficulties to have the experience of adults in their lives giving up on them. If a child is to move towards autonomy, then s/he needs to have a sense of belief that autonomy is possible, in order for it to *be* possible. Yet in the face of continuing despondancy in pupils, the teachers' task of sustaining this belief can be a very daunting one. The first example given below illustrates this.

For a teacher to communicate a sense of belief requires an attitude which consistently shows a sense of trust in the natural regenerative capacities of the healthy psyche to take over, when it is time for each child. The teacher might communicate this by being emotionally alongside the child, supporting, making expectations, yet not pressurising. In such circumstances, it is as if the teacher holds the faith that the child will become less troubled. In some situations, someone is needed to carry this belief for the child, in the hope that the other adults in the child's life, and the child him/herself, will renew this sense of faith for themselves. Children themselves find ways of making statements of belief about themselves. The example of Alan is given below.

Example: A bottom-set GCSE group

When I met with a teacher who faced daily difficulties and pupil apathy in a bottom-set GCSE science group in a mainstream secondary school, the teacher acknowledged that it seemed that the pupils in this group had had the spirit knocked out of them, and that he felt as if he was having the spirit knocked out of him in trying to work with them. What mattered perhaps more than anything else here was this teacher's response to his sense of frustration, and the extent to which he would be able to find, and communicate, a sense of belief in these pupils.

Example: A child's own statement of belief about himself

It is important for children to have opportunities to internalise the sense of belief in themselves. This example comes from the work of a small group in a tutorial class setting. In tutorial class children sometimes made statements of intent about ending their placements. Alan, who came from a religious family, chose an explicit way. We were looking together at a book about gods and goddesses, and talking about the power of Uranus to elicit change and innovation. Alan turned to the wall, closed his eyes and prayed. He then informed the group that he would not be coming to the class when he transferred to secondary school, at that point ten months away. Against the odds, that is actually what he was able to achieve. Ironically, this was a boy in whom I found it difficult to have faith (although I hope I did not communicate this to him!) and I took seriously his expression of his renewed ability to call upon his own faith in himself.

Example: An ex-pupil's comment about what made a difference to her

In a training session with a group of support service teachers, one teacher told of his chance meeting with a 17 year old ex-pupil after she had left a local support unit for 'disruptive' students. The girl reported that her life had improved significantly. When the teacher asked her what had made the difference, the girl said that at the support unit, 'they didn't stop believing in me'.

Exercise: Showing belief in the children

/*

The pair or group is asked to consider that they are a staff group from one school who have been asked to work on the following issue: about to join the school is a new member of staff who does not have much experience in working with pupils with challenging behaviour or low self-esteem. The staff of this school have adopted Rogers' core conditions as part of their statement about how they wish to work. They recognise that children with low self-esteem find it difficult to believe in themselves – in their own goodness and in their potentials, and that if the children are to develop these beliefs, they need to get a sense that significant adults believe in them.

Your task is to prepare a way of briefing the new member of staff about this.

Openness towards reparation

Working with disturbing children in educational settings involves finding and teaching the 'teachable' part of each child, and making alliances with the positive aspects of the child's interaction, interests and attainments. The child, however, because of experiences and adaptations (such as defences), may not yet be able to sustain positive relationships, or may initially rebuff attempts to make alliances with his/her potential. This is what happens in the testing-out process. A child will of course test out where s/he stands with adults, and children with emotional and behavioural difficulties often test out over and over again. When such testing-out takes place it seeks to elicit responses in the teacher which enable the child to feel safe, and so be able to get on with the risky business of learning.

Example

In a film about Bruno Bettelheim's Orthogenic School in Chicago (Horizon, *Bruno Bettelheim*, BBC, 1986), a former pupil, as a middle-aged adult, reflects upon the testing-out which he made when he was at the school as a child:

> As I arrived at the Orthogenic School, Patty was the one who greeted me, and I knew, as children know, I guess, that this lady liked me. But knowing that didn't make me happy. What had to happen was the process of testing. And with the kind of hatred I had for women, at that stage of my life, that process became very graphic. The fellow who has a parent who is some-times nice and sometimes horrible begins to think that that's the way the world is. In my own case that's the way it was. At the time when I came to the school, as I was confronted with Patty, who was an exceptionally fine human being, and a very affectionate and decent human being, I wasn't able to accept the affection, which caused even more anger. Every human being wants to accept the affection. But if you condition yourself to not accepting affection because if by accepting it you only let yourself in for the next downfall, you put yourself in a position where, by accepting it, you're asking for your own destruction. So you find yourself in a position where you don't dare to hope that the affection is for real and you keep testing to find out if it is for real. That's the process whereby, step by step, you find out whether it is. Maybe that explains my own need to hurt those who would be nice, because in that environment, I needed to find out whether or not the affection would continue to come.

Klein's work helps in understanding some of the issues and dynamics involved in such situations. Klein argued that throughout life we struggle with the tension of trying to reconcile the splitting and healing of our consciousness, the images we have of others, and our relationships to them. She suggests that a significant psychological task is to learn to contain the anxiety that ensues when the images of the good and the bad are inte-grated, to tolerate their feelings of shame (features of what she terms the 'depressive' position). However, if the anxiety overwhelms the individual, s/he regresses to what Klein termed the paranoid-schizoid state, the position of fundamental splitting and alienation. Klein uses the word 'position' to emphasise that the depressive experience is not a fixed stage in the life cycle but a recurring experience. (These dynamics are considered in more detail in Chapter Two, section on 'Anxiety and separation'.)

We continually face the problem of sustaining a 'whole' image of those to whom we are close. Hirschhorn (1988) describes the reparative process as being shaped by several interdependent moments of experience. He argues that the reparative process emerges when we first become aware that we have hurt someone we value, and that in learning to repair our relation-ships to others, we learn to affirm our own value. He suggests that in repairing our relationships, we overcome our tendency to split off our feelings of badness and project them onto others. Rather, we see others and ourselves as both good and bad, as whole. In order to experience shame, Hirschhorn says that we must overcome the anxiety of facing our pettiness by working through a set of complex feelings: we enter the depressive position. In doing the work of reparation we are no longer grandiose. We affirm our limitations and therefore the inherent value of our life in the face of its limitations. By sustaining our feelings of shame in the depressive position, we do not simply relieve our feelings of guilt but restructure our relationships to others.

Facilitating the capacity for reparation involves providing opportunities for reparative experiences, over and over again. The example of John and his temper tantrums (given in Chapter Two, section on 'Anxiety and separation') is pertinent here. On the only occasion in which John broke something during a temper tantrum, my purposeful lack of immediate response was used by John to offer reparation: he offered to repair the object he had broken. The child's own moves towards reparation are worth so much more than those made in response to pressure, since they are related to changes in the child's inner world. 'Reparation rests on a symbolic process, on the transformation of meanings attached to particular symbols of our inner life' (Hirschhorn 1988: 212). When reparation takes place, the internal constructs of troubled children change, providing further possibilities for emotional growth and learning.

Exercise: Reparation

*/**

Consider occasions where you have been able to make reparative gestures. Reflect upon:

1 the emotions which you had to face up to in order to make the gesture;
2 the impact of the gesture upon the relationship.

The implications of the theme of reparation in work at the organisational level are discussed in Chapter Nine. The notion of working with openness towards reparation links closely with the concept of 'emotional holding', discussed in Chapter Four. Coming to the end of our consideration of attitudes, I turn next to examine the issue of observing and assessing needs, and then consider in subsequent chapters the more 'active' ingredients of facilitating emotional growth and learning.

OBSERVING AND ASSESSING NEEDS

The way we behave is not random. Behaviour always has a meaning, and is symptomatic of that meaning. In Chapters One and Two I explored the sorts of issue which give clues to the meanings which might underlie behaviour. A working hypothesis of the possible meaning of behaviour can help build a picture of what a pupil's needs might be. The more accurate a working hypothesis about a child's difficulties, the more precisely we are able to meet her/his needs. The role of careful observation is fundamental here. Observation of *how* things are done rather than *why* can be much more instructive. This is because of the unconscious nature of the child's search for what is needed, whereby children 'give unconscious cues that indicate what they are looking for in key relationships' (Casement 1990: 31). Observations which assess such needs form the basis upon which the adult can make the necessary affective responses, thus providing the emotional qualities to support growth.

In the introductory chapter (see Figure 1) I described the capacities available for learning and development as a function of inter-personal and intra-personal experience, reflecting subjective experiences of the present and the past, and the experience of family, friends and the school environment. If we are to understand children and their needs fully, it is necessary to observe and make assessments in relation to these multi-dimensional, interactive processes. Yet, traditionally, observation and assessment have fallen a long way short of this. In his review of developments in the identification and assessment of special educational needs, Cline (1990) identifies four modes of assessment: focus on the learner, focus on the teaching programme, focus on the zone of potential development, and focus on the learning environment. To understand the multi-faceted nature of observing and assessing need, it is useful to consider these four modes briefly.

Cline (1990) argues that focusing observation and assessment fairly exclusively upon the learner is commonly used and is encouraged by the prevailing pattern of resource allocation under the 1981 Education Act. Such a focus has disability, or deficit, as the basis of its hypothesis, and assumes that the individual's traits are those which are inhibiting learning, that normative tests are a valid means of providing a picture of the child's strengths and weaknesses, and that teaching based upon the results of such tests will lead to improvement. Such an exclusive focus upon the child fails to take process and interaction into account.

Assessment which focuses on the teaching programme has at its base, Cline (1990) argues, the hypothesis that the curriculum is not well suited to the needs of the child, and it aims to match the curriculum more closely to the child's skills by analysing learning tasks. According to Cline, in this model the specialist teacher passes technical knowledge to class teachers, and the parents and children participate passively. Such a 'transfer-of-knowledge' assumption about teaching and learning may lead to focus on lower-order skills. It is useful to consider ways in which access to the teaching programme can be enhanced, but if the potential difficulties of the deficit model are to be avoided, then the teaching programme must be viewed in the context of *interaction with* other factors involved in facilitating or inhibiting learning.

Where the focus of observation and assessment is on the zone of potential development, Cline (1990) states that the underlying hypothesis is that the teacher is not making full use of the child's emerging skills and abilities. By identifying the zone of potential development of the child, through carrying out standard tasks and monitoring the child's performance, one may develop a picture of the assistance which the child requires. This approach looks at what the child can *almost* do. It depends on the availability of a specialist teacher, and the class teacher is thereby perceived to play a relatively passive role.

Observing and assessing needs in relation to the learning environment (Cline 1990) examines the conditions in the environment which facilitate success. Through methods such as classroom observation, diaries and oral self-assessment, the different perceptions of the learning environment can be analysed. The implication of this approach is that the most useful area for observation and assessment lies in the interaction between the child and her/his learning environment.

When one focuses on the child and his/her interactions, diagnostic labels become largely irrelevant (Rogers 1978). The child's experience of interaction is the crucial issue in the relationship between emotional factors and the capacity for learning. It is thus the last of the four modes identified by Cline that potentially may be the most useful in relation to emotional factors and learning. Interaction and relationship are the key, and to assess them requires a process-oriented perspective, which examines the various factors as a set of dynamic processes. The task is to assess the child *in relation to* other factors which promote or inhibit learning. I now examine these, taking in turn the following areas: child–teacher; child–peer; child–school as a whole; child–family; the child's subjective experience.

Child–teacher interaction

One might observe the feelings aroused in oneself by particular children. The projection of feelings by troubled pupils onto teachers was considered in Chapter Two. It is difficult to be on the receiving end of difficult projections, but this does provide an opportunity for the teacher. If we are able to have some perspective on the feelings that are aroused in us, so that we do not become overwhelmed by them, or caught up in them, then there is the possibility that we might listen to them. We are then able to ask the question, 'What feeling has the child pushed into me?' If we are able to do this, then we are beginning to be able to receive, to experience a communication about the child's experience. This may be a communication which the child has not yet been able to make in any other way. What we are made to feel may convey important diagnostic clues for understanding otherwise elusive communications (Casement 1990). In the example referred to in the section on 'Projection' in Chapter Two, I felt John's sense of turmoil, not knowing what was happening, wondering if I could cope and wishing I could give up and finish the suffering. The struggle to maintain some perspective on these feelings enabled me to understand them as communications of John's experience. Awareness of the feelings we are receiving from children is a means of helping understanding of what might be happening for the child in the here and now, and of logging changes in experience over a period of time.

Being aware of projections can serve the useful functions described above. Building into an assessment the dimension of feelings aroused in adult workers also helps to ascertain the capacities for tolerance which people have in the situation. 'The dividing line between a "problem" behaviour and an acceptable behaviour is one of degree and tolerance; how often is it a problem and to whom . . .?' (Sambrooks 1990: 41). Our tolerance levels are crucially linked to our capacities to manage disturbing feelings which are projected onto us. Being aware of this, and understanding its significance in the developing dynamic of relationship, may in itself help some people to develop their capacities for tolerance, particularly where opportunities for careful reflection upon the interaction are available.

To use the notion of projection as a sole assessment technique is insufficient. Sometimes it can be difficult to disentangle one's own feelings from the experience of those projected onto us by someone else. Experiences of projection should be backed up with careful observation. Some emotional difficulties are not well communicated through projection, particularly perhaps where the person is withdrawn.

The messages, signals and cues given by each child through overt messages, posture and other non-verbal behaviour invite the adult to 'think of me as this or that kind of person', or 'behave towards me in this or that kind of way'. The teacher can learn much by reflecting upon the sort of interaction which the child seems to be asking for. Such reflection can be aided by the following sorts of question (some of which are adaptations of a personal communication by Helen Green):

About roles:
- What kind of role does the child seem to be wishing you to enact?
- What kinds of pressure produce which kinds of demand by the child?
- Do you feel you need to take special care with him/her? If so, how?

- How does the child react when winning, losing, being left out, getting his/her own way, or not getting his/his own way?

About boundaries:
- How does the child expect you to react if s/he breaks rules? For example, does s/he expect a particular kind of punishment?
- Does s/he get into trouble? If so, what is it about?
- Does the child habitually break your rules or fail to conform to routines?
- Does s/he respond to explanations?
- Does s/he find it difficult to accept corrections from others?
- What happens when time is up?

About context:
- How does the child react when s/he meets you in other places, e.g. the corridor?
- Does the child behave differently with you, or seem to feel differently in different situations, i.e. more/less structured, when directed or less directed by you, when taking part in solitary activities or those which require interaction?
- Are some routines with this child more stressful than others?

About your understanding:
- How do your answers to these questions inform your understanding of the child's subjective, inner experience, or personal constructs?
- How might the child's constructs be inhibiting him/her from emotional development or learning?
- What process of communications might help the child communicate more, and engage with you undefensively?
- For what manner of intervention is the child ready? For example, how conscious is s/he of his/her behaviour and feelings? How much is s/he able to acknowledge areas of difficulty? Is s/he close to being able to reframe particular personal constructs?

Child–peer interaction

Child–peer interactions can be rather complex. Yet, where it is emotional factors which inhibit learning, observing these interactions can be a significant part of appreciating the nature of the child's functioning in the learning environment. The process of observation can take a number of forms, and choice of an appropriate form will depend on the circumstances. Various possibilities are suggested below. In these suggestions there is inevitable overlap between observing child–peer interactions and teacher–child interactions. (Some of the suggestions below have been adapted from Mongan and Hart 1989.)

- *Diary description:* An attempt to record everything that occurs during the period of observation. The period might be relatively short. Detail is important here – body language, facial expression, quality of relating, etc.

- *Diary of affective responses:* This refers to the keeping of a diary about a particular child in which key impressions of the child's emotional world are noted, e.g. moods, showing/acknowledging feelings, reporting of significant events from outside school. This might be kept on a daily basis as a series of key words or phrases.

- *Time sampling:* One might observe a pupil's behaviour for an amount of time (e.g. an hour) at five-minute intervals to ascertain a picture of the child's functioning, e.g. trying to note in what ways and circumstances the child is on or off task. The observation has to be frequent enough to produce the required profile of the child; the usefulness of observing particular behaviours, and the use to which these data will be put, need careful consideration.

- *Event sampling:* This technique requires a record to be kept of each occurrence of a defined type of behaviour in a given period of time. Example: Observe Jane for twenty minutes each day, during which each occurrence of a particular behaviour is recorded. It can be helpful to concentrate upon how this behaviour manifests, and the surrounding circumstances.

- *Using profiles/checklists:* One might choose to observe the detail surrounding what appear to be key characteristics for a particular child, for example:

  - body language and eye contact;
  - anxiety level;
  - how the child relates to oneself;
  - dependence/independence;
  - response to praise or failure – can the child tolerate being corrected, or to bear to not know?
  - response to winning or losing: can the child bear to compete or to lose?
  - anger: can the child use it? Is the child afraid of it?
  - does the child engage in solitary or mutual play?

These types of characteristic have been developed into various sorts of profile, e.g. the Bristol Social Adjustment Guide (Stott and Marston 1971), the profiles in Achenbach and Edelbrock (1983) and Reardon *et al.* (1979), for assessment against normative criteria. The Bristol Social Adjustment Guide is based on assumptions and perceptions about behavioural norms, rather than analysing interaction, and can be time-consuming to complete. In contrast, the child-profile format shown in Figure 11 is designed to provide a quickly obtainable 'snapshot' of a child in a particular situation. It can serve as a useful focus for discussions between teachers about differences and similarities in perceptions of interactions. It may also be used to gauge the changes in a child's functioning over a period of time. (It was originally developed by Paul Greenhalgh and Linda Murgatroyd for use in the London Borough of Hackney's tutorial class service.)

Child–school interaction

This section relates to the relationship between the child and the wider institution of the school. Here one might be concerned both with the qualities of interaction and relationship between staff and pupils, and broader questions of ethos and culture which provide the framework within which relationships take place. The former raise questions of teachers' sensitivity and tolerance of stress, as well as their capacities to communicate to children with care, consideration, acceptance, respect and to encourage a sense of personal worth. Such issues may be related to inter-staff relationships – how much do the staff collaborate and support each other? Those factors which affect the ethos and culture of the school are considered in Chapter Nine.

The nature of the interaction between children and the school as an organisation is largely determined by the extent to which the school acknowledges that it has a responsibility to educate for emotional/behavioural development, and how explicitly the school aims to act to include all children in positive and developmental learning. For example, how are people in the school encouraged to work with the uncomfortable feelings aroused in work with troubled children? How does the school work proactively with personal and social defence mechanisms (see Chapters Two and Nine)? How do the school's organisation and structure facilitate productive interaction between staff and pupils? Does the school recognise that personal and social development does not happen by chance, but may be encouraged through, for example, guidelines and an active policy for Personal and Social Education (e.g. DES 1989e)? Has the school formulated/implemented/reviewed a behaviour policy, which builds on the recommendations of the Elton Report (DES 1989c)? Is the behaviour policy the basis for early observation and assessment? Does the policy provide for consistent, yet flexible approaches across the school? Is the policy realistic – does it enable people to cope better with each other? Does the policy provide staff with positive strategies for managing behaviour? Are such strategies seen in relationship with positive strategies to facilitate learning? Is there an appropriate curriculum, in terms of courses and modes of accreditation offered? Further attention is given to policy development in Chapter Nine.

Child–family interaction

Parents know a lot about their children which can inform a teacher's

Section A: Evidence of the Child's Anxiety/Ability to Cope

	not clear yet	very often/ a lot	usually/ quite a bit	sometimes/ a little	hardly ever/ hardly at all
Restless and unsettled					
Moves about the classroom inappropriately					
Appears worried, miserable					
Is tight and held-in					
Dominates group situations					
Fights with other children					
Bullies other children					
Is a victim of bullying/verbal abuse					
Wets or soils					

	not clear yet	hardly ever	sometimes	usually	very often
Can be assertive where necessary					
Responds to provocation from peers without over-reacting					
Accepts not always having own way					
Accepts being the loser in a game					
Able to take turns					
Able to wait for what s/he wants					
Able to share valued resources					
Able to share attention					
Respects other children's privacy					
Respects other people's property					
Values/takes care of own belongings					
Can tolerate unexpected events/changes in routine					
Can accept adult authority					
Able to relate with physical contact					
Considers the feelings of others					

Liked by other children			
Can make and keep friends			
Can independently negotiate with peers and take responsibility for the consequences			
Can cope with difficulties on a task without becoming unduly upset			
Values/takes care of own work			
Shows pleasure in own success			
Appreciates other children's achievements			

Section B: The Capacity to Acknowledge and Work on Difficulty

Able to acknowledge own feelings of sadness, anger etc.			
Able to acknowledge own difficulties			
Accepts responsibility for own behaviour			
Able to use play to work on problems			
Can accept adult intervention			
Can **engage** in discussion about an area of difficulty			
Can **initiate** discussion with an adult about an area of difficulty			

Section C: The Child's Ability to Work on Tasks

Has adequate concentration span			
Can accept help with a task when necessary			
Can responsibly select from a range of choices			
Sustains interest in an activity until completion			
Uses own initiative when planning and carrying through a task			
Can aim for quality of achievement through correction/revision/editing			
Can be co-operative with peers in group situations			
Can be co-operative with peers in unstructured play situations			
Is able to use art-form(s) to express creativity			
Is able to use the written word creatively and imaginatively			

Figure 11 Child-profile format

understanding of the child. The sharing of such knowledge is a starting-point to see how parents and teachers can work together to help the child. Family dynamics may often have a powerful effect on the development of a child's personal constructs, or ways of experiencing the world. Where a child is persistently disturbing to others, some appreciation of the family dynamic may be helpful in teasing out the issues for which the child is seeking resolution. Possible areas for exploration include the following (originally developed by Linda Murgatroyd and Paul Greenhalgh for use in Hackney's tutorial class service):

- the child's position in the family/home;
- significant events in the child's life;
- how the child is seen by various members of the family/household;
- the parents' views on how the child sees other members of the family/household;
- the child's interests, hobbies, and patterns of social contact;
- how the child's difficulties are seen and dealt with at home;
- the parents' perception of the child's experience of school.

In addition, in order to understand the child's personal constructs, it may be useful for the teacher to understand something more of the family dynamics. One might ask about the quality of the child's relationships with other family members. There may be other issues which the teacher might want to assess, and be able to do so in ways other than asking direct questions. Are the parents able to show sensitivity, and tolerate stress; are they able to communicate love, acceptance and encourage feelings of personal worth; and what is the quality of the relationship between the parents – e.g. does each parent feel secure and well-supported by the other?

The child's subjective experiences

Given the significance of the child's emotional construction of his/her reality in opening access to development and learning (see Chapter One, section on 'Affect and learning'), it is important for the teacher to understand something of the child's subjective experiences. Dockar-Drysdale (1990) writes of listening carefully to the vital symbols in all forms of communication. The child's perceptions of the learning environment and his/her patterns of interaction both at school and at home provide information about the child's subjective constructs of the world. With regard to the child's perceptions of the learning environment and patterns of interaction, one might explore the child's awareness of strengths and weaknesses both educationally and socially; likes and dislikes in school; subjective experience of school; perceptions of his/her own needs; significant relationships with family and peers; and how s/he spends time out of school. The extent to which the child is able to acknowledge feelings and difficulties provides a measure of the extent to which s/he is ready to work on the difficulties, or is in need of defensive mechanisms. This also gives a picture of the extent of the child's ego functioning. Dockar-Drysdale (1990) suggests that assessment of the degree of ego functioning might take account of the following: feelings of guilt, capacity and extent of dependency, unconscious merging with others, capacity for empathy, capacity to deal with feelings, capacity for communication, ability to make use of modelling experiences, extent of depression, and patterns of aggression.

Further evidence of the child's subjective constructs may be obtained by the use of projective techniques. These are so called because they invite the child to project aspects of inner experience into a particular exercise. Projective techniques enable the child to speak metaphorically, through the use of image, about their experience, fantasies and preoccupations. Speaking particularly of the Rorschach test, but making comment which apply to a range of projective tests, Cox and Theilgaard (1987: 87) say that they enable the 'inner world to be safely explored through the non-intrusive, evocative promptings of ambiguous stimuli', and that they keep 'the mind's door open to the unconscious' (1987: 188). In Chapter Five, I give a more detailed explanation of this idea and of issues involved in facilitating such work in educational settings. The reader, at this point, might refer particularly to the example of Ishret, in the section on 'The role of image and metaphor in helping emotional growth' in Chapter Five, on communicating about inner experience. In this example, I illustrate how Ishret's making of a drawing enabled her to communicate, given the way in which she engaged with my hypotheses (which did not interpret but which stayed within the metaphor provided by Ishret), something of her subjective constructs. Projective techniques need to be employed sensitively; the issues discussed in Chapter Five are applicable here. Teachers should not make psychological interpretations to children about art work or projective tests, but *stay within the metaphorical framework provided by the child.* Some projective techniques, e.g. the Rorschach, may be used only by suitably qualified personnel. With sensitivity and with discernment, most may be more widely used, and these are listed below.

- Winnicott's 'squiggle game': the adult draws an incomplete line or shape and the child is asked to complete the drawing in whatever way s/he likes (Winnicott 1975).
- Unaided fictional writing.
- Retelling a story, for example by sequencing. Sequencing cards may be used to make up a story.
- The draw-a-person test. Here the child is simply asked to draw a person.
- Kinetic family drawing. The child is asked to draw a picture of his/her family, with each person doing something.
- A fantasy drawing, e.g. the child is given an outline drawing of a

spaceship and asked to describe or draw what the inside of his/her spaceship looks like.

- Sentence completion, e.g. sentences which elicit feelings about school, home, peers, siblings; or what mum, best friend, worst enemy, etc., would say about one.

The fruits of observation provide the basis upon which to meet the children's needs with regard to emotional growth and learning. The processes of facilitating such work are considered in subsequent chapters.

SUMMARY

- Given that *how* one responds to an emotional need is as important as *what* one does, one's attitude is highly significant.
- The question of attitude is also highly significant in relation to accepting and being accepted by troubled children, in order that a relationship can be established which is not based on defensive manoeuvres and within which change becomes possible.
- To facilitate the development of troubled children, adults significant to them need to show Rogers' core conditions: realness or genuineness, acceptance and trust, and empathic understanding.
- The experience of adult communications of a sense of belief in children enables children to develop a sense of belief in their own goodness and autonomy.
- Openness on the part of adults towards working through the processes of reparation provides a framework within which inner damage and personal constructs which inhibit children's development can be repaired. Reparation is related to the capacity to accept ambivalence, and forgo our own grandiosity (characteristics of Klein's depressive position).
- The ability to meet children's needs is enhanced by the capacity to observe and reflect upon *how* things are done.
- Observation and assessment are most useful where they consider the child *in relation to* other factors which inhibit or promote development and learning; the teacher, the learning environment and the whole-school ethos, the relationship of the child with peers and family, the child's perception of experience.

4

EMOTIONAL HOLDING

INTRODUCTION

In earlier chapters I discussed how difficult, distressing and intense feelings can impede and get in the way of learning. The way in which we respond to such feelings is crucial for emotional growth and increasing children's capacity for learning. The concept of 'emotional holding' relates to the way in which we might pay attention to these difficult feelings.

In our early lives our growth and development take place largely in response to the qualities of emotional experience provided by significant adults. Of troubled children, Rollinson writes, 'their growth is not via the intellect primarily, but through *actual emotional experience* – only after which occurs the fusion between thought and feeling' (1992: 10, my emphasis). This chapter is concerned with the provision of one of the key aspects of emotional experience, that of emotional holding. The idea comes from the work of Winnicott, and it refers not to an action, but to a process. Emotional holding is the holding and containment of disturbing feelings which are inhibiting the capacity for relationship, emotional growth, and learning; it involves demonstrating that distressing feelings can be tolerated, helping children to manage feelings, think about them, and understand some of their meaning. Such holding is crucial to development: if I had to use one phrase to describe the most significant aspect of my own work with troubled children, it would be 'providing emotional holding'.

In educational settings, difficult behaviours and feelings are often responded to on the *content* level, ignoring communications on the *relationship* level. The danger in this is that such an approach can continue until the relationship becomes so frustrating or painful that one party gives up out of desperation or anger (Watzlawick *et al.* 1974). Hence the importance of emotional holding as part of a process of interventions. Where the child is not yet ready or able to contain disturbing feelings for him/herself, the adult has a important role in helping this process, to hold or contain the anxiety of disturbing feelings in a way which enables children to learn to contain it for themselves. This is a complex task, particularly where children have not developed sufficient capacity to trust, or have very limited ego functioning.

The considerations in previous chapters of the importance of one's attitude, and the assessment of the meaning of a child's behaviour, lay the foundations for considering emotional holding. In a holding environment the adults have the capacities to hold the anxieties aroused in themselves. There is a reliable provision of trust and affirmation, and stability of emotional climate. 'Only in a climate of affective stability can maturational processes flourish, promoting the differentiation of self and object-representations' (Jacoby 1990: 61). In providing a holding environment the adult strives to be reliable, to be attentive and sympathetically responsive to the child's explorations, and to see and feel the world through the child's eyes – to be empathic. Within such an environment a child can be helped to hold and manage intense and disturbing feelings. Reliable holding means that the immature and weak ego of the child is made stronger by the ego-support that the adult is able to give, having the child in mind as a whole person. Through the holding of the adult there arises in the child in the course of time a sense of trust in the adult and the environment, and there comes about a relationship between adult and child which Winnicott refers to as 'ego-relatedness' (Davies and Wallbridge 1990).

The aim in such relationships is to help children with hitherto poorly functioning egos to take greater responsibility for their behaviour and learning, to become more autonomous. This involves supporting children to be more in touch with their own feelings; to be better able to respect the feelings of others, and to be more reflective and able to think about problems and talk about them rather than act them out; to be better able to contain their own anxiety, and to introject rather than project their own anxiety and pain; to be better able to be self-aware, and to gain and act on insights; and to be better able to appreciate and seek effective support.

Children with very limited ego functioning – those to whom Dockar-Drysdale refers as unintegrated children – may not, because of their adverse experiences, believe that the adult is to be trusted to behave kindly or to understand their predicament. Winnicott's idea of holding is described by Bowlby as being very similar to his idea of providing a secure base, and to Bion's notion of containing. Bowlby argues that in providing a secure base from which to explore and express thoughts and feelings, an adult worker's role is analagous to that of a parent who provides the child with a secure base from which to explore the world. A basic task of emotional holding is the provision of a secure physical and emotional base from which the child can make actual and metaphorical sorties into the outside world and to which s/he can return, knowing that there will be a welcome, physical and emotional nourishment, comfort if distressed, and reassurance if frightened. In essence, this role is one of being available, ready to respond when called upon to encourage or perhaps assist (Bowlby 1988).

The child's development of the capacity to contain, manage and think about disturbing feelings brings with it the development of a more effective ego. The teacher's provision of emotional holding might be called 'ego-provision'. It is as if the adult offers the child an 'auxiliary ego' to provide structured help for the child to contain disturbing feelings. This helps children develop the notion of having an inside and outside, a 'psychic skin'. Working with these processes of emotional holding could be described as an aspect of the 'hidden curriculum'. Providing emotional holding is not a discrete activity. One works on these ego-providing processes during involvement with children in whatever activity is under way – cookery, maths or whatever. The focus for the adult is upon understanding and attitude as the basis for developing skills, rather than the easy application of learned techniques. The necessary skill is in one's art and sensitivity towards people, rather than the application of techniques. The capacity to provide emotional holding emerges out of one's own growth. As Rogers (1961: 56) says, 'The degree to which I can create relationships which facilitate the growth of others as separate persons is a measure of the growth I have achieved myself.'

The task of providing emotional holding demands a process-oriented approach which is developmental over a period of time. With what Dockar-Drysdale calls 'archipelago children', who have islets of ego growth in a chaotic sea of integration, the aim is to achieve integration by turning the archipelago into a continent. Where there is panic – which is anxiety manifested as a tantrum, rage, despair or physical symptoms – the ego-providing task is to enable the child to 'know that adults understand and can contain panic and that it is not inevitable, that he can be helped by anticipation and support' (Dockar-Drysdale 1990: 183). So the recovery of learning for troubled children is facilitated by providing particular qualities of experience which promote the necessary psychological development. 'It is not enough to give emotionally deprived children good experience, we must also help them to keep the good things inside them, or they will lose them once more' (Dockar-Drysdale 1990: 99).

The focus in this chapter on providing appropriate qualities of experience for ego-provision forms the basis upon which, in the next chapter, to discuss help for children with egos which are already functioning, but haphazardly, so needing further support. The latter might be termed 'ego-supporting' issues. (The distinction between ego-provision and ego-supporting is made by Dockar-Drysdale 1990.) When one works at an ego-supporting level, one works explicitly within the realm of conscious awareness, placing a higher premium on the role of language and discussion with the child. Not all development can be willed, or directed by the ego, and Chapter Five develops the related theme of 'letting go' of the child sufficiently for the child to explore imaginative and symbolic realms, in order to help the renegotiation of relationships in the inner world, and hence also in the outer world. The processes of emotional holding, of strengthening, of using image and metaphor and also of working with the group (explored through the following chapters) are in dynamic relationship with each other. Progress does not take place neatly from one 'stage' to another, but through simultaneous work at multiple levels.

The processes described in this chapter are relevant to work at the individual, small-group, classroom and whole-school levels. For children's anxiety and disturbing feelings to be worked with effectively, both individual adults and the organisation of the school or other community as a whole should provide emotional holding. There is now a wide body of literature which indicates the ways in which schools contribute to the behaviour and attitudes of pupils, and a wide range of experience in effective schools which confirms this (e.g. Reynolds 1985). A school 'by its conventions, discipline and curriculum can continue and confirm children's alienating experiences. On the other hand, a school can support, stimulate and demonstrate care for those children already in difficulties, thus preventing or arresting their maladjustment' (Laslett 1982: 19). That this view is now widely accepted is exemplified by Mongan and Hart's argument that schools:

> must accept their own responsibility for examining how the dynamics of schooling may be contributing to 'problem behaviour', and what might be done both to ease the problems pupils are currently experiencing and, where possible, to prevent the same problems arising with the next generation of pupils.
>
> (Mongan and Hart 1989: 35)

Preventative work focuses on the whole context in which 'problem behaviour' occurs, not just on the pupil or pupils; it seeks to make adjustments within that context which will help to prevent problem behaviour from occurring or reoccurring; and it directs the adjustments towards accommodating the needs believed to lie behind the behaviour, rather than simply trying to suppress or control it (Mongan and Hart 1989). The provision of emotional holding at an organisational level is considered further in Chapter Nine.

This chapter explores the holding of disturbing feelings and behaviour through processes such as providing boundaries which give emotional containment, containing anxiety whilst also giving sufficient space for exploration and autonomy, responding helpfully to projections, demonstrating understanding, and providing a 'mirror' and a 'safety net'. This series of processes provides what might be termed a 'framework for

110

emergence' of children with inadequate egos who are at the mercy of their distressing feeling. In times when one's vulnerability increases, the importance of holding increases. In educational settings children's vulnerability occurs on a regular basis in a range of beginnings and endings which happen as part of school life, and this chapter considers the implications of emotional holding for practice at such times. Helping children recognise feelings and manage their own behaviour might also be said to relate to moral development, and this is discussed too.

PROCESSES OF EMOTIONAL HOLDING

Providing a well-bounded container

In providing emotional holding for difficult feelings, one might imagine providing a container for those feelings, and consider how one's actions, words and organisation serve to create and strengthen the container. What happens at the boundaries of the psychological container is of particular significance in how the container is defined and perceived, and therefore in its effectiveness. The provision of emotionally containing boundaries is part of providing emotional holding. An example of a boundary is the way in which the teacher manages communication with the class: a request to listen or to put up hands makes a very different communication from an order not to shout out. When setting boundaries and expectations, positive rather than negative frameworks can be used.

The frameworks for boundary setting are particularly useful where they relate to the needs of the group as a whole and of individual children. In an institutional setting, providing emotional 'holding' may be defined as an 'affirmative response to chaotic behaviours where the "carer" essentially is attempting to boundary the "boundaryless" individual in such a way as to achieve a meaningful space for both of them' (Adams 1986: 3). Providing a boundary for the boundaryless individual is a complex task. It requires conscious reflection upon one's relationships with, and interventions on behalf of, the children with whom one works.

The behaviour of troubled children who are at the mercy of their feelings sometimes expresses primitive affect, and presents severe challenges to the management of boundaries. But for children to be able to feel containable within boundaries is crucial for their development.

> It cannot be over-emphasized how frightening it is for adolescents, as for little children, to feel that no one can hold them or that they can scare or control their adult mentors. . . . Some adolescents cope [with problems of control] by excessive inhibitions; others throw internal inhibiting factors overboard and tend to experience all control as coming from outside – in the form of parents, police and teachers,

etc. Adults are seen as the only source of authority unless and until the adolescent can be helped to recognize concern and responsibility for himself – to be his own authority in fact.

(Box 1978: 149)

As Casement writes, 'A child who is not given appropriate limits goes in search of them' (1990: 183). Maintaining firm, overt boundaries in the face of considerable acting-out is one way of demonstrating that the child and his/her difficult feelings can be emotionally held.

Example: Terry

Seven year old Terry had been attending a tutorial class group for just over a year when he was about to make his second change of school within the year. Since he had begun his attendance at tutorial class his parents had ceased to live together. His entry to the second new school was to come after a period of over two months when his mother refused to let him attend any school. Terry had been particularly omnipotent and recent events in his family seemed to have reinforced this tendency. In the tutorial class group, despite initial good progress over several months, at the time of his non-attendance at school he became particularly challenging. As he faced his next school, the situation must have been very frightening for Terry: would he face rejection yet again, or would he be containable? At this point he was only able to test this out in one way. Upon his entry to the new school, Terry conformed and tried hard in some ways, whilst also going through a period of acting-out in which he would shout verbal abuse at his class teacher, and sometimes run out of the classroom, fleeing situations of difficulty. The class teacher's responses, which demonstrated that he was going to be in charge and to have his expectations met, served to demonstrate that he was determined to hold Terry as someone who could participate within and contribute to the life of the class.

In the face of severe and/or continuous abuse of boundaries by children, a teacher or other worker might feel like giving up on the situation. A 'process' view of development (see the introductory chapter) helps the worker to continue to restate expectations about boundaries whilst maintaining empathy for the child's dilemma. This may require the ability and practice of confronting the child in an emotionally non-threatening way.

These might be viewed as 'discipline' issues. The difficulty with the word 'discipline' is that it can imply a one-sided process, by implication benevolent, patronising or authoritarian. However, the notion of providing emotionally holding boundaries implies a framework within which children have the opportunity to learn something for themselves – an important ingredient in moving towards autonomy. The notion of discipline has limited value without an opportunity to learn self-discipline. It is indeed necessary for discipline to be imposed where self-discipline is not possible, but as soon as some self-discipline becomes possible then opportunities for it need to be provided alongside a gradual withdrawal of imposed discipline. Emotional holding cannot be provided without group control, and

112

refers to the deployment of a series of skills in the context of a well-ordered environment. Winnicott (1984: 96) comments that 'maturational processes depend for their becoming actual in the child, and actual at the appropriate moments, on good enough environmental provision'.

For Winnicott there was no such thing as a human relationship between adult and young child unless the adult *managed* the situation – there had to be a holding environment (Davies and Wallbridge 1990). Winnicott believed:

> that a democratic society relies upon the individuals within it at any one time who are mature enough to identify with the wide circle that comprises the whole of that society, as well as being able to identify with narrower groups. . . . This mature social sense comes from a balance between boundary and space within the individual, which means that there has already been a working through of the conflict between impulse and control, so that the individual is able to find the whole conflict within the self as well as being able to see the whole conflict outside the self in external (shared) reality. . . . The antisocial individual cannot make use of boundaries in the world of shared reality . . . as a representation of those within himself, because control has not yet become internalised. He is thus forced (where there is hope) to provoke actual strong management from society.
>
> (Davies and Wallbridge 1990: 145)

The need to provide boundaries whilst also facilitating the internalisation of control leads to a number of tensions. These are further elaborated in Figure 12.

Exercise: Setting limits

/*

Members of the group are asked to consider that they are staff members of the same school, and that they have been asked to work on the following issue: About to join the school is a new member of staff who does not have much experience in working with pupils with challenging behaviour. The school staff believe that it is helpful for pupils' development for them to have clear boundaries, but that limits should be set in a non-threatening way. This is one of your whole-school policies.

You have the task of briefing the new member of staff about how to do this, and why. What will you say/do to brief the new member of staff?

Problem:	Need to provide emotional holding to enable child to feel safe	— Need to encourage responsibility and autonomy
Action:	Provide emotional holding, be 'in charge' of agenda and set consistent expectations	— Provide appropriate opportunities for negotiation
Problem:	Need to provide accurate picture to child	— Need to enhance self-esteem
Action:	Importance of reflecting-back cf. punishing	— Valuing the child, positive reinforcement etc.
Problem:	Need to confront	— Need to avoid being emotionally threatening
Action:	Avoid reinforcing resistance	— Operate within the child's frame of reference

Figure 12 Tensions in setting boundaries

Containing anxiety whilst giving space for autonomy

A fundamental ingredient of providing emotional holding is the containment of anxiety. This requires the teacher to contain anxiety on behalf of children until they can do this for themselves, which involves the paradox of allowing children to experience some anxiety, so that they may learn to manage the containing process independently. The paradox of providing boundary and space relates, respectively, to needs for psychological safety and psychological freedom. Adams (1986) likens this process to holding an object on behalf of someone else, and being trusted not to drop, lose, break, damage or keep it. Adams compares the held object to a cup of tea, and suggests that if the holding person drank some of the tea, this would not be holding, it would be exploitation; if the person spilt some of the tea it would not be holding, instead it would be dropping, disregarding, not taking care, being care-less; and dropping the cup would be indicative of the holder's impatience. If the tea is returned, the other person has to let go. It is important, Adams maintains, to avoid becoming like a 'too good' mother, who might hold the cup to the other person's lips, thereby dominating to such an extent that exploration would be inhibited.

The effective holding environment incorporates sufficient space for the development of the capacity for exploration and autonomy and sufficient boundary for the development of consistency and stability (Adams 1986). Winnicott, thinking of an adult's responsibility for identifying the infant's fluctuating needs for boundary and space, invented a game which he used to diagnose both the quality of a parent's holding environment, and the infant's emotional reponse to adult care. During a consultation, Winnicott would place a spatula between himself and the tiny infant, just out of reach. At the sight of this the infant would probably make some gesture to secure the object in order to place it in his or her mouth. Adams (1986) explains the three probable responses that a parent might make in this situation:

1 The parent notices that the infant is salivating, and for some personal benefit, such as tidiness, moves the object firmly out of the infant's reach and proceeds to distract the infant away from the desired spatula.
2 The parent notices the infant's deep attention to the spatula and that the infant is salivating and, anticipating the infant's desire, places the spatula in the infant's mouth.
3 The parent reads the infant's desire and *interacts* with this desire by pushing the spatula just near enough for the infant to reach out and secure the object. This results in a sense of achievement and exploration as the infant places the spatula in his/her mouth.

This third response illustrates the subtle co-operation which parents and other adults can give, which supports yet does not dominate, and which is the basis of Winnicott's concept of holding (Adams 1986).

Example: Tyron

When 9 year old Tyron was referred to tutorial class, his educational psychologist commented, 'The school staff think he's the worst thing since the history of the world began.' Tyron was having violent tantrums, requiring a number of staff to be involved in physically restraining him, several times a week. In my initial interview at the school, I was asked to meet with a group of five members of staff, who all spoke of traumatic experiences with Tyron. The situation was clearly fraught, and the school staff were losing their desire and capacity to provide emotional holding for Tyron. One of the ways in which I tried to provide some emotional holding for the staff was by suggesting that perhaps Tyron needed to have his tantrums at the tutorial class, rather than with them. Tyron made a speedy and positive emotional engagement with his tutorial class provision, and the immediate tension between him and the school relaxed.

At this time, Tyron had recently begun the school year with a young teacher who provided a cushion for Tyron's use, in an alcove in the classroom. When he felt moody or unable to work with the other children he was allowed the privacy of his corner, where he would take his work, or simply day-dream. Tyron's tantrums disappeared, and he was able to meet the common expectations of the classroom for most of the time. This teacher provided emotional holding for Tyron by empathising and interacting with his moods and desires, and providing a boundary which demonstrated awareness of his needs whilst maintaining the expectation that he belonged in the community of the classroom. I associate the emotional holding that this teacher provided with the comment of analytical psychologist James Hillman: 'stillness, darkness, coolness and patience may provide the cave in which to hide until the night is over' (1967: 34).

Immediate responses to projections

The projection of difficult feelings onto other people, which happens as a result of intolerable anxiety, is discussed in Chapter Two. When a child pushes his or her bad feelings into teachers, the first task is not to get emotionally caught up in the difficult feelings oneself. Yet there is a natural, unconscious and sometimes very strong urge to retaliate in response to projections. Projections can arouse intense feelings. In order to avoid being overwhelmed by such feelings and to retain the capacity to think, it is important to manage the difficult projected feelings, and to avoid knee-jerk reactions to them, thereby avoiding the natural tendency to retaliate.

It sometimes takes considerable internal resources and reflection not to succumb to such pressures. But simply to react unreflectively to projections offers the child no further understanding of the dilemma, and may reinforce the child's difficulties. So the manner in which key adults respond to the projections of troubled children may offer the possibility either for increased awareness, or for an emotional 'stuckness' to be reinforced. Responding to projections thus requires, on the part of the adult, self-knowledge, self-management and the capacity to manage one's overt response. To respond to projections effectively is to provide a dimension of emotional holding, demonstrating that distressing feelings can be tolerated, thought about and understood. (I do not use the term 'tolerated' in a permissive sense, but in the sense of being emotionally tolerated by the adult.)

Winnicott argues that

> Good teaching demands of the teacher a toleration of the frustrations to his or her spontaneity in giving, or feeding – frustrations that may be felt acutely. The child, in learning to be civilized, naturally also feels frustrations acutely, and is helped in becoming civilized not so much by the teacher's precepts as by the teacher's own ability to bear frustrations inherent in teaching.
>
> (Winnicott 1964: 202–3)

And Dockar-Drysdale writes:

> Only an integrated person, involved and aware of involvement, can experience reaction consciously, that is to say, knowing that it is a reaction. An unintegrated person may or may not be aware that he or she has reacted, but in context such a person can only react and may know nothing about this afterwards.
>
> (Dockar-Drysdale 1990: 18)

When we react consciously we are also more likely to be aware of our own individual inner 'hooks', which attract particular projections to us. This involves recognising the areas of vulnerability in ourselves which attract particular projections. It is important as well to develop an awareness of one's own feelings, and the ability to differentiate between which feelings belong to oneself and what one is made to feel by someone else. With self-knowledge one is better able to manage oneself. If one is able to make statements about one's own feelings in response to projection, this makes explicit the feelings or reactions stirred up by an event, whilst avoiding judgemental comments. Such statements, which might be called 'I' statements, may provide a form of feedback which is difficult to negate since it is expressed in the form of an individual identifying his/her own feelings. It is also important, in order to avoid reinforcing negative self-esteem, to differentiate clearly between disapproval of a particular action and disapproval of the child in general.

To make these comments is not to say that negative feelings should never be aired. Winnicott stresses how essential it is for negative feelings to be not only identified, but occasionally expressed. He points out that when a child experiences a mother or other adult who appears to show only love, the child is faced with the illusion of carrying all the negative feelings of their relationship and thus fears that s/he is not loved or liked at all. Winnicott (1984) argues that love is the basis for the totality of care which facilitates maturational processes, and that love includes hate. An expression of negative feelings which takes place unconsciously, in retaliation, may serve to reinforce a child's difficulties. In such a situation, the child has not had the experience of the dilemma being held and reflected upon, but has the destructive potential of the negative feeling reinforced. In contrast, a conscious expression of negative feelings by the adult might be usefully made when the timing is appropriate for the child to reflect upon the experience.

Demonstrating reflection and understanding

For the child to be able to make projections, and also to work on them within a holding environment, enables emotional reactions to become converted into thought – for some meaning to be given to the action of projection. It is as if young and unintegrated children do not know they have a mind until the parent or other adult helps them to know that they have it. In educational settings the teacher's task is to *demonstrate* that difficult feelings can be reflected upon, can be thought about and have some meaning. It is not appropriate for the teacher to give the child interpretations about what might be happening in his/her inner world. The distinction between demonstration and interpretation is an important one: the former is the task of the teacher and the latter the task of the psychotherapist.

The developmental processes which occur between the significant parent and an infant give clues about the processes of making appropriate processes in the classroom. Jacoby refers to:

> the important prerequisite that the infant's magical omnipotence and its spontaneous 'exhibitionist' activities be received by the mother with pleasure and empathic mirroring. . . . Gradual inevitable disappointments of the child's boundless needs enable boundaries to slowly crystallize, constellating the possibility that omnipotence fantasies and the hunger for admiration eventually may mature into adequate ambitions and realistic self-esteem. Under optimal conditions, the empathetically mirroring mother-figure will be gradually internalized. In other words, optimal maternal empathy lays the groundwork for development of a healthy self-esteem.
>
> (Jacoby 1990: 67)

Similar experiences may be provided by teachers sensitive to children's emotional development. In order that a child can learn to feel and contain anxiety, the adult needs to allow the child a tolerable level of anxiety, and to support the child without dominating him/her. In learning situations, this issue is not a question of cutting up the curriculum food smaller and smaller, and spooning it into the child's mouth in bite-sized pieces. One function of providing support is to think about the meaning of what is happening. Where anxiety is evacuated in the form of a projection there is a need for the adult to contain the evacuated, projected feeling, and to understand, tolerate and think about it. The adult's demonstration that s/he is thinking about an event might be made through the acknowledgement of her/his own feelings in a situation. The adult might speculate verbally about the child's feelings, or verbally reflect, non-judgementally, upon a difficult event after it has happened. The child then has the experience of having the horrid feeling not only tolerated by the adult, but also understood. The experience of the adult's capacity for reflection gradually enables the child to internalise this capacity for him/herself.

Where a child is overwhelmed by intense feelings, the adult's task might be – as it was with John (see below) – to demonstrate that one can have a relationship with intolerable feelings other than being possessed by them, so showing that such feelings can be borne, tolerated and lived with. Where the teacher is able to think about the meaning of the behaviour, and communicate something of this thinking, the child has the experience of the receptive adult's mind taking in the child's feelings, reflecting upon them and discerning their meaning. Where the child experiences reflection upon his/her state of mind, s/he is gradually able to internalise the container, and develop a mind that can hold more thought. The child then perceives her/himself more in relation to the world of meaning. Where the adult is non-judgemental and apportions no blame (which is different from the business of setting limits and boundaries), the child experiences an attitude on the part of the teacher which takes the 'symptoms' seriously. The understanding teacher communicates that the 'symptoms' express something of necessity in the child's individual existence. This implies that the 'symptoms' belong to the child's psychological health, in the sense that they are necessary precursors to emotional growth.

Example: John

In Chapter Two (section on 'Anxiety and separation') I described John's temper tantrums. During the first months of his placement at tutorial class John disintegrated into rage when apparently small things went wrong. Whilst John was in his tantrum state, I was made to feel as if I was in turmoil, not knowing what was happening to me, wondering if I could cope, and wishing I did not have to be with this material. I considered that my task was to soldier on, to turn up to sessions and somehow learn to live with John. Being able to do this provided the rudiments of the container which John needed. Although I felt his pain, I did not carry it for him. Rather, as container, I was holding on to the feelings which were intolerable for him. During the tantrums I said that I would physically hold him whilst he was out of control and until he could manage himself, and that even though it felt like he wanted to smash the place up, I was not going to let him do so. I acknowledged his anger and rage. As the tone of his emotions changed, I suggested that, some day, he might be able to be sad rather than angry.

Just as I have described children's behaviour as a form of communication, so the behaviour of teachers and other key adults is a form of communication to children. Dockar-Drysdale (1990) writes that such symbolic communication by the adult is the vehicle which provides the necessary early emotional experiences for the child. Listening carefully to the vital symbols in all forms of communication, and exploring their meaning, enables the adult to demonstrate understanding of the symbolic meaning in the way in which s/he responds. The aim is to show the child that s/he can have a symbolic experience which can feel real, be 'realised' or experienced internally, and be stored (Dockar-Drysdale 1990).

Providing mirrors and safety nets

Another aspect of the holding function can be likened to providing a mirror to reflect back to the child, and to providing a safety net of holding as the child comes to be able to contain more difficult feelings for him/herself. Providing emotional holding through mirroring involves empathically reflecting behaviour traits and symptoms back to the child. Empathy is important, and requires that the teacher quietly verbalises what can be seen by all, rather than intruding or 'psychologising'. Neither is this a question of making accusations or judgements about the child – rather, it is a process of enabling the child to *own* feelings. Mirroring might involve a non-judgemental commentary on observed behaviour, in order to increase the child's awareness of his/her behaviour. In order to increase the child's capacity to articulate and talk about feelings, in mirroring the teacher might also name feelings which the child *might* be experiencing, for example, saying to a particular child that it seems frustrating for him/her to be a loser in a game. If the child feels judged or emotionally intruded upon, the difficulty might be reinforced. One way of avoiding judgement and intrusion is to make suggestions, such as, 'I'm going to have a guess at the feelings you might have just now – it's only my guess, and I might be wrong . . . '. With John, some of the mirroring I gave took the form of verbalising the difficulty he seemed to have in receiving an equal share, and not more than others, of drink-time biscuits or ingredients for cookery.

For Winnicott an important facet of the *mutuality* of communication between child and adult is the adult's reflection back of the child's qualities (Davies and Wallbridge 1990). The child needs a consistent picture of him/herself reflected by a significant adult if s/he is to build an integrated identity (Menzies Lyth 1988). Gradually, through the experience of mirroring, the child becomes more aware of his/her actions, of taking his/her own responsibility for behaviour and of providing his/her own emotional holding. The containing qualities of boundaries become internalised, and the child develops a greater capacity for thought.

The child then becomes more aware of the links between feelings and behaviour, and recognises behaviour traits which others might find difficult. The adult:

> is the sounding board against which [the child] can try out his personality. [The adult] is the one who holds the mirror so [the child] can see himself as he is. . . . The therapist-teacher is alert to recognise the feelings the child is expressing and reflects those feelings back to the child in such a manner that the child gains insight into his behaviour.
>
> (Axline 1989: 136, 140)

Reflecting back to the child evidence of ways in which s/he is changing is also important. Doing this makes an alliance with the child's growing capacities and helps counter resistance to change. Change is frightening for all of us, so such resistance should not be underestimated. As a girl who had previously been very withdrawn was preparing to leave tutorial class, I commented that there were a number of settings in which people had noticed she had changed. 'But *I* don't think I've changed!', she retorted. It is all too easy to assume that one's perception of the way in which another person is changing is shared by the other person, but often this may not be the case. With unintegrated children, reflecting back evidence of ways in which they are changing can help to promote ego development.

As the child becomes more autonomous and is gradually able to hold and contain more affect or anxiety for her/himself, the teacher should play an increasingly distanced role: The adult now serves to provide a safety net in the holding process. That one is providing such a safety net can be communicated by showing that one is ready to *listen*. This helps the child to develop an awareness that situations can be held or contained with words, and at the child's own initiation or request. The skills specific to listening and counselling are considered in Chapter Six.

Exercise: The experience of emotional holding

*/**

Think of a relationship in which you have had the experience of being emotionally held. This might be a relationship in your personal life, or a professional relationship in which you have experienced support which has been particularly valuable to you. What were the qualities of that relationship which made emotional holding possible?

Exercise: Providing emotionally containing responses to disturbing feelings

/*

Members of the group are asked to consider themselves members of staff at the same school, and to imagine the following scenario: about to join the school is a new member of staff who does not have much experience in work with disturbed or disturbing pupils. In the school's whole-school policy there are some guidelines on providing emotionally containing responses to disturbing feelings. The staff have agreed:

- to try to be aware of difficult feelings aroused in themselves by challenging behaviour;
- to try to avoid 'knee-jerk' reactions;
- to demonstrate to children that difficult feelings can be tolerated and thought about (thereby showing that one does not have to be 'possessed' by the disturbing feelings);
- to reflect back to children about their behaviour in a way which does not make a judgement about the child as a person;
- to talk openly about feelings, and particularly to encourage people to acknowledge their own feeings;
- to try particularly hard at times when children are likely to feel especially vulnerable, for example, at the beginnings and ends of sessions, days, weeks and terms.

Your task is to introduce the new member of staff to this aspect of your policy. Previously the school has found that just giving new members of staff documents to read is not a very effective way of helping them to participate in the school's policies, and you are asked by the head to find a more interesting and effective way. How will you do this, and what will your briefing consist of?

Ineffective holding

In order to understand better the processes of holding, it is useful to consider the characteristics of ineffective holding. Symptoms of ineffective holding are demonstrated in situations such as these:

> most pupils who end up having on-site provision made for them do not exhibit intolerable behaviour while in the unit. But few of them transfer their good behaviour back to the classroom or corridors. Many are lost to exclusions and suspensions for incidents that occur

during break, lunchtime or en route to another part of the building.
(Mongan and Hart 1989: 121)

The task of containing anxiety on behalf of the children when they are at a stage when they cannot do it for themselves becomes dysfunctional in the following sorts of circumstance (after Bruce 1983). The first is when staff deny the anxiety that they themselves might feel, or avoid the main task by setting up parallel activities, such as organising endless case conferences. The staff's taking flight into theory might also represent a defence against the painful aspects of providing emotional holding. The second is when staff get overly angry – suggesting unchecked retaliation in response to projections; or when staff do not get angry enough – suggesting possible collusions, failures to maintain boundary setting, or being emotionally swamped by feelings difficult to tolerate. The third is when staff become overidentified or underidentified with the children. In overidentification, staff may receive secrets in a manner which encourages the children to think 'You're the only one who understands me.' This may result in a breakdown of appropriate boundaries between adult and child. Underidentification takes place when the adult has little or no feeling for, or empathy with, child/adolescent aspirations. Fourthly, over-reliance on institutional structures may be another symptom of flight from the painful experience of providing emotional holding for unintegrated children. This happens, for example, where staff have a rule for everything, and rigidly impose the rules without seeking to understand the dilemmas of the children. Fifthly, staff may fail to provide adequate holding where they withdraw from involvement with the children into themselves and/or each other. In the latter case, intense liaisons between staff may develop. And sixthly, when staff choose not to pursue and maintain responsibilities for emotional holding, this may become manifest in a variety of ways, such as what might be called 'splintering', or recruiting many specialists into the system.

Holding is likely to be effective where the image of the container meta-phorically describes the emotional qualities of the provision being made for children. Emotional holding is particularly important in relation to beginning and ending situations in schools and residential homes. It is to these situations that I now turn.

BEGINNINGS AND ENDINGS

The provision of emotional holding is especially important for children at times of particular vulnerability. Beginnings and endings mark times of transition when we are unsure what will happen next, and so these are times when anxiety is particularly likely to be aroused. In schools, beginning work with new teachers, and the beginnings and ends of years, terms, weeks, days or lessons are examples of such situations. In each of these examples, the holding experience provided by a key adult is lost, and there is a hiatus before the next and perhaps quite different experience begins. A beginning also requires the loss of the previous situation. Experiences of loss may be aroused by events within schools – the leaving of a class member, or the end of a period of time of being taught by a particular teacher. These issues are eloquently considered by Salzberger-Wittenberg:

> The more unstructured and strange a new situation, the further we are removed from what is familiar physically, mentally or emotionally, the more disoriented and terrified we tend to feel . . . however mature and capable we are, we continue to harbour some dread of helplessness, of being lost, overcome with fear of disintegration. Even if we have mastered other like situations, we dread that our abilities will not be adequate *this* time or to *this* situation. . . . we feel threatened with not knowing *where we are, what we are, who we are.* We need to test, and fear to test, whether our painfully acquired internal equipment, which is the basis of our sense of self, will stand up to the new experience . . . We are afraid that we may lose knowing ourselves, our identity, when all familiarity has gone and we dare to risk being face to face with the unknown. . . . These feelings . . . are an inevitable concomitant of any true beginning. Indeed the negative capability of being in a state of not knowing is a prerequisite for learning and discovery. For if we are too frightened to allow ourselves to be open enough to have an emotional experience of newness we also shut ourselves off from the perception of something different, from discovering anything new, producing anything fresh. If, however, we do not thus rigidify our thinking and our affects, we pay the price of the agony of helplessness, confusion, dread of the unknown – of being in a state of beginning once more.
>
> (Salzberger-Wittenberg *et al.* 1983: 7–9)

Where such issues are addressed in children's experiences of beginnings, the children are helped to make more effective and creative use of what will happen in that situation, and anxiety is less likely to be an inhibiting factor.

Example

Some of the emotional implications of beginnings were demonstrated by a group of specialist support service teachers, who were asked at the beginning of a twelve-session course to think of the feelings aroused in themselves. They acknowledged anticipation; expectation; hope – for example, that the course would help build self-confidence; irritation (at things which had not been clear); and anxiety (one course member had previously given up a course for this reason). Also acknowledged were the following questions: 'What is my place in the group going to be?'; 'Can I concentrate for long enough?'; 'Is the course going to be intrusive?'; 'What am I going to be asked to do?'; 'What will the relationships be between sub-groups of people who already know each other?'; 'What will my relationship be with my peers who have not been chosen to come on the course?'; 'What kind of people will other course members be?'; 'What sort of competition and power struggles will there be between group members?'; 'Why was I chosen to come on this course?'; 'Am I up to being a member of this course?'; and 'Am I worthy enough to be on this course?'

The responses in the last example were made by a group of successful, self-aware adults; how much more potentially frightening might beginnings be for unintegrated children! There is a whole range of beginning situations in educational settings in which it is helpful to consider such issues: when children enter new groups, have new teachers, start new terms and school days, and so on. Upon the entry of a new child into a group, is the situation actively addressed, for example, by encouraging empathy in other members of the group by asking them to remember and reflect upon what it was like for them when they joined a new group? (Such issues are considered further in Chapter Seven, in the section on 'Group stages'.) Do support teachers adequately take account of holding and beginning issues when first meeting a child? This meeting will have a disproportionate affect upon the use the child is able to make of the intervention. In cases where an initial meeting is part of exploring further support for a child, the importance of such an interview lies in the manner in which the teacher relates to the child, opening channels of communication and beginning to demonstrate possibilities for acknowledging difficulty within a safe framework, and enabling the child to perceive, and build upon, emotional strengths.

The impact of a new beginning in the family may have potent repercussions for a child's learning in school. The classic example is the arrival of a new baby, about which a child may have all sorts of ambivalent feelings. The child may well realise that the feeling of pleasure is what 'should' be publicly acknowledged. But envy and anger about his/her position in the family being usurped may also be present: the more the child senses that these are feelings to be denied the more likely it is that they will manifest through the child's behaviour. Conversely, the more the child is able to acknowledge ambivalence, the less likely s/he will be to get 'stuck' on one side or the other of the range of feelings.

Exercise: The impact of beginnings

*/**

Think of a recent beginning you have made, such as starting a new job, working in a different role or with different groups, starting a new course. Better still, if you are at the beginning of something right now, reflect upon that.

1 What feelings does being at this beginning arouse in you?
2 What are your hopes?
3 What are your anxieties and fears?
4 How might your feelings affect the way you behave in the new situation?
5 Do your feelings affect the way you are able to take up and make use of opportunities in the new situation?
6 How do you take account of your own experience of beginnings in the way that you manage beginning situations for the groups you work with?

I consider below some ways in which difficulties over endings show themselves in educational settings, and explore some of the underlying issues in these situations. I go on to use the concept of emotional holding to inform a discussion about managing endings.

The difficulties and dynamics of endings

In schools some children experience breaktimes and lunchtimes as particularly difficult. Some otherwise well-functioning primary schools in inner London have such a large proportion of children who find playtime breaks so fearsome, and who become so aggressive and chaotic during and after them, that the schools have ceased to have morning or afternoon breaks. This pattern of breaktime behaviour in these schools is at variance with their pattern of much better behaviour during lesson-times. This would suggest that there is a significant proportion of children who are appropriately emotionally held by their teachers during classes, but who have not yet been able to cope autonomously with the loss of their teachers, and their holding function, at breaktimes. 'As responses to the risk of loss, anxiety and anger go hand-in-hand. It is not for nothing that [these words] have the same etymological root' (Bowlby 1988: 79).

In educational circles, the endings faced by teachers and pupils are often denied. Children with emotional and behavioural difficulties may particularly seek to deny endings, and can often 'act out' their difficulties on this issue. Routine endings may evoke the pain of the risk of attachment to the teacher or the group, or the child may be overwhelmed by feelings of anxiety about what might happen next. The ends of group sessions with troubled children can be particularly fraught, especially when those relatively new to a group are present. It appears to be common, when teaching troubled children, for potential or actual conflicts to become heightened just before the ends of sessions, and the endings can be difficult to manage. Children might seem to want to burst out of the group as if they did not

126

really have to finish or go through the transition of leaving one place and arriving in another. Sometimes troubled children might leave in a manner which makes the teacher feel 'dumped upon'; a child's quip might seem to destroy the session's achievements, or an insult might project the experience of the difficulty onto someone else. But the prevailing culture in educational establishments generally denies the significance of endings. The end of the academic year is a prime example: it seems to be common practice for teachers who are leaving to tell their pupils this as late as possible. So much for emotional preparation! Perhaps it is difficult for teachers to acknowledge that endings matter, for to do so might arouse guilt, perhaps associated with conscious or unconscious feelings of abandoning the children.

Let us explore some of the underlying dynamics associated with endings. Endings are emotionally powerful phenomena in that they evoke a range of feelings. They evoke feelings in regard to the present loss, and they may evoke unresolved feelings from previous losses. Endings also evoke feelings about how one related to the opportunities in the situation which is ending: what were the opportunities which one missed, and what were those which were taken and maximised? Our missing and taking of opportunities may evoke ambivalence at the ending of a situation. But it may be very difficult to hold this ambivalence in our minds: in theoretical terms, we may find it difficult to experience both sides of the ending in what Klein would call a 'depressive' manner. So one side of our ambivalence can easily get left out of what we acknowledge at an ending. This can arouse the urge to dump a one-sided perception of experience at an ending, and this is particularly likely with children and young people who have not yet learned to own and manage difficult feelings.

The capacity to work through loss is closely related to the capacity for attachment. As we have seen, Bowlby's work demonstrates the biological urge for attachment, for bonding. How we experience and sort out our early attachments in infancy has important consequences for our psychological health. Secure attachment is generated where the child is confident that the parent-figure will be available, responsive and helpful if needed. With this confidence, the child feels bold in explorations of the world. Those children who are most stable emotionally and who make use of their opportunities are those who have significant adults who encourage the child's independence, yet are available and responsive when called upon. A child who has not been able to make satisfying attachments might be afraid to allow her/himself to become attached to anyone for fear of a further rejection, with all the associated agony, anxiety and anger. Such a child may have a defence against expressing, or feeling, the desire for close, trusting relationships.

If we have secure attachments we are better able to deal with loss. Separation is easier if those things which are left behind can be held in mind and remembered. 'The anxieties and pain which accompany [ordinary ending situations in the lives of students and teachers] are rarely faced, yet how these experiences are dealt with is of great importance in determining what of the past can be retained and used creatively in the present and future' (Salzberger-Wittenberg *et al.* 1983: 139). Those who are not able to keep a good image of things lost inside themselves find change, even everyday or routine changes, very difficult. Without a sense of inner security, change can feel like disorganisation and disintegration. It can seem like an attack on one's sense of identity. If the issue of loss is not worked upon, then the attachment to the previous situation or person is denied, and our good internal image of it becomes precarious.

> Attachment is so central to our security in childhood that it becomes embedded, ineradicably, in the meaning of safety and reward for the rest of our lives. Hence changes which disrupt the specific patterns of attachment upon which anyone depends will disrupt their ability to experience life as meaningful, and plunge them into grief, however rational these changes may seem from the point of view of someone with other attachments. . . . When a pattern of relationship is disrupted in any way for which we are not fully prepared, the threat of continuity in the interpretation of life becomes attenuated or altogether lost. The loss may fundamentally threaten the integrity of the structure of meanings on which this continuity rests, and cannot be acknowledged without distress.
>
> (Marris 1986: ix, 21)

Endings also offer opportunities. A well-made ending might involve a complete experience of loss, a mourning of that which is lost, and an acknowledgement of what sort of an experience it was, but also the need to move on in order to grow. If, in the sadness of loss, the good memory is not attacked but taken inside oneself, the memory and ability to re-experience it will sustain one. If well made, endings can offer the possibility for reinforcing ego development through further differentiation of feelings. The termination phase of a group situation potentially offers special opportunities to work on and through the feelings associated with earlier separations, which have not yet been confronted or resolved. According to Whitaker (1985), experiences which are psychologically significant for some individuals in a group may occur only towards the end of the group's life because it is only then that really significant affective resonances occur.

A number of emotional stages to endings have been recognised: denial, anger, guilt for what could have been done differently, grief and sadness. If one gets stuck at any of these stages, those left unfinished are likely to carry over into the next beginning. The way in which things end attains a special significance. Endings tend to be taken as giving the final picture of what has gone before, and can crucially affect the nature of what is learned and internalised from the relationship. Every change, internal or external, means leaving something behind in order to encounter something new.

> Every change involves a loss and every loss needs to be properly 'mourned' if there is going to be real growth and progress. By 'mourning' . . . I mean the kind of conscious and unconscious re-adjustment necessary whenever something of importance has been lost and the subsequent reorientation to the new reality takes place, which now includes that absence. This . . . involves an inevitable assessment of that which has gone, and our relationship with it. A picture or internal vision is built up and coloured both by the feelings associated with the experience or person while it was there and by our success or failure in adapting to the loss. . . . A real, successful mourning . . . and ending will be one in which the real value can be appreciated and sadness felt without either idealisation or over-whelming destructiveness. . . . With either of these extremes, . . real mourning is avoided. . . . [The] capacity to experience the ending of a good experience and to keep it 'good' in the mind demands a considerable amount of psychic health. If someone leaves us, for example, even temporarily, we can defend against really missing them by playing down how important they are for us. We can even say that we never needed them anyway, they weren't all that good, so who cares if they are not there any more. Alternatively we can deny the fact that we have been left and pretend to ourselves that we did the leaving. It is far more comfortable in one sense to do the finishing than to allow someone else to be in possession of something one wants and will no longer be able to have. . . . There is the possibility open to us of actually spoiling something to make the leaving easier.
>
> (Dyke n.d.: 2)

If we leave with resentment, then there is a sense in which we are still attached to the situation, and this undermines our functioning in the new situation. As Hendrick (1989: 4) puts it, 'Unless you can say Thank You, you can't say goodbye.'

Implications for the management of endings

These emotional issues in endings have practical implications for work with children. In what follows I consider the implications of managing routine endings, the experience of losing a personally significant teacher or group of relationships, and then ending 'rituals'.

In relation to routine endings in organisational life, children need warning and emotional preparation. For children in difficulty, feelings of loss and separation may be aroused regularly at various points in the day: coming up to playtime, dinner break, the end of the day. Children struggling with ego development need warning of how much time there is left before it is time to pack away, before it is time to finish a session, a day, a week, a half-term or a term. Some might need the teacher to help them bridge these gaps. In relation to handling the end of term, Dyke (n.d.) suggests that such strategies as talking of plans for next term, clarity over dates, indications that the relationship will continue despite physical absence, can all help the child avoid the feeling of disintegration. It is helpful to avoid the assumption that holidays are enjoyable and eagerly awaited. Not only is this untrue for many children, but it may reinforce feelings of desertion, of being too awful to remain with, and foster ensuing resentment. By demonstrating sensitivity to the real feelings underlying manic excitement, the teacher may lessen the child's need to act out, making it more possible for something good to be preserved and taken away. Where children may feel that everything might fall apart during a break, some may project their anxiety, seeming to be feeling quite happy about the holiday but instilling in the teachers a great worry about how they will cope and what will happen. It is important that the teachers recognise this and do not themselves act out the anxiety, and that efforts are made to provide safe ending experiences which minimise the possibility of acting-out by the children. It may be helpful for the child to take something home from school to look after during the holiday, thus providing a concrete link and reminder of relationships in school. When sending reports to parents, anxieties aroused in children about this can be helped by going through the reports with the children beforehand. In schools there are often a number of children who are absent during the last few days of term. This might be an indication of not being able to stand endings – giving up before actually ending – and schools often collude in this situation.

A child's loss of a personally significant teacher or group of relationships presents another management issue. Children with emotional and behavioural difficulties put teachers through so many trials that the teachers might not feel that they have any personal positive significance for the individual child, and so minimise the significance of an ending. Yet Quinton's (1987) research shows that girls who had experienced 'bad parenting' and who presented problems in school grew up to remember the good experiences of their teachers and were able to make use of these experiences in the way they mothered their own children. When significant relationships come to an end, 'if the group and persons in it have become important, if there has been substantial investment in the experience, then individuals may be faced with acute feelings of separation and loss' (Whitaker 1985: 363). When children experience repeated changes of teacher, this may elicit the feeling that no one wants to stay with them, provoking anger, depression and acting-out of rejection. In preparing for the ending of a relationship there needs to be space for anger, loss, acknowledgement of what will be missed, sadness. All concerned need the opportunities and time to think through and talk about what the separation will mean to them.

> [T]he less opportunity to prepare for a loss, the less predictable or meaningful the event itself, the more traumatically will the whole structure of meaning be disrupted, and the more insecure thereafter will the attachment seem, when its loss can be so sudden and unforeseen.
>
> (Marris 1986: x)

All those concerned in impending loss need to anticipate the ways in which they will feel pleased or relieved, the things they will most miss, the things they will not miss at all, and so on. If we cannot afford to be sad, a huge amount of experience is unavailable to us.

Emotional preparation requires time, and needs to take place in various ways. When a teacher is due to leave a school, leaving emotional preparation entirely to the last-minute parties is to miss opportunities to think about the meaning of the experience and the relationships, to help the children take these experiences 'inside' themselves, and be able to carry them forward and make use of these memories in the future. Expectations about preparing for endings might be made explicit to the children: 'I don't think people can say a real hello until they've said a real goodbye.' We cannot go forwards until we have thought about what we are losing. If a child is leaving the class, then talking, writing and drawing about what will be missed can facilitate the consolidation of the developments the child has made. The child's fantasies of what s/he might remember afterwards help her/him to think about what s/he can take forward and build upon, what s/he takes to the new situation. This reduces the possibility of the child falling into the defence of simply leaving the experience behind. It can be useful to invite group members to construct agendas for the remaining sessions of the group. Whitaker (1985) suggests that the adult might ask group members what they hope might happen before the time that the group ends, or acknowledge that there might be things that group members would really like to do or to talk about before the group ends to avoid the disappointment of these things not happening, so that opportunities can be made to provide these activities or discussions.

It has been my experience in working with teachers in consultation groups that concern is commonly voiced about children who seemed to make progress, and then regress when they transfer to a new class. In such situations I have asked whether the former teacher might help the child to use the memory of the previous good relationship in the new situation: 'Whilst you're with Ms/Mr X, I wonder if you can remember the good things from last year, take them with you inside yourself, and use them there?' Where there might be an element of grieving for a satisfactory but lost relationship, it is possible for the lost attachment to give meaning to the present. 'Recovery from grief depends on restoring a sense that the lost attachment can still give meaning to the present' (Marris 1986: 149).

Ending routines and 'rituals' can be a useful management tool for providing emotional holding. It has been my experience with groups of troubled children that endings can be particularly traumatic times. A session which has been particularly creative can sometimes degenerate at the ending. Since the various endings in which we are involved with children may potentially arouse so much anxiety, it is useful to create frameworks in which the uncertainty of the endings is minimised. One way of doing this is to provide a regular routine for the way in which the group finishes each session. Similarly, when it is time for a child to leave a group an expected format can again be useful. When an element of ritual is involved, messages can be expressed symbolically and with a sense of heightened meaning for the individual.

Example

When children left my tutorial class groups (which happened as each individual became ready) the leaving was marked in a number of ways. The child would be invited to make a final drawing or piece of writing which expressed how s/he wanted to say goodbye to the class, and which would be kept at the class to symbolise that those who remained would keep the child in mind and remember him/her. Each child was given a (homemade) portfolio in which to carry and protect the work they had made at the class, to symbolise that what had been experienced there was worthy of care and protection, and that the internalisation of experience would endure. Finally, there would be some special food, and cards specially prepared by the other children. At the presentation of the cards group members would be asked in turn to make some comment to the child who was ending, which would often include a statement about what they would remember of the child who was leaving.

To summarise, in response to ending situations with all children, but particularly those who are troubled by anxieties, we can make a significant difference to the child's experience of the ending by making the following interventions: preparing for and talking about an ending well in advance; giving the child a reminder of when one will next see her/him and thinking of ways of bridging the gaps; voicing to the child that an ending might be a difficult time because it might make her/him feel sad, or angry; and, for everyday endings, having a regular routine, an expected way of taking leave.

It feels appropriate to end this section with another eloquent quotation from Salzberger-Wittenberg.

If we can . . . remember our mentors with more love than anger, with more gratitude than grudge, then we will be able to hold on permanently to something of the goodness gained in those relationships. It implies that the past is not obliterated, nor the loss denied. It

132

involves us in some sadness and missing what we have had, and yet, out of appreciation, endeavouring to keep it alive in our minds. The past can never be ignored or undone. We can try to kill it off inside ourselves but by doing so we cut ourselves off from our roots and parts of ourselves. We then feel insecure and have no inner store on which to base our future. Alternatively, if we preserve the externally lost relationship within our minds, we are able to build on the inner groundwork we have developed, and feel we have some internal resources with which to face the future hopefully. This makes it possible to enter a new relationship without denying or smashing up the past, but rather by transferring the good feelings from the past and the hope gained thereby to the new situation.

(Salzberger-Wittenberg *et al.* 1983: 154)

Exercise: The experience of endings

*/**

Reflect upon childhood experiences of being left by adults who mattered to you, and the feelings which were aroused in you at such times. In what ways did these feelings affect you?

Exercise: The experience of loss and separation

*/**

Reflect upon how your own life has prepared you to work with the losses and separations of others.

Exercise: What do you need to say goodbye?

*/**/***

Think of a shared situation which you are in at the moment in which the relationships are valuable to you. This might be a training course, a friendship, a working relationship, a group or team experience. Imagine that this experience is about to end, and reflect upon what you need to say a meaningful goodbye. Include what you need to do for yourself, and what you need to do in relation to the other people with whom you have participated.

Exercise: Providing emotionally holding endings

*/**

Consider the various ways in which you might enhance the emotionally holding nature of the various endings which you manage in the setting in which you work.

THE LINK WITH MORAL DEVELOPMENT

Theories of moral development provide another 'filter' to help think about an appropriate level of emotionally holding responses. The concern here is not with moralising. 'Those who hold the view that morality needs to be inculcated teach small children accordingly, and they forgo the pleasure of watching morality develop naturally in their children' (Winnicott 1984: 15). Winnicott argues that moral development is related to emotional growth in the following way: it is linked to the capacity to experience a sense of guilt, and it takes place where conditions enable trust, and belief in and ideas of right and wrong, to develop out of the working through of inner processes relating to the personal superego. Winnicott viewed the capacity to act and feel responsible as the capacity for concern.

This part of his theory owes much to Melanie Klein. The conditions necessary for the development of this capacity, briefly put, are

1 Integration of the ego. There has to be a whole person, with an inside and an outside, who can contain the anxiety within the self. 'I am' has to come before 'I am responsible'. At this stage the ego is beginning to be independent of the mother's auxiliary ego.
2 Object relationships in which there are elements of love and destruction . . . though there has come to be some appreciation of the difference between fact and fantasy.
3 The mother is seen as a whole person, separate from the infant, and in the process of becoming permanent.

(Davies and Wallbridge 1990: 74)

In relation to these developmental processes, Winnicott argues that

we have to provide . . . in infancy and childhood and adolescence, in home and in school, the facilitating environment in which each individual may grow his or her own moral capacity, develop a superego that evolved naturally from crude superego elements of infancy, and find his or her own way of using or not using the moral code and general cultural endowment of our age.

(Winnicott 1984: 105)

We come to learn to be less dependent upon our inner judgemental voices, and to be able to construct our own judgements and values about the world around us and our place in it.

Keeping in mind the notion of the various levels of moral development can enable adults to respond to children at a level of meaning which makes most sense to them. Kohlberg's theory of moral development provides a workable tool. Theories such as his explore a child's reasoning at different levels when facing issues of genuine moral conflicts, rather than issues of good manners. Basing his work on cognitive and experimental psychology, he interviewed children over a number of years to ascertain the reasons why stealing was judged to be wrong. He developed a series of stages of moral development, which are said to apply to people aged 9 years and over. These are shown in Figure 13. Kohlberg argued that children and young

The pre-conventional level

Stage 1: Punishment and obedience
Reward and punishment determine goodness and badness.
Sticking to rules backed by punishment.
Obedience for own sake.

Stage 2: Instrumental purpose
You scratch my back and I'll scratch yours.
Following rules only when in one's immediate interest: acting to meet one's own interests and letting others do the same.

The conventional level

Stage 3: 'Good boy – nice girl'
Conformity to stereotyped images of being good: one gets approval by being nice.

Stage 4: Law and order
The rules are fixed: one does one's duty and has respect for authority.
One fulfils duties to which one has agreed.
Rightness involves contributing to the group or institution.

The post-conventional, autonomous or principled level

Stage 5: Social-contract
Personal opinions are relative and there is a need to reach a consensus.

Stage 6: Universal ethical principles
Right is defined by individual conscience in relation to ethical, abstract principles.
One follows self-chosen ethical principles, and acts in accordance with those principles.
Respect for the dignity of human beings as individuals.

Figure 13 Kohlberg's stages of moral development

people cannot comprehend arguments more than one stage in the sequence beyond their own. Adult thinking which is more complex than the child's – i.e. by more than one stage in the sequence – is likely to be void of meaning and so rejected, thus providing no motive for change.

Kohlberg argues that development through the stages of moral development takes place in order through the sequence, and that a shift to the next stage happens when we feel uncomfortable in functioning at a particular level. As we move through the stages our perception of the social system widens, and we become increasingly able to think abstractly.

Most adults in society are said to operate at stages 4 and 5. Whilst it can be useful to hypothesise the stage at which a particular child or young person might be functioning, care must be taken in doing so. It is not possible to make judgements about moral development on the basis of isolated pieces of behaviour, since different children might perform the same action for different reasons. Therefore any hypothesis about the functioning of a particular child needs to be based on a holistic view of the child.

Given that children are said to find it difficult to comprehend arguments at more than one stage from their own, and actively to reject such thinking, to use these stages as a tool in relation to children's levels of functioning can be helpful. An adult's response to various sorts of testing-out and acting-out will be ineffective unless pitched at a level of moral development appropriate for the child. It would be inappropriate, for example, to appeal for consensus when a child believes that actions are made to satisfy one's own needs. Similarly, it might be difficult for a child to comprehend an appeal to respect authority, if s/he believes that punishment is the only method of demonstrating the 'badness' involved in disobedience. In working with children on moral development, role-play is a potentially helpful means of learning to develop empathy, and of learning to consider alternative forms of action using abstract forms of thought.

Exercise: Recognising and helping moral development

*/**

1 Reflect upon an incident when you have put forward some sort of moral reasoning to a child. Assess the stage of the child's thinking, and the stage of your response, in terms of the Kohlberg model.
2 Reflect upon a developmental issue which you are currently working on with a particular child. Make a hypothesis about the child's functioning in terms of Kohlberg's scale. What can you learn from this, and the above discussion, to help you formulate an appropriate response?

The following two exercises relate to material from the whole of the chapter.

Exercise: Emotional holding at times of difficulty

*/**/***

1 In your experience, are there particular times in the school routine when emotional and behavioural difficulties tend to manifest?
2 Try to think of responses which provide emotional holding at such times in relation to:

   – individual children;
   – the class group;
   – the whole school community of children.

Exercise: Using the concept of emotional holding for problem-solving

*/**/***

Think of a problem which you are currently facing. It might be a problem in relation to an individual child or the class or school organisation.

1 What are the factors in your identified problem which get in the way of learning?
2 Use the concept of emotional holding as a tool to consider the dynamics of this problem, and how you might work with it. How is your understanding of the situation affected?

SUMMARY

- Emotional holding involves containing disturbing feelings, and demonstrating that they can be tolerated, thought about, understood and managed. The provision of emotional holding by the adult helps the child's internalisation of these processes for him/herself, and helps his/her ego development to proceed.
- Adults provide emotional holding through their relationships with children by making a well-bounded countainer for 'boundaryless' individuals, to create a meaningful space for all concerned; by containing anxiety whilst providing appropriate space for exploration and autonomy; by being aware of the way in which projections are responded

to, containing the anxiety aroused in oneself, and seeking to avoid unconscious retaliation; by demonstrating that one can have a relationship with difficult feelings other than being possessed by them; by showing that a difficult feeling can be lived with, thought about and understood; and by empathically mirroring or reflecting back behaviour traits.

- The processes of holding enable the child to experience reflection upon his/her state of mind, and gradually to internalise the container, producing a mind that can hold thought.
- Processes of holding become general features of classroom practice through:

  - setting clear and meaningful boundaries and maintaining expectations in a manner which provides emotional holding and security;
  - keeping feelings, including the difficult ones, on the classroom agenda;
  - developing strategies for particular individuals on the basis of observed needs;
  - empathically reflecting back a child's behaviour, thus helping the child to increase awareness of the link between behaviour and feelings, talk about problems rather than act them out, and respect the feelings of others;
  - providing positive frameworks for reinforcing expectations;
  - being particularly vigilant to provide emotional holding at times when boundaries are vulnerable, e.g. the beginnings and ends of sessions;
  - working to both immediate and longer-term strategies;
  - taking account of the child's stage of moral development;
  - structuring the curriculum to take account of the anxiety and risk generated in trying to learn (this will be considered in Chapter Eight).

- Processes of emotional holding may also usefully be reflected in work with parents of children experiencing emotional/behavioural difficulties and in whole-school special educational needs policy and organisation.

5

USING IMAGE AND METAPHOR IN COMMUNICATION AND DEVELOPMENT

Where symptom was, there metaphor shall be.

Wright 1976

INTRODUCTION

In this chapter we come to consider that just as we have seen that behaviour has meaning, so do the images expressed in play, stories and the arts.

Where growth and development appear to be stuck, or to be regressing, there is a natural urge to will development forward. It is as if we might want to say, 'If only his or her ego could be strong enough, then all would be well.' But as Donnington (1963: 149) says, 'it is not within the direct power of the ego to bring about transformation and renewal; the most the ego can do is open itself to the process'. This point that development cannot necessarily be willed is a crucial piece of understanding. However effective ego-provision is, some areas of growth emerge from deeper levels within the human psyche. When we work with making images, for example in play, story making, painting and sculpture, we often work with elements of the unconscious. Through using the symbols of metaphor and image, which are expressions of unconscious aspects of psyche, we are able to make new connections in our inner worlds, and from within find sources of new possibility. In psychotherapy one might endeavour to articulate the meanings of such symbols. In educational settings – particularly through the arts and English curricula – work with image provides opportunities for children to express inner, subjective meanings *symbolically* through metaphor, and to explore and reformulate these meanings by working within the metaphor. Teachers of the arts and English curricula are required to teach technique. But within these subject areas in particular, teachers can provide important opportunities for growth through using image, by being aware of the metaphorical dimensions of such work, and by integrating an understanding of these dimensions into their broad curricular role. Because art activities encourage thoughtful perception and depth of emotional experience, Mary Warnock (1977) suggests that more arts in the curriculum would probably be of greater social and educational value than pastoral or counselling services.

Piaget developed the idea that in order for the child to understand something, s/he must construct it for her/himself, must reinvent it. The ability to symbolise is one of the foundations of learning, and this ability is helped by the capacity to use the imagination. Where learning is impeded by emotional and behavioural difficulties, the imagination has become stuck, fixed, as if the children have become psychologically frozen. It may also be the case that troubled children do not yet have the language or the ego strength to communicate very much verbally about their difficulties. Images and metaphors are mediums which help development, by providing a vehicle for us to relate to those frozen aspects of the personality, and helping to unfreeze them.

In the second and third sections of this chapter I consider the role of using metaphor and image in educational settings with troubled children, and how to facilitate such work to help growth and development, using a number of case studies. Some readers may first wish to consider the theoretical starting-points.

DEFINITIONS AND THEORETICAL STARTING-POINTS

The imagination has long been understood as a source of creativity. A sixteenth-century alchemical dictionary describes the imagination as 'the star in man'. Coleridge saw it as 'the living power and agent of all human perception', and Yeats thought of images as 'living souls'. More recently, fantasy and drawing are described by the University of Nottingham's School of Education (1991) as 'powerful tools for developing self-understanding'. It is through the use of image that we can imagine new possibilities for ourselves:

> To tell a story is often to make images . . . We cannot take a step in life or literature without using an image. Not only does each image tell its singular story, but that story invokes another.
>
> (Hardy 1975)

The metaphorical aspects of imagery are particularly significant for our concerns in this chapter. The Greek *metaphora* comes from a verb which means 'to carry across'. Metaphors carry across psychic contents from the inner world to the outer world. They are a way of proceeding from the known to the unknown (Nisbet 1969). Metaphor allows us to go into unconscious realms, and to explore unknown aspects of ourselves. 'Metaphor seems to have the capacity to touch the depths before the surface is stirred. Its efficacy . . . has something to do with the [person]

140

being touched from *within*, rather than entered from without' (Cox and Theilgaard 1987: 109). So metaphors evoke the unconscious world (Rothenberg 1979) and mediate between unconscious and conscious realms. Metaphorical images expressed in play, art or story form are potential routes of communication for the expression of conflicts and possibilities. Anna Halprin, founder of an early dancers' workshop in the USA, says, 'In art you give expression to that which lies deep inside you and, having given expression to it, you receive back a vision which is a map by which you can set your other goals' (in Roose-Evans 1987: 13). Metaphorical work thus provides opportunities to experience and find one's own meaning, to think and to develop richer relationships. Metaphor is 'the beginning of thought itself, if you regard "thinking" as the ability to perceive and identify new relationships' (Williams 1991: 36).

The therapeutic value of the metaphorical image is its capacity to say several things at once, its so-called polyvalency. This is because metaphorical expression uses symbolic imagery. From a psychological point of view, it is particularly important in this work to understand the significance of symbols. The word symbol derives from the Greek word *symbolon*, which combines *syn*, meaning together or with, and *bolon*, meaning that which has been thrown. The basic meaning of symbol is thus 'that which has been thrown together'. When considered psychologically, symbols become energy-evoking and -directing agents (Campbell 1969). The work of Jung brought huge advances in our understanding of the importance of symbols, enabling us to work with the concept of symbol as 'a living thing, . . . an expression for something that cannot be characterized in any other or better way' (Jung 1971: 474, 476). Elsewhere Jung says, 'because there are innumerable things beyond the range of human understanding, we constantly use symbolic terms to represent concepts that we cannot define or fully comprehend' (Jung 1964: 126). The crucial function of a symbol, for Jung, is that it expresses in a unique way a psychological fact incapable at the time of being grasped by consciousness. 'A symbol has a subjective dynamism which exerts a powerful attraction and fascination on the individual. It is a living, organic entity which acts as a releaser and transformer of psychic energy. . . . a symbol is alive' (Edinger 1973: 109).

Jung clearly differentiated between symbols and signs. In contrast to symbols, signs are visible, uni-dimensional indications, which make connections between things which are already known. Metaphor sits midway between sign and symbol, since one half of metaphor is known to consciousness (Samuels 1985a). What matters in work with children in educational settings is the *metaphorical* use a child can make of a symbol: is the child able to imagine, use image, enter the story of an image? Through the individual's use of metaphor to express and play with inner images, inner resolutions emerge, which are more meaningful to the individual than externally imposed resolutions. Changes which emerge from one's own inner world tend therefore to be more closely integrated within the developing personality. Symbols expressed through images may emerge before corresponding behavioural change.

> clear images may emerge into consciousness before the corresponding behaviour is anywhere near to being able to be given up or not given up as a matter of choice. There is often a splitting between image and corresponding affect which is used defensively (intellectually, for instance) in order to delay affective (moral) responsibility and autonomy.
>
> (Redfearn 1985: 105)

An effective holding environment provides the 'potential space' to work on further necessary behavioural change and the development of creativity. In Winnicott's notion, potential space (Chapter One, section on 'Emotional needs and learning') is a relaxed place, where play, and an overlap between the internal and external worlds, contribute to self-realisation. Potential space partakes of the dream and fantasy world, and the world of shared reality, at once. 'It is the place where experience builds upon experience, where the world is continually "woven into the texture of the imagination", so that new patterns of imagining emerge and a man is able to be truly original' (Davies and Wallbridge 1990: 167). It is within potential space that symbols originate (Cox and Theilgaard 1987). Growth of the imagination does not take place in response to direction or coercion: non-judgemental permission is necessary. Using metaphor and image as a means of communication and development requires an approach in which the emphasis is invitational rather than adversarial; permission-giving rather than coercive; catalytic, spontaneous and enabling rather than predetermined and reductive.

This area of work derives in many ways from Jung's work with what he called 'active imagination'. Active imagination involves giving attention to an internal image, and can be done in many ways including dance, painting, drawing, work with clay, story telling and every other kind of artistic medium. 'Every form of active imagination initiates this essential dialogue between curiosity and the imagination. Such dialogue is an interweaving of conscious and unconscious; it is the ultimate source of creativity' (Chodorow 1991: 6). Active imagination involves letting the images happen rather than directing them, and respecting the images as sources which help the story move onwards. Active imagination is a way of coming to terms with the contents of the unconscious within the unitary reality of creative fantasy (von Franz, in the introduction to Hannah 1981).

THE ROLE OF IMAGE AND METAPHOR IN HELPING EMOTIONAL GROWTH

I now explore the functions that work with image and metaphor can fulfil in educational settings: holding and containing feelings, communicating about inner experience, resolving conflicts of feeling, and facilitating access to the individual's potential (Greenhalgh 1988). Each of these areas is examined in turn.

Holding and containing feelings

Children might not be able to articulate difficult feelings verbally for a variety of reasons. They might not have the vocabulary, they might not be conscious of the feeling, or the feelings might be too frightening. Dockar-Drysdale (1990) comments that one of the most noticeable absences in emotionally deprived children is the scanty use of verbal communication. Disturbing feelings may be expressed non-verbally through image: 'emotions are crafted into distinct materialised shapes' (Hillman 1979: 134). Since the feelings are expressed symbolically there is a sense of distance and safety from the disturbing nature of the feelings. So one might say that metaphors and images themselves provide emotional holding for feelings. Commenting about his own psychic struggles, Jung (1977: 201) wrote, to 'the extent that I managed to translate emotions into images . . . I was inwardly calmed and reassured. Had I left images hidden in emotions, I might have been torn to pieces by them.' The creative representation and concretisation of psychic contents which are emotionally charged, and therefore long to be expressed, normally bring relief (Jacoby 1990). Jung's colleague, von Franz, comments that the symbols of image act as a 'net in which to catch the unspeakable mystery of the unconscious' (von Franz 1980).

Exercise: Using imagery to show feelings

*/**

Think of as many ways as you can of encouraging children to show imaginatively what it is like to have a particular feeling (e.g. fear, happiness, sadness, anger, etc.).

Communicating about subjective experience

Metaphor provides a means of expression for the child's point of view, and a channel of communication which is psychologically acceptable to the child. It is psychologically acceptable for three reasons. First, it does not require the use of a linguistic vocabulary. This is important as children might not have developed a sufficiently large or adequate vocabulary. Even if one is an articulate adult, 'the deepest feelings cannot be put into words. Language fails' (Cox and Theilgaard 1987: 60). Second, the use of metaphor avoids the need for the child to erect, reinforce or hide behind defences. It allows the adult/teacher to approach painful areas obliquely, tangentially, at a rate which is determined by the child's psyche. The use of metaphor invites and does not threaten, evokes and does not invade. '[The image] is always tailor-made. Yet it is tolerable and acceptable to the [person] as she comes to terms with hitherto unacceptable parts of her experience' (Cox and Theilgaard 1987: 53). Third, metaphor reaches those parts of psychic experience which cannot be known through thought, putting us in touch with parts of ourselves that are too far away or too close for us to see in ordinary life.

How might the teacher make sense of metaphorical communications, in educational settings? Whilst it is not appropriate for teachers to make psychologial interpretations of metaphorical material, developing a metaphorical *hypothesis* can play a significant part in empathising with the child's experience.

Example: Ishret

This example shows how image and metaphor can be used by a child to communicate about inner, subjective experience.

When she was aged 8, Ishret's situation was referred to the tutorial class service. She had been considered an elective mute in school. She rarely made any verbal communication and seemed never to initiate contact with anyone, nor ever to express any feelings. When she came with her father for an initial visit to the tutorial class, I asked if she would like to do a drawing while I talked with her father. She drew a picture of a girl trapped with her siblings in a cage suspended over a fire in a witch's house. At this point Ishret was able to communicate very little verbally, but I ascertained what Ishret was able to acknowledge or deny about the picture by asking questions which needed answers simply in the affirmative or negative. Given the responses which Ishret was able to make, I took the drawing to be an eloquent description of the way in which Ishret was at the time experiencing life. Through minimal use of language, she could acknowledge that the witch had made a powerful spell. When asked what the girl in the drawing might do to escape, Ishret gave the impression that she could not begin to imagine such a possibility. Later in that meeting, I spoke of one of the purposes for Ishret's attendance at tutorial class as being to find a way of escaping from the witch.

During Ishret's part-time placement in the tutorial class group the witch theme emerged again from time to time in her stories and pretend plays. Over many months in drawings, stories and plays with other children, whenever Ishret had a girl trapped in a witch's den, she could not find a way to escape. On one or two occasions the group spontaneously became involved in plays about escaping from the witch, and whilst others would find their way out, Ishret was not able to. Eighteen months after starting in the tutorial class group, when she was beginning to participate more in relationships and to initiate interaction, Ishret wrote her own story in which the girl made her escape from the witch's den. Symbolically, it was as if the spell had been broken.

Example: Sonya

In the following story, written together by a girl called Sonya and tutorial class teacher Mary Brown, the girl was able to write about a witch, and then verbally acknowledge that she was often like this witch. The story thus provided Sonya with the means to communicate about her inner experiences, and, in particular, her fears about how powerful and terrible she might be.

> Once upon a time there was a little witch. She was an evil little witch. What she liked doing best was making spells and catching children and turning them into frogs. The children were frightened of her. She was sad because she didn't want to be spiteful. She wanted to be friends with the children, but all the children didn't like her, because she shouldn't change them into frogs.
>
> She's going to stop it, but she can't help it. She's trying to get rid of her spells but she can't because it's difficult. She tried to bury the spells in some sand and she done it but people comed on the beach and one of the children sat on the spell and they changed into a frog.

Resolving inner conflicts

Working with metaphor enables us to relate to unconscious aspects of our psyches, and to engage with aspects of our psychic experience which we might otherwise repress. Using metaphor has the potential to change the relationships between the various aspects of our inner world. Working with metaphor has metamorphic and transformative power, and has the potential to resolve conflict at an unconscious level. 'Metaphor is our means of effecting instantaneous fusion of two separated realms of experience into one illuminating, iconic, encapsulating image' (Nisbet 1969, quoted in Cox and Theilgaard 1987: 95).

There is considerable agreement in the fields of psychology and art on the role of metaphor in resolving affective conflict. Artists have widely acknowledged the role of metaphor in exploring and resolving the conflict of feelings. For example, Coleridge speaks of the faculty of the imagination as 'that reconciling and mediating power' (quoted in Cox and Theilgaard 1987: 136). In psychological terms, the imagination takes us to the emotional core of a difficulty, and can also lead us *through* it (Chodorow 1991). Jung (1973a: 191) explains why symbols are needed to resolve psychological conflict. 'Conflict can only be resolved through symbol. . . . [Symbols] . . . facilitate the much needed union of conscious and unconscious. This union cannot be established either intellectually or in a purely practical sense, because in the former case the instincts rebel, and in the latter case, reason and morality.' Cox and Theilgaard argue their case for the role of metaphor in resolving psychological conflicts in the following terms:

> The poetic metaphor exerts its synthesizing effect by building a bridge between the ikonic mode of the right and the linguistic mode of the left hemisphere. Thus, it also enhances the exchange between

145

unconscious and conscious realms. Thereby it helps in the establishment of genuine insight. . . . The therapeutic potentiality of an image depends not only on its capacity to surprise and its dynamic freshness, it also utilizes its inherent synthesizing power. The active organising principle acts below the level of consciousness and is linked with emotion. . . . Symbols reconcile inner forces which are not evident in the province of discursive logic.

(Cox and Theilgaard 1987: 96)

Example: Richard

This example shows how Richard was able to use metaphor to work on some of his emotional conflicts through playing with a puppet. I will first give some background to Richard's situation.

Richard was referred to the tutorial class service when he was aged 9. He was described as disruptive at school, and involved in incidents of stealing and lying. Richard had spent his early years alone with his mother. At the time of referral, mother had had two children by a new partner, who was apparently emotionally and physically heavy-handed towards Richard. When Richard began part-time attendance with a tutorial class group, he presented overanxiously as a perfectly good boy, who had strict – and rather judgemental – morals, and who avoided becoming messy. Given the nature of Richard's experiences during the rest of the week, there seemed something unreal and defensive about this persona. I hoped Richard would be able to find a way of bridging and healing the splitting of good and bad (a defence associated with Klein's paranoid-schizoid state – see Chapter Two), so that he could live more realistically and creatively with these two sides of himself. This meant that the 'good' boy would have to find a way of tolerating and working with the 'bad' parts of himself. Some of my early attempts to facilitate this were too blatant, overt and unsubtle. For example, I asked Richard to write a story called, 'The Day I Became Messy'. Richard, who regularly wrote independently and ably, was not, at that point, able to tolerate the thought of such a theme. It was possible to use activities like cookery to think a little with Richard about being messy.

It was mainly through symbolic language that Richard was able to do the emotional work he so much needed. He took a liking to the witch puppet, which he used as a ventriloquist uses a dummy, to represent himself and the witch in dialogue with each other. Richard was finding a way to voice the nastiness and cruelty of his witch, and thereby to explore symbolically his relationship with his own nasty and cruel impulses. This enabled him to work towards resolving the conflict between the parts of his personality. As Marion Milner comments, 'Psychic creativeness is the capacity for making a symbol' (1971: 148). *Gestalt* psychology uses the technique of creating dialogues between the 'bits' of a person (for example, see Oaklander 1978): Richard was able to work towards forging his own *Gestalt*, or perception of wholeness.

Example: Melissa

One of Melissa's stories made a strong impression on me as an example of metaphor being used to resolve inner conflicts.

Melissa's situation was referred to the tutorial class service when she was aged

146

7. She was described as being extremely withdrawn and finding it very difficult to make friends. Her school report indicated little progress over three years. Melissa had been given additional individual attention in school over a two-year period, but this had not enabled her to make progress. At the point of referral her literacy and numeracy skills were at a very early level, and her lack of imagination in painting and craft work was commented upon. In his report of referral the educational psychologist described Melissa as very lacking in self-confidence, finding it very difficult to participate, to be spontaneous or to play, and seeming overwhelmed and crushed by anxiety. In her time with the educational psychologist it was striking that when Melissa felt that she did not know the answer to a question, she went silent and looked down as if she had done something wrong. The educational psychologist commented that she might feel much of the time that the safest thing for her to do was to say nothing and do nothing, and he posed the question which he thought Melissa faced: 'Dare I disturb the universe?'

In my initial meeting with Melissa's mother at the tutorial class she disclosed that the father had sexually abused Melissa when she was in infancy, by rubbing his erect penis against her on a number of occasions. Mother and father had then split up, and at the time of referral the father had not lived in the house for a number of years.

Melissa began attending a part-time tutorial class group, and, after a four-month period, I was surprised when Melissa said that she would like to climb a beanstalk. So I asked her to write a story entitled, 'Climbing the Beanstalk'. In the story Melissa climbed the beanstalk, and set free some other children who had been trapped by the giant at the top. She then descended the beanstalk and, when the giant attempted to follow, she 'chopped and he fell dead into his grave'. Melissa's social and academic functioning had, by this time, begun to improve, and I made the hypothesis to myself that Melissa might now be beginning to stand up to her inner ogre. Upon hearing Melissa read her story, in order to acknowledge something of the psychological import of what I thought might be happening, I commented joyfully to her, 'The ogre is gone now!'

Three months after this incident, when I next met Melissa's mother, she described Melissa as more outgoing, confident, open, and showing initiative. Melissa continued part-time attendance at tutorial class for another year, whilst these developments were consolidated. During this time her school described her as 'integrated' rather than on the fringe', more assertive, telling other children if they annoyed her, asking to work with particular children, and having a go at everything. Her self-confidence had markedly improved, and she was making progress in academic attainments. By this time she had a number of apparently rewarding friendships.

Speaking to the title 'The Soul of the Giant', Jungian analyst Dr D. Baumann (1989) told a traditional Romansch story which involved the killing of giants. He viewed the giant as the power complex which takes over the whole personality and leads one to isolate oneself from others. In fairy stories – which express archetypal themes – the giant is overcome not by strong emotion or straightforward intellect, but by the capacity for calculation. This talk suggested to me a series of strong symbolic associations to the dilemma which Melissa had faced.

Example: Peter

Some of Peter's story is told in Chapter Six, section on 'Supporting children's relationships with peers'. At this point I would like to refer to his engagement with a long story of many chapters which he wrote over a number of months, a story which enabled him to work with metaphor towards the resolution of some inner conflicts.

147

Peter's situation was referred to the tutorial class service when he was aged 9. In school there was concern about his isolation from his peers, his difficulty in sorting events logically, either orally or on paper, and his slow progress in number work. The educational psychologist wrote that in class Peter was noticeable because of his difficulty in relating appropriately to both adults and children. With adults, he unwittingly adopted an overfamiliar manner, attracting attention by waving, smiling and calling out. With regard to children, he seemed to misinterpret their behaviour, believing that they were picking on him or laughing at him when often they were not involving him at all. At the same time, though, his behaviour could irritate them to the point of retaliation, a point of which he seemed unaware. Peter was a ward of court. His situation was referred to the tutorial class service after a short period of work with the family at a local child guidance clinic. There were concerns that Peter's difficulties might be related to distorting defences (see Chapter Two). A piece of evidence from school to support this concern was a comment of Peter's class teacher: even when doing drawing based on close observation work Peter still drew from his imagination.

During Peter's part-time placement in a tutorial class group, there was a period of a number of months when he would use part of almost every session to write a long, long story. He began to refer to this as his 'novel', called *The Black Horse*. His drawing of the black horse showed it to be a heavily armoured, rectangular, tank-like vehicle, on wheels. I give some extracts from his story by way of example of the metaphorical explorations Peter was going through:

> One day a boy called [Peter] . . . had invented a tank called the black horse he liked to go on adventures. Tomorrow he would set sail. He would start these gallant adventures by helping people, and by saving their villages. a man called Horace wanted to stop [Peter] from helping people by causing havoc, and killing some of the people . . . [Instalment 1].

> The black horse has some protection now and it can fit one more person inside. . . . [Instalment 2].

> now [Peter] has been very doubtful. the black horse has now gone into a town where [Peter] and his crew are very scared. the black horse rides deeper and deeper in the town . . . [Instalment 3].

> the town was far away . . . the black horse was in a trance and was very scared. karl [another boy in the group] wanted to cry. the black horse stopped outside the hideout. horace was laughing . . . [Instalment 4].

There were many adventures and struggles which Peter and the black horse team had with Horace and his men, in chapters with titles such as 'Death Swamp' and 'Pits of Death'. The final instalment, number 41, came some months later:

> After successive wins, the black horse team were really surprised that the rattlesnake team didn't win at all. That evening the team sat down to eat chicken chop suey, cooked in oyster sauce. In a moment, the black horse was flying over the mountains, until they reached England. [Peter] drove to Landsdowne Drive. Pleased to see them, the teachers rushed out and the staff got ready to greet them. The whole school got a glimpse of the black horse team. Congratulating them stepped out [Headteacher's name] presenting [Peter] with the cup of destiny.

Peter had, through the symbolism of his story, fought many inner battles, and knew unconsciously, and *in his own time*, when he was ready to take the cup of destiny through full-time reintegration into his mainstream school. At a review meeting fifteen months after the beginning of his tutorial class placement, it was noted that Peter had made some good friends and was now able to work well with other children. He was more able to take criticism from his teachers, tolerate the frustration of not always having his own way and accept changes in routine. Testing by the educational psychologist indicated that his performance on a test of basic computational skills had improved at least two years in the preceding year. It is noteworthy that Peter's access to mathematics increased even though this was not a major element of his work at tutorial class, and he had not received a disproportionate amount of maths support in school. After this review meeting, arrangements were made for Peter to terminate his tutorial class placement and to reintegrate full-time into his mainstream school.

Providing access to potential

The philosopher of psychoanalytic ideas Gaston Bachelard (1987: 110) says, 'Rather than the will, . . . Imagination is the true source of psychic production. Psychically, we are created by our reverie . . . Imagination works at the summit of the mind like a flame.' Exploring imaginatively through symbol is a way of both discovering and communicating about what is latent and emerging in the individual's psyche. This process is linked to the development of what Jung termed the self, the dynamic centre of the psyche which expresses the unity of the personality as a whole. For the individual child, the self grows through processes of imaginative, internal, sophisticated trial and error, termed deintegration and reintegration (Fordham 1969, Ryce-Menuhin 1988).

Work with Mary provides an example of how using metaphor and image can provide access to hitherto untapped potential.

Example: Mary

Mary is the pupil referred to in Chapter Two in relation to the influence of parental difficulties upon the child; further background on Mary's situation is given there. In the example which follows, Mary had been attending the part-time tutorial class group for about nine months. Her academic and social potentials were becoming evident in a variety of ways in the class, at home and at school.

One day in tutorial class, Mary (then aged 8 years) and the others in the group decided to play at 'hospitals'. I was asked by Mary to be a patient, and agreed. Mary pretended that there was a wound on my arm, and treated it by bringing me a leaf and a toy snake, which I was instructed to hold together on the wound as a poultice. On a later occasion, Mary wanted to write a story, which she first dictated to me. It is called 'The Sun and the Moon':

> Once upon a time there lived the sun and the moon. They used to fight. One day they didn't fight. The sun said, 'Good morning, how are you doing?' The sun went to the moon's house. The baby sun and the baby moon were playing. They put on the television and the babies liked it. They giggled and had their dinner. They had their bottle, then they went to bed.

Psychological work suggests that such play and stories are far from meaningless. In the pretend play about the hospital, Mary put herself in the position of a healer

– it seemed that in some way she was beginning to be able to imagine healing. From the hundreds of objects available in the room (there were shelves containing many miniature objects) she chose two which can be symbolic of healing. The leaf creates food for the tree – the tree of life. In the context of our play, and in my own mind, I associated the snake with the emblem of Asclepius, divine healer of classical times. When the snake and tree are linked, the snake represents 'the awakening of dynamic force, the genius of all growing things' (Cooper 1978: 146). The potential for healing was taken further in the sun-and-moon story, and illustrated by the changing relationship between the sun and the moon. Analytical psychologist Bani Shorter (1987: 59) comments that 'Sol and Luna, as they were called by the alchemists, do in fact rule together in the human psyche.' In most cultural traditions sun and moon represent the universal father and universal mother. For Mary, these two fundamental principles in psyche 'used to fight', but now they were able to go to each other's houses, and their children played together.

In Jungian terms, the example of Mary might be viewed as the child making contact with the 'collective unconscious'. Jung established the existence of this aspect of the psyche in addition to the personal unconscious. It serves as a repository of 'symbolic memory' across cultures and time. At the time of this play and story by Mary, her inner world seemed to be opening up to the freedom of being able to imagine greater realms of possibility.

FACILITATING WORK WITH IMAGE AND METAPHOR

Having considered the role of image and metaphor in communication and development, we now turn attention to facilitating work with image and metaphor in educational settings.

This work involves allowing children to engage in open-ended imaginative work, showing that products of the child's imagination are taken seriously, talking about the work within the metaphorical framework provided by the child, and valuing and honouring children's metaphors and images. These issues are discussed in the sections which follow. It is first necessary to acknowledge the importance of play, drama, stories, myths and fairy tales.

Play and drama

The Inner London Education Authority's pack *The National Curriculum: A Planning Guide for Primary Schools* (ILEA 1989) has a section entitled 'The Importance of Play (from 3 to 11)'. Since it demonstrates the serious concern with which an education authority might take the issue of play, it is worth making a substantial quotation from the document:

Play is of vital importance to the development of children's understanding. . . . It is an essential means of exploring, expanding and representing experiences, both cognitive and emotional; it provides a major vehicle by which children gain access to the curriculum and remains important throughout the primary age range from 3 to 11. In a world where increasingly pressure is upon us to succeed or fail in achieving pre-set goals, the need for education to find generous room for playful activity is pressing. It is cognitively and emotionally necessary to nurture it and essential to ensure that provision for play reflects the cultural knowledge and experience of all children.

An essential starting point for the growth of understanding is the child's self-directed and spontaneous activity. . . . We need to consider four important values of play which are of special significance to the child in school. . . . a) Play as a means of coming to terms with oneself, other people and the world. b) Play as exploration/ investigation/problem-solving. c) Play as practice. d) Play as symbolic representation. Children learn in many different ways and successful matching will depend upon the teacher's skill in providing for this range and fitting it to the child's learning needs. Observation of children at play provides a valuable tool for the assessment of both development and learning.

The range of activities to enhance learning and to support programmes of study should include the following possibilities. Coming to terms with oneself and others through role play. . . . Opportunities for imaginative reflection and projection through creative play, in symbolic and dramatic activity, music, visual media, movement and language. In this respect play must be seen as a fundamental mode of representation.

(ILEA 1989)

Winnicott (1964) argues that the capacity to play shows that the child is capable, given reasonably good and stable surroundings, of developing a personal way of life, and eventually of becoming a whole human being. Piaget takes a similar view:

> It is indispensable to [the child's] affective and intellectual equilibrium . . . that he have available to him an area of activity whose motive is not adaptation to reality, but, on the contrary, assimilation of reality to the self, without coercions or sanctions. Such an area is play, which transforms reality by assimilation to the needs of the self, whereas imitation (where it constitutes an end in itself) is accommodation to external models.
>
> (Piaget and Inhelder 1969, quoted in Davies and Wallbridge 1990: 62)

Davies and Wallbridge (1990) suggest that Piaget describes here the difficulties in moving from the pleasure principle to the reality principle, and that he is very close to Winnicott in concluding that an area of activity in which play is included is indispensable for the transition to be made. 'Teaching, if it is to be profitable, also takes place in this overlap of play areas (i.e. between teacher and child)' (Davies and Wallbridge 1990: 65–6).

151

Children stuck in emotional and behavioural difficulties are often unable to play. It is as if something in their life has touched an aspect of the psyche which has become fixed, and the psychological 'life space' becomes static. In play, the imagination may open up the potentially fluid environment between component parts of the psyche. Jung explains this in terms of archetypes (collective and instinctive organisers of experience) which awaken a person's psyche and thus allow it to become involved in spontaneous activity. In such activity one becomes involved in fantasies not of the conscious realm, but from a deeper source of creativity, from the stuff of which dreams are made.

For children with emotional and behavioural difficulties play is particularly important for the following reasons. Firstly, fantasy is the forerunner of inner reality, and play links the individual's relationship with his/her inner reality with external or shared reality. Secondly, play provides a framework for an initiation into relationships which have an emotional charge and meaning. In Dockar-Drysdale's terms, this reflects the capacity to represent symbolically emotional experience which has been realised internally. Play, then, is transitional (in the sense that Winnicott used this term): one neither controls significant others, nor is at the mercy of one's own instincts. Thirdly, play facilitates the development of symbols and their use in metaphor, and this helps the development of thought. Fourthly, play provides space within which the imagination can work and move. And fifthly, play allows the pattern of each child's individual being (in Jungian terms, the self) to be nourished and to emerge.

Adults' understanding of the environmental qualities which facilitate play profoundly affect the sorts of play in which children engage. It is the free and protected space for children in play and drama, the permission to be themselves, the adult's understanding, acceptance, recognition of feelings, and capacity to clarify what the children think and feel that help them enhance their self-respect (Axline 1989). To maximise its therapeutic effect, play should take place in a regular, structured way – not just anywhere, at any time, with anyone (Dockar-Drysdale 1990). The child needs a setting in which the adult provides relaxed, reliable and emotionally contained experience. The facilitating adult is able to participate appropriately with the child in play, to let the child be absorbed in his/her own play, to provide the experience of an emotionally containing environment, and to think actively about what is happening for the child. Winnicott (1974) refers to a therapeutic relationship as an area of mutual play, in which both parties give each other the space in which creative activity can occur, and in which each can use the space between subjective and 'objective' reality, illusion and 'reality' in a creative way. For the adult to be playful implies that s/he has ready access to nourishing sources of fantasy, and might thus be better able to participate with the child in the same collective fantasy (Foukes and Anthony 1984). With regard to letting the child become absorbed in play, the child needs to be able to 'forget' the adult, yet have confidence that the adult is available – available both externally and in the child's mind – if needed. 'The child [plays] on the basis of the assumption that the person who loves and who is therefore reliable is available and continues to be available when remembered after being forgotten' (Winnicott 1974: 55).

Example: John and Carol

This example of the potential of play is taken from work with John, who was referred to in Chapters Two and Four. (His background was described in Chapter Two, section on 'Defences against development'). John had been omnipotent, challenging and unable to trust. A year into his part-time placement in a tutorial class group, John was regularly playing pretend families, working particularly well with a girl I refer to as Carol. In this play there were at times, especially at first, intensely bitter 'sibling' squabbles and a screaming baby full of anguish. I found that being witness to some of this play was very uncomfortable for me and I was constantly asking myself whether I should step in as an overt holder or limit-setter. However, I knew that I had to allow the children to take their own experience as their starting-point and then work from that, if they were to be able to reformulate their sense of life experience. Indeed, they did gradually create other experiences for themselves. Pretending to be brother and sister sharing a room, they nestled down in blankets next to each other. A baby-voiced John squeaked seriously to Carol, 'Don't go away, I want to stay close to you.' In this event, John was beginning to move from omnipotency and to be in touch with dependency, itself a pre-condition of independence. John was only able to let himself experience trust and intimacy in relationships after he had explored them through play.

One day four months later, John and Carol were pretending to be a young married couple. Carol became pregnant. With quiet dignity and tenderness John cared for his young wife and, at the end of the play session, after Carol had given birth and nursed her baby, John offered the observation that Carol was a good mother. The children behaved as if something special was happening that morning. It surely was; John was beginning to be able to recognise the qualities of a good mother somewhere inside himself. In their play, John and Carol were exploring their budding ability to be more available to integrate and tolerate diverse feelings (characteristic of Klein's 'depressive' possibilities). Play with peers offers a valuable medium for the re-enactment of parent–child relationships and inter-sibling rivalries and the exploration of issues of conflict.

Play is often perceived as relating to the primary phase of education (e.g. ILEA 1989). In the secondary phase, many of the opportunities of play present themselves in drama. Although drama is more formalised and conscious, make-believe is an inherent part of both forms of expression. Dramatic play is a basis for imitation and identification, requiring of the pupils the processes of trying-out, developing and testing attitudes and ideas, and the reorganisation of knowledge and experience, which necessitate creative thought.

Exercise: One's own capacity for play

*

Use paper and coloured pens or paint, or some plasticine or clay, and allow yourself to draw or sculpt an image to the theme, 'Myself and Play'.

Stories, myths and fairy tales

Stories, myths and fairy tales play an important role in stimulating emotional development. Mary Wilson (1983) suggests that good literature is a very rich source for the study of human feelings and behaviour, and argues that in listening to or reading stories, children can extend their experience vicariously to include a wide variety of people and circumstances. Since stories have an emotional content, she argues, the children can become involved with these fictitious people in such a way that their imagination is stimulated, and they begin to be able to appreciate the affective realm of both other people and themselves. This point is developed by Rustin and Rustin (1987), who argue that fiction is important, in children aged 5–11 years, for beginning 'the more obvious development of an inner identity independent of and sometimes hidden away from parents; the in-between space between family and social world which children begin to negotiate in these years is vitally connected with their developing sense of personal self' (Rustin and Rustin 1987: 2–3).

Myths and fairy tales differ from other stories in that they use a symbolic language to speak of archetypal themes, with motifs that are common to all cultures, and independent of geography and time. Myths are generally more complex than fairy tales in that they reflect and incorporate the specifically religious traditions of a culture, in what might be described as a collective dream (Campbell 1974). Sen (1988) speaks of the remarkable nature of cross-cultural concurrences, saying that ancient civilisations, and different cultures and religions the world over, appear to express universal ideas. Jung said that people may unconsciously 'live a myth': myths live within people, in the unconscious, motivating one towards certain forms of experience and behaviour (Jacoby 1990). The work of Joseph Campbell has also played a significant part in enabling us to understand that the individual is carried by myth into society in a deep, participatory way, and that myths are not things that just happen 'out there' in the external world, but are also psychological experiences which take place within a person's psyche. Also, because they deal with archetypal themes, myths potentially offer insights into the development of both individuals and societies. When themes which are emerging within a number of people coalesce into a

154

myth which catches the attention of a whole society, then new myths are made. The ongoing development of myths can have a profound effect on the course and outcome of a society's problems and predicaments.

Turning more specifically to consider fairy tales, I have often observed that reading a fairy tale to troubled children of primary age and older can elicit responses of a kind different to those produced by other sorts of story. It is not unusual for children who normally avoid eye contact to overcome this inhibition whilst listening to fairy tales, or for those who find it difficult to sit still or listen to do so with rapt attention. Resulting from the distillation of themes across time and cultures, fairy tales contain maps of inner reality, providing a mediating link between the inner and outer worlds.

> Fairy tales are the purest and simplest expression of collective unconscious psychic processes. . . . They represent the archetypes in their simplest, barest, and most concise form. . . . [Every fairy tale brings together] one essential psychological meaning which is expressed in a series of symbolical pictures and events and is discoverable in these.
>
> (von Franz 1982: 1)

Bettelheim (1978) explains the significance of fairy tales for children as providing an opportunity to mesh the fantasies of the conscious with those of the unconscious and to allow them to deal with symbols without anxiety. He argues that for a story to enrich the life of a troubled child it must give full recognition to the child's disturbances, and suggest solutions to problems which perturb him/her. Fairy tales stimulate symbolic experience and offer symbolic possibilities for difficult emotional tasks, such as learning to be able to tolerate loving and hating the same person. In contrast, Bettelheim argues that the prevalent parental belief is that a child must be diverted from what troubles him/her the most, such as formless, nameless anxieties, and chaotic, angry and even violent fantasies. 'Contrary to what takes place in many modern children's stories, in fairy tales evil is as omnipresent as virtue' (Bettelheim 1978: 8). The fairy tale communicates to the child that a struggle against severe difficulties in life is unavoidable, that such a struggle is an intrinsic part of human existence. It is for this reason that 'unexpurgated' versions of fairy tales are recommended. Bettelheim speaks eloquently of the significance of fairy tales for troubled children:

> these stories speak to [the child's] budding ego and encourage its development, while at the same time relieving preconscious and unconscious pressures. . . . In order to master the psychological pressures of growing up . . . a child needs to understand what is going on within his conscious self so that he can also cope with that which goes on in his unconscious. He can achieve this understanding, and

155

with it the ability to cope, not through rational comprehension of the nature and content of his unconscious, but by becoming familiar with it through spinning out daydreams – ruminating, rearranging, and fantasizing about suitable story elements in response to unconscious pressures. By doing this, the child fits unconscious content into conscious fantasies, which then enable him to deal with that content. It is here that fairy tales offer unequalled value, because they offer unequalled value to the child's imagination which would be impossible for him to discover as truly on his own. . . . The form and structure of fairy tales suggest images to the child by which he can structure his daydreams and with them give better direction to his life. . . . [W]hen unconscious material is to some degree permitted to come to awareness and worked through in imagination, its potential for causing harm . . . is much reduced.

(Bettelheim 1978: 6–7)

Exercise: Living fairy tales

*/**

Write or tell the story of your life in the form of a fairy tale. Use fairy-tale-like characters to represent the major influences upon your life.

A facilitating environment for work with image and metaphor

The features of a facilitating environment are reflected in the processes described in Chapters Three and Four. In such an environment there is trust and reliability, and the adults have the capacity to hold the anxieties aroused in themselves, are clear about boundary setting, consistently communicate a sense of belief in the children, and organise the environment to respond to individual capacities for autonomy.

Teachers may demonstrate that they take the role of metaphor and image seriously by using cross-curricular activities which incorporate play, drama and stories. The notion of 'taking seriously' should relate to all aspects of work with metaphor and image: attitudes towards such work, how children's work with metaphor is 'received' and responded to, the arrangements for pieces of work to be displayed and stored, how the children are encouraged to think of its significance and remember it, and so on. Such actions are all communications about the value ascribed to creativity through imagery, and demonstrate to the children the honouring of metaphorical work by the teacher.

156

When working with art for therapeutic purposes, the concern is not with producing beautiful works of art, but with painting spontaneously, exploring one's experience of the world in a personal and open-ended way, with no 'right' way of doing it (Liebmann 1986). When a child undertakes such art work, s/he is extremely sensitive to the sincerity of the adult (Axline 1989). When a child is engaged in a creative task, the adult's task is to remain available to respond to a request for support, and at the same time not to intrude; the child needs to feel safe enough to immerse him/herself in the task. I often think that this sort of safety has been achieved during those times when children in the classroom, after a period of deep reflection, look up and enquire, 'Mum . . . ' or 'Dad . . . '. At such times children seem to show not just a sense of safety, but being immersed in reverie. 'Reverie [aids the memory of] the imagination. In reverie we re-enter into contact with the possibilities that destiny has not been able to make use of' (Bachelard 1971: 12). Reverie requires 'a physical setting in which we are freed, for the time being, from the need for immediate practical expedient action' (Milner 1971: 164).

In seeking to relate to metaphorical images, one should not suggest what children should draw, as it is essential that the ideas should be entirely their own. The facilitator needs to be patient, and each child needs to be able to say for him/herself when the drawing or other work is finished. Describing art as giving palpable form to the imagination, Adamson (1984: 6) comments that 'the spectator is given the great privilege of being allowed into the secret garden of dreams'.

Once the child has completed a piece of creative work which involves some sort of metaphorical and symbolic dimension, it is important to allow the child to take the lead about how much discussion takes place. Too much adult curiosity may be unhelpful to the child. Analytical psychologist James Hillman (1967) describes curiosity as the antithesis of allowing the unconscious to produce symbols with highly individual meanings in its own way and its own time. It is important to appreciate the potential of symbols: emerging from the unconscious, symbols speak not of psychological causes of situations, but of purpose, of the thing that is wanting to express itself and come into life. This idea (based on Jung's concept of teleology) implies that the symbols which emerge through the imaginative creativity of children become most valuable when the imaginative work is valued by adults as gifts to the children from the unconscious.

A facilitator helps something forward and avoids overt direction. I will explore this role further, in relation to work with image and metaphor, by referring to my work with Dave and Jenny.

Example: Dave

Over a two-and-a-half-year part-time placement in a tutorial class group, Dave's series of paintings formed part of his developing capacity to explore imaginatively, and to be open to the wider possibilities of learning and relationships. Each of the large and detailed pictures, in what eventually became a series of seven, took several sessions to complete. The series is illustrated in Figures 14–20.

Dave had been referred to the tutorial class service when he was aged 7, and severely underachieving in his mainstream school. He was described by the educational psychologist as being loud, disruptive and attention-seeking in class. He was provocative to both children and teachers, and aggressive towards other children. He was very restless and could not easily settle to class work. The school staff were also concerned about his sexually explicit play. When alone with an adult he presented very differently from when with his peers. In the former situation he would regress, sucking his fingers and talking in a 'babyish' voice. Dave performed overall at a well-below-average level on the WISC(R) test, but his subtest scores were very scattered, between a good average ability and a limited level. The educational psychologist found it difficult to say how reliable these results were as an estimate of Dave's ability since he did not always seem bothered to try. However, at other times he did not seem to understand what was required of him. At times he spoke rather indistinctly and his expressive vocabulary was poor.

At the beginning of Dave's part-time placement in a tutorial class group, the theme of his very first drawing was not his own, but that of a well-known fairy tale. Dave needed a lot of help to put the basics of his drawing down on paper. At this early stage of his placement he found it difficult not only to have confidence in his ability to draw, but also to use his imagination and to symbolise. It was some months before Dave initiated the first of his own imaginative drawings, and there were weeks between each drawing. When he had finished each picture I asked him if he wanted to talk about it. Invariably he gave vent to a torrent of stories, rushed and inarticulate, much of which I did not follow. However, I listened, and through showing my interest and taking the lead from what Dave said, I demonstrated that I regarded his work as having meaning.

Dave's seven pictures were as follows:

1   Figure 14: A large complex building, 'the flats', has stereo equipment very prominent, and black angry smoke in the sky, obscuring the sun.
2   Figure 15: 'The swimming pool Haggerston' is the title of the second picture, which has many dark tunnels and passages.
3–5   Figures 16–18: Monsters emerge. Some have open mouths, sharp teeth, and emit rays. Others, like little devils, are in battle with a knight on a horse.
6   Figure 19: A 'spaceship' is confronted with a large notice, 'A Dead End'.
7   Figure 20: A block of flats, a sweet shop, a book shop, a museum, a letter box, a bright street light, a path, and labels reading, 'The Street', 'The High Road', 'The Path', 'The World'.

Dave's pictures tell their own story in their own personal way. What follows are simply my associations, as a hypothesis, rather than an interpretation. From a state of being out of contact with the imagination and the ability to symbolise, Dave was able first of all (Figures 14 and 15) to sense and express something of his psychological home located in the unconscious. In the pictures of monsters (Figures 16–18) there is the sense of speaking the unspeakable, of finding a way of depicting his persecutory monsters and, in so doing, confronting them. In Figure 19, the cul-de-sac, it is as if something has been found which needs to be reconsidered. Lastly, in Figure 20, Dave pictures a community with access to educational resources, communication between people, and a light to light the

Figure 14 Dave's picture no. 1

Figure 15 Dave's picture no. 2

Figure 16 Dave's picture no. 3

Figure 17 Dave's picture no. 4

Figure 18 Dave's picture no. 5

Figure 19 Dave's picture no. 6

Figure 20 Dave's picture no. 7

path to the world. At the time of the last picture, Dave was better able to make use of educational resources in that he was involved in and making achievements in his school work, and he enjoyed a much-improved quality of relationships.

An early attempt by all those involved with Dave to end his tutorial class placement met with a regression in behaviour in school and at home. He then had further tutorial class support, which ended just before his transfer to secondary school. Two years into secondary school, he continues to make pleasing progress.

Example: Jenny

Jenny was referred to the tutorial class service at the age of 7, described by her educational psychologist as the most deprived child he had ever met. In school she was unable to concentrate and was sometimes found scavenging in the school dustbins. Although her performance in psychological tests gave the sort of indication of moderate learning difficulties which would often provoke a referral to special school, in this case the educational psychologist felt that Jenny had not had the necessary life experiences for the psychological tests to be a valid reflection of her potential. Jenny was one of seven children; it was said that her father was an alcoholic, who used to lock his children in a cupboard and who used to abuse Jenny sexually. Her mother had died when she was 4, whereupon the seven children went to live with their aunt and uncle, who had seven children of their own. The local authority made a claim for custody of the children, which was lost.

During her time in the tutorial class group, there was a period when Jenny seemed to be obsessed with houses. She drew houses over and over again, and made models of houses in wood, in clay, in board. In facilitating her metaphorical explorations, I provided the space and the support for her to do this. I considered

162

Jenny's need for space to construct and reconstruct her house to be particularly important. At this point Jenny did not use her houses as the starting-point for stories, but, talking with her at a descriptive level about what she had made, I tried to communicate the importance of what she was creating. Architect and psychoanalyst Olivier Marc writes, 'The child who is giving birth to himself, having sensed in himself the existence of the basic archetypes which give structure to the development of consciousness, will begin to draw his house' (1977: 80). The house is a building upon which aspects of the self can be projected, becoming, in Bachelard's view (1969: 6), 'one of the greatest powers of integration for the thoughts, memories and dreams of mankind'.

Jenny's interest in houses is but a brief indication of one of the ways in which she made use of her tutorial class placement. Jenny's literacy, numeracy and social skills developed to the extent that, towards the end of her primary school life, it was considered appropriate for her to transfer to a mainstream secondary school.

Staying with the metaphor

If a child wishes to talk about a piece of her/his imaginative work with an adult, the potential of the symbols to take the story forwards is best made use of where the symbolism is talked about *as a story, within the framework provided by the child* – that is, by staying with the metaphor. This gives the child further opportunities to relate to the symbols, thus exploring their potential multiple meanings, and perhaps leading the story on to new possibilities. It also enables the child to go at his/her own pace, to not reveal anything that s/he does not wish to, and to maintain – from a conscious point of view – the safety of the 'at-one-remove' of metaphor. It also means that the teacher maintains his/her role by staying outside the realm of interpretation of the symbols.

Where the child wishes to talk about the created piece of work, a continuation of the symbolic dialogue may be encouraged by asking open-ended questions which stimulate the child to consider further possibilities. For example, if the child draws a sinking ship, the adult might ask open-ended questions to find out what happens to the people. If the child seems stuck, the adult might offer a range of possibilities from which the child might choose, for example, 'Do the people drown?', 'Can they swim?', 'Are there any rescue craft?' To such suggestions the child might add his/her own options.

The adult's attitude and approach towards such a task is of the utmost importance. Key elements in this process are the manner in which the adult waits and accepts what emerges. 'The attitude of letting be . . . is the highest form of care. . . . Releasement is detached involvement. . . . We wait, however, not passively but as saints and animals wait – in prolonged alertness to the unknown, the strange, the wonder' (Avens 1984: 100–2). This waiting means that one must acknowledge to oneself the mystery surrounding that which will emerge. Analytical psychologist Barbara Hannah (1981: 13) tells the story of a rabbi who answered, in response to a question about why God spoke directly to his people much less often than in former times, '"Man cannot bend low enough now to hear what God says" . . . We shall only hear what God or the unconscious says by bending very low.' Waiting for emerging images by 'bending very low' can be described as having a symbolical attitude. Robert Hobson (1985) speaks of expectant waiting, being ready to receive what will emerge and lead forward. 'Whether a thing is a symbol or not depends chiefly on the *attitude* of the observing consciousness' (Jung 1971: 475).

Example: Jason

In order to appreciate better the example I give of following the symbol of Jason's work within his metaphor, some background information is provided. Jason had been referred to the tutorial class service when aged 9. He was described by the educational psychologist as seeking to obtain a lot of individual attention from his class teacher, finding it difficult to get interested in class work on his own. In the absence of individual support he tended to become restless and provocative to other children. Upon testing he was found to be functioning well within average limits, but his sense of his own history was not developed.

Jason's mother married and had two children when she was very young. When Jason was just under 2, his mother left him, his brother and her husband to go and live abroad. The boys were taken into care. Subsequently, the father found another partner and the brother was taken to live with him and his wife, but Jason was initially excluded because neither adult felt able to look after a child so young. Jason did eventually join them but the marriage did not last. He was looked after by his grandmother and then again taken into care. Meanwhile Jason's mother had separated from her second husband. The children were returned to her. When Jason began his tutorial class placement, his mother had recently had a baby by her new partner. Jason had had a soiling problem in the past, and at the time of referral he still sometimes soiled himself on his way home or in the evening, but not at school.

In the tutorial class group children would often use the sandtray and miniatures to make a world in the sand (see Appendix Two). The first sandworld made at tutorial class by Jason – see Figure 21 – had, on one side, a neatly ordered and well-functioning farm. On the other was a land of wild and dangerous animals, with two divers on a dinghy sailing on a lake in which there were sharks. On the ridge dividing the two areas were some trees and, in a position from which it could have a view of both sides, a panda. I did not voice to Jason my thinking that the two parts of the sandworld might describe two psychologically split parts of Jason's internal world (see Chapter Two, section on 'Defences against development'). It was not surprising, given Jason's experiences and his psychological need for emotional protection from other people, that in his emerging story there was such a definite split between the well-functioning and the devouring aspects of life. There was a sense in which Jason, at that point, had come to need the firmness and solidity of the ridge to keep out the devouring forces. Nor did I mention to Jason my fantasies about the way in which the panda might be involved in relation to the split. Instead, Jason and I spoke about what we could concretely see before us in the sandworld: we thought together about some of the qualities of pandas, and what the panda might do next in the story. In my verbal discussion with Jason, I stayed with the metaphor.

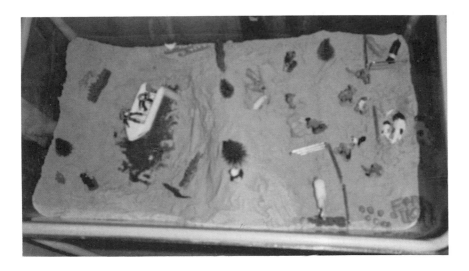

Figure 21 Jason's first sandworld

Where empathy, trust, and the child's obvious comfort with such a discussion allow, some people would make a link to the outer world by asking a question along the lines of, 'Where are you in this story?' or 'Where does this happen in your everyday life?' In order to avoid a possible regression through fear, the child needs to have a considerable degree of ego strength to support and think about such a question.

Example: George

Twelve year old George made a sandworld in which there was some 'sinking sand'. I asked him how the characters in the sandworld felt when they were caught in the 'sinking sand', and he was able to give a descriptive response. I asked if there were times when he had those feelings in his life. George was able to acknowledge that he did, and to acknowledge for the first time his experience of such feelings, and when they occurred. We then returned to the symbolic; I asked him if anything could be done in his sandworld to help overcome the problem of the 'sinking sand'. He suggested that rafts of concrete could be effectively fitted. I asked him to do this physically in his sandworld, thus continuing his metaphor. I said that I hoped that he would be able to take the concrete rafts away inside himself and be able to make good use of them if and when it might be necessary.

In a group setting, where the group is familiar with the necessity of respecting the emerging story of a member of the group, and can avoid being intrusive or making derogatory remarks, it is possible for the group itself to be helpful, by making spontaneous metaphorical associations. The child who has made the image is thus given access to a greater richness of

165

associations with which to continue imagining the story. In Chapter Seven the role of the group is considered in more depth.

Exercise: Using image and metaphor

*/**/***

1 Make a list of all the ways in which you use image and metaphor in your work.
2 Brainstorm as many more practical ways of working with the imagination and metaphor as you can.
3 Note how the ideas might be used within the delivery of the National Curriculum.

SUMMARY

- Where inhibited by emotional factors, development cannot proceed through will or ego strength alone. Image and metaphor have a value in helping exploration at an inner, symbolic level.
- Using image and metaphor helps the individual's psychological fluidity in imagining possibilities and resolutions.
- Using image and metaphor helps to hold or contain difficult feelings; communicates about the individual's perception of experience; helps to resolve conflicts about feelings; and facilitates access to potential.
- Facilitating work with image and metaphor involves providing a reliable and trustworthy environment, active appreciation of the value of play and drama, active appreciation of the value of myths and fairy tales, and, where personal development and not the quality of the finished art work is the aim, supporting but not intruding upon metaphorical and imaginative exploration.
- Metaphorical symbols should be discussed in educational settings within the metaphorical framework provided by the child. In cases where the child has adequate understanding and ego strength, links to the child's experiences in the external world might usefully be made.

6

STRENGTHENING THE PERSONALITY

INTRODUCTION

In this chapter I consider ways in which teachers and other workers can work to strengthen children's emotional resources further, by making effective use of their verbal interactions. Previously we considered providing emotional holding and staying with the metaphor of symbolic imagery, and in these processes the teacher works with children to meet their developmental needs without necessarily making the processes explicit to the children. The focus was upon the need for the adult to demonstrate understanding of the child's dilemmas, and to provide an auxiliary ego, or to relate to developmental issues through metaphor. An environment which provides emotional holding forms a context in which further strengthening can take place. In this chapter the focus is upon the adult working alongside the more autonomous child to help the child's development of emerging ego strength, by explicitly addressing at a conscious level issues which are troubling the child, or relationships which are proving difficult. This chapter, then, is concerned with 'ego-supporting' processes (Dockar-Drysdale 1990), which help the child develop further ego strength.

A brief reminder of the function of the ego is in order here. The faculties of the ego relate to conscious awareness: it has the function of mediating between inner and outer worlds, and discriminating and managing feelings. Ego-strengthening work seeks to raise the children's awareness of themselves, their feelings and actions, to enable them to enhance the capacity for autonomous decision-making, and to be able to take responsibility for the consequences of their decisions. Ego-strengthening work thus involves assisting children to develop an increasing level of conscious awareness, to differentiate a growing range of feelings – for example greed and envy, feelings of loss – and to be aware of managing them. It also involves helping children to take in and remember their goodness, to have a good internal

167

image of themselves which can be sustained through actual or perceived difficulties. So there is an important link between building self-esteem and developing ego strength. When a child's ego has become what Neumann termed 'integral', it has the capability of assimilating and integrating positive and negative factors 'in such a way that the unity of the personality is guaranteed and is not split into antagonistic parts' (Neumann 1973: 58). When the ego is integrated within the psychic structure, it can function as an 'observing ego', and so help one to watch, monitor and manage oneself.

With regard to developing the ego strength of children of low self-esteem, the child's development of the capacity to hold an internal image of her/his own goodness depends on the 'internalisation' or taking in of sufficient experiences of her/his own worth. The child's sense of goodness partly develops through the way in which one experiences being trusted and valued by peers. Helping children to develop the capacity to relate to others in productive ways serves to enhance the value which the children accord to relationships. This entails helping children with poor self-esteem to develop awareness of themselves in relation to others, and to help them to develop a range of negotiation skills. In the first part of the chapter I consider ways of supporting children to make better relationships, by thinking about interventions within a group context.

Another significant way of demonstrating a child's worth is through relationships with key adults, and as children become more aware of their actions and feelings, the adult has the task of maintaining the expectation that difficulties can be talked about rather than acted out. These processes demand an effective use of counselling skills, and those aspects of counselling which are most concerned with one-to-one discussion are considered in the second part of the chapter.

SUPPORTING CHILDREN'S RELATIONSHIPS WITH PEERS

As we improve our capacity to be aware of, and to manage, our own feelings we become better able to manage our relationships with others. This is particularly the case with 'negative' feelings such as envy and anger. Un-integrated children tend to relate to others without being able to manage such feelings, and behave as if they are victims of their feelings. Where children have little capacity to tolerate feelings of anger, despair, loss, etc., they are likely to act the feelings out in their behaviour and project the intolerable feelings onto others. Children with little ego strength may quickly resort to snatching or verbal and physical abuse in response to a small but provocative comment from a peer.

Part of the ego-strengthening process involves helping children to develop the skills of negotiating with others – for example, negotiating the borrowing of a piece of equipment, or how a game might be played. The success of such negotiations depends on the children's awareness of their own feelings, and those of others. In helping children to develop these skills, the teacher might develop the habit of asking, for example, 'How else could you say that?', or 'How do you think that makes "so and so" feel?' These issues are kept on the classroom agenda where such questions are quietly but regularly asked by the teacher. Such interventions might be developed into role-plays of rude and polite ways of asking for things (personal communication: Helen Green). The teacher might ask the children to try to recognise when they might not be able to manage a situation alone, and to help them find 'face-saving' and unprovocative ways of asking for help.

We also develop ego strength from the feedback we receive about how we are valued. It is particularly important for unintegrated children to have an experience of affirmation which is consistent over a period of time. One way of giving such affirmation is for the adult to demonstrate that each child is a valued member of the group. It is vital that there are opportunities for children to experience this, in as many ways of possible. The more children feel they have something to offer, the more able they are to perceive themselves as being valued members of the group. In the small-group setting of tutorial class sessions, children would regularly bring fruit, sweets or biscuits to share at drinks-time. The opportunity to have a copy of a piece of work printed from the computer, to take home or back to the mainstream school, was relished. Every session began with newstime – a sharing of news of events or moods since the previous session. In this, everyone had something to offer, and the starting-point for each session for each child was his/her individual experiences.

Example: Matthew and Peter

This example concerns the work of two children who attended the same tutorial class group from different mainstream schools. The background to Peter's story was described in Chapter Five, section on 'The role of image and metaphor in helping emotional growth'. I will briefly describe Matthew's background.

Matthew was referred to the tutorial class service when he was 7 years old. In his mainstream school he was disliked and victimised by other children, and easily provoked into avoidance behaviour such as running out of school and fighting. He was described as extremely disruptive in class, spoiling his own work and that of others, shouting, interrupting others by snatching books and tools for no apparent reason, and running out of class if approached. At the time of his referral he had recently been suspended for kicking his teacher when she intervened in a fight. Whilst agreeing to a part-time tutorial class placement, the headteacher expressed the view that he did not imagine that Matthew would be able to reintegrate productively full-time into mainstream school, and that he really needed a special school placement.

The educational psychologist who referred Matthew to tutorial class provision described him as displaying signs of great anxiety, such as badly bitten nails and much activity. He was said to be seriously underachieving in school, being of overall above-average ability as measured on formal assessment, yet being a virtual non-reader. The educational psychologist reported that when she asked about his father, Matthew gave three different stories of where his father was, as if he was confused about what was acceptable, and his anxious behaviour was accentuated at these times. Matthew's mother had acknowledged to the educational psychologist that there had been violence within the marriage, which Matthew had witnessed, and which led to separation when Matthew was 5 years old. There had been incidents of fire-setting at home, and Matthew had started to fight with neighbouring children who he felt were picking on him. Mathew's mother reported to the educational psychologist that the fights often seemed to be provoked by children asking where his father was. It was only subsequently, and after I had worked with Matthew for some time, that his mother acknowledged to me that her previous husband had not been Matthew's father, but that she did not want Matthew to know this.

Within a tutorial class group, Matthew and Peter spent several sessions working and playing together on the theme of the *Ghostbusters* TV programme. As well as writing stories around the theme, they made *Ghostbuster* equipment-packs which they wore on their backs and used in several pretend plays. Through this, they were able to fantasise about and explore their own internal capacities to know what it is to be on one's own ground, to stand in relation to something else, and to act in accordance with this knowledge. This is but one example of the many activities in Matthew's and Peter's placements.

The way in which Matthew ended his part-time eighteen-month tutorial class placement seemed to be a very clear metaphor about the ego strength which he had developed. During his last session he chose to use a computer graphics program to make a drawing of a room with a door, keyhole and key. Matthew's unsolicited comment about the room in his drawing to which the door gave access was, 'This is the space where I can think better. Now I've got the key to it and that's why I'm leaving.'

After he had reintegrated full-time into school for a few weeks, I made a visit to the school. The reflections of Matthew's class teacher were also an indication of the ego strength which Matthew had developed. His teacher remembered that in the past when something was difficult for Matthew, he used to erupt. Then the school had gone through a phase of Matthew being able to talk about his difficulties. Then Matthew could write things down, using the system of diary-writing in the class. At the time of his full-time reintegration into school his teacher described him thus: 'If he's finding something difficult, he can take responsibility for writing it down quietly, and, if he needs to talk to me about it, to approach me at an appropriate time.' In his final year of primary school, some while after his tutorial class placement had ended, Matthew passed the necessary tests and interviews to be awarded a place at a highly selective secondary school.

Peter's leaving drawing had the caption, 'Action force is very important. Goodbye!' This annotation seems to capture Peter's developed capacity to act with more thought, or, in psychological terms, to have at his disposal and use his acquired ego strength. So these examples show several ways in which Matthew and Peter had developed and internalised effective and strengthened egos.

For children with low self-esteem the experience of being a valued member of the peer group is essential if they are to internalise a greater sense of self-worth. So groups must be managed in order to provide these sorts of opportunities.

Example: Circle-time

One way of providing opportunities for children to have the experience of being a valued member of a group, in mainstream settings, is an activity called circle-time. Circle-time is used to encourage pupils to listen carefully to what others are saying and to respond supportively. Primary headteacher Murray White describes circle-time activities in his school:

> I ask all the teachers to begin circle-time each day with the class sitting on the floor in a circle. . . . The teacher says an incomplete sentence, gives an example to finish it off, then the child next to her repeats the phrase and puts her own ending to it, and so on. . . . 'What makes me laugh is . . . My favourite TV programme is . . .'. Even a round where a child chooses a fruit she would like to be . . . After registration and an opportunity to share with everyone anything that has happened during the time the children have been apart, comes the section of the Special Child for the Day. . . . First, the child is presented (often by yesterday's holder) with a badge . . . 'I am Special'. Then she is asked to leave the room while a discussion takes place about all the nice things that can be said about her . . . It's important to get the children to preface their remarks with phrases like, 'I think you . . .' or 'I believe that you . . .'. In this way the recipient accepts it and cannot contradict it. Teachers record the comments while they are being said and the sheet is presented to the child.

(White 1989)

The significance of supporting children to become more self-aware and to make better relationships is reflected in developments in active tutorial work and personal and social education programmes in the middle and secondary school phases. There is now a wide literature in this field (for example Baldwin and Wells 1979, Ballard 1982, Button 1974, 1981, 1982, Canfield and Wells 1976, Leech and Wooster 1986). The contribution which an understanding of group dynamics can make to helping children experience themselves as valuable members of groups is considered in Chapter Eight. The use and management of the formal curriculum to foster the growth of self-esteem and methods of positive reinforcement is considered in Chapter Nine.

Exercise: Rounds to build self-esteem

*/**/***

Think of questions/statements which could be used as the beginning of rounds in a 'circle-time' type activity. You could begin with:

My favourite day is . . .
Something which turns me off is . . .

> **Exercise: Developing activities to build ego strength**
>
> */**/***
>
> Invent a game to encourage children to develop the capacity for taking turns or being a loser in a game.

HELPING YOUNG PEOPLE TO RESOLVE THEIR OWN PROBLEMS: USING COUNSELLING SKILLS

The Elton Report (DES 1989c) spoke of the value of counselling skills for teachers (see Chapter One, section on 'Affect and learning'). Pastoral staff may have opportunities for one-to-one discussions: subject teachers have the task of integrating appropriate aspects of counselling skills into their classroom work. Teachers have a good starting-point for effective counselling of pupils: 'Ask anyone about their most significant experiences in learning, and they will almost certainly start talking about the people who taught them' (Salmon 1988: 38).

Let us begin this consideration with the invitation to do an exercise to explore the function of counselling.

> **Exercise: Images of the role of counselling**
>
> */**
>
> Imagine that you are wanting someone to help you out with some sort of issue which concerns perceptions or feelings. You decide to approach a colleague, friend or counsellor to ask for a discussion.
>
> 1 What would you be looking for from the person who counsels you?
> 2 What sorts of response from this person would be of benefit to you?

The British Association of Counselling defines the task of counselling as giving the 'client' an opportunity to explore, discover and clarify ways of living more resourcefully and towards greater well-being. The prime aim of counselling is to help the individual discover solutions to his/her own problems. The following comments by Carl Rogers (1942: 29) about therapy apply equally to counselling situations: 'Therapy is not a matter of doing something *to* the individual . . . it is instead a metter of freeing him for normal growth and development, of removing obstacles so that he can again move forward.' Nelson-Jones (1988) identifies a number of ways of looking at and approaching counselling:

172

- as a relationship, in which the emphasis is on the quality of the relationship with the child or young person;
- as selectively deploying a repertoire of skills, depending on the needs and states of readiness of children/young people;
- as self-help, the overriding aim being to work with the notion of personal responsibility to help children to help themselves;
- as a tool to help people to become better choosers;
- as a process of interactions.

Counselling can be compared with other approaches by contrasting the extent to which the young person is included or excluded in the problem-solving process, and the extent to which the process is problem-centred (primarily focused on the problem) or child-centred (primarily focused on the child's relationship with the problem). From these two continuums a matrix showing four styles of helping can be formulated, and this is shown in Figure 22.

The counselling style takes the child or young person rather than the problem as the starting-point, and involves the child in solving the problem. In this approach the person using counselling skills does not need to formulate a solution. The aim is to help the child find the solution to the problem, and to learn as much as possible through the problem-solving process, so that when s/he faces another problem s/he is much better equipped to deal with it. Counselling seeks to be empowering and ego strengthening.

There are dangers in using a counselling approach, against which one needs to draw boundaries. Using counselling skills does not involve seeking opportunities for vicarious pleasure through voyeurism, or intruding or persecuting by using so-called counselling to interrogate the child. Neither does counselling involve 'infantilising' the other person. Counselling seeks to enable the other person to take greater responsibility for his/her own problem-solving.

The process of counselling centrally involves the holding of anxiety and

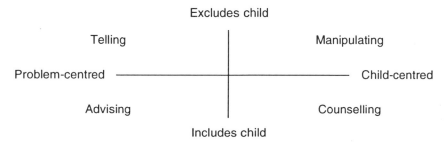

Figure 22 Four styles of helping
(adapted from De Board 1983)

disturbing feelings (discussed in Chapter Four) as the emotional context for effective work. The skills required for effective counselling are considered below in terms of relating to the other person's life space, containment and confidentiality, boundaries, initial structuring, listening and responding, clarifying and summarising.

Relating to the child's life space

In Chapter One we considered the way in which we develop subjective constructs to make sense of our experience, these constructs forming the basis for the experience of meaning, and hence for the way in which we take up learning. In considering with a child or young person what might be getting in the way of learning and relationship, it is essential to relate empathically to the young person's subjective meanings, since 'in all relationships the other person is seen in terms of the internal world of the perceiver' (Casement 1990: 125). Each individual's subjective view of the world may be termed his/her 'life space', a concept which was first put forward by the psychologist Kurt Lewin. The life space is the psychological 'force-field' around every individual which determines and limits behaviour (De Board 1983). Similarly, from Kelly's point of view,

> social relations are constructed out of mutual perceptions. . . . If [two people] each constantly approaches the other through categorizations that make no reference to that person's subjectivity, they cannot enter into a relationship. Most broadly, it is our willingness and ability to view people *psychologically* that defines how far we can understand and appreciate them.
>
> (Salmon 1988: 98–9)

A strong thread in the argument of this book has been the need to understand behaviour as a form of communication. 'When behaviour is recognized as communication this can often be seen to contain cues for the care-giving world, indicating unmet needs and an unconscious search for these needs to be adequately attended to' (Casement 1990: 110). Casement (1990) refers to the expression of needs through behaviour as a form of 'unconscious hope'.

One of the first tasks in meeting the emotional needs of another is to understand and relate to the life space of the other person. This is not an easy task since every individual experiences situations, events and life differently. Furthermore, the individual may well develop defences (see Chapter Two) to prevent unwanted exposure or violation. A climate of trust is necessary for the young person to welcome the adult voluntarily into his/her life space. When this fails to happen, the counselling work will be ineffective and the young person will put his/her energy into defending his/her inner life from possible attack. Once a person using counselling skills is invited into the young person's life space, that confidence needs to

174

be respected. If the young person feels criticised or judged, this can be damaging to the counselling process. To a person whose sense of self is insecure, feeling criticised may evoke a sense of threat. A person who feels threatened within a counselling approach is most likely to respond by ejecting the counsellor from his/her life space (De Board 1983).

The role of the counselling approach is to help the young person to focus on his/her problem. Having gained the young person's confidence, the adult using counselling skills can help the young person to explore his/her life space as follows (De Board 1983): people tend to push un-pleasant facts and memories to the back of their mind and then do their best to forget about them. The young person might be able to acknowledge or 'remember' something which s/he would sooner forget but which may have a bearing on the current problem. The person using counselling skills can help the young person see things from a different angle, and to consider possible outcomes and implications of certain courses of action. The 'counsellor' thus enables the young person to consider an aspect of the problem which s/he would not otherwise have done.

If young people are able to discuss their problems there are likely to be strong associated feelings.

> Sometimes the main component of a problem is an emotion such as feelings of love or anger towards someone which cannot be ex-pressed. Some people are closely in touch with their feelings and can express them openly and clearly. Others appear to be dissociated from their feelings, and are not able to express them or appear not to know that they have any. . . . In effective counselling, the counsellor provides the opportunity for the person to express their feelings.
>
> (De Board 1983: 82).

Where the emotion is a significant part of the problem, this helps to elucidate the issues which might be contributing to the problem.

A person's life space is subjective, an expression of the world as that individual experiences it. Given the complexity of individual personalities, everyone has different ways of formulating her/his own experience or reality. We need to be able to imagine and fantasise in order to consider all sorts of options and possibilities about our potential, but if we get en-trenched in a particular fantasy it may inhibit our capacity for relating to others and working effectively with problems. For instance, events are experienced differently by each individual, and each person remembers the facts of an event in a way which reflects and reinforces her/his own experience of it. De Board (1983) suggests that perhaps the most common area of fantasy relates to self-perception: how do I see myself – am I capable and successful or a failure and incompetent?

Because life space is unique to each individual person, any solution to a problem must relate to that life space. Marris (1986) argues that people have a tendency, when having to make adaptations or changes, to assimilate reality into their existing structure, and so avoid those aspects which cannot be assimilated. He suggests that changes in one's emotional structure seem to be possible only gradually, within the limits of what can be assimilated at any one time. The construction of a life space which has meaning to the individual is cumulative, so the more fundamental the revisions which have to be made, the more the emotional structure is threatened and the more emotionally disruptive revision becomes. Any resolutions suggested by a 'counsellor' are often inappropriate, and probably rejected, because they are based on another viewpoint and different experience. The words 'If I were you . . . ' are unlikely to be helpful: direct advice or guidance which demands a change of long-held beliefs is likely to be rejected (De Board 1983).

Boundaries in relationship

Whether a young person rejects help will in some part be affected by the degree of skill of the counsellor in relating to the young person's feelings. It can be very difficult to expose problems, vulnerabilities, inadequacies or fears. For this reason a counselling approach has to take place in a climate of safety, in which it is possible for difficult feelings to be aired, thought about and understood. The processes of providing emotional holding, a 'container' for difficult feelings explored in Chapter Four, are pertinent here. The adult helps to create a safe 'container' by paying attention to the boundaries of what it is appropriate to have inside the container and what belongs outside it. Confidentiality is one form of boundary which marks those things which it is appropriate to keep inside the container. I invite you to explore the significance of this boundary through the following exercise.

Exercise: Confidentiality

*/**

Have you ever shared some very personal information with someone else on the understanding that what you have said is confidential, only to discover later that the confidentiality has not been respected? If so, can you remember how you felt about the confidence not having been kept, and how you felt about the person who betrayed your trust? Would you trust that person again?

Reflect upon any experience you have had of confidentiality being broken (or discuss this with someone else): how did it feel? What were the consequences?

(Adapted from Langham and Parker 1988)

The way in which boundaries are set is very important for the development of containment. Anxieties and feelings of being stuck in a certain problem can produce intense feelings which may make the young person feel overwhelmed. Boundaries are necessary to help people to feel safe to explore the emotional issues underlying a presenting problem. In relation to counselling situations, boundaries delimit those things which belong *in* the work, and those things which belong *outside* it. Psychological boundaries involve recognising what is appropriate and inappropriate in the counselling relationship. Such boundaries delineate what the adult will introduce into the relationship, as potentially helpful for the young person; and experiences which might inhibit the effectiveness of the work, which the adult avoids introducing into the relationship.

Recognising and working with psychological boundaries demands a significant measure of self-awareness in the adult. Is one managing to be aware of both one's own feelings and those of the young person? How much of oneself is one bringing into the interaction: for example, is one using self-disclosure deliberately and in the interests of the young person? The idea of realness or genuineness (see Chapter Three) shows the need for personal involvement in the interaction. Teachers and other workers reveal aspects of themselves through their verbal, vocal and body messages, their availability, their written communications, and so on. In some cases verbal disclosures of a more personal kind may be appropriate where they serve the interests of the young person. Disclosing something about oneself, such as one's own feelings, may help free young people to talk about themselves. Appropriate disclosures may help the adult to be perceived as being involved and genuine, rather than using a facade (Nelson-Jones 1988).

Nelson-Jones (1988) acknowledges grave dangers in inappropriate disclosures during counselling: the adult may become overinvolved or overidentified with the young person, and if the focus of the work shifts to the adult, the adult lives vicariously through the child. Where the relationship is no longer primarily focused on the interests of the child, then the work will cease to be effective. The young person will be less inclined to trust in the adult, and to take the risks necessary to explore the problem. Sometimes the adult may unconsciously relate to the young person in a way which seeks to meet the adult's needs for approval and intimacy. The adult might have positive or negative feelings towards young people based on unresolved areas in his/her own life. There can be strong impulses to 'make things all right' for the young person, rather than stay with painful experiences and enable the young person to come to his/her own resolutions. These issues highlight the importance of self-awareness regarding the motivation for self-disclosure.

Exercise: Personal boundaries

*

This exercise is designed to help you to reflect upon those aspects of yourself which might require particular vigilance in using a counselling approach.

What are those aspects of your personality which might inappropriately get into the counselling situation? (Examples might be a tendency to be judgemental, or to rush in with one's own solutions, or to collude, or to make the other person feel better rather than experience their pain, etc.) It can sometimes be difficult to reflect upon these sorts of issue, which might in some way reflect one's own emotional problems. So it could be helpful to 'reframe' your thinking about these issues by expressing them in another way: try drawing these aspects of your personality, or making representations of them in clay or plasticine. If you do this, also draw the boundary or make the container in which you might metaphorically keep and observe these aspects of yourself.

Another psychological boundary in the counselling approach relates to the use of criticism. (This was mentioned above, in the discussion on life space.) De Board (1983) argues that people can often feel threatened when they are criticised and the automatic psychological responses to this are fight or flight. The fight response may involve criticising in return. The flight response may involve moving away from the topic as quickly as possible, or making excuses. Such a defence mechanism for protection from perceived threat is put into operation by the young person who feels criticised. Once damaged, it takes a long time to re-establish the climate of openness and trust, which is essential for the effective use of counselling skills (De Board 1983).

Sometimes the boundaries around the counselling work may need to be modified, or negotiated with the young person. An example of this is found in circumstances where it might be appropriate to break the boundary of confidentiality. I invite you to explore this issue through the following exercise.

Exercise: Breaking the boundary of confidentiality

*/**/***

Consider the areas in which you might wish to break the boundary of

---

confidentiality with a child or young person with whom you have a counselling relationship:

- discovery of the child's stealing;
- the young person's use of drugs for non-medical reasons;
- sexual abuse of the young person;
- violent acts by the child;
- physical abuse of the child;
- others.

1 On what grounds, and acting in the interests of the young person, would you break the boundary of confidentiality?
2 If you break the boundary of confidentiality, what implications does this have for your working relationship with the young person?
3 How would you negotiate a change in the boundary of confidentiality with the young person?

(Adapted from Langham and Parker 1988)

Listening and empathic responding

What I need is a good listening to.

Children's Society Advertisement

When we are listened to and we feel that we are being heard from the point of view of our own experience, we feel that our subjective perceptions are being affirmed. In relation to issues which cause us anxiety or other forms of disturbance, it is only when our current perceptions are affirmed that we mobilise the capacity to embrace wider perceptions. So when working as a listener, the more we can be aware of the subjective perceptions of the other person – and ourselves – then the more likely it is that the communication will be effective.

We listen potentially with our whole body and mind. Sensitive listening is 'a skill as well as an attitude' (Rogers 1978: 11). Listening of a high quality is marked by the giving of undivided and thoughtful attention in a way which communicates genuineness, acceptance and empathy (Rogers – see Chapter Three). In interpreting what we hear, we are influenced by many different factors. So often we tend to see the world from our own point of view, conditioned by past experience, our present internal state, and our expectations of what is going to happen. The danger is that some of these factors can get in the way of hearing (see Chapter Two, section on 'Symptoms of blocked communication'). An important task in listening is to not mix in one's own ideas, so not 'laying on' the other person anything that person did not express (Rogers 1978). Langham and Parker (1988) argue that the skill in accurate listening is to be able to step out of our own subjective reality, our internal frame of reference, into that of the young person. For example, when an adult in a counselling relationship accepts the young person's subjective reality, apparent 'lies' or 'untruths' are listened to from the perspective of this information being what the other person wants us to know about them, for the present. If we view the situation from the young person's subjective reality, we view it from the perspective of the other person's internal frame of reference. If the adult does not perceive the young person's view of him/herself, then s/he remains in an external frame of reference with regard to the young person's world, and effective counselling is inhibited.

Exercise: Listening

*/**/***

Consider three questions:

1 How do you communicate that you are giving your full attention when listening?
2 What might inhibit you from active listening? (Consider those emotions or experiences which are difficult to hear.)
3 When working effectively, what are you actively listening *for?*

Exercise: Knowing that one is being listened to

*/**/***

How do you know that you are being fully listened to? Make a list of all the ways in which a listener communicates that s/he is hearing and understanding what s/he is being told.

Gendlin (1981, quoted in Nelson-Jones 1988: 37) suggests that 'If you only listen, and indicate whether you follow or not, you will discover a surprising fact. People can tell you much more and also find out more inside themselves, than can ever happen in ordinary exchanges.' I would like to consider key skills of empathic responding and reflecting before going on to explore the skills of clarifying and summarising.

Effective dialogue is aided when the adult communicates that s/he has accurately understood the young person's frame of reference, which re-quires responding with empathy. The importance of working with an empathic attitude was considered in Chapter Three. In terms of specific responses, Nelson-Jones (1988) suggests that empathic responses are taking place when the young person perceives that the adult counsellor wants to understand how s/he sees things, mostly knows what s/he means, usually senses or realises what s/he is feeling; and appreciates how the things s/he experiences feel to him/her. Empathic responding is not happening, Nelson-Jones argues, where the young person perceives that the adult counsellor understands the words but not the feelings; where the adult thinks the young person feels in a certain way because that is the way the adult has felt; when the adult does not realise how sensitive the young person is about some of the things discussed; and when the adult's response is so fixed, automatic or predictable that the young person does not feel that s/he is getting through. Responding empathically might entail the counsellor making *exploratory* responses which help the young person to articulate and explore (where appropriate) those more personally relevant, emotionally tinged and potentially threatening areas of his/her experience (Nelson-Jones 1988).

One way of showing that one has understood what the young person is trying to say is to reflect back significant aspects of what one has heard. The notion of reflecting is similar to that of mirroring, which is discussed in relation to emotional holding (Chapter Four). I use the term 'mirroring' to refer to reflecting back behaviour traits or patterns which one notices in the child. The purpose of reflection is to convey to the young person that one has understood what s/he has said from the point of view of his/her frame of reference, to show that one is picking up the literal meanings of the young person's words, and also the accompanying vocal, body and other unconscious messages. Reflecting back key aspects of the discussion also provides the child with feedback about the meaning of what is said. In the process of reflecting, the adult seeks to convey understanding both of the *content* of what is being said, and of underlying *feelings*. The listener might reflect back to the speaker the content, feelings, or both, depending on the needs and states of readiness of the young person (Nelson-Jones 1988).

There is an important distinction between *accepting* what is being said, and *approving* of what is being said. In the latter case, the counsellor may be seen as colluding with the young person. This is unhelpful, because it could encourage the young person to become dependent upon the adult, and thus be allowed to avoid responsibility (Langham and Parker 1988). In the former case it is the other peron's subjective experience of events which it is important to accept.

Clarifying and summarising

The adult counsellor may need to check out his/her perception of what a young person is saying in order to establish that the young person has been correctly understood. By checking perceptions of what has been said, the adult checks his/her understanding of the young person's frame of reference, thus avoiding talking at cross-purposes. The process of clarifying also helps the young person to be aware that the counsellor genuinely wants to understand his/her perceptions.

Nelson-Jones (1988) differentiates the process of clarifying into what he refers to as encouraging 'self-talk' and helpful questioning. The adult encourages self-talk by helping the young person to focus on his/her own role in the issue under discussion. The significance of this is related to the tendency which we all have to avoid dealing directly with problem issues or experiences which make us feel uncomfortable. In encouraging self-talk, the adult keeps the focus on the young person. The adult's focus on the young person's feelings increases the probability of the young person being able to talk about him/herself (Nelson-Jones 1988).

Another way of helping another person to focus on his/her own role in a situation is to encourage him/her to make 'I' statements. When we use the first person singular – 'I' – we own our own messages. We all have a tendency to avoid owning difficult feelings and thoughts. 'I' statements make the difference between, for example, 'People are concerned about your behaviour', and 'I am concerned about your behaviour.' Young people can be encouraged to make 'I' statements if the adult uses them him/herself, and by the adult responding in ways which make use of the word 'you', as though the 'client' had made an 'I' statement, even when s/he has not (Nelson-Jones 1988).

'Clients' can be encouraged to own their problems by enabling them to acknowledge difficulties. The extent to which someone is able to acknowledge a difficulty gives an indication of his/her readiness to work on that difficulty. Nelson-Jones (1988) gives the example of a mother who says she has a troublesome child and who may want to define the child as the problem. The way in which that issue is worked upon may enable the mother to come to see that it is possible to look at the issue in terms of herself in relation to the child. Providing opportunities for someone to reflect on his/her feelings about an issue, within a non-judgemental framework and an environment of trust, is a vital aspect of the process of helping someone to come to acknowledge a difficulty.

Another feature of the process of clarifying relates to the way in which questions are framed. Effective questioning involves sensitivity to the types of question and the timing of questions. The sorts of question to avoid include (Nelson-Jones 1988):

- too many questions, which may lead to defensiveness or dependence.
- leading questions. Such questions put the answer into the young person's mouth, e.g. 'You like this lesson, don't you?'
- closed questions. Closed questions restrict the other person's options for responding, often giving only two options, 'yes' or 'no'. A closed

question, such as 'Do you like lessons with Mr X?', contrasts with an open version, such as 'What do you feel about lessons with Mr X?'

- too probing questions, which are 'likely to create anxiety and resistance because they seek to elicit material that clients may be neither ready nor willing to disclose' (Nelson-Jones 1988: 74).
- poorly timed questions, e.g. asking someone to examine his/her contribution to a difficulty at a time when s/he is full of emotion.

In contrast, useful questions are open-ended. Questions which lead to further exploration of a problem are more likely to begin in ways such as, 'Could it be that . . .?', 'What would happen if . . .?', 'How . . .?' It is also helpful for questions to be framed within the young person's frame of reference. Nelson-Jones (1988) distinguishes between questions which seek elaboration, specification, or to elicit personal reactions. Elaboration questions might ask the young person to expand on what s/he has already started talking about. Specification questions seek to elicit detail that helps the young person clarify his/her concerns. For example, if a girl says that someone bothers her, one might ask her to say what it is about this person that bothers her. Other types of specification questions might ask the young person what s/he means, exactly, or for a specific example to be given. Seeking to elicit the client's personal reactions involves exploration of his/her thoughts, feelings and subjective meanings. Questions which seek such reactions include, 'How do you feel about that?', 'Do you have any thoughts and feelings about . . .?', 'I'm wondering about what the meaning of all this is for you' (Nelson-Jones 1988).

Exercise: Responding empathically and questioning helpfully

***

The group is asked to consider that they are part of a staff group from one school who have been asked to work on the following situation: A new member of staff is about to join the school who does not have much experience in working with pupils with challenging behaviour. As a staff you have worked on the importance of responding empathically and questioning helpfully, and you have built these ideas into whole-school policy on responses to challenging behaviour.

The group's task is to plan how the school should introduce the new member of staff to this aspect of the policy. Previously the school has found that just giving new members of staff documents to read is not a very effective way of helping them to participate in the school's policies, and you are asked by the head to find a more interesting and effective way. How will you do this, and what will your briefing consist of?

Summarising provides a form of closure at the end of an interaction, but it can also be used within the discussion. In summarising, the adult offers feedback to the young person about the whole situation as presented. By being able to understand the young person's frame of reference for a particular situation and more generally how that person experiences the world, the adult can help the young person to gain new insights into the situation. The adult might wish to explore alternative frames of reference for the situation, proposing various hypotheses of understanding. (This process of reframing is described further in Chapter Nine.) Developing wider frames of reference might help the young person to understand the issue in different ways and to imagine a greater range of meaningful responses. There is a tendency in us all to have favoured ways of perceiving ourselves, others and our problems, and this may become emotionally locked into a rigid system of perception, which inhibits psychic fluidity. Exploring the possibility of different perceptions may help young people to reconceptualise their problems. The adult might ask, for example, 'Can you imagine any other way of viewing the issue?', 'How do you think he or she views the matter?', 'Could you have done it differently?', 'What do you really want out of the situation?', 'Do you feel that there is any other interpretation?' (Nelson-Jones 1988).

Reframing one's perceptions can be a powerful tool for strengthening young people to work with an issue which, in the previous frame, seemed immensely difficult. It is important that it is the young person that makes the connections between the different frames, not the counsellor. Langham and Parker (1988) contrast the skill involved in looking at the problem from the young person's own perspective, and allowing her/him to make any conections s/he feels are relevant, to a situation in which the adult sees the whole situation quite clearly, formulates the solution and offers an explanation from his/her point of view. In the latter case, the adult has constructed a bridge, and expects the young person to walk across it. As a result, the young person may well become defensive, and effective communication between the two is therefore blocked. When the young person plays no part in the construction of the bridge, s/he remains unsure of it: to be confident, the young person will need to construct his/her own bridge (Langham and Parker 1988).

Example: Thomas

In this example I tell the story of an initial meeting I had with a child to illustrate the way in which a counselling approach was used to help in the development of ego strength. I describe the initial meeting I had with Thomas to explore with him the possibility of having a tutorial class placement. To understand the example, it is necessary to give a brief background to Thomas's situation – this forms the basis of the information which I had during my meeting with him.

Thomas's situation was referred to the tutorial class service when he was aged 9. The educational psychologist had commented that Thomas was beginning to despair about ever being able to begin to read. Thomas was one of six children. He had been known to the schools psychological service since the age of 3, when concern was expressed about the difficulty he had in communicating. He had spent two years in a language delay unit, a placement which had finished two years prior to the tutorial class referral. At the time of referral he was described as isolated, poorly motivated and underachieving in his mainstream school. He appeared to the educational psychologist as remote, silent, preoccupied and demoralised. The educational psychologist thought the heavy 'doom and gloom' approach of his father's religious sect – with its chapel in the family's front room – might be one factor in inhibiting Thomas's development. Furthermore, at the time when I first met Thomas, relationships between his new teacher and the class were precarious.

I met Thomas in school. He appeared, hunched and quaking, as one of the most overtly anxious children I have ever met. When we talked about the possibility of him having a part-time placement in a tutorial class group, he asked question after question about what happened there: 'What if . . .', 'Can you . . .', and so on. As a way of beginning to facilitate the development of Thomas's ego strength, I tried to recognise and verbally reflect back the steps towards autonomy and responsibility that Thomas was able to make in that meeting. After nearly three-quarters of an hour of Thomas asking 'What if . . .' type questions, I stopped him and summarised, saying that I was pleased that he could do what he needed to satisfy himself that tutorial class would be OK for him. I asked him if he had enough information for now, and if he could hold his other questions till he came to look at the class. His affirmative response enabled me to say that I was pleased he could know when he had good enough information for his needs, and that he could take responsibility for wanting to find out more about the class and being able to wait until the appropriate time to do this.

Exercise: Creating a helping relationship

The following ten questions were developed by Carl Rogers (1961: 50–5). Reflect upon your own capacities in relation to them.

1 Can I *be* in some way which will be perceived by the other person as trustworthy, as dependable or consistent in some deep sense?
2 Can I be expressive enough as a person for what I am to be communicated unambiguously?
3 Can I let myself experience positive attitudes towards this other person – attitudes of warmth, caring, liking, interest, respect?
4 Can I be strong enough as a person to be emotionally separate from the other?
5 Am I secure enough within myself to permit the other person his/her separation?
6 Can I let myself enter fully into the world of his/her feelings and personal meanings and see these as s/he does?
7 Can I accept each facet of the other person which s/he presents to me?

185

8 Can I act with sufficient sensitivity in the relationship for my behaviour not to be perceived as a threat?

9 Can I free the other person from the threat of external judgement?

10 Can I meet this other individual as a person who is in the process of *becoming*, or will I be bound by his/her past and my past?

Exercise: Self-assessment of skills in emotional holding and strengthening

*

This profile relates to discussions in Chapters Four, Five and Six. It is not meant to contain an exhaustive list of skills, but rather is presented as a possible tool for reflection. You may wish to rate your skills in providing emotional holding and strengthening on a scale of high/medium/low. Deployment of your skills will vary according to context and mood. Do this exercise either in general terms, or in relation to a specific context. Reflect upon your scores. You may like to do the exercise again at a future date, and look at how your results compare.

To be empathically available.	H M L
To be able to be involved, yet also detached, and non-collusive.	H M L
To 'get alongside' the learner non-intrusively.	H M L
To be able to be non-judgemental.	H M L
To be able to be non-directive as well as directive.	H M L
To demonstrate awareness of the child's inner world.	H M L
To have perspective, to be able to stand back, let go and relate to, rather than identify with, the child.	H M L
To contain extremes of behaviour without retaliation, whilst setting appropriate boundaries.	H M L
To be able to confront in a non-threatening way.	H M L
To challenge creatively.	H M L
To control self-destructive responses in children.	H M L
To be consistent and reliable in meeting the child's needs.	H M L
Not to provide immediate solutions.	H M L
To listen to and affirm the child.	H M L
To relate to the child's inner frames of reference.	H M L
To reinforce positively and develop ego strengths.	H M L
To recognise the feelings the child is expressing, to appreciate, value and reflect them back.	H M L
To clarify your understanding of the child's experiences.	H M L

To be able to respect confidentiality.   H M L

To be able to help the child with *how* to think rather
than *what* to think (or feel).   H M L

To offer the possibility of the experience of trust.   H M L

To respect the child's capacity for solving his/her own
problems if given the opportunity to do so.   H M L

To be sensitive to the process of establishing transitional
objects – dolls, games, etc.   H M L

To facilitate an exploration of the inner world of images
and creative processes.   H M L

To help the child make connections between
experiences.   H M L

To ask questions which stimulate curiosity about the
external world.   H M L

To be able to appreciate and respect colleagues' feelings,
concerns and anxieties.   H M L

To show that you are taking the child seriously and
recognising the uniqueness of his/her experience.   H M L

To relate effectively to school policy on discipline and
contribute to providing a caring and purposeful
community.   H M L

To be able to seek support from other agencies if
necessary.   H M L

To have space within oneself to think about the child
and the meaning of her/his behaviour, rather than
pre-judge.   H M L

To be able to contain your own anxiety, live with
uncertainty, and not project your own anxiety and
pain, or act out.   H M L

To be aware of your own internal experiences.   H M L

To contain and know your own violent feelings so that
these do not become acted out upon the children.   H M L

To concentrate fully and suspend your own anxieties and
concerns.   H M L

Consider and prioritise those skills most important for you to work on
for your development.

SUMMARY

- Strengthening the personality implies working to support and
strengthen the child's ego. Increased ego strength brings greater
awareness of the feelings and how to manage them.

- This chapter has considered ways of working to engage children and young people at an explicit and conscious level in thinking about troubling issues and the management of relationships.
- Children are encouraged to experience themselves as valued members of the group where they are helped to develop negotiation skills, and where structured activities, e.g. circle-time, are used to build the sense of self-worth.
- A counselling approach is based on understanding and relating to the individual's subjective experience, or his/her 'life space', and aims to help the individual discover solutions to his/her own problems.
- A counselling approach requires the adult to be very clear about appropriate boundaries for discussion, for example, boundaries relating to confidentiality and self-disclosure.
- When listening within a counselling approach one tries to understand from the perspective of the other person, and to respond empathically, using the skills of reflecting, clarifying and summarising.

7

WORKING WITH THE GROUP
DIMENSION

INTRODUCTION

I now turn to consider group phenomena. The processes and skills considered in previous chapters are relevant to group settings. But the import of the group itself has a powerful effect on interactive processes, and since schools are organised around groups, group issues need to be considered in their own right.

The role of the teacher is significant in relation to group dynamics. In recent years the role of the teacher as a 'facilitator' has become increasingly recognised. This shift has been supported by developments in active and flexible learning, and the government's Technical and Vocational Educational Initiative. This widening of the teacher's role increases the complexity of group dynamics in the classroom. 'The responsibility entailed in the nurturing role is much more subtle and delicate than that seen in the directive role. The facilitative leader is often a person much more conscious of the enormous responsibility he has taken on than the directive leader' (Douglas 1978: 138–9).

Emotional or behavioural difficulties are given expression in relationships, in groups, and so the dynamics of group relations can bring into sharp focus the issues and problems demanding attention. For unintegrated children a key area of difficulty is a lack of the capacity to work and play with others in groups. Mongan and Hart (1989: 26) write, 'If the behaviour of pupils was to be improved, consideration needed to be given first as to how to enable pupils to work effectively in groups.' Yet this can sometimes feel so difficult that such a strategy is often ignored in favour of individualised activities. Croll and Moses (1985) showed that children can expect to spend, at most, only 3.2 per cent of their time receiving individual attention from the teacher. Left to work individually for the greater part of their day, children identified by their teachers as having behavioural difficulties spent twice as much time distracted from what they were supposed to be doing as other children.

189

Yet the group can be a powerful tool for promoting positive interaction. The first part of this chapter explores the opportunities which groups present for facilitating children's emotional development and learning. However, being in a group presents any of us with a wide range of demanding issues, particularly concerning the relationship between our individual identity and the identity of the group. The struggles which this issue presents in groups can elicit a number of defensive group processes. The second section of the chapter considers group phenomena which inhibit development. It is important to understand such phenomena, since 'unless one understands the character of the helping medium which one is considering using one cannot even begin to make plans and decisions about . . . how to plan the effort and how to proceed while using it' (Whitaker 1985: 32). The third section of the chapter considers the impact of group size and stage upon dynamics. The final section draws out the themes considered and highlights issues to take account of when leading groups to facilitate development and learning.

These issues in working with group phenomena are pertinent to any group. They therefore have implications for working with staff groups, a theme which will be further considered in Chapter Nine. Those group phenomena which inhibit development are more overt and blatant where group members have limited skills in negotiating and relating with others, or in being aware of and managing themselves. Hence they are particularly pertinent to work with children with emotional and behavioural difficulties.

By way of tuning into the issues of group phenomena, I invite you to consider the following exercise.

Exercise: What helps and what gets in the way in groups?

*/**/***

Consider the experience of a group which you belonged to. Reflect upon what was helpful and what got in the way of development in that group. Think about these issues both from the perspective of the group as a whole, and in relation to the development of yourself as an individual. Where there tensions between these two aspects of development, and if so, what were they?

This exercise may be used as an evaluative tool of the group process in existing working groups. In such circumstances it may be sufficient for group members simply to consider what has been helpful and what has got in the way of development in the group.

OPPORTUNITIES FOR PERSONAL GROWTH AND DEVELOPMENT IN GROUPS

In this section I consider the functions of the group in relation to the opportunities for personal development presented by the group itself as a helping medium. Recognition of the positive potential of groups is an aid to promoting the positive aspects of group processes. So I ask, 'What meaning can the group itself bring to the search for the recovery of learning?' By way of an answer, I present five images of the group as a helping medium: the group and the churn, the group as a bridge between internal and social reality, the group as matrix, the group as kinship, and the group and the pluralist psyche.

The groups which provide the context for the examples cited in this section of the chapter are tutorial class groups, each of which comprises about six children with emotional and behavioural difficulties from different schools, attending for half-days, usually on a twice-weekly basis. (See Appendix One for a description of the work of the tutorial class service.)

The group and the churn

Hassan said, 'Wouldn't it be good if Shaheena could have some of my noisiness and I could have some of her quietness!'

The concept of the group as a churn relates to the notion of the emotionally contained environment. A churn is a form of container. The physical act of churning involves agitation and stirring in order to aid transformation into another substance. Two features of physical churning relate to the churning involved in group work.

Firstly, churning requires continuous action for a long enough time to effect changes. In relation to group work, this calls for continuity both practically and psychically. Psychological continuity can be provided partly through the use of structures which provide elements of ritual in the group's life. An example of ritual structures in the tutorial class setting was my division of the half-day sessions into four phases: newstime (when children took turns to share news or concerns of their own choice); worktime (when each child was given work on appropriate aspects of the curriculum); choice-time (when children made use of the varied resources of the room, including the resource of the teacher for help with negotiation, to follow friendships and activities of their choice); and ending, with a coming together for drinks and a story or a game.

Secondly, in the act of churning, the substances in the container move against each other. This is an important precursor to transmutation into a new substance. In a group churn, experiences and ideas are turned over in the mind. A group is an environment in which people can observe what others do and say and then observe what happens next. Even when a person

191

may appear to be doing nothing more than watching or listening, s/he might be noting events which may have a particular personal meaning. For example, someone who has always been afraid to make challenges may be observing others make challenges. A group is also an environment in which people can receive feedback from other members about their own behaviour or participation in the group. Receiving feedback from others in the group is one of its main advantages as a context for helping personal growth. Group members can gain information about the impact of their behaviour on others. In a group, new behaviours can be tried out in an exploratory way. Within the containing environment of an established group, a child might productively try out new behaviour patterns which are not part of his/her established repertory.

The group provides opportunities for the child to explore personal meanings and the sense made of life experiences, in relation to a wide range of identifications with others and provocations by others. Freud articulated these processes in terms of 'suggestion' and 'imitation'. Bion (1989: 175) preferred the idea of 'valency', which he defined as 'the capacity of the individual for instantaneous combination with other individuals in the established pattern of behaviour'. Provocations and projections enable others in the group to feel things which they have not felt before, or to rediscover aspects of themselves which have been projected or denied. 'External changes rub up against parts of oneself that were not available before ' (Khaleelee and Miller 1985: 373).

These potentially valuable experiences in groups provide, in relation to some types of small-group work, an argument for the value of a limited amount of acting-out. This provides a safe space within which a child's communications through behaviour, which s/he may not yet be able to express in any other way, may be received and thought about. Murray Cox (1990) argues that the group *as a whole* carries the transferences of feeling and that the group together can often bear the intensity of a group member's difficult feeling when the individual cannot.

The group as a bridge between internal and social reality

'In some cases the addition of other children in the play contact brings out feelings and attitudes that could not show up in individual contact' (Axline 1989: 100). In Chapter Five (section on 'Facilitating work with image and metaphor') we considered the significance of play for emotional growth and learning, and looked at some play experiences of John and Carol, who had been particularly omnipotent and wilful children, apparently stuck in the black and white of what Klein calls 'paranoid-schizoid' experience. In making pretend play they were able to make use of the group environment to engage with each other in ways which enabled them to re-enact parent–child relationships and sibling rivalries, explore issues of conflict, and reformulate their subjective constructs in relation to these experiences. The group is a potentially helpful context for such possibilities.

The group also provides a ready-made social context in which the membership provides a forum of social attitudes and expectations. In the group the inner realities of children, as expressed partly in behaviour, are continually exposed to, and sometimes confronted by, what might be called the 'group ego'. This process is continually at work in groups, even though it might not always be expressed in the mature way in which Anna once said, at the beginning of a newstime, 'I'm concerned about Simon's behaviour.' Exposure to the 'group ego' generates the need for each group member to develop responses at an ego level, which are acceptable to the group. Adult interventions can help the child discover the links of meaning between the inner world and social reality. The adult's feedback to the child – of a difficulty or a change – might be given in relation to the child's social reality in the group. The child is thus both required by the group, and helped by the adult, to link inner and outer experiences and the experience of community, and this contributes to the child's ego development. Exposure to the 'group ego' can be particularly valuable for the development of omnipotent children.

Example

In Chapter Four I told something of Terry's story. When he, as a 7 year old, joined the tutorial class group, he was extremely challenging. In the group there were three somewhat macho 10 and 11 year old boys. Terry's desire for a respected and valued place in the group meant that he really took note of the other children's comments about his exaggerated stories and rudeness.

For children who have been emotionally deprived, and whose capacity in life has been damaged, the group setting offers the experience of reliving more positive experiences, over and over again, in concrete forms. The deprived child is thus enabled to internalise gradually a wider range of possibilities in relationships.

The group as matrix

Groups might come to have a symbolic as well as a practical significance for their members. Miller and Rice (1967) termed such groups 'sentient' groups. A significant symbol in facilitating emotional development is that of the matrix, the womb (Cox 1990). Within a known group, the individual potentially has a familiar place, a sanctuary, a sense of safety, of belonging and of trust. Where a group functions as a matrix, the group member can feel free to express and clarify a range of feelings. In defining group developmental goals, Mongan and Hart (1989: 127) place the generation of a sense of belonging – a feeling that 'I am accepted and trusted as a member of this group' – as the first on their list. This is related to what they describe as the development of a sense of achievement ('I have achieved something worthwhile for myself and my contribution to the work of the group is valued') and of shared influence ('I help to decide what goes on in this room, my opinion counts, I take responsibility for my own learning and behaviour').

Example

By way of example I refer to work with Terry, mentioned above. Very soon after Terry had joined the tutorial class group, he and the other boys decided that they wanted to play together at pretend wrestling. This became a frequent activity over the months which followed. As they showed themselves able to respect the boundaries which I had initially imposed, fairly soon I was able to withdraw in my role as boundary setter. I watched this group negotiate and agree changes in the rules, praise each other, warn each other to 'be careful of Terry because he's smaller', and extend the activity into new forms of games. I verbalised what I could see about ways in which they were learning to trust and feel safe with each other.

Cox (1990) maintains, with reference to therapeutic processes in groups, that the therapist is there 'to trust the group. . . . The root is trust; it grows in trust.' Where there is trust, there can emerge the characteristics defined by Bion (1989) as good group spirit: i.e. a common purpose, a common recognition of boundaries, the capacity to absorb new members and lose old ones, freedom from internal subgroups having rigid boundaries, each individual member being valued for his/her contribution to the group and having freedom to move within it, and the capacity to face discontent within the group.

When children themselves recognise the importance of the maintenance of trust in the group, it can sometimes stimulate a high degree of ethical awareness. I provide a vignette involving two children I have already described.

Example

When George returned, somewhat reticently after a missed session, Andrew and Richard asked, 'Why did you tell us George was away because his grandmother had died? You should have just told us he was going to be away. It was for him to tell us the rest if he wanted to.'

In ongoing groups, where individual members leave as they are ready, and new members join established groups, there are opportunities for issues relating to endings, beginnings, loss, separation, greed, envy and feelings about the individual's place in the group to be reworked over and over again. This provides each individual with renewed opportunities to work on his/her subjective constructs about such issues.

The group and kinship

The group provides opportunities for its members to make related, 'living' contributions to each other. In the tutorial class group it was noteworthy how often children brought sweets, crisps, biscuits, fruit and drink to share at drinks-time. It seems that by helping others the capacity to help oneself is constellated. In an early work on groups, Ginott (1961: 6) says, 'The therapeutic process is enhanced by the fact that every group member can be a giver and not only a receiver of help.'

Here we are talking of kinship. Jungian analyst Molly Tuby writes,

> The circle . . . the exclusiveness, the faithfulness are all reminiscent of tribal initiation into another stage of consciousness. . . . The kinship archetype is powerful and eternal; when it is activated it should be recognised and honoured, at the same time as [individual] consciousness changes and grows.
>
> (Tuby 1988: 3)

A sense of kinship evokes the development of a sense of attachment to the group and those in it. When this happens there is the opportunity for relationship, perhaps unconsciously, with what the group as a whole symbolises, and this has a potentially powerful effect upon individual growth. Strubel develops the theme:

> The group as a symbolic wholeness constellates the wholeness of the individual. . . . only if each individual may be himself, only if each may bring his individuality as a specific contribution to the group, does the group realize itself as a symbolic wholeness. . . . The wholeness of the group and the wholeness of the individual are constantly in relation to each other.
>
> (Strubel 1983: 292)

In groups, shared themes and kinship build up through associative processes, in which each person makes contributions out of her/his own associations to what has gone before. Issues which are important to a particular person can be explored within the context of a prevailing theme in the group.

> The potential for benefit lies in the opportunity to explore issues of potential importance under conditions in which a number of people are involved and the shared character of the situation leads to courage and support. . . . an individual finds a theme manageable even though threatening because it *is* shared and because much mutual support for exploring it exists in the group.
>
> (Whitaker 1985: 36–7)

The sense of kinship is supported by the group's evolution of particular attitudes and behaviour patterns, or 'norms' and belief systems. The kinds of belief system on which a group operates are of critical importance and can make the difference between a sterile or even destructive group and a useful one. The evolution of group norms can serve as a means of helping some members to feel safe, for example by allowing group members to express anger in particular ways. Some norms and belief systems have the effect of widening the boundaries of the group, making useful explorations of personal issues possible. For example, the shared belief that 'we all have problems sometimes' supports a group and its members as a positive medium for help, since, if everyone has problems, no one need feel ashamed of talking of problems (Whitaker 1985). Whitaker develops the notion of a 'group solution' as a wider concept than norms and beliefs but encompassing both of these, and she builds the notion into a model of group functioning called 'group focal conflict theory'. In this theory, a facilitating solution is regarded as one which deals with fear, and allows for the safe expression of wishes related to fear. Fears are thus contained and, at the same time, group members can confront and explore the associated impulses and feelings. In a group the motive to precipitate a conflict might relate to a wish which feels risky and which cannot be acknowledged, such as a wish to be close to others, or to be nurtured or loved. Whitaker (1985) argues that during periods when a group is operating on some facilitating solution, processes which she terms comparison, feedback, spectatorship and behavioural try-outs are likely to go on in a co-operative, useful and constructive manner. Bion (1989: 136) examined the relationship between co-operation and on-task behaviour in groups: 'Organisation and structure are the weapons of the work group. They are the product of co-operation between members of the group, and their effect once established in the group is to demand still further co-operation from the individuals in the group.'

From the above discussion it is evident that processes relating to the development of a sense of kinship go beyond individual adjustment and the internalisation of 'acceptable' behaviour. Each group member can begin to establish areas of agreement and disagreement with the group, and thus become less dependent and more of an individual. This process is both helped by, and a product of, co-operative learning methods. Such methods help the development of higher-quality cognitive strategies; the improvement of understanding through discussion and controversy; the improvement of long-term retention from the continual restatement and reformulation of new ideas; the enrichment of ideas through exchanges between pupils of different background, achievement levels and experiences; and the increase in motivation for learning (Mongan and Hart 1989: 129).

How does working exclusively with groups of troubled children relate to these issues of kinship, from the adult's point of view? Foukes and Anthony comment:

maladjusted children can be exceedingly demanding, and drain us of our feeling . . . but no unilateral relationship in human society is a good one. . . . unilateral giving is bad for both sides. It is always therapeutically wise to expect something in return, even from the most psychotic child, for whom the act of giving may become the act of redemption. . . . In the group . . . it should be shown:
1) That unilateral receiving is not therapeutic for the child.
2) That unilateral giving is not healthy for the adult.

(Foukes and Anthony 1984: 226–7)

Foukes and Anthony add that the establishment of a reciprocal relationship is as good an indicator of development as any.

The group and the pluralist psyche

The preceding discussion has indicated the value of individuals coming into contact with different individuals in groups. I want to take the issue of difference in groups further, by arguing that the group, because of its pluralist nature, provides a valuable resource for helping to get in touch with, and tap the potential of, inner resources, since psyche is also pluralist in nature.

Bion (1989: 133) argues that, 'There are characteristics in the individual whose real significance cannot be understood unless it is realized that they are part of his equipment as a herd animal and their operation cannot be seen unless it is looked for in . . . the group.' He also says (Bion 1989: 54), 'I consider that group mental life is essential to the full life of the individual.' We seek and find our potential through pluralistic experience, and often look for this in groups. But do we just need the group externally? There is a sense in which we need, and have, groups inside ourselves. Psychically, we are each a group. Joseph Redfearn (1985) has written to the title *My Self – My Many Selves*, and Jung (1973a: 508) argues, 'The self . . . is of a conglomerate nature. It is, as it were, a group. It is a collectivity in itself and therefore always, when it works most positively, creates a group.' With reference to group relations theory, Colman (1992: 94) refers to the 'concept known as "group in the mind" which expresses the ever-present group consciousness of individuals even and especially when they are most isolated and functioning most separately from others'.

How are we to relate to our 'inner group(s)' for our personal development? An ecological parallel is relevant here. We live at a time when ecology is writ large in the collective psyche. When considering troubled children, ecological analogies are increasingly in use. Mongan and Hart (1989: 72) speak of 'socio-ecological perspectives', and Upton and Cooper (1990) write about an 'ecosystemic' approach to behaviour problems in schoools. The value of an ecological, holistic approach was also discussed in the introductory chapter of this book.

Let us examine a direct ecological parallel. The BBC's *Horizon* television programme (broadcast 14 May 1990), *The Legacy of the Volcano*, documented the scientific study of the regeneration of the vegetation and animals around Mount Saint Helens in the Rocky Mountains of the USA, after its 1980 eruption. As a result of this study, new ideas are emerging about the regeneration of plant and animal communities. The areas which recover best and fastest are those where there is *greatest diversity of environment.* The lesson seems to be that if one is going to plant, aim to have a mixture of things around, and so maintain the diversity.

This lesson is relevant to the benefits of groups for personal development. With regard to organic growth in the psyche, the group provides the facilitatingly diverse context for development. In working with a variety of tutorial class groups, I came to appreciate that the more diverse they were, the more effective they seemed to be. It is the very diversity of the group which helps us to discover and relate to the continually dynamic diversity within ourselves and of our relationships with others.

The above discussion has elaborated a number of ways in which groups provide opportunities for personal development. Enabling groups to manifest these potentials is a task that calls for skill, since the teacher or other adult is inevitably also struggling with group phenomena that get in the way of development. It is to these phenomena that I now turn.

GROUP PROCESSES THAT INHIBIT DEVELOPMENT

An awareness of group phenomena that inhibit growth enhances the adult's capacity to work effectively with group processes in the service of facilitating individuals' development and learning. Group processes which can inhibit development arise in all manner of groups – groups of adults and of children – and are likely to be most obvious where the individuals within the group have difficulty containing and managing disturbing feelings.

In order to get a feel of the sorts of issue pertinent to this discussion, it is worth noting Wells' (1981) remarks upon the parallels between the relationship of an individual with a group and the relationship of an infant with his/her mother. Both experiences elicit struggles over the issues of fusing/joining and separating/isolation; both potentially elicit a sense of being nurtured and of frustration; and in both, strong ambivalent feelings are aroused. The last relates to the experience of both love and hate simultaneously, to the generation of the defence mechanism of splitting and projective identification in order to cope with ambivalence, and to the struggle with the tension between engulfment and estrangement.

Group issues are discussed below in terms of defensive norms and beliefs, the toleration of difference, contagion and regression, and task avoidance and regression. The impact of such phenomena depends largely upon the skill of the group leader to work with them preventatively, diagnostically and remedially. To be able to work effectively with processes which inhibit development can have a powerful effect on group experience. Kurt Lewin's research (e.g. 1948) on the forces which drive and/or restrain change in the work situation led him to conclude that working with the factors restraining or inhibiting change is a more effective way of facilitating it than simply reinforcing those forces which drive towards it.

The group phenomena considered here are likely to operate upon individuals in the group in an unconscious manner. This has an impact upon the sorts of fantasy which are harboured by individuals within the group. The dynamics of any group generate fantasies which are commonly held in the group. The fantasies of a group have a part to play in constructing a belief system about what is, and is not, possible in the group.

Defensive norms and beliefs

The positive influences of group norms were considered in the first part of this chapter. Norms and belief systems can also constitute powerful defences in groups. Group norms may serve to suppress feelings which group members find difficult to tolerate, and thereby to keep group members comfortable; but such norms may also reduce or constrict the value of the group by restricting the areas in which individual and group exploration can occur. If such defence mechanisms become a (conscious or unconscious) collusion between group members they have the potential for targeting flak at particular individuals within a group, for example by one person being made the scapegoat. Negative norms and beliefs may be damaging in the direct sense of facing individuals with something which they cannot tolerate, or by placing them in a position where they are blamed or attacked (Whitaker 1985).

Such group dynamics generate norms and beliefs which serve to mask competition and rivalries within the group. Since competition and rivalries are difficult to face up to, groups develop ways of avoiding these issues. Some rivalries which groups commonly avoid are those which relate to the various individual needs and wishes in the group. The question arises of whether the meeting of the wishes or needs of other people threatens the possibility of one's own wishes being met. In unconsciously seeking to mask rivalries, groups may thus generate the belief, for instance, that no one wants to be different in the group, or that no one in the group is interested in certain activities or fostering certain attitudes, whilst everyone in the group is interested in other particular activities or fostering other attitudes.

In circumstances where difficult feelings are present in a group, the group might allow one person to believe that s/he is the only one with a particular feeling, as if s/he becomes a 'carrier' for the group of a particular impulse. This is the mechanism through which group members may (unconsciously) take on particular roles within a group. An individual may

199

thus become isolated within the group, and this mechanism enables other group members to maintain the myth that the particular feeling does not 'belong' to them as individuals. The scapegoat is the particular individual to whom these same feelings or wishes have been ascribed and who is then isolated and scorned for possessing the feelings. So long as scapegoating persists, others are allowed to avoid acknowledging the same feeling or behaviour in themselves. If a group leader keeps the scapegoat in the centre of attention to 'help' that particular individual, this simply continues the pattern of scapegoating in a disguised and devious form. Sometimes, when one person is being criticised or blamed, the underlying dynamic produces displacement activities. Anger which really belongs to one person is displaced onto another, usually because the attackers then feel safe from retaliation, abandonment or other negative consequences.

When group fantasies emerge which relate to the behaviour or motivations of most individuals within the group, these fantasies most often remain unchallenged by the group, *even when* contrary evidence is available to all those engaging in the fantasy. The danger of differentiating feelings in a group is that it might become clear who feels what, and who carries what, and who brings which vulnerabilities to the group. It may often feel easier for individuals in groups to live with a fantasy about a group's behaviour, rather than checking it out. When an individual feels something different to the group's fantasy, this can feel very risky, both for that individual, and for the rest of the group: 'like individuals who reject shadow elements of themselves by projecting them out into the environment, the group will create victims rather than face dealing with diversity and difference' (Colman 1992: 98).

Toleration of difference in groups

In groups we are all faced with the difficulty of tolerating individual differences, differences between ourselves and others. Often unconsciously, we will seek 'sameness' in a group of which we are a member, as a way of avoiding difference, since recognising difference implies recognising different needs, and again, by implication, rivalries within the group. Our strong tendency towards conformity is linked to the experience that 'to be original, or different, is felt to be dangerous' (Rogers 1961: 348). Difference is therefore unconsciously avoided in order to maintain the sense of safety associated with sameness. When faced with the range of such pressures that always exist in groups, it becomes difficult to maintain, struggle with and experience ambivalences, and so in groups we easily slide into omnipotence. We might be driven in such a direction, for example by inner voices which say, for instance, 'Shut up, I want to speak, I can contribute as much as you. I want my two-penny-worth!'

The above discussion suggests that it can feel very risky to acknowledge difference in a group. As soon as the difference of one group member becomes clear and acknowledged, it is possible that the other group members may reject that individual or psychologically eject him/her from the group. Groups most often function to avoid any examination of the differences between members, by taking flight into other 'safer' issues. The struggle between being part of a group and being an individual can be very difficult to deal with.

Where teaching is organised in mixed-attainment (a notion preferred to mixed-'ability') groups, teachers may both recognise the potential of this form of organisation, and yet find some of the issues which get in the way of learning in such groups difficult to cope with. Although teaching mixed-attainment groups demands a high level of organisational skill, the organisational issues in themselves become easier when some of the underlying group dynamics issues are addressed. Of particular importance is the capacity of people to tolerate differences between members of a group. A group may find it very difficult to come to terms with various individual needs within it, since, once different needs are acknowledged, a rivalrous situation exists, which elicits the question for group members, 'Are one person's needs going to be met at the expense of other people's needs?' Hence the significance of the teacher's role in validating and organising for difference. Differences of all sorts can be celebrated: cultural difference, differences in individual interests and areas of attainment, and so on.

So, to summarise, the fear of difference within a group derives from the fear of rivalrous or envious feelings. To feel envy of someone else, or to feel the envy of others, can be frightening, since it may heighten the possibility of emotional (or even physical) attack.

Contagion and regression

Feelings of envy or fear of attack which may be aroused in group dynamics provoke anxiety, particularly when they re-evoke previous disturbing experiences. When one is anxious the temptation to act out the difficult feeling and to project it onto others becomes stronger. Panic takes hold of individuals more easily in groups, and groups can sometimes develop particularly intense moods or atmospheres. Quite suddenly, for example, a group can be in a panic, or start behaving hysterically. The process of 'contagion' was first articulated by Freud. It occurs when group members experience a conflict between strong impulses to express a feeling, and a strong pressure (from the ego or super-ego) to suppress the impulse. The individual who initiates a particular behaviour may have weak inhibiting forces, and this initiation then makes it possible for the others to express the feeling (Redl 1956). When groups are 'caught up' in frantic feelings, it can become difficult for group members and the group leader to maintain the capacity to think, and this is particularly so when emotional or physical attacks are likely.

Sometimes groups can be overwhelmed by experience akin to that of the state Melanie Klein described as the 'paranoid-schizoid' position (see Chapter Two). Reed and Palmer argue that group activity of an omnipotent kind:

> may be precipitated by what are seen as threats to the group from outside, or by anxieties arising within individuals about their relationship to the group. These amount to the same thing, in that the felt threat is to what may be a very primitive fantasy of the group, on which the individual feels he depends for his survival. . . . Behaviour is directed towards safeguarding the survival of the group, not by realistic measures, but by designating sources of protection and deliverance on the one hand, and of malign influence and destruction on the other.
>
> (Reed and Palmer 1972, Lecture 2: 10)

Some regressive features are more prominent in what the literature defines as large groups, i.e. those of over sixteen members. When feeling insecure in a group, for example feeling that one has no allies within the group, an individual group member may seek to protect him/herself and may resort to withdrawal from the group, either seeking to leave the group, or withdrawing emotionally.

> Finding no external good object to which he can relate, he mentally clings to some secret idea or relationship which he feels to be secure. An alternative means by which the individual seeks to survive the stresses of the large group is to allow his personal ego boundary to dissolve, so that he loses himself in the mass of feelings of the group. As a group process this leads to a progressive *homogenisation* in which all individuality is lost. . . . Homogenisation provides the individual with the protection of individuality.
>
> (Reed and Palmer 1972, Lecture 3: 10–11)

People tend to get thrown back to regressive stages under pressure. Another factor which induces regressed states in groups is the entry of a new group member. When a new child joins a group which has become settled and on-task, the group will often regress, with the teacher feeling that s/he is 'back to the starting-point' with the group. This issue is picked up again in the section below on group stages. All groups experience regression at times: the inhibiting factors discussed in this section become reinforced when a group gets stuck in a particular stage as a coping strategy.

Task-avoidance in groups

Bion's innovation in working with groups was to treat the whole group as his patient, and he gave interpretations to the group rather than to

individuals. Bion argued that effective work in groups is constantly inter-
rupted by things from other contexts which push them off task. Whenever
the group is working, it can behave as if a 'basic assumption' is held in
common by all the members, which will affect the activity of the group. By
this Bion meant that groups often seem to behave in a particular mode, 'as
if' all the members hold a basic assumption in common. The basic assumption relates to unconscious group fantasies about the kind of action which
is required to secure the group's survival. These assumptions are seldom
voiced. When:

> one kind of basic assumption threatens to overwhelm the group and
> make work unproductive, the teacher has to try to find ways of
> mobilizing another, so that new forces can come into play and be used
> by the group in an increasingly mature and responsible fashion.
>
> (Richardson 1975: 223)

According to Bion, there are three distinct emotional states in groups
from which 'basic assumptions' can be deduced. He described these states
as 'dependency', 'flight/fight' and 'pairing'. I consider each of these in
turn. First of all the dependent group:

> When the shared map of the group is based on the dependence
> assumption, members behave as though they had access to a person
> or object which is able to supply all their needs, without their having
> to do anything except wait and receive. Correspondingly, they feel
> themselves to be weak, ignorant, inadequate and vulnerable.
> Capacities which they are able to use elsewhere disappear in the
> climate of dependence.
>
> (Reed and Palmer 1972, Lecture 2: 11)

Of the dependent group Bion says:

> one person is always felt to be in a position to supply the needs of the
> group, and the rest in a position in which their needs are supplied. . . .
> As the culture becomes established, individuals . . . begin to show
> their discomfort. One quite frequent phenomenon is the emergence
> of feelings of guilt about greed.
>
> (Bion 1989: 74)

When a group becomes taken over by a culture of dependency, what the
leader says or does is sooner or later bound to be a disappointment. The group
has to work to maintain the fantasy on which, it is felt, their survival depends.

> When the leader's behaviour does not fit the role he has been cast in,
> it is ignored or explained away. Another member may be un-
> consciously assigned the role of a disciple or high priest who explains
> and justifies the words and actions of the leader to the other members.

Alternatively the leader may be manipulated to show the love and power he appears to be hiding, by giving him problems to solve.

(Reed and Palmer 1972, Lecture 2: 12)

If the teacher takes the role of leader with a dependent group, the group, although in some ways willing to collude with this, may also become frustrated. In such situations the teacher:

must contrive to be reliable while continually urging the class to question his omniscience, challenge his opinions and realistically accept his human limitations. And at times he will create situations in which members of his class take his role, and become accepted as alternative leaders in a basically dependent culture, using their own expertise as he uses his when he is the accepted leader.

(Richardson 1975: 223)

In the 'fight/flight' group, task avoidance proceeds through flight away from the task, or 'fight' with peers.

In the flight–fight culture the danger is that the group will either destroy the teacher or itself by the unleashing of its own hostile impulses or withdraw from the situation altogether. And so the role of the teacher is to channel the aggression into an attack on ignorance and apathy, so that the class rediscovers its powers of co-operation in a learning situation and uses its leaders in a constructive way.

(Richardson 1975: 223)

In the 'pairing group', collusive pairings between group members are entered into as a way of avoiding the task at hand. The pairings may be felt to be collusive by those group members who are excluded from them. Pairing takes place to some extent in all groups, mostly unconsciously. Pairings may take place in many different ways, based for example upon projection, empathy, the desire for sexual liaison, or the ability of some members of the group to relate to others in an honest, direct and personal manner. Reed and Palmer explain the dynamic:

the hope is built up of creating a group which will be free from all the frustrations and disappointments of most human relationships. This process leads to a shared idea of a group which is highly idealised. All the negative aspects of human relationships are projected outside the group, onto external authorities, careers, marriages and social systems.

(Reed and Palmer 1972, Lecture 2: 13)

Richardson relates this dynamic to the role of the teacher:

In the pairing culture, the danger is that the group rests in the lazy hope that two members will continue indefinitely to carry responsibility; individuals then become frustrated because their hope of some perfect product from these two is never realized. Here the teacher's role is to break up the task and give each pair or small group a manageable part of it to tackle. In this way achievement becomes possible, because no one any longer supposes that one pair can be left to produce the magic solution.

(Richardson 1975: 223)

Tourquet (1974) explores the paradoxes in the relationship between the basic assumption and the 'work group'. The latter is a term used by Bion to refer to that aspect of group functioning that is the 'real' task of the group. Tourquet explains how the basic assumption group inhibits development: 'its primary task arises solely from within its own midst and is pursued solely for the satisfaction and the internal needs of the group'(Tourquet 1974: 356). The basic assumption group, however, is not always entirely negative in its effects. Tourquet compares and contrasts the basic assumption and the 'work group', and, noting the oscillatory and paradoxical relationship between them he observes that as an individual leaves the basic assumption way of life, s/he experiences loss: loss of satisfaction of his/her need to belong, loss of a sense of unity, cohesiveness and so on. This produces an attraction back into basic assumption group ways, which can 'give man a breathing space and enable him to return refreshed by the strength of fraternity to face his aloneness' (Tourquet 1974: 369). In earlier chapters it has been pointed out that psychological mechanisms related to defences may be mobilised to support or inhibit growth. Similarly, a sophisticated work group seeks to mobilise the relevant basic assumption group in support of its work.

I now consider the impact of group size and stage, and then turn to the facilitation and mobilisation of helpful aspects of group life.

GROUP SIZE AND STAGE

Group size

In the field of education, much is made of the significance of class size, but more from the perspective of the relationship of class size and individual attainment than from a consideration of the group dynamics issues. These are considered below in terms of the impact of group size on individual identity, the arousal of primitive feelings, the development of a shared understanding of the group, the stability of relationships in the group, and the group's relationship with the wider organisation.

Groups of more than sixteen people are regarded in the group relations field as 'large groups'. In large groups it is more difficult for us to hold onto our own sense of individual identity. One way of holding in one's mind an image of a group of which one is a member is to include an image of each individual group member. A large group is a group which is too big for this to happen (Reed and Palmer 1972). Tourquet argues that a group of twelve is the optimum size for a single group member to encompass so as to take in the rest of the group as individuals, and that sixteen is the very upper limit for this capacity. In large groups a sense of individual identity often develops by individuals identifying in some way with the figure-head. Clearly these issues have implications for the organisation of classes in schools. A group dynamics perspective reinforces the value of dividing class groups into subgroups, particularly when questions of individual identity are pertinent to the task, e.g. for subjects such as personal and social education, for activities such as problem-solving approaches which require mobilisation of social as well as learning skills, and for younger or less autonomous children whose sense of identity is not yet well developed.

In large groups primitive feelings are more likely to be aroused than in smaller groups. Large groups tend to arouse – in both group members and leaders – feelings that the group holds together somewhat tenuously and that conflict and tension might relatively easily break out. A sense of group cohesion can relatively easily change into a dynamic of 'everyone for him/herself'. This can create a difficulty for group members in retaining their own sense of individual boundaries. The larger the group the more emotionally 'primitive' it tends to be. These issues reinforce the need for class groups and smaller groups to be managed in different ways.

In large groups several factors combine to prevent the development of a shared understanding or 'map' of the group. In consequence the capacity of individual members to relate productively to ambivalence in the group is more precarious. Reed and Palmer (1972) suggest that one factor which might inhibit the development of a shared map of the group is a spatial factor. They argue that, given the large size of the group and the space in which it physically operates, the individual cannot always register the effect of her/his contributions on others, and so does not know what feelings are being left with them.

> Nor can he register with others the effect of their words and behaviour upon him, and consequently he may become the reposi-tory of feelings and fantasies, originating from others, but whose origins he cannot trace. He feels angry, or shut out, or safe, and does not know why, though he may invent a reason in order to feel in control of the situation.
>
> (Reed and Palmer 1972, Lecture 3: 6)

According to Reed and Palmer, another factor which prevents the development of a shared map of the group is that of quantity. In a large group there is too much happening for each individual member to take in:

In fantasy the individual feels himself engulfed. He cannot locate any clear boundaries, of membership, roles or topics, such that he can encompass the group and form a distinct idea of it in his mind; the experience of the group is unencompassable. Without an idea of a bounded group it appears to be difficult for the individual to separate his good and bad feelings about it, so that he can idealise the group and project its bad aspect onto the outside world, as he can in a small group.

(Reed and Palmer 1972, Lecture 2: 7)

This reinforces the significance of the leader's role in working with group boundaries.

Reed and Palmer suggest that another factor to take account of in the development of a shared map of the group is that of time. In large groups which last for a length of time, the individuals may have difficulty in remembering the facts and putting them together into a coherent framework.

The individual's ability to tolerate the resulting sense of confusion is diminished by his need to feel that what happened is in some way intelligible. This leads to the generation of myths, that is, of simplified and emotionally heightened accounts of events, which become generally accepted, even in the face of facts which do not fit the story. The individual may have experienced an event differently, but feels he cannot trust his judgement or memory, in face of what is apparently a universally-held belief. Evidence is therefore suppressed, and the myth becomes highly resistant to modification.

(Reed and Palmer 1972, Lecture 2: 7)

A large group which remains undifferentiated, in terms of emotionally meaningful relationships between members, tends towards instability and is liable to be caught up in impulsive activity or frozen into sterile rigidity. If not provided with structure, the large group frequently breaks down into smaller groupings, either spontaneously or through conscious decisions of the members. Reed and Palmer note three common patterns: firstly, polarisation into two opposing factions – a group and an 'anti-group'. Secondly, there is the formation of an active small group, in the limelight, with others who participate vicariously. The third form of division is into multiple subgroups. This suggests the need to provide structures which link relationships within the group to the whole group identity, and to harness the tendency towards division in larger groups proactively and creatively.

Tourquet (1974) suggests that a key issue in large groups of between twenty and thirty people is the 'institutionalisation' of the individuals as a way of saving individual group members from the constantly threatening feeling of emotional annihilation. In large groups individuals face the task of searching for and finding something which can represent individual wholeness and the wholeness of the group and the wider organisation. The individual forms an internal picture of the organisation which stands for its totality. The extent to which an individual is able to mobilise such a model and his/her own internalised image of individual wholeness determines the capacity of the individual to link his/her personal development with the aims of the organisation. Schools are an example of many institutions which assemble periodically for large meetings, of which the main emotional purpose seems to be to reinforce each member's internal model of the organisation.

> Through contemplating meetings, persons, or objects, which are regarded as symbols of the institution as a totality, members are able to carry on their work within their own department or unit, with an enhanced ability to relate their work to the aims and values of the whole.
>
> (Reed and Palmer 1972, Lecture 3: 16)

Without such opportunities, Reed and Palmer argue, the members of an organisation may come to regard it and its leadership as what object relations theorists would refer to by the term 'bad objects', as figures in whom they have no emotional investment.

Group stages

Issues concerning the vulnerabilities experienced by individuals within groups at the beginnings and endings of times when groups meet have been discussed (Chapter Four, section on 'Beginnings and endings'). A range of other issues is presented by the dynamics of group stages. In group dynamics literature the affect of group stage is well documented, and these have important consequences for schools.

Example

In an in-service training session for newly qualified teachers, one of the teachers noted that after he was just getting on top of the demanding process of getting a group settled, on several occasions other pupils were sent in from another group. He observed that on each occasion this seemed to put the whole group process right back to the beginning again. An understanding of group dynamics issues can help avoid this sort of difficulty, and so help functioning groups to pursue their primary tasks.

Groups develop and change their character over a period of time. Their preoccupations are likely to change according to the stage of the group's life. At some time or another, all groups are likely to be faced with issues such as group members questioning their own acceptability within the group, yearnings for closeness and nurturance, anger and its management, issues of power, control and autonomy, personal aspirations and the hopes, fears and despairs associated with them, envy, and personally held fears and guilts. The extent to which an individual's needs are met at the beginnning of the group's life disproportionately affects the individual's capacity to participate productively in group tasks. When first joining a group, or at the beginning of a group's life, individuals are likely to have a number of concerns. (For example, the concerns of a group of teachers embarking on a course are given in Chapter Four, section on 'Beginnings and endings'). These concerns are likely to relate to the questions shown in Figure 23.

Initially, the individual in a group achieves a sense of belonging through becoming in some way identified with the leader, and by developing a sense of the leader's stance on the issues in Figure 23.

Group leaders/teachers can be more effective if they are also aware of the processes which a collection of people go through in establishing themselves as a group. Tuckman (1965) identified a number of stages in the life of a group, which are shown in Figure 24.

Tuckman also argued that when new members join a group, the group has to rework the previous stages that it has gone through.

When a group has matured and is working effectively, it is able to manage productively the tensions shown in Figure 25.

Process

Safety:
>Will I be emotionally and physically safe in the group?

Acceptance:
>Will I be liked or disliked? How will I be treated?

Participation:
>What will my place in the group be?

Task

Definition:
>What will we have to do and what are we meant to achieve?

Competence in relation to task:
>Will I be able to do what is expected of me?

Hierarchy of achievement:
>How will my competencies compare with those of others?

Leadership and group management

Who will be in charge?
How will the rules be made in the group?
What will I feel about the way the group is run, and how will I respond?

Figure 23 Concerns at the beginning of a group's life

Stage 1 Forming

The group discovers the task in hand and the rules which govern it. They also have to learn about each other.

Stage 2 Storming

During the initial stage a false consensus is often reached. This is challenged in ways which reveal interpersonal conflicts but lead to new rules. The developing trust of group members is tested here.

Stage 3 Norming

Feelings and views are exchanged as norms and practices are established and their limits explored and tested by group members.

Stage 4 Performing

Levels of performance are no longer hindered by the processes of the previous stages. The group is now able to focus on the task in hand.

Figure 24 Stages in the life of a group
(after Tuckman 1965)

- Links a whole image of the institution and clarity about the group's goals and purposes.

- Shares leadership functions and responsibilities among group members.

- Maintains supportive values and beliefs and facilitates expression and resolution of difficult feelings.

- Facilitates communication, reflection and the development of mutual understanding on the group's tasks and processes, and makes modifications where appropriate.

- Balances group productivity and individual needs, enabling individuals to relate to whole images of the group and of themselves as individuals.

- Balances group identity and cohesion on the one hand, and the capacity to respond flexibly in the environment on the other.

- Selects procedural and decision-making arrangements flexibly and efficiently.

- Works productively with difference, e.g. differences can be expressed and conflict tolerated, minority viewpoints are taken into consideration, the different abilities of group members are valued and made use of.

- Accepts with ambivalence new additions and the losses of group members.

Figure 25 Managing the tensions: characteristics of an effectively functioning group

The notion of the whole image of a group or organisation is significant in helping to work against the splitting and other defence mechanisms. This notion is discussed further in the following section (and also in Chapter Nine).

Exercise: Observing group processes

***

This exercise is for groups which have worked together for a period of time (e.g. a staff group or a course group). It is designed to enable group members to observe and discuss group processes. The exercise is based on a role-play which is watched by some members of the group, with briefs to observe specific aspects of group process.

The facilitator should prepare sufficient role cards for every member of the group. Some role cards assign the role of 'task group member'. Others give the briefs for the observers. Each observer has a different brief. They might be as follows:

- Please collect evidence on the ways in which the group members help and support each other.
- Please collect evidence of rivalry within the group.
- Please collect evidence of the way difference is dealt with by the group.
- Please collect evidence of ways in which the group as a whole and individual members avoid engagement with the task.
- How do anxieties manifest in the group?
- In what ways are group norms and beliefs expressed?

Group members are asked to select role cards at random. Those who receive 'task group member' cards are asked to sit together so that they can work as a group. This group then undertakes a task, which those with 'observer' cards observe and consider in relation to their individual briefs. The task for the task group is read out by the facilitator. It might be as follows:

> I would like you to imagine that this whole group has asked you to consider how it has worked as a group over the last *x* weeks/this term [the time period should be specified]. You have been asked to prepare a brief report about this, which can be given to the whole group. You have *x* minutes [the time period should be specified] to complete this task.

The facilitator manages the time boundary for this exercise. I have found that twenty minutes is not inappropriate for a task such as this: it is sufficient but not too long a time for the observers to do their

---

tasks, and under pressure of time, group processes in the task group may be more obvious.

When the time is up for the task, each member of the task group is asked to say very briefly how s/he feels at the end of the exercise. This debriefing is an important step in the ensuing discussion. Each observer is then asked to give feedback according to the brief s/he has been given. There should be opportunities for group members to comment about the observers' feedback. There then needs to be ample time for a general discussion about the issues raised in the exercise: a lengthy period of debriefing is necessary so that feelings can be processed, and general principles about group processes can be elucidated.

FACILITATING AND MANAGING GROUP PROCESSES

In reviewing the discussion of this chapter so far, I now turn to extrapolate some key functions in facilitating and managing group processes in groups which are concerned with the development of the individuals within them. In general terms, the management of groups designed to facilitate developmental processes requires, according to Menzies Lyth (1988), clear task definition and sustaining the values, roles and boundaries to achieve the task; the capacity to keep in mind the whole group and each whole child; the capacity to mitigate defences (in oneself and others) and anti-task behaviour; and the modelling of good 'management-cum-ego' functioning. Bearing in mind the teacher at work with emotional/behavioural factors in learning, in the discussion which follows I highlight a number of significant leadership and management functions: the capacity to reflect upon process, self-observation, establishing the group as a symbol, boundary control, issues of emotional containment and dependency, supportive group norms, and working with difference and facilitating multiplicity of experience in groups.

Reflection upon process

The significance of 'process thinking' has been a theme throughout this book. This is particularly important in relation to group phenomena, as these are so complex. Douglas (1978) emphasises that the effectiveness of group leaders in facilitating emotional development is determined by their capacity to examine and work with 'process' as well as 'content', i.e. with the dynamics, the interactions and the affective realm as well as with the subject-matter of the activities. Working with process as well as content suggests that the group leader needs to be able to work with the many-layered inter-relationships of group members' contributions – group and

212

individual dynamics, conscious and unconscious intentions – as well as the overt subject-matter of the contributions: 'an adult's capacity for listening and seeing beyond the face value of opinions contributes to the function-ing of the group' (Barrett and Trevitt 1991: 203). Douglas argues that the key skills in working with group processes are the ability to observe, the ability to assess the group's situation, and the ability to make appropriate interventions. The teacher's effectiveness increases to the extent that s/he can enable group members to make use of the group in what Whitaker (1985) describes as a 'medium for help'.

> The conductor's responsibility *to* the group and its members can be stated in general terms as an obligation or duty to do everything he can, to the best of his ability, to work towards [the] purpose of utilizing the group for the benefit of the members. His responsibility *in* the group, that is, while actually conducting it, is to be clear about instrumental purposes [purposes which can contribute towards the achievement of the overall purpose], attentive to events as they unfold, and ready to anticipate and note the consequences of his behaviour and to regulate his behaviour according to how it bears on instrumental purposes.
>
> (Whitaker 1985: 378–9)

Whitaker (1985) also suggests that a group leader, as part of the work of reflection, has the following tasks: to develop, refine and expand an under-standing of each person in the group; to keep in touch with the dynamics of the group as a whole and as it develops over time; to keep in touch with one's own feelings and to note one's own behaviour and its consequences; and to perceive connections between the group and individual dynamics.

Self-observation

If one is reflecting in a process-oriented way then one is including oneself as part of the equation of evaluation. Given the range of feelings which are part of group life and the projection of painful feelings, a group leader has to act as a projection receptacle and has to be able to bear being used for this purpose (Tourquet 1974). So for the leader of a group to become aware of his or her own feelings can significantly help him/her not only to control his/her expressions and behaviour appropriately, but also to be able to contain feelings which are aroused in reaction to the losses, hurts and needs of others. The use of the leader/teacher's observing ego is essential here. A group leader is like an ego, Janus-like, looking inside and outside (the group and him/herself) as participant and observer (Tourquet 1974).

Group processes and interactions are enormously complex, and it is a demanding task to forge and maintain self-awareness in the face of such

213

dynamic complexity. By way of example of some of the issues which group leaders face in this regard, I refer to Whitaker's (1985) series of questions which group leaders might consider in relation to their role and the group dynamic. What are the implications for the group of the group leader becoming fascinated by the circumstances of problems of one member to the detriment of the rest of the group? What are the implications for a group leader's relationship with a group if someone in the group violates a personally held norm or a norm which the leader/teacher considers essential to the continuing usefulness of the group? Is it possible that sometimes the group leader/teacher gets caught up in the same fears as group members and colludes with some 'restrictive solution' (i.e. an adaptation which reinforces defence mechanisms)? Whitaker acknowledges that since groups move too quickly and the import of events cannot always be registered in time, all group leaders/teachers are bound to miss some of the opportunities for development presented by group events, and to take actions in the group which may be inappropriate to helping the group with its primary task. She maintains that if an issue is important within the context of a particular group's dynamics, it will enter the group in a similar form, thus providing further opportunities for exploration.

Given the possible negative impact upon the leader of group dynamics, leaders also need to be vigilant about the personal effects of working with such potentials. To some degree everyone in authority uses his/her role as a defence against anxieties, by, for example, developing a sense of detachment. Some detachment is necessary to gain perspective, but there is a danger in taking this too far: 'The role may in extreme cases become so important as a form of defensive organisation that the task it was designed to carry out suffers' (Reed and Palmer 1972: 12). There are many fine lines to be mediated here. The need to demonstrate genuineness, trust and empathy (see Chapter Three) has to be balanced with developing skill in coping with the pressure which large groups generate. 'The danger is that the form of personality organisation which is developed becomes a rigid persona, a platform manner which the individual is unable to relax or modify' (Reed and Palmer 1972, Lecture 3: 14).

Symbols of the whole group

The group does not become an emotionally important, or sentient, group for the individual – from which s/he derives symbolic meaning – unless it can be developed in the individual's mind as a good symbol. This skill involves developing symbolic structures which reflect the potential wholeness of the group in its totality – its vision, its task, the value of the group as a medium for the task, and how this might translate for the individuals within it. This is difficult since it requires work with the paradoxical struggle of facilitating a positive identity with the group, and of developing individual identity within the group. Where group members relate (either consciously or unconsciously) to the symbolic structures of group wholeness, this will inform the nature of the psychological contract which they make with the group, giving their participation greater meaning. Symbolic reminders of wholeness also offer a further level of containment for potentially destructive group dynamics and work against defences such as splitting.

Boundary control

The boundary of the group helps to define it, and holds the persons and things of a group together. It may function partially through the timetable on which the group expects to meet, the regular nature of the membership of the group, the expectations regarding the group's activities. The role of the group membership helps to define the boundary of the group, which has implications for the feelings aroused when group membership changes.

The leader's work on boundary control relates to both the physical and psychological boundaries. Physical boundary control involves issues to do with the way in which group members physically enter and leave the group – their manner of coming in and going out, their presence or absence in the group, and so on. Psychological boundary control is much more complex, and relates to the management of issues which psychologically belong inside or outside the group. For example, what 'material' brought to the group is confidential to the group? In what circumstances might confidentiality be broken, and how might this be negotiated with group members? Are there times when the group's actions have implications beyond the group for the rest of the organisation? Are there times when it is appropriate for the group leader/teacher to refer to events which happen outside the group within the boundary of the group, and what are the implications for the group dynamics of so doing? The communications about such boundaries have implications for group identity, the capacity of individuals to engage with the group and the group's relationships with other groups in the environment. (The last of these issues is considered after the following example.)

Example: Joining a group

This is an example taken from work with a group of adults. Twelve teachers came together as participants in a twelve-session course. In the first session they were asked to reflect upon what they needed from each other in order to be able to learn effectively together over the subsequent sessions. These reflections were then shared and discussed, and formulated into an informal contract. The flip-chart version of this was pinned on the wall in subsequent sessions of the course, and for the first few sessions participants were asked if they wanted to make any further comments about the contract, for example, whether they wished to add anything further or there was anything which they were unhappy about.

Two of the participants were not present at the first session of the course. At the beginning of the second session these two teachers were welcomed onto the course, they were given feedback from the previous week, the contract was explained, and they, along with the rest of the group, were invited to comment, or make any changes.

It was not until several sessions later these two teachers were able to acknowledge that, even though the contract had been explained to them and they had been invited to contribute, it had never been meaningful to them and they had never felt part of it because they had not been part of the group when it had been formulated.

The contract represented a significant part of this group's identity, of its boundary – who and what was in the group and who and what was outside. Even when I, as facilitator, considered that I had gone to some lengths to facilitate identity and engagement through this boundary mechanism, the two participants referred to had not, subjectively, felt able to engage in the contract.

Another aspect of boundary control is the management of the interface of the group and its environment. The group's relationship with its environment presents a further dimension of determining group identity – what the group is and what it is not. An important element of a group's environment is the other groups operating in the environment. Studies have shown (e.g. Higgin and Bridger 1965) that inter-group relations often involve much rivalry and the emergence of myths about each other's experiences. So an aspect of boundary control is the management of the relationship of a group's perceptions about itself with its perception of other, perhaps rival, groups in the environment.

Issues of emotional containment and dependency

It is important not only that individuals within the group feel emotionally contained by the group leader/teacher (see Chapter Four) but that the group *as a whole* feels safe, emotionally contained. The teacher might demonstrate his/her capacity to contain the group, at one level, through a range of practical measures, such as reliability in relation to time-keeping, the organisation of children's work, the management of classroom re-sources and the upkeep of displays and other aspects of the environment. The sense of group safety will be further established and maintained by the teacher through his/her management of tensions, rivalries, conflicts and fears between group members. In addition to these management functions, the teacher who is also able to demonstrate the capacity to understand, tolerate and reflect upon the difficult feelings which emerge in the group provides a significantly more meaningful 'container' for, or sense of safety in, the group. With such a sense of safety group members are able gradually to give their trust to the group and its processes, and thus open themselves to greater possibilities of change and growth.

If members of the group do not experience the group situation as a safe

216

enough environment they will not stay in it, but will either flee or psychologically insulate themselves from the experience. Feeling safe enough means:

> experiencing a degree of ease, trust and confidence in self and others which makes it possible to stay in the group and begin to take risks in it. This does not imply comfort or the absence of all threat or challenge. 'Too safe' is sinking so comfortably into a customary or preferred interpersonal position that nothing new is experienced or tried. 'Unsafeness' is feeling so perturbed and alarmed at the bad things that could happen that the only way to protect oneself is to get away.
>
> (Whitaker 1985: 226)

Group members may establish routes of safety within a group by operating within what Whitaker terms 'restrictive solutions', such as interacting only with the leader, withdrawing into solitary activities, disowning their own problems, interacting with subgroups but avoiding the whole group. Whilst such adaptations enable members to feel safe, Whitaker argues, they also avoid the risks of emotional development. They have value where they can be used incrementally to build up a greater repertoire of ways of feeling safe within the group. The danger is that the boundaries within which the individuals are operating become so narrow that little in the way of useful exploration, social comparison, feedback etc., can take place (Whitaker 1985). It is part of the leader/teacher's task to monitor this aspect of the group's functioning and look to ways of helping members give up 'restrictive solutions' in favour of being open to emotional growth and development within the group.

Another fine line with which the group leader is working is that of dependency. In containing disturbing feelings one is not seeking to take the pain away, to make things feel better, but to demonstrate that there can be thought and understanding of the feelings. Yet for this process to happen there needs to be trust, some way in which the children can feel dependent upon the adult (Chapters Two and Four). Since children with emotional/behavioural difficulties often have to struggle both to avoid omnipotence and to achieve the capacity to allow themselves to be dependent, and then to move into a more genuine independence, testing out in relation to dependency is an important part of the developmental process. So in some ways it is a necessary and healthy part of group experience. But the danger is that dependence might be used as a form of defence against the task (see section on 'Group processes which inhibit development' in this chapter). Managing the fine lines and subtle meanings in relation to dependency in groups is a complex task.

During the final phase of a group's life, the issue of emotional containment is highlighted: a sense of threat can escalate, particularly, Whitaker

217

(1985) points out, if the prospect of separation resonates sharply with important and unresolved feelings and fears on the part of a number of members (see Chapter Four, section on 'Beginnings and endings').

Establishing and maintaining supportive group norms

In the earlier sections of this chapter both the value and the dangers of group norms were discussed.

> Balint explains that collaborative group norms follow from the leader's behavior in allowing everyone to be themselves, to have their own say and in their own time . . . instead of prescribing the right way to deal with the problem under discussion, opening up possibilities for group members to discover the right answer.
>
> (Perlman 1992: 186–7)

Helping a group to establish and maintain supportive group norms (Whitaker 1985) is generated partly through the sense of safety in a group. The group will be more effective in promoting emotional growth and learning if members can establish norms which are helpful and supportive to members in expressing their feelings and trying out new behaviours. The question is how to help group members feel safe *and yet also* be prepared to take risks without resorting to threatening others. An important way of establishing and maintaining supportive group norms is by making use of events in the group for the benefit of group members (a notion introduced by Whitaker 1985). One can make use of group events for members' benefit on either a collective, i.e. whole-group, or an individual basis. The sort of issue that one might work with on a collective basis is given in the following example.

Example: Feedback to a group

I observed a teacher in a high school introduce a topic to a class, described by the teacher as not engaging well with the subject. In their first lesson on a new topic the members of the class were invited to work in groups and to brainstorm what they already knew about the topic. The activity went very well – the students were all actively engaged in the task, and each small group had lively discussion and produced large diagrams which logged their discussions. Given this teacher's concern about the psychological contract this group was making with its task, I was surprised when the teacher did not appear to make use of the successful way the pupils had worked together on this activity. By deploying our knowledge and experience of group dynamics, teachers/group leaders might comment upon such experiences as the above to establish and reinforce supportive group norms, and so enable the group to build on positive experiences and to develop and extend its work.

In terms of interventions which make use of the group for the benefit of individual members, it is possible for teachers and other group leaders to intervene to enable group members to reflect upon their experiences of the group, and to make use of this shared experience in relation to the particular needs of individuals within the group. Group leaders have a role in establishing both a general ethos, and particular structures or activities, which invite group members to bring their individual experiences of the group into the arena of group discussion. There are a number of ways of doing this, including sharing a personal view or opinion, supporting individuals in acknowledging feelings, giving and reinforcing feedback to others in the group, acknowledging the new accomplishments and understandings of other group members, and emphasising an important breakthrough (Whitaker 1985). Once the group leader/teacher is successful in facilitating these sorts of process within the group, s/he potentially has a further role in making explicit the links between different group members' experiences. For instance, 'So does that help you to see that if you do . . . that makes so and so feel . . .'. Children may also be helped to achieve insight into their problems of social adjustment by the leader/teacher non-judgementally reflecting back to them the manner in which they interact when working and playing with the others.

Working with difference and facilitating multiplicity

Working to promote positive attitudes towards difference and pluralism in the group is one of the most essential yet perhaps one of the most difficult tasks in facilitating group processes for the benefit of members. The defence mechanisms which work against the acknowledgement and valuing of difference are strong: those managing groups walk a fine line between maintaining a positive *group* identity and enabling children with emotional difficulties to develop more of their own *individual* identity. Being both an individual within the group and yet a fully participating member of the group, without identifying with one extreme or the other, demands significant internal resources. For it demands the capacity to be able to struggle with these competing demands, weigh them up, acknowledge them, without falling victim to impulsive desires. In Kleinian terms, this is the capacity to experience 'depressively', rather than in a paranoid-schizoid manner (see Chapter Two).

Example: An open-ended group task

This example is drawn from work with adults rather than children. It serves as a demonstration of the processes under discussion.

In a training session on the development of counselling skills the group of about twenty people faced the open-ended task of deciding how they were going to use a forthcoming session. There was first a period of uncomfortable quietness in which there were some very tentative and short comments of a very general nature. Then one or two people made some practical suggestions, there was a rush by a good number of group members to take up these suggestions – it was as if everyone wanted to join immediately the bandwagon of a possibly viable suggestion. I commented that perhaps it was difficult to be an individual in the group. The group members were able to take stock of what was happening and individuals were able to voice a number of different needs and desires. Some sessions later some group members commented on the usefulness of being helped to be an individual in the group.

The facilitator's task is to allow difference to be possible in the group, in relation to feelings and the inner world, and the more obvious overt behaviours, interests, cultures, attitudes which manifest in the external world. This might involve acknowledging to group members the value of, and the struggle we have with, difference and the multiplicity of experience. In relation to this issue the function of the group leader also lies in enabling group members to experience the many-sidedness and ambiguities of life in the group, in contrast to relating largely out of fantasies, assumptions and omnipotence. Such a group is likely to be able to relate to the leader by being:

> able to entertain ideas and feelings of trust and support without seeking to create a concrete embodiment of a wholly dependable and supporting leader or institution. Actual leaders and institutions are regarded with a blend of trust and mistrust, the appropriateness of which is (from time to time) assessed.
>
> (Reed and Palmer 1972, Lecture 2: 15)

Being able to tolerate and incorporate the capacity for what Klein termed 'depressive' experience includes the group being able to face and mourn its own ending, when it is about to disband. (See Chapter Four, section on 'Beginnings and endings'.)

> If the ending is accepted and worked for, with all the feelings of let-down, anger and regret for lost opportunities which this entails, its members may be released to use what they have got out of the group in other groups and situations. In practice people often behave as though the dissolution of the group would be the end of them too.
>
> (Reed and Palmer 1972, Lecture 2: 16)

Members of the group then fall back into 'paranoid-schizoid' experience, inventing other tasks, planning reunions, or alternatively killing off the psychological contract with the group prematurely to avoid the pain of the closing stages.

One way of demonstrating and modelling the struggle with many-sidedness is for the teacher to voice a range of feelings about various events in group life – to acknowledge pleasure at success, and disappointment when things go wrong, for example. One way of doing this relates to the way one acknowledges and deals with the mistakes that one has made oneself. Where the teacher/group leader makes mistakes in relation to particular individuals in the group – perhaps, for example, through a lack of patience or some other insensitivity – then some form of reconciliation or apology initiated by the group leader can be very helpful not only for the individual concerned, but for the group as a whole. The leader thereby demonstrates that that particular group can be one in which the inner omnipotent voices (for example saying 'I'm right') can be struggled with, and aid reconciliation and the development of relationships of a more balanced kind.

The skills discussed in this fourth section of the chapter are relevant to managing and facilitating not only groups, but also the wider organisation. The relationship of these arguments to managing the school or other organisation is considered in Chapter Nine.

Exerise: Managing and facilitating group processes

*/**

Reflect upon the group(s) which you manage or facilitate. What are your areas of strength in facilitating groups? Which skills would it be useful for you to pay particular attention to, to help your development as a group manager/facilitator?

Exercise: What do you need from peers in groups?

*

Think about a group which you are soon to join, or a group of which you are currently a member. What will or do you need from your peers in that group?

***

As a group exercise this is appropriate at the beginning of a group's working life, e.g. at the beginning of a course, or the coming together of a new team.

Consider what you will need from each other to help your work together.

SUMMARY

- Group processes exert a powerful impact upon development and need to be considered in their own right.
- The group offers much potential as a medium for helping with emotional growth and learning. Groups offer each individual the

possibility of assessing his/her own experience against that of a range of other people, and thus of coming into contact with hitherto unrealised aspects of him/herself. The group offers significant opportunities to bridge the experiences and feelings of inner realities with a range of social realities. It is as if there is a 'group ego' against which one can test and assess oneself, which forms both an expectation and a measure of development. Groups potentially offer the experience of a matrix, a womb, which nurtures the capacity for trust. Groups provide powerful opportunities for meaningful relationships with others through the experience of kinship. Groups provide diverse environments, reflecting the needs of the pluralist psyche.

- However, groups can also be anxiety-provoking and even frightening. Group phenomena can also serve to inhibit development. There is always a struggle for individuals to experience reflectively both the need and desire for individual identity and the need and desire for group identity, without furthering one of these at the expense of the other. Groups develop defensive norms and beliefs against anxieties. It is particularly difficult for group members to come to tolerate and be able to work with difference within the group. Tasks may be avoided through the mechanisms of dependency, flight/fight or pairing. Defensive and regressive processes in groups can become 'contagious'.

- The impact of group size and stage also have significant effects upon the dynamic of groups.

- Managing and facilitating group processes in a way which supports emotional growth and learning requires clear task definition and sustaining the values, roles and boundaries to achieve the task; the capacity to keep in mind the whole group and each whole child; the capacity to mitigate defences and anti-task behaviour (in oneself and others); and the modelling of good 'management-cum-ego' functioning (Menzies Lyth 1988).

- Managing and facilitating group processes requires the capacity to reflect upon process, and considerable self-awareness. Groups are helped where symbolic structures of their wholeness are provided; where boundary control issues are well managed; where there is emotional containment and the opportunities for some dependency without this reinforcing defence mechanisms; where supportive group norms are established and maintained; where events in the group can be related to the needs of individual members; and where it is possible to acknowledge and explore differences in experience in the group.

- These group phenomena are relevant to any group. They are particularly obvious and pertinent where the individuals' capacities for awareness and management of feelings are at an early stage of development – hence their particular importance in work with children with emotional/behavioural difficulties.

8

MEDIATING THE CURRICULUM

INTRODUCTION

The curriculum is the planned learning offer of the school (Watkins 1989), with, among others, its moral, social, cultural dimensions. Given the requirements of the 1988 act, and often repeated aims about 'developing the full potential of every individual', teachers include personhood in the curriculum (Watkins 1989). The processes explored in Chapters Three to Seven inclusive are vital in facilitating the development of personhood, of enhancing the capacity for learning in children with emotional/behavioural difficulties, and are of significance for the way in which teachers deliver the curriculum. In particular I have hitherto explored ways in which adults can facilitate the emotional development of children, and thus enable those inhibited by emotional difficulties to participate in the curriculum better. Teachers encounter in learners a range of resistances, defences, and anxieties (which were discussed in Chapter One). In delivering the formal curriculum, teachers can find opportunities to help children to develop the necessary emotional resources for learning by providing the particular qualities of relationship discussed in earlier chapters, i.e. emotional holding and ego strengthening. It is the quality of teacher–pupil relationships, particularly teachers' capacities to provide emotional holding and strengthening, which determines the effectiveness of the strategies discussed in this chapter. This is a vital point, since it is the containment of potentially disturbing feelings that creates space in which there can be thought. It is as if thinking is made possible largely by the availability of internal emotional space for this activity. The strategies discussed in the second part of the chapter have an impact on supporting the necessary emotional development for learning when teachers bear in mind the holding and strengthening processes as a 'filter' for considering *how* the more practical strategies can be made use of.

Anecdotal evidence from my own work as an advisory teacher suggests that, with the pressures of the content and testing of the National Curriculum, teachers in the primary phase are finding it increasingly difficult to keep in mind the whole child when delivering the curriculum. In this chapter I examine current issues in curriculum planning for individual needs, in terms of a series of tensions. On a day-to-day basis the teacher faces many tensions in relation to planning for individual needs – pressure of time, and the tensions resulting from one's own feelings about those students who might be perceived as needing 'extra' time. In the first part of this chapter I consider the broad social, cultural and political influences upon educational organisations' capacities to meet individual learning needs. I explore the tensions encountered in terms of tensions between learning as 'process' and as 'content', between centralisation and decentralisation in curriculum control, between 'process' and 'objectives' models in curriculum planning, development and evaluation, between entitlement and expediency in curriculum organisation and access, and between active/participative and didactic/transmissive teaching and learning styles.

The second part of the chapter considers the more practical aspects of mediating and differentiating the curriculum to take account of emotional factors in learning. A child's developing ego strength is more likely to be mobilised for learning where the teacher builds bridges to the curriculum and organises the classroom and activities to maximise learners' opportunities to experience success. In the second part of the chapter I explore these tasks in relation to what I describe as the 'anxiety–risk ratio', the use made of curriculum-based assessment, teaching and learning styles, the structuring of learning tasks, promoting access to materials and resources, and positive reinforcement. Success in learning provides valuable and tangible opportunities for the learner to experience a sense of her/his achievement and potential for further success. When teachers take account of such factors as these, and deliver the curriculum in a manner which meets learners' affective and emotional needs, this benefits all pupils. Near the end of the chapter is a note about the particular needs of gifted and able pupils.

The teacher has an important role in mediating the curriculum so as to prevent manifestations of unease which disrupt learning. It goes without saying that the quality of classroom management has a significant effect on the manifestation of behavioural difficulties, and that classroom management has a significant preventative role. This notion is reflected in Galloway and Goodwin's (1987, quoted in Mongan and Hart 1989: 91) more general comment: 'The most effective procedures for preventing, rather than treating, disturbing or maladjusted behaviour are a by-product of processes which aim to raise the overall quality of education for *all* pupils in the school.' The main focuses of this chapter should be considered in the context of an acknowledgement of the issues for effective and proactive classroom management, which is provided through the following exercise.

Exercise: Preventing disruptive behaviour in the classroom

*/**/***

This activity may be conducted as a ranking exercise. You may like to make the statements below available on cards. Group members can then be asked to rank the cards in levels of importance, either as an entire set, or in the three subsets indicated.

The teacher

- The teacher *feels* prepared.
- The teacher has an awareness of his/her own non-verbal messages and a capacity to make use of non-verbal communication.
- The teacher feels and appears relaxed.
- Teaching by example: the teacher models attitudes and behaviour expected of the pupils.
- The teacher has the ability to turn negative comments into positive experiences.

The curriculum

- A variety of activities and methods are used.
- Objectives for the lesson are made clear early on, and pupils understand what these are.
- The curriculum is delivered in the context of a plan to ensure continuity and progression.
- Learning tasks cater for the range of learners' attainments in the group.
- The needs of all pupils are considered in lesson planning and delivery.
- The lesson plan is flexible.
- There is some choice of activities.
- The teacher evaluates his/her own lessons.
- The teacher uses questions to check comprehension.

Classroom management

- The teacher is perceived to be fair by pupils.
- The classroom layout is suitable for the task.
- Materials and resources are accessible for pupil use.
- Pupils are admitted in an orderly way.
- Pupils leave the room in an orderly way.
- Lessons get off to a brisk and interesting start.

- Routines, expectations and ground rules about learning and behaviour are made clear.
- The teacher is aware of what the whole class and individual pupils are doing.
- The class is given feedback on performance during/at the end of the lesson.

However skilful the teacher is in putting into practice the features identified in the above exercise, pupils' emotional needs require attention through planning to meet individual needs.

TENSIONS IN CURRICULUM PLANNING TO MEET INDIVIDUAL NEEDS

The first tension I examine is that between *learning as process and learning as content*. Managing teaching and learning to meet these needs requires as much emphasis on *how* people learn (the process of learning) as on *what* they learn (the content of learning). The notion of learning as process is currently being reinforced in a number of ways. First, at a time of rapid social and technological change 'the most essential needs of tomorrow's citizens . . . will be those skills which are of general application . . . together with positive and flexible attitudes' (Everard and Morris 1990: 191). Secondly, the developing understanding of special educational needs as a function of interaction within a social context (highlighted in the introductory chapter) also reinforces the notion of learning as a 'process'. Referring to the Warnock Report (DES 1978), Ainscow and Florek (1989) suggest that 'post-Warnock thinking' acknowledges that any child might experience difficulties in school at some stage and perceives educational difficulties as resulting from an interaction between what the child brings to the situation and what the school has to offer. This implies that teachers should take responsibility for the progress of all children in their classes and that support should be available to staff as they attempt to meet their responsibilities.

Such developments help us to view learning as a 'process', with the emphasis on learning how to learn, and how to be open to and evaluate new concepts (Ferguson 1982). This enables teaching to be viewed as a 'purposeful interaction intended to promote learning' (Tomlinson and Kilner n.d.: 6). Such thinking indicates the importance of making the curriculum offered to all children more responsive to the needs of individuals. Tomlinson and Kilner (n.d.) argue that the current emphases of government-financed flexible learning initiatives are corroborated by current educational theory and research.

However, the introduction of the National Curriculum has tended to reinforce the concept of learning as 'content'. The more negative effects of the Education Reform Act upon learners with emotional and behavioural difficulties – e.g. the effects of open enrolment and the publication of exam and Standard Assessment Test results (see introductory chapter) – have reinforced what Ainscow and Florek (1989) term 'pre-Warnock' thinking. This is based on the assumptions that a group of children can be identified who are different from the majority, that the problems of these children are a result of their disabilities or personal limitations, and that once such a group has been provided for, the rest of the school population can be regarded as 'normal'.

These tensions in the perception of learning as 'process' or 'content' are a reflection of tensions between different values in society, a debate which is currently overtly politically driven. As Morrison and Ridley (1989: 41) point out, 'the curriculum is value-based. It is founded on the principle of protection and neglect of selected values.'

This brings me to the second tension to explore, that between *central-isation and decentralisation in curriculum control.* Individual needs might best be catered for where the curriculum is determined as close to the learner as possible, or in partnership with the learner, i.e. where curriculum control is decentralised. Educational organisations are 'structurally loose' (Weick 1976), and despite the Education Reform Act and its implement-ation, a relatively decentralised approach remains since decision-making is diffused through all levels of the educational system, the diversity of institu-tions is increasing, and some teacher autonomy is retained. Shipman (1990: 126) argues that 'the evidence . . . points to the continuing ability of teachers to move the service in the direction dictated by their experience with children in the classroom'.

However, factors which reinforce central curriculum control have strengthened massively. The introduction of a centrally determined cur-riculum and league tables might be seen to serve to reinforce Handy's notion that 'schools see their students as products' (1989: 173). The way in which the National Curriculum is taken up with questions of delivery, with attempts to specify objectives and end points in learning sequences through levels and statements of attainment, has 'serious implications for the status of the learner. Failures of curriculum can be "explained" by blaming the child for not learning efficiently, for being "different" in a negatively viewed way' (Thompson and Barton 1992: 14). Where such views take hold it becomes increasingly difficult for the teacher to mediate the curriculum in the interests of the learning of pupils with emotional/behavioural difficulties.

The tension between *'process' and 'objectives' models in curriculum planning, development and evaluation* refers to the difference between those models which embrace a 'process' view of learning and those which are premised on learning as an exclusively rational activity. Kelly (1989) argues that

227

objective, rational models fail to allow for individual interests, ambitions or autonomy. It is process models that are more likely to help teachers cater for individual needs. Preedy (1988) notes that process models assert the importance of negotiation in the curriculum, and aims to accommodate different perspectives between teaching colleagues, between teacher and student, and between students. However, Kelly (1989) asserts that Her Majesty's Inspectorate have hitherto been committed to an objectives approach to curriculum planning, and suggests that the demands for accountability in education also tend to encourage the use of objectives-based curriculum models.

With regard to evaluation of the curriculum, objectives-based curriculum evaluation models, which rely on positivistic, quasi-scientific, quantitative methods, contrast with the 'process' model approach of reflective and qualitative approaches to evaluation, which stress the interaction between the curriculum, learner, teacher and context. The process approach emphasises teachers' understanding of learners' individual needs and the importance of a variety of learning methods and opportunities. Currently, the trend of emphasising learning processes is reflected in the widespread use of pupil self-evaluation and profiling. (These are discussed further in the second part of the chapter.) However, the underlying focus on 'output' models of evaluation, which seek to quantify learning outcomes, has been strengthened by assessment procedures related to the National Curriculum, and by the notion of examination league tables. This focus has been bolstered by factors like increased parental and political concern, and competition between educational institutions premised on declining roles and closures. The increasing use of 'pencil and paper' Standard Assessment Tests, and the recent reductions in coursework assessment for GCSE, reinforce the trend towards the use of objectives-based curriculum development models.

There is a tension between *entitlement and expediency in curriculum organisation and access* which has arisen as a result of the Education Reform Act (1988). The Act established in law the principle that each pupil should receive a broad and balanced curriculum which is also relevant to his/her individual needs. 'That principle must be reflected in the curriculum of every pupil. It is not enough for such a curriculum to be offered by the school. It must be fully taken up by each individual pupil' (DES 1989d: 2.2). Section 1 of the Act states that all pupils are entitled to the whole curriculum, not just the core. In the context of an 'entitlement curriculum', every teacher has a teaching responsibility to pupils with special educational needs. The National Curriculum Council (1989b: 1) links this responsibility to the process of teaching all pupils. 'Participation in the National Curriculum by pupils with SEN is most likely to be achieved by encouraging good practice for all pupils. Special educational needs are not just a reflection of pupils' inherent difficulties or disabilities; they are often related to factors within schools which can prevent or exacerbate some problems.' Delivering the curriculum in a manner which meets children's affective and emotional needs has benefits for all pupils.

However, a legal entitlement and consequent work to promote access to a prescribed curriculum may not be the most effective means of catering for individual needs, because of the potential mismatch between content and need. Hart (1992) points out that these legal requirements are encouraging schools to group children in 'sets' according to their attainment:

> Urging teachers to differentiate their teaching further at a time of general overload of work may make the task seem so daunting or so unrealistic that teachers may well conclude that the only sensible solution is to revert to setting or separate grouping of children in order to fulfil their responsibilities for providing for differences while rationalising the use of scarce resources. There is anecdotal evidence that this process is already under way in both primary and secondary schools. . . . One of the reasons for the abandonment of streaming, setting, remedial classes and so on in the past was our growing awareness of the impact which such groupings could have upon teachers' and pupils' expectations and upon the learning opportunities made available.
>
> (Hart 1992: 10–11)

The tension between *participative and transmissive teaching and learning styles* continues. Kyriacou (1991: 1) argues that 'effective teaching is primarily concerned with setting up a learning activity for each pupil which is successful in bringing about the type of learning the teacher intends'. This takes place where a range of learning opportunities cater for individual needs, and particularly so where responsibilities for learning are extended to the learner. 'Learners do best when they know what they are supposed to be doing and can take responsibility' (Shipman 1990: 30). A number of initiatives have sought to increase learner responsibility, for example, the formative stages of Records of Achievement work (in which learners evaluate their progress and set further goals), the Flexible Learning Project's encouragement for teachers to negotiate targets with learners, and TVEI's encouragement of learning activities which foster problem-solving, enterprise, and work in groups. The nationwide nature of such initiatives indicates that participative learning is increasingly at least considered by schools and colleges.

In contrast, didactic methods of teaching, which assume a relative degree of learner passivity and a more uniform delivery, are less likely to take account of, or to meet, individual needs. Yet 'It is still largely the case in many organizations that the prevailing orthodoxy is the conventional, "didactic" and teacher-centred approach' (University of Keele 1992a: 16). The continued dominance of transmission teaching is explained by Dennison and Kirk (1990) in terms of a number of factors. These are the ready fit of the transmissive approach within the existing institutional framework of educational organisations, its easier adaptation for accountability purposes, the relative ease of designating objectives, designing teaching programmes and examining students, the security which the didactic exam-oriented mode provides, and the relative 'tidiness' of transmission modes in contrast to the perceived 'messiness' of experiential methods. Dennison and Kirk suggest that teachers prefer the conventional mode because their knowledge is subject-based. Hargreaves (1982: 195) comments that a 'teacher's authority ultimately rests in the authority of his subject. For such a teacher his subject expertise is absolutely central to his identity.' The introduction of the National Curriculum, along with the publication of test and exam results, has reinforced the subject-based focus.

I have highlighted a range of tensions in relating the curriculum to individual needs. This range provides a background against which teachers operate in their day-to-day work of making the curriculum accessible to learners with a variety of needs. In the following section, I discuss the issues involved in differentiating the curriculum to meet special educational needs related to emotional/behavioural difficulties. In doing so, I take some of the generally accepted approaches to differentiation, and add a perspective about developing the necessary emotional or inner resources for learning.

DIFFERENTIATION AND EMOTIONAL FACTORS IN LEARNING

Differentiation is the term given to the process of planning and delivering the curriculum, teaching methods, assessment methods, resources and learning activities to cater for the needs of individual pupils. The legal requirement of the Education Reform Act for the curriculum to be relevant to individual needs rests uneasily with the range of background conflicts in providing a differentiated curriculum which were considered above. In what follows I consider ways in which the forces which support the meeting of individual needs may be harnessed in more direct and practical ways, and with particular reference to emotional factors in learning.

A framework for organising the curriculum to benefit all children becomes most achievable where its underlying principles are consistent across the school. A whole-school policy can usefully ensure that principles for facilitating access to the curriculum are reflected in all curricular areas. The National Curriculum Council (1989a: 8) points out that pupils with special educational needs are likely to have even stronger needs than other pupils for 'positive attitudes from school staff who are determined to ensure their participation in the National Curriculum'. Maximising access to the curriculum for all pupils, through differentiation of the curriculum, is now widely recognised as good practice. 'Within any group of pupils there will be a wide range of ability and experience. This calls for a flexible approach allowing for differentiation to provide success and challenges for them all' (National Curriculum Council 1989a). Ainscow (1989) argues that teachers are able to meet individual needs where they know well pupils' existing skills and knowledge, interests and previous experiences, where they help pupils to establish a sense of personal meaning about the tasks and activities in which they are engaged, and where teachers organise classrooms in ways which encourage involvement and effort. Weston (1992) suggests that a most important aspect of differentiating the curriculum is the structuring of learning activities within the classroom to ensure that all learners can perform to the best of their ability. This reflects what the DES has termed a 'dispersed' approach (Stradling and Saunders 1991), in which attempts to encompass the needs of all attainers are made within the provision and policy for all pupils in a year group, subject area or whole school.

Organising activities to maximise successful learning outcomes is particularly important for children experiencing emotional difficulties, since their ego fragility may be reinforced by their failures in learning tasks. A key factor in mediating the curriculum successfully for pupils with emotional difficulties is the teacher's appreciation of what might be termed the 'anxiety–risk ratio'. This refers to the ratio between the amount of risk experienced in a activity, and the amount of anxiety which might be experienced by the learner. Unconscious anxiety can be a major factor in impeding learning and development (see Chapter Two). Risk-taking and 'reinventing' to make an idea one's own, so much a part of learning, may reinforce or trigger other latent or actual anxieties for the child. One of our tasks as teachers is to enable the child to achieve success at the limits of the autonomy of which s/he is capable. For this, learning tasks have to arouse some, not too much, anxiety and yet involve the child in enough risk to get a sense of being able to be independent. For the teacher to pay attention to the anxiety–risk ratio is particularly important for those learners who are negotiating emotional barriers to learning. Pupils with special educational needs are likely to have stronger needs than other pupils for 'a climate of warmth and support in which self-confidence and self-esteem can grow and in which all pupils feel valued and able to risk making mistakes as they learn, without fear of criticism' (National Curriculum Council 1989a: 8). The limits of autonomy might more effectively be incrementally pushed further when the starting-point for learning takes account of the child's particular vulnerabilities and capacities to take risks. There may be an unconscious internal pressure for the child to test whether s/he is as useless as s/he feels, or whether there is a possibility that s/he may be of some value. If the child can experience a sense of his/her own success and value, that is the basis upon which it is possible to build a more positive and regenerative self-esteem.

A further, key, underlying emotional issue in providing a differentiated curriculum is the management of difference within the classroom. The difficulties we have in acknowledging and coming to terms with difference in groups were explored in Chapter Seven, as were some ideas about managing difference in groups. In relation to mediating the curriculum, the issue of difference between learners manifests itself in many ways: different prior knowledge, skills and experiences, different interests, different pace of learning, different preferred learning styles, different expectations, differing parental support, different patterns of engagement, different attainments, etc. As Weston (1992) points out, differentiation is premised on diversity. She argues that 'it will be more difficult or impossible in future to ignore diversity within classrooms which has always existed but will be now much more fully and publicly documented' (Weston 1992: 6). In managing the emotional aspects of differentiation, it is the teacher's capacity to work with difference which becomes significant. For example, to what extent does the teacher create a climate in which differences are not only tolerated but valued? How does implementation of the school's equal opportunities and multi-cultural policies contribute to learners' understanding and valuing of difference? How does personal and social education contribute to this dimension? How does the school (or other organisation) help staff to value the different contributions which they make?

Exercise: Managing difference

*/**/***

1　In what ways do you enable differences to be valued in your practice?
2　How might you extend your practice in this area?

The technical issues in differentiating the curriculum are shown in Figure 26. The various aspects of this diagram are explored below in relation to curriculum delivery and emotional development. It is the intention here not to elaborate the technical aspects of differentation, but to highlight the emotional aspects of the processes involved.

Curriculum-based assessment

The assessment of pupil progress, and the use of such assessments as a basis for further teaching, are a significant element in meeting learners' individual needs. This is the case in relation to the teaching of all children (e.g. DES and the Welsh Office 1987). There is an essential link between

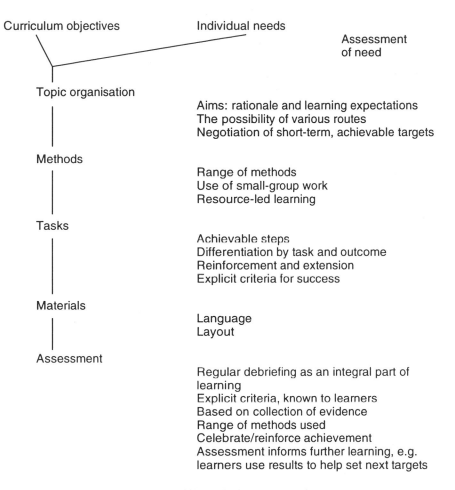

Figure 26 Differentiation: an overview

diagnostic assessment and effective task differentiation (Weston 1992). It is necessary to know what a pupil already knows, understands and can do before the teacher can effectively facilitate his/her success in a task. Information about pupils' functioning in terms of knowledge, understanding and skill is particularly important for those children for whom the anxiety–risk ratio is of significance in their learning. In line with a recurring theme in this book, I suggest that it is useful to have a sense of *how* the child learns, as well as the content, or *what* s/he has learned. The capacity to be aware of how a child learns may provide important diagnostic cues which help understanding of the pupil's subjective world, or personal constructs, and which can be used to help engage the child in learning in a way which is

233

personally meaningful and relevant. Where the teacher is able to make the sorts of observations and assessments suggested in Chapter Three, section on 'Observing and assessing needs', a wealth of evidence is provided about the way in which the child engages with the curriculum.

It is vital to know as accurately as possible 'where the pupil is at' if the teacher is to respond appropriately to match learning tasks to knowledge, understanding, skill and the child's anxiety and capacity to risk, in a way which enables the pupil to achieve success and develop autonomy. Such a matching exercise also requires the teacher to be aware of the skills needed by pupils to undertake each particular learning task. Knowledge of what a pupil can do does not necessarily indicate in what way the pupil will proceed with learning. Daniels (1992) argued that different children may go through different routes to develop the same learning outcomes, and that teachers need to question their assumptions about starting-points in relation to outcomes, since different pupils have different needs in terms of the sequencing of activities.

Assessment is most effective where it supports learning and motivates learners. 'Assessment is inseparable from the teaching process since its prime purpose is to improve pupils' performance' (DES 1985b: 51, para. 134). The process of formative, ongoing, assessment is most helpful when it provides feedback which enables each learner to know what s/he can do well, to recognise his/her achievements and have them recognised by others, to know what is expected of him/her, and to have targets for future work. Where assessment is an integral part of learning, a sense of purpose is achieved by using criteria for success which are known to the learners (i.e. the learner knows the focus for assessment before undertaking the task). It is also important to use a range of methods of assessment, including self-assessment, to collect evidence as a basis for assessment, and to make use of assessments to help set further targets.

Weston (1992: 6) defines differentiation as 'the process of identifying, with each learner, the most effective strategies for achieving agreed targets'. Setting targets can be developed into personal action plans, based on a shared assessment of the current situation by teacher and pupil, in which pupils set goals for future work. Weston (1992) points out that working with more detailed profiles of individual learners demands the active participation of the pupil, a process which will affect the pattern of teacher–pupil relationships in many classrooms. Differentiation challenges classroom relationships to be more affectively creative. The process of negotiation required in shared assessment and goal setting allows at each point the 'psychological contract' (Handy and Aitken 1986) between teacher and pupil to be renegotiated and strengthened. Where the pupil has sufficient ego strength to participate in this process, it helps him/her to become more engaged and the teacher to have a mandate from the learner for further work. Pupils with special educational needs are likely to have stronger needs than other pupils for 'partnerships with teachers which encourage them to be active learners, helping to plan, build and evaluate their own learning programmes wherever possible' (National Curriculum Council 1989a: 8). It is imperative that negotiated goals relate to the pupil's development of autonomy, and that they make sense to the child's subjective perceptions of his/her needs.

Teaching and learning styles

Some of the current conflicts relating to the use of participative and transmissive teaching are acknowledged in the first part of this chapter. Here I briefly consider the use of varied teaching and learning styles to meet individual needs. There has been much research which shows that we all learn in slightly different ways. Kolb (1984), for example, differentiates a range of learning styles which variously favour concrete experience, reflective observation, active experimentation and abstract conceptualisation. A four-fold model is reflected in many psychological theories, such as Jung's typology of thinking, feeling, intuition and sensation (Jung 1971), and the four members of a person's nature with which the educator works in Steiner education (Edmunds 1979, Steiner 1965).

Where learners have opportunities to make use of their preferred learning styles they have greater opportunities for success in learning. Where anxiety is a significant factor in inhibiting a child's learning, the need to demonstrate clear examples of success and to enhance ego strength, indicates that more concrete methods of exploration and learning may be more appropriate in the early stages of development, moving towards the more analytic approaches as appropriate. Where it is impractical to select particular methods for particular pupils, it is important that the teacher uses a range of methods, thus enabling each pupil to have regular opportunities for enhanced success in learning by sometimes being able to use a personally appropriate method. The use of a range of learning approaches within a classroom makes powerful communications about catering for difference and diversity (issues addressed in Chapter Seven). Using a range of methods provides opportunities to generate collaborative experiences, and, if necessary, to train children in such approaches (see Chapter Six).

The value of group work for learning is being increasingly recognised in recent years (e.g. Dunne and Bennett 1990, Galton and Williamson 1992). The potential power of the group as a means of stimulating emotional growth and development was explored in Chapter Seven, where some of the advantages of using group work to stimulate learning were mentioned. Ainscow (1989) argues that co-operative learning can have an effect on academic outcomes, self-esteem, social relationships and personal development. Some children with emotional/behavioural difficulties find working in groups very threatening. The issues involved in the arousal of threatening feelings in groups, and the implications for managing emotional process in groups, were considered in depth in Chapter Seven. With regard to using group work to deliver the curriculum, Figure 27 indicates useful stages in training pupils for group work, a process which minimises the sense of emotional threat, and so helps to facilitate success. There are many practical strategies for delivering the curriculum using group-work approaches, e.g. Hunt and Hitchin (1985), Jenkin (1989).

Learning tasks

One of the teacher's tasks is to enable the child to achieve success at the limits of autonomy of which s/he is capable. It is particularly important for those learners who are negotiating emotional barriers to learning for the teacher to pay attention to the anxiety–risk ratio. When the starting-point for learning takes account of the child's particular vulnerabilities and capacities to take risks, the limits of autonomy will be more effectively pushed further. Below I consider the structuring of learning tasks to take account of emotional factors, in terms of relating the tasks to the learners'

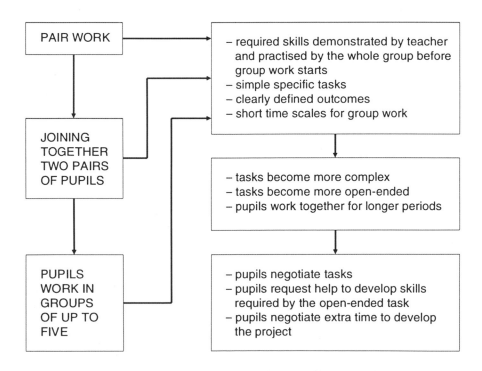

Figure 27 From work in pairs to work in groups
(Spillman 1991)

experiences, providing appropriate combination of stimuli/tasks, and providing bridges when confidence wavers.

Teachers can help to provide a bridge to involvement in learning, for those pupils who resist, by relating teaching and learning to pupils' own experiences. Personal construct theory, considered in Chapter One, section on 'Affect and learning', indicates that children need to construct their understanding of the curriculum out of their own real experiences. Ainscow (1989) argues that effective teachers help children to understand that there is meaning in what they are learning, and give a high priority to explaining the purpose of learning. The teacher has a vital role in linking the previous experience of children with the areas of potential learning. 'It is when teachers, through background experience or imaginative empathy, can enter into the life engagements of the young learners in their class that real educational breakthroughs are likely to occur' (Salmon 1988: 84). Sylvia Ashton-Warner, in describing her teaching of Maori children in New Zealand (1980), speaks powerfully of the need to relate to the children's experiences.

> in daring to 'hear' these children, to relate personally to them, Ashton-Warner managed to grasp something of their real experience. It was, in the end, her affirmation of this experience, by making it the curriculum of her teaching, which proved the turning point in the children's learning to read.
>
> (Salmon 1988: 55)

Where the curriculum and individual experience speak to each other, empowerment of the learners takes place. 'From the school they learn the ideas and principles by which to understand their own and other experiences, and the skills to influence their own situations' (Watkins 1989: 47). Where a learner can use his/her own subjective experience as a means of engaging more meaningfully with an issue, the potential is created for him/her to relate to the task imaginatively and creatively.

Where learning is inhibited by emotional difficulties, some of the difficulties may be projected (as explained in Chapter Two) onto a variety of people and things, with the consequence that the child might genuinely believe that it is other people or things which are the sources of the difficulties. Yet in order to engage in the problem-solving and explorations necessary for independent learning, the child needs to develop the capacity to empathise with other people. Those children who are struggling to establish boundaries between their own feelings and those of others also struggle to be able to empathise with others. Helping development in these areas requires that learning tasks be related to pupils' individual experiences of feelings. Feelings can be kept on the agenda in classrooms by explicitly referring to and exploring them in relation to the curriculum. We all have feelings, and this is a field in which each person's contributions are valid, since they relate to subjective experience. Egan (1992: 115) points to the value of a curriculum related to feelings when he reminds us that 'in oral cultures, in literature, in film and T.V., it has always been recognised that important meaning can very effectively be communicated by embedding it in affective images'. He makes what he describes as an 'uncontentious observation' that 'students' imaginations are more readily stimulated by content which engages their emotions than by content that doesn't' (Egan 1992: 71). Here, I am suggesting that we keep feelings on the classroom agenda both in terms of the *content* of the curriculum and to reflect on the *process* of learning together.

Examples of the ways in which feelings may be included across the curriculum are as follows:

- making use of pupils' own experiences, life stuations and feelings as a component of learning activities;
- relating the curriculum content to an affective message which identifies the 'transcendent human qualities' in the topic, and humanises the content in terms of how it relates to human hopes, fears, intentions or other emotions (Egan 1992);
- allowing pupils to explore the part emotion plays in people's lives;
- enabling pupils to explore the nature of relationships;
- allowing pupils to explore how people behave in the face of obstacles and pressures;
- suggesting that pupils explore their own affective responses to particular themes, such as 'Things I am afraid of', 'I wish I was somebody else', 'Things I like and things I hate', 'Things I wish I could do';
- asking pupils to evaluate an area of the curriculum, a lesson or an activity in subjective terms.

Example

I worked alongside a humanities teacher with a class of 12–13 year old boys in a setting where group work was not much used. We asked the class to work in groups and present their research to the class in the form of a poster. In the debriefing of this activity, I suggested to the class teacher that he elicit more of the students' affective responses to the experience. In this setting where such work was not yet the norm, this teacher was surprised by the depth of perceptions of the students. It also seemed to me that including the affective realm in a discussion about an activity which had required the students to take responsibility for their own learning helped the development of a positive and enthusiastic working alliance between this class and their teacher.

Learning may also be related to individual experiences by involving pupils in their own 'action-planning'. This involves asking pupils to set their goals for their own learning and negotiating a shared agreement with them. Maximising the amount of responsibility a learner can take for his/her own learning facilitates the development of ownership and involvement (Eraut *et al.* n.d.). Negotiation about setting goals may be facilitated by and recorded in a pre-prepared and simply written format. Making explicit the skills involved in learning tasks helps the pupil to develop a sense of ownership in his/her learning and to keep a record of progress. This process also helps the learner to develop an awareness of her/his increasing autonomy. Again, simple written formats for peer- or self-assessment can be used. The more user-friendly these are, the better. These processes may be part of the ongoing, formative process of Records of Achievement.

Let us now consider the provision of learning tasks and stimuli to take account of the anxiety–risk ratio. For this, learning tasks have to arouse some, but not too much, anxiety whilst also involving the child in enough risk for him/her to get a sense of being able to be independent. Mongan and Hart argue that:

> Perhaps the most complex aspect of teaching is that of acting as facilitator to children's learning. If the materials provided are too structured, they remove the need to develop personal skills and judgement. However, an approach which is too open-ended may make children feel vulnerable if they have no experience of exploring situations and being encouraged to come to different conclusions in a secure atmosphere.
>
> (Mongan and Hart 1989: 145)

Figure 28 shows the possibilities for differentiating the curriculum by using varying combinations of stimulus and task. The first approach requires that the task be open-ended enough, and the stimulus materials accessible enough, for all pupils to participate at their own level. (This is often referred to as differentiation by outcome.) The second approach uses differentiation by task. Learners are set different tasks in relation to the same stimulus material. The third approach provides different stimuli of varying degrees of difficulty and the learners are asked to do the same task. In the fourth approach learners are given different tasks in relation to particular stimuli. This last approach has the danger of teachers' expectations limiting learner attainment, and it also removes the motivating power of choice (Spillman 1991).

However well the teacher structures the tasks, learners who lack confidence, have poor self-esteem or who have repeatedly experienced rejection or failure may balk at the invitation to learn. It is not uncharacteristic for children with poor ego development or low self-esteem to respond to being given a learning task by protesting, 'I can't . . .'. The teacher's skill in mediating frustration blocks is a vital determinant of whether a pupil persists with a task. When a learner's confidence wavers the teacher provides a bridge to learning by employing skills in ego strengthening.

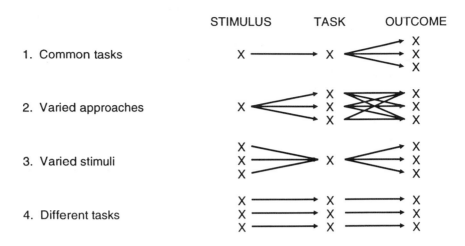

Figure 28 Differentiation by task and outcome
(Spillman 1991)

(The notion of ego strengthening was discussed in Chapter Six.) With regard to deploying skills in ego strengthening for a particular learning task, it can be useful to remind the pupil of his/her success in similar tasks. In psychoanalytic terms, the inner world of children with emotional difficulties might be viewed as being inhabited by a variety of 'self-attacking objects', in the face of which it is difficult for the child to maintain a sense of his/her own goodness, or positive capabilities. So the child may not be able to mobilise the belief that s/he can be 'good' in a particular skill area. In these circumstances, it can be useful to have tangible evidence of the pupil's previous successes close at hand, not to wield threateningly over the child, but to reinforce the child's capacity to overcome his/her internal fragility, and his/her disbelief in being able to be the source of good, worthwhile production. Wall displays which affirm the children's success can be particularly helpful in this situation – 'Look, you did something similar here, do you remember?' It can be useful to demonstrate that the skills the pupil has developed already can be used to master the present learning task, or that the new learning task might be a relatively small step.

Promoting access to materials and resources

A person's capacity to tolerate frustration is linked to the state of his/her ego development. Since children with emotional difficulties are often struggling to develop effectively functioning egos, it is not surprising that it is a common characteristic of such pupils to become frustrated in learning tasks, and to give up on them. This characteristic is not necessarily related to intellectual development, and teachers can also find it particularly irritating to witness pupils giving up when they do not lack intellectual ability (whereas they may lack ego strength). The flexible organisation and design of materials have a role in helping children to overcome poor frustration tolerance. Ainscow (1989) argues that effective teachers store materials and equipment in a flexible way which enables them to be located whenever they might be needed, thus enabling immediacy in meeting individual needs, and learner's autonomy to be catered for. The good design of teaching materials can reduce the inhibiting effect of frustration blocks and increase a child's access to the curriculum. Figure 29 provides a checklist of considerations in designing materials to provide access to the curriculum.

Positive reinforcement

The features and importance of formative assessment were acknowledged earlier. The *process* of collecting assessment data, and the sharing of that data between teachers and learners, is perhaps of greater significance than the data themselves. Reviewing work provides opportunities for teachers to reflect back to pupils their success, a process vital to the internalisation of self-worth. Review processes offer significant opportunities for the celebration and reinforcement of achievements. When one has low self-esteem, success and achievement have to be experienced over and over again for the internal picture one has of oneself to be changed. Rogers' notion of genuineness (see Chapter Three) is pertinent here. In terms of its emotional worth, praise for a small but real success has more value than hollow, perhaps undeserved, praise for the sake of praise. For the teacher to make the most of positive reinforcement s/he should be on the look-out for appropriate opportunities to give children feedback on their successes. A positive reinforcer may be defined (Sambrooks 1990: 48) as 'any event which, if given, increases the likelihood of the previous behaviour being repeated'. Research shows that teachers generally routinely provide positive feedback in relation to academic achievements, but are much less likely to give positive reinforcement in social developments. Effective teachers provide positive reinforcement in both the formal and social curricula. This may entail supporting a pupil with as light a touch of encouragement as is necessary to help her/him to make new steps and to recognise and comment upon these new steps. It is important for pupils' ego development that improvements in social interactions are recognised and commented upon by teachers.

Example: A teacher observation

As part of an in-service training course, some teachers had chosen the task of observing a particular child with a view to (in the often-used expression) 'catching

Requirements
Do the materials assume:

- prior knowledge?
- prior experience?
- prior skills?

What skills are needed to participate successfully, and do these relate to the skills of the students?

Accessibility
Are the materials explicit about aims and purpose?
Can the materials be used by a group/individuals?

Relevance
Are the materials relevant to:

- your purposes?
- your students' experiences?

Language
Reading age:

- Are common rather than unusual words used?
- Is the reading age of the text appropriate for all students?

Introducing new words:

- Can the new words be introduced in relation to an activity?
- Can the root word and reminders of spelling be given?

Phraseology:
- Are literal rather than metaphorical sentences used?

Sentence structure:
- Are short sentences used?

Layout
Is the material eye-catching?
Are the graphics and the medium appropriate?
Is double spacing used between statements and treble spacing between sections?
Is print size largish?
Is there an appealing ratio of text, pictures, diagrams, charts, etc.?
Are key words emphasised?
Is the sequence clear?
Are illustrations, particularly maps and diagrams, set in a frame?

Flexibility
Do the materials allow learners to start at different places?
Do they cater for a variety of levels?
Do they allow learners to move at different paces?
Do they provide a framework of achievable steps and a structure for success?
Do the materials provide open-ended possibilities for different levels of achievement?

Do the materials facilitate:

- understanding?
- transfer of skills and understanding to other situations?
- extension of skills and understanding?

Figure 29 Designing materials to enhance access to the curriculum
(formulated with reference to FEU/Training Agency/ Skill 1989, Currie 1990)

him/her being good' as often as possible, and on these occasions making verbal, positive reinforcements. One teacher reported her story to the group as follows: 'I chose a girl, aged 6, to observe, and I watched her really closely for three days. The only time I saw her doing anything that could be considered good was when she remembered to wear her coat and to hang it in the right place.' The teacher told her story rather apologetically, and was asked by other members of the group whether the girl usually managed to wear her coat and hang it up. When the teacher replied that the girl did not, the other members of the group asked if she gave the girl some positive reinforcement for this. When the teacher said that she did, the others wanted to know what happened. The teacher acknowledged, still rather apologetically, that the girl had smiled. The other teachers then enquired whether the girl often smiled, and the teacher, saying, 'No, I hardly ever see her smile, actually', began to smile herself as she understood more of what had happened in giving some positive reinforcement to the child.

The importance of positive reinforcement has been stressed by social learning theory, or behaviourism, which is based upon the assumptions that most human behaviour is learned through recognisable processes of reinforcement, and that it can therefore be modified. This school of thought considers behaviour to be situation-specific, not pre-determined or measurably influenced by unconscious or emotional forces. The method is based on the assumption that criteria can be developed which reflect objective perceptions of external reality. In my view the value of this approach to emotional development and learning lies in the contribution it can make to ego strengthening, through positive reinforcement.

Skinner (1973) suggests some guidelines for giving positive reinforcement, in order to encourage individuals to do more of the same:

- Be specific, with as much information as possible. Speak of specific achievements, not all-round standards.
- Be immediate – give the pat on the back today, rather than waiting for the stage of reviewing work.
- Make the targets achievable; small, frequent wins are more reinforcing than one big win.
- Keep it unpredictable, because the unexpected bit of praise counts for more than the counted-on commendation.

This last 'rule' might not always be appropriate for children with entrenched emotional and behavioural difficulties; it might be more important for unintegrated children to be clear about behavioural goals, and to receive positive reinforcement from the teacher when these are achieved. Some children, because of their resistance and defences (see Chapter Two) to development and learning, may seem to want to function in classrooms on their own terms. (There is a discussion of omnipotence in Chapter Two, section on 'Anxiety and separation'.) This might lead some disturbing children to try to manage their relationships with the teacher through using, for example, a combination of disruption and seduction. When this happens, it is tempting for the teacher to avoid 'trouble' by adopting a *laissez-faire* attitude in which the pupil might be perceived as 'doing what s/he can'. Yet, in doing so, the teacher might be colluding with the pupil's defences, and thus reinforcing the pupil's difficulties. In such a situation, it is helpful for the pupil to sense that the teacher is not collusive, but rather is able to provide boundaries and be empathic. The teacher thus retains the authority to define the expectations of the pupil, although this might be put into practice through collaborative negotiation. For example, to generate a framework in which positive reinforcement is possible, the teacher might decide with the pupil the time period over which specific expectations are to be monitored (e.g. half-day, day, week, as appropriate), and then, at the end of the defined period, reflect back to the pupil and positively reinforce the pupil's developments in relation to the defined expectations.

When a child has low self-esteem, any positive self-related feelings can disappear quickly, as if overwhelmed by the child's negative or depressing feelings. In such cases it is important for teachers to find concrete, tangible ways of logging and reflecting positive achievements. Photographs, journals, wall displays, badges and charts all have a role here. It can be useful to keep a camera close to hand so that positive participation in group activities might be visually recorded. A display of photographs is a tangible method of recording and reinforcing success in activities, such as group work or games, which might otherwise have few tangible results.

Example: Achievement boards

Gardiner (1991) writes of the 'achievement boards' which are pinned up in every classroom at Henley County Primary School in Suffolk. Children write up their own successes onto the achievement board and applaud those of other pupils and staff. If a child is reticent about displaying aspects of his/her success, the teacher will add something. The rich variety of contributions on the walls gives some idea of just how wide the definition of achievement is in this school.

> Offerings range from 'Well done David for concentrating and finishing your written work', or 'I have improved my spelling' to 'I walked a ten-mile walk on a very rainy day and got drenched.' Staff do not try to impose their own concept of what constitutes an achievement; that is something which the children are encouraged to discover for themselves. The children keep 'This is my Life' books, fill in 'What's special about me' sheets and achievement diaries, and have drawn up a code of conduct for themselves. . . . Staff saw self-assessment by pupils as particularly important, commenting that parents enjoyed reading them more than teachers' reports. . . . [An evaluation of previous practice had] revealed that 90% of the children thought that the record folders 'belonged' to [the headteacher].
>
> (Gardiner 1991: 10)

The keeping of records of achievement, containing examples of achievements and negotiated between teacher and pupils in regular review meetings, enables pupils to feel a sense of 'ownership' in the process. Pupils with special educational needs are likely to have stronger needs than other pupils for an 'emphasis on profiles of achievement which encourage self-assessment and which record all that pupils have achieved and experienced in both the National Curriculum and the curriculum as a whole' (National Curriculum Council 1989a: 8). Records of achievement are based upon the idea of positive reinforcement, the celebration of successes, and the encouragement of pupil autonomy. They provide opportunities for teachers and learners to link and reflect upon agreed goals, attainments achieved and further developmental needs. '[T]he more pupils can take responsibility for keeping their own records of progress the better. . . . it gives pupils real responsibility for monitoring and planning their own learning' (Hall 1992: 23). Where pupils are involved in the keeping of their own records of progress and achievement as part of a planned process, this serves to acknowledge, and help the development of, the child's autonomy. Records of achievement also aid the transition from school to further education, training or the workplace, since they function as a transitional object – providing a tangible demonstration of the fact that one has achieved something worthwhile – and help to make sense of where one has come from: because of pupil ownership of the process, pupils are part of the valuing, and so the record of achievement also helps the pupil to avoid the need to rubbish the ending in order to be able to leave (Griffiths 1993).

With children of a young age-group similar functions have been fulfilled, and parents have been incorporated in the process, by the use of home–school diaries. These enable teachers, parents and pupils to communicate with each other in a way that provides positive reinforcement for the pupil on a regular and consistent basis. It is important that all parties understand the reasons for, and intentions behind, the use of the diary, so that it does not become negatively reinforcing.

The use of badges provides a further method of providing positive reinforcement which is concrete and tangible.

Example: Badges of affirmation

An acting headteacher of an inner London primary school found herself to be the school's fifth acting headteacher in less than two years, and the school was experiencing an increasing incidence of behavioural difficulties amongst pupils. She availed herself of some of the commercially available badges which have various messages of praise upon them. The headteacher tells the story of how, with the use of such badges, assemblies turned from being quite tricky occasions to being well-ordered gatherings, to which the children looked forward. There was much anticipation in the air as the headteacher went round each class teacher, in turn, asking for nominations for which children were to receive the positively reinforcing badges.

245

Exercise: Positive reinforcement

*/**/***

Think of as many meaningful ways as you can of making positively reinforcing communications.

Exercise: Catch them being good!

*

Choose one or two pupils with whom you work who regularly present difficulties. Try to catch them being good as often as you can, and tell them the achievements they are making.

The needs of gifted and able learners

Giftedness is often thought of as a phenomenon which presents the individuals concerned with outstanding opportunities and possibilities. So it does. Yet bright lights cast dark shadows. A gifted young person may be presented with a range of dilemmas. S/he may feel misunderstood by the family. If s/he does not experience his/her gifts as being acceptable within the peer group s/he may learn to hide them. S/he may, at some unconscious level, feel 'better', more 'advanced' than the parents or teachers. This feeling may arouse fear which may need to be defended against, for example by becoming omnipotent, or by feeling that s/he does not have to grow up (Ryce-Menuhin 1987). We considered in Chapter Two how, when we face difficulties, we may unconsciously, if not consciously, attempt to split them off and push them away. Where giftedness becomes associated with difficulty, the gift may be hidden, or denied, or split off into some discrete activity which may only seem possible in very particular circumstances.

The issue of being different from our peers presents a struggle for us all – and this is much more difficult for adolescents. The issue of difference was discussed in Chapter Seven and earlier in this chapter. Where a gift accentuates a young person's difference, the internal pressure to deny the gift may become reinforced. The danger of the young person splitting off parts of him/herself then becomes greater.

Exercise: What is it like being a gifted and able pupil?

*/**/***

The purpose of this exercise is to relate with empathy to the sort of dilemmas a gifted and able child might face.

Each participant is given a blank card.

   Instruction: Imagine you are a gifted and able pupil. Think about the sorts of experience/feeling you have. In role as a gifted/able pupil, write a paragraph which is an entry into your personal diary. You may wish to write about events/feelings relating to school, family or friends.

   Collect in the completed cards, and hand them out at random, asking participants to read out to the group a selection of the writings.

I am suggesting that there is a critical relationship between the affective realm and a young person's capacities to make use of his/her gifts. If the school is to help in this, it has to counter any tendencies towards splitting. This is partly a question of the school demonstrating a tolerance of differences, finding a range of ways of valuing the pluralist nature of its learners. It is also a question of finding ways of helping the gifted young person to integrate the gift within his/her view of him/herself, and to have a positive experience of integration within the school community. As the so-called 'Fish Report', *Educational Opportunities for All?* (ILEA 1985), said, integration is a process not a state. The process of integration is facilitated by staff–pupil relationships as well as by the school's organisational structures.

Since the experiences, feelings and attitudes of teachers have a significant influence upon effectiveness, it is appropriate to consider the subjective realm of the teacher in relation to gifted pupils.

Exercise: What is it like teaching the gifted and able?

*/**

The purpose of this exercise is to discover what feelings may be aroused in teachers when working with the gifted and able.

The statements below may be given out as a stimulus for discussion in pairs or very small groups. The groups are asked to discuss whether they have ever felt any of these responses. Group members are asked to give brief examples of their experiences, being as frank as they feel able to be.

- Resentment at feeling you should do extra work to produce extension activities.
- Feeling threatened by pupils' superior intellect and/or verbal challenges.
- Stimulated by the intellectual challenge and curiosity of the pupils.
- Feeling guilty because you are not stretching the pupils as much as you might be.
- Finding it difficult to understand pupils who are creative in unorthodox or obscure ways.
- Envy that your own talents are not as well developed as those of your pupils.
- Anxious about not knowing what to do to meet the pupils' developmental needs.
- Protective about the pupils coming over as different from their peers.
- Pleased that the pupils share your strong enthusiasm for your subject.
- Bewilderment at the pupils' erratic motivation patterns, despite their ability to do the work.
- Admiration for the pupils' accomplished achievements.
- Feeling sorry for the pupils because of the nature of their relationships with peers.
- Concerned that although the pupils seem intellectually gifted, they do not seem to be coping emotionally.
  (with acknowledgements to Elizabeth Cowne for her contributions)

The school may cater for the affective aspects of the learning needs of gifted and able pupils in a number of ways. There are a number of curriculum delivery models which can be used to do this. It is generally recognised that curriculum extension and enrichment are needed. Extension refers to going further than peers in relation to the same content (i.e. greater depth within the topic), whereas enrichment refers to the provision of greater breadth and variety. Some schools provide opportunities for curriculum acceleration, i.e. undertaking the same course of study as peers but faster. It is sometimes argued that grouping able children together provides a further model of curriculum delivery, but Her Majesty's Inspectorate found, with regard to grouping, that 'no system appeared to be uniquely suited to the needs of the very able' (DES 1992: 13).

Whatever curriculum delivery model is used, there are a number of principles which are important in supporting the learning of the gifted and able. Firstly, the *processes* of using and applying skills, concepts and values become more important than factual *content*. Secondly, higher-order thinking skills which require application, analysis, synthesis and evaluation should be encouraged. Thirdly, also to be encouraged are problem-solving activities such as making hypotheses, predictions, and judgements. Fourthly, open-ended questions, with appropriate expectations, facilitate imaginative and extended responses. Fifthly, the involvement of able pupils in the planning of their work should provide opportunities for selectivity to encourage identification of the most important learning activities in a particular cycle. Sixthly, the integration of complex moral issues into learning activities helps the development of able pupils.

How does the school organise itself to support the sorts of mechanism outlined in the above two paragraphs? A variety of ways may be explored in the following exercise.

Exercise: How does your school cater for the affective and learning needs of gifted and able pupils?

*/**/***

1 What are the departmental arrangements for developing, supporting and monitoring the differentiation of the curriculum?
2 What are the strategies for teacher development and support?
3 Are there appropriate cross-curricular opportunities for extension and enrichment activities?
4 Are mentor arrangements encouraged with staff and adults other than teachers?
5 How is PSE and tutor time used to explore issues of difference and to foster mutual understanding?
6 Would a young person feel 'safe' to refer him/herself through the school's pastoral structure if s/he felt the need for counselling?
7 In what ways does the school build partnerships with parents in order to form the sorts of collaborative relationship which might be needed to encourage a young person to make use of his/her giftedness?
8 How are the school's policies for the gifted and able reviewed and evaluated?

A flexible learning environment

In the introduction to this chapter, the principles of classroom management for the prevention of disruption were considered. We have explored some of the tensions in planning for individual needs, and the affective aspects of differentiation. Let us move towards the close of this chapter by briefly considering the nature of the classroom environment which takes account of the concerns expressed here. The teacher's capacity to differ-

Briefing
Topic objectives
Tasks summarised

Tutoring to negotiate targets
Targets negotiated which are relevant to individual needs and course objectives
Negotiation recognises differences between learners
Agree action: what will be achieved by when
Learners develop negotiating, summarising and clarifying skills
Small group context: pupils exert peer pressure

Learning experiences
Individual and group work
Emphasise active involvement, related to shared meaning
Emphasise the responsibility of the learner
Provide for different learning experiences based on individual needs

Resources
Access to a wide variety of resources
User-friendly categorisation and classification
Integration of information technology
Preparation of learners on how to access resources

Support
Teacher as facilitator
Feelings kept on the classroom agenda

Review and assessment
Learners involved in recording and presenting learning outcomes
Learners benefit from each other's experiences
Debriefing of content and process of learning
Learners and teacher assess and evaluate progress

Management
Planned, consistent, systematic
Clear framework within which to work

Figure 30 The key features of a flexible learning environment
(formulated with reference to materials produced by the London Flexible Learning Project)

entiate the curriculum by taking account of emotional factors in learning in the various ways discussed above is enhanced where the learning context is a flexible one. The government has in recent years encouraged the development of flexible learning, for example through TVEI projects. Two key objectives in flexible learning are 'To meet the learning needs of students as individuals and in groups through the flexible management and use of a range of learning activities, environments and resources [and] to give the student increasing responsibility for his/her own learning within a framework of appropriate support' (Eraut *et al.* n.d.: 11).

A flexible learning environment takes account of individual experience, different paces in learning and so on, and is organised to support learners' autonomy. Winnicott's notion of a facilitating environment is one in which the amount of support provided matches the child's changing needs for attachment and autonomy. A facilitating environment thus provides a flexible and adjustable balance between boundary and space. Developing flexible learning approaches enables teachers to provide this balance between boundary and space. In the secondary phase, flexible learning initiatives have been extended through the work of TVEI projects. Figure 30 summarises the key features of an environment which provides opportunities for flexible learning.

A flexible learning environment which is effective is underpinned by a supportive institutional ethos. Such an ethos is likely to bring a recognition of the important interconnections between how learners and staff relate with each other, a premium on openness, a feeling of being able to take measured risks, a strong sense of identity with the organisation, support for individuals to contribute to the community, and help for every learner to feel s/he is contributing something of value and being valued as a person as well as a learner (Eraut *et al.* n.d.). The link between ethos and organisation brings us to issues which will be considered in the next chapter, on managing the organisation.

First, I present some opportunities, through the following exercises, for further reflection upon this chapter.

Exercise: Case studies in mediating the curriculum

*/**/***

Given below are descriptions of three children. In what ways would you help these children to gain access to the curriculum?

Roger
Roger has been described as very withdrawn, and gives the impression of a 'frozen' child. He appears to lack confidence. He avoids eye contact, and often seems to be somewhat hunched. His academic attainments are low, although teachers have remarked that when he gets to know teachers who are able to give him some attention, there are signs that he begins to 'come to life', and his achievements improve. He does not speak much in school, but when he does speak his language is appropriately constructed.

Roger usually associates with a couple of other boys in the class, although the relationship between these boys seems rather sterile and empty. He interacts with the other children in the class as little as possible: others are reluctant to join in with him, without expressing particular objections to doing so.

He is able to join in structured activities (e.g. board games), but finds unstructured play or expressive arts difficult.

Tina

Tina is underachieving across the curriculum in her written work, although orally she appears to be quite bright. Her concentration span on written work is short. In basic skills she is getting behind her peers. In lessons she can seem quite demanding, as she often appears to need work to be individually set, and she finds it difficult to get started and then to sustain concentration and to complete pieces of work. She can appear to spend significant amounts of lesson time disrupting the work of other children. She seems to have a knack of knowing just how to provoke and 'wind up' other children, so disputes are not unusual. She has been known to be rather confrontational with teachers; teachers perceive this to happen when Tina feels threatened.

At the same time, Tina has got what some people describe as 'charm'. Others describe this as being good at manipulation. This makes her quite difficult to deal with in school – different teachers seem to develop very different approaches and boundaries in relation to her.

She has a clique of peers who seem to follow her lead. She has a paradoxical relationship with others in the class, who seem to be wary of her, yet also rather courteous towards her.

Robert

Robert has on occasion been described by his peers as 'mad'. He seems to live in a world of his own. Some of his habits – such as using particular grimaces – appear to be slightly obsessional. He appears to plod mechanically and fairly unsuccessfully through his academic work: teachers have a sense that most of the work does not seem to be relevant to him. Sometimes he becomes passionately interested in particular subjects, and then he will put in a lot of effort.

He has an extremely vivid imagination, and his art work shows a very individualistic style. He enjoys using various art media to express fantasies, but he is not very interested in learning art techniques. Recently there is some indication that when given the opportunity to manage an extended and complex arts project he is able to do so. He has also begun to be able to relate other areas of the curriculum to such projects.

Robert has spent a long time being very isolated from his peers. It is sometimes remembered that when he was younger he would sit and rock on his chair, and make 'silly noises'. Recently he has been able to get into more conversations on a one-to-one basis when a teacher to whom he feels close has enough time. Teachers are still sometimes unsure how much of his conversation relates to his own fantasies and how much to shared realities. Robert is more accepted by his peers than he used to be, but there are only one or two peers in the school with whom he seems to have something like a friendship.

Exercise: Self-assessment of curricular skills

*

Assess your own skills on some of the issues considered in this chapter. Use this checklist to help you take pleasure in your strengths, and to highlight your developmental needs.

	Low				High
The anxiety–risk ratio	1	2	3	4	5
Curriculum-based assessment	1	2	3	4	5
The range of teaching and learning styles used	1	2	3	4	5
Relating teaching and learning to pupils' experiences	1	2	3	4	5
Designing materials to enhance access to the curriculum	1	2	3	4	5
Providing bridges when confidence wavers	1	2	3	4	5
Positive reinforcement	1	2	3	4	5

Select one or two categories (e.g. your highest- and lowest-scoring categories). Which aspects of these strategies do you consider you do well, and in which areas do you have developmental needs?

Exercise: Making recommendations to improve access to the curriculum

*/**/***

Imagine that you are a member of staff at a school in which the governing body has requested that the school should work on improving access to the curriculum for pupils with emotional/ behavioural difficulties. You are (a) member(s) of a working group which has taken on the task of drawing up a set of proposals about this. Outline your proposals.

We have now examined issues about meeting individual needs, and ways of differentiating the curriculum to take account of emotional issues. This last exercise poses some wider organisational issues: 'we cannot look at the curriculum in any whole-school or whole-person sense without also recognizing the overlap with organization and climate' (Watkins 1989: 47). It is to these issues that the next chapter turns.

SUMMARY

- Whilst delivering the curriculum, teachers have opportunities to provide emotional holding and strengthening.
- Learning is a function of processes of interaction between the learner, teacher and the learning environment, and teachers have a vital role in mediating the curriculum to cater for emotional factors in learning.
- Current tensions in curriculum development to meet individual needs include tensions between:
  - learning as a process and learning as content;
  - centralisation and decentralisation in curriculum control;
  - 'process' and 'objectives' models of curriculum planning and evaluation;
  - entitlement and expediency;
  - participative and transmissive teaching and learning styles.

- Differentiation, an important means of facilitating access to the curriculum for all children, should in particular address the 'anxiety–risk ratio' in relation to emotional factors in learning.
- Differentiating the curriculum to take account of emotional factors in learning requires that particular account be taken of:
  - curriculum-based assessment to support and motivate learning by enabling teachers to know what pupils can do, and providing opportunities for joint goal setting;
  - the range of teaching and learning styles used, to provide for diversity and preferred learning styles, and to help create collaborative classrooms;
  - the structuring of learning tasks to match skills needed with pupils' levels of functioning, to relate the tasks to pupils' experiences, and to enable the teacher to provide bridges when confidence wavers;
  - the availability and design of materials;
  - providing positive reinforcement for success, of both the academic and social curricula, in tangible ways;
  - the affective as well as the learning needs of gifted and able pupils.

- Providing an environment for flexible learning opportunities enhances teachers' capacities to respond to pupils' emotional/behavioural needs.

9

MANAGING THE
ORGANISATION

INTRODUCTION

In this chapter the focus is on the links between emotional growth and learning and the issues of managing the organisation. Fullan (1991) suggests that management involves getting things done by working effectively with people. In recent years there has been much debate about managing the processes which produce effective schools and other organisations. The wide body of research which demonstrates the influence which the school has upon a child's achievements (e.g. Mortimore *et al.* 1988, Rutter *et al.* 1979), was reinforced by recent submissions of evidence to the Committee of Inquiry into Discipline in Schools, chaired by Lord Elton (Galloway 1990). Research has shown that schools which achieve higher levels of outcomes have certain typical internal conditions, that these differences are systematically related to the school's culture or ethos, and that the school's culture is amenable to alteration by the concerted action of the staff. This research suggested that in effective schools, organisational factors – such as a supportive climate within the school, clear goals and high expectations for students, a system for monitoring performance and achievement, ongoing staff development and in-service, and parental involvement and support – are consistent with the school's culture. Hopkins (1991: 58) makes the point that organisational characteristics alone do not inform our understanding of the dynamics of developing schools as organisations, and that there are further 'process factors' which 'lubricate the system and "fuel the dynamics of interaction"'. Fullan (1985) suggests that process factors are related to the process of leadership, a guiding value system, intense interaction and communication providing support and pressure both horizontally and vertically within the school, and collaboration in planning and implementating initiatives. Fullan asserts that school improvement requires a direct and primary focus on organisational factors: 'Strategies are needed that more directly affect the culture of an organisation' (1988: 29).

The work of the schools effectiveness movement provides a context for examining the way in which management processes relate dynamically to emotional factors in learning. There is a dynamic interplay between the capacities of individual staff members to participate effectively in the organisation, the management mechanisms and organisational culture to support staff in their tasks, and the organisation's relationship with the anxiety provoked by the emotional/behavioural difficulties of children and young people. Individual members of organisations have a range of subjective perceptions about their organisation which affect their capacity to work within it. In addition, work with troubling children increases the anxiety levels of staff, and so the subjective realms of staff's experience become a significant factor in managing the organisation. It is the task of management to provide an effective organisational base which, where necessary, takes account of such dynamics in enabling staff to fulfil their tasks – the task of particular concern here being that of facilitating emotional growth and learning. Whilst the debate of this chapter draws upon work in school settings, the processes are equally pertinent to other child care establishments.

Irrational and unconscious mechanisms play a role in staff's capacities to fulfil their tasks. The importance of subjective perceptions in the management of people in organisations is becoming increasingly recognised. Shipman (1990: 58) comments that in decision-making 'the part played by reason will be limited'. Kakabadse et al. (1988: 93) comment that 'Managing relationships forms the greater part of a manager's job.' Everard and Morris (1990: 135) point out that 'most negative behaviour occurs because people feel unsure or threatened'. The work of Jaques (1955), Menzies Lyth (1989) and Hirschhorn (1988) demonstrates the way in which individual defence mechanisms might become anti-task social defence mechanisms within the organisation. Helping staff to develop their effectiveness in relation to such dynamics might involve exploring issues concerning the toleration of differences, ways of dealing with resistance, the projection of difficulties onto others, the impact of anxiety, and the role of fantasy in constructing what appears to be possible. The more one embraces holistic notions of personal and organisational development, the more one becomes able to manage and mitigate anti-task phenomena, and to make use of one's role to relate to and meet the individual needs of 'clients'.

A further issue which currently arouses strong feeling in staff is the huge amount of change that is required of schools, the impetus for much of which is external to the immediate school environment (e.g. the implementation of the Education Reform Act, relationships with Training and Enterprise Councils, and new legislation heralded in the White Paper *Choice and Diversity* (DFE/Welsh Office 1992). The literature on educational change now demonstrates increasing recognition that emotional factors have great significance in staff members' capacities to participate productively in organisational change. For example, Hinson (1991: 13) notes that 'attempts to induce changes in any system are likely to encounter some form of blocking or resistance by those who want to preserve the status quo'. Such factors are now recognised to be of fundamental importance in creating 'learning institutions' which can be responsive to children's needs in a rapidly changing society. The experiences of uncertainty which change brings are subjective. Merton (1968, quoted in North 1988: 167) writes that people 'respond not only to the objective features of a situation, but also to the meaning the situation has for them'. Murgatroyd and Reynolds (1984) make use of work by Ellis (1962) to suggest that fantasies about organisations affect organisational behaviour. Moss Kantor suggests that:

> organisational change is stimulated not by pressures from the environment . . . but by the *perceptions* of that environment and those pressures held by key actors. . . . Innovations and change . . . are bound up with the meanings attached to events and the action possibilities that flow from those meanings.
>
> (Moss Kantor 1983: 281)

Fullan (1991, quoted in University of Keele 1992b: 31) argues that 'educational change is a process of coming to grips with the multiple realities of people who are the main participants of implementing change'. Marris (1986) demonstrates that all change involves loss and anxiety, and that organisational change threatens the occupational identity of staff and their confidence in their own competence.

Whilst an overt impetus for change may be to help institutions become more effective, staff members may not always experience change in this way, particularly when people feel burdened by the amount of change required of them. Menzies Lyth (1988) argues that when the task as originally defined becomes too difficult, or when pressures result in unrealistic task definitions, there is a danger that the main, 'primary' task will be, perhaps implicitly, redefined. At such times, 'task may implicitly slip over into anti-task; for example, the education system not being realistically oriented to maturation and preparedness for life in society but to providing for dependency needs which may be anti-maturational' (Menzies Lyth 1988: 226).

When the task is perceived as being more difficult or demanding than one is prepared for, or when anxieties about the task threaten one's task performance, then defences emerge. Since the interaction of staff in organisations is of a dynamic nature, individual defences can become adopted by groups, and these can become institutionalised into what may be termed social defences. The first part of this chapter considers those defences which manifest themselves as social phenomena, and which inhibit the effectiveness of an organisation's work. The second part considers the implications of social defences for facilitating effective work and providing an effective organisational base. The processes discussed in previous chapters are pertinent here. For example, group work issues are faced by adults in their direct work with children, and also by staff in working with the dynamics of staff groups. In relation to providing an effective organisational base for emotional development, Menzies Lyth (in Dockar-Drysdale 1990) suggests the need to consider a number of issues: the way in which the whole institution operates, staff roles and functions, the maintenance of proper boundaries and the provision of opportunities for staff to deploy their capacities fully. These issues are considered in the second part of the chapter.

SOCIAL DEFENCE SYSTEMS

Throughout the preceding chapters, the facilitating and inhibiting power of communication has been a recurring theme. Dockar-Drysdale's (1990: 154) comment that 'All acting-out results from breakdowns in communication' is pertinent not only to interactions between adults and children, but to relationships between staff members in an institution.

> The real task of humane institutions can in a sense be described as relating to dependency needs; for example, . . . meeting educational needs. [Such a task cannot] be effectively accomplished only by gratifying dependency needs, but these needs are there and the institutions must relate to them somehow. These institutions have, therefore, as their work task a function that is close to an anti-task phenomenon. This puts them at risk.
>
> (Menzies Lyth 1988: 233–4)

It was shown in Chapter Two that when we face an anxiety-provoking situation, we are all inclined to take action, probably unconsciously, which helps us to avoid that anxiety. Psychoanalytic work shows that one of the most significant factors determining the way in which an organisation operates is the avoidance of anxiety by individuals within the organisation. Individuals might, for example, unwittingly pass on anxiety to other people, and the transmission of anxiety may thus get in the way of individuals being able to fulfil their primary tasks within an organisation. Anxieties may also be generated by organisational change, as discussed in the introduction above. Marris's (1986) research shows that, during periods of organisational change, anxieties experienced by individuals centre upon a struggle to defend or recover a meaningful pattern of relationships. Because of pressures and uncertainties, we can *feel* powerless, even when we are not. In the face of feelings of such powerlessness, work groups manage their anxieties by developing and deploying social defences. This may involve the creation of social systems which support systematic role violations. 'The social defences *externalize* individual defences' (Hirschhorn 1988: 56).

Unfortunately for task performance, members of institutions are also likely to seek satisfaction of personal needs that are anti-task; very often they need to mitigate the stresses and strains of the task itself and of confrontation with the human material on which the task is focused. In other words, members try to establish a social system that also acts as a defence against anxiety, both personal anxiety and that evoked by institutional membership.

(Menzies Lyth 1988: 228–9)

The significance of the creation of social systems which support systematic defences is better understood in the context of understanding the organisation as a system. The *Shorter Oxford Dictionary* defines a system as 'a whole composed of parts in orderly arrangement according to some scheme or plan. A set or assemblage of things connected, associated or interdependent, so as to form a complex unity'. Similarly, systems theory regards organisations as entities consisting of connected, interdependent parts, and individual behaviour is viewed within the context in which it occurs. The behaviour of one component of the system is considered to affect, and be affected by, the behaviour of others; systems are intrinsically dynamic in nature.

The systems view looks at the world in terms of relationships and integration. Systems are integrated wholes whose properties cannot be reduced to those of smaller units. . . . The activity of systems involves . . . the simultaneous and mutually interdependent inter-action between multiple components. . . . systems thinking is process thinking.

(Capra 1982: 286–9)

Schools can of course also be viewed as systems – open systems which interact with their environment:

members of a group can function as a system, and engage in co-ordinated activity, without necessarily meeting together to do so. The staff of a school can work to a common policy, and manifest shared feelings about particular issues affecting the school, when they are teaching in separate classrooms.

(Reed and Palmer 1972, Lecture 2: 2)

Killeen (1993) argues that schools as systems produce outputs which are both acceptable and unacceptable, the latter manifesting, for example, as failed pupils, failed teachers, and school-girl pregnancies. In the post-Education Reform Act era, the unacceptable products become even more unwanted. What happens to these aspects of the school as a system?

The study of social defence systems was pioneered by Jaques, a Kleinian psychoanalyst and specialist in organisations, who was impressed by 'how much institutions are used by individual members to reinforce individual mechanisms of defence against anxiety, and in particular against recurrence of the early paranoid and depressive anxieties described by Melanie Klein' (Jaques 1955: 478). He postulated that the defence against anxiety is one of the primary elements that bind the individuals within an organisation together.

Organisational defences are more likely to occur where the organisation fails to take its members' personal identities seriously. Blishen's research suggests that young people view schooling, with its relentless bell-ringing and herding in large groups, as disrespectful of personal identity. Blishen comments that however involved pupils are in their work, upon the ringing of the bell they must instantly switch to another lesson, teacher and wavelength: when structures and timetables are rigid, they act to eliminate any really personal contact with teachers, who become 'aloof authoritarian people, instead of ordinary companionable human beings' (Blishen 1969, quoted in Salmon 1988: 61). An organisational culture which affects its 'clients' in this sort of way undoubtedly affects its staff in similar ways, thus reinforcing the tendency towards social defences.

Hirschhorn (1988) suggests three modes in which social defences develop. He refers to these as the 'basic assumption', 'covert coalition' and 'organisational ritual' modes. Following the work of Bion (see Chapter Seven), Hirschhorn (1988: 57) argues that the basic assumption group 'acts as though it believes or assumes that a cohesive group mind exists and can be sustained *without* work or development'. Staff groups can feel as if they have a purpose and a life independent of the conscious and collaborative efforts of their individual members. Basic assumption behaviour thus expresses people's primitive wish to create a benign environment in which there is collusion with anti-task phenomena. 'When the group's tasks promote anxiety, the basic assumption experience enables members to limit their feelings of isolation and depersonalization' (Hirschhorn 1988: 57). Hirschhorn argues that what he calls the organisational ritual mode of developing social defences is impersonal in character. 'The defensive process is entirely externalized onto a set of mandated actions and does not depend on the emotional propensities of particular people. It helps all group members depersonalize their relationship to their work' (Hirschhorn 1988: 67).

One of the manifestations of such depersonalisation is the education system's implicit definition of knowledge as constituting a kind of hierarchy.

> Those areas of understanding which have an undeniably personal character – the expressive as against the instrumental spheres of knowledge – represent the lower levels in the hierarchy. So in the school curriculum, art, music, drama or dance are subjects with typically lower prestige than maths, chemistry or physics.
>
> (Salmon 1988: 62)

Salmon's comments provide an illustration of depersonalisation mechanisms found in schools, mechanisms which reinforce the tendency towards the creation of social defences. Depersonalisation is also the foundation of neurotic behaviour. 'We act out and we stay out of touch with reality by discounting the reality of other people and of ourselves. Thus the organized ritual reproduces the fundamental characteristic of neurotic behaviour at the social level' (Hirschhorn 1988: 67).

The various types of social defence are similar to the various means of defence outlined in Chapter Two. I explore below some social defences commonly operating in school situations, viz. splitting, denial and distortion. As with personal defences, these categories are a tool to help understanding; in practice they may often overlap or even defy categorisation (Jacobs 1982).

Splitting

In Jaques' (1951) early research, which was based on a small engineering company, he explained that the difficulties encountered in negotiations between management and worker representatives, even where there were generally good labour relations and high morale, were based on the operation of social defences against anxiety. He suggested that the workers had unconsciously split the management into 'good' and 'bad', the 'good' ones being the ones they worked with daily, and the 'bad' ones being those with whom they negotiated. The workers, by projecting their good impulses onto the managers in the work situation, were able to maintain good working relations with them. However, the workers' hostile and destructive impulses were projected onto their representatives, who then deflected them against the 'bad' managers in the negotiating situation.

Splitting can take place in all sorts of interpersonal and organisational situations. From a psychodynamic perspective, Hirschhorn (1988) explores the particular dynamics underlying the splitting which occurs in the relationship between managers and those managed.

> Managers trust subordinates *by projecting their own image of the good into them.* To be sure, they imagine that the subordinates are trustworthy by rationally assessing them. But to *feel* trusting, they must also irrationally see the reflected images of their own good internal objects in the experience of their subordinates. *They imagine that the subordinates are like the good parts of themselves.* (That is why narcissistic leaders cannot judge the character of their subordinates. They are compelled to see only the inflated or grandiose images of themselves in their 'trusted' subordinates.) . . . People find it hard to sustain whole images of others and themselves, for wholeness itself creates anxiety. People become anxious and uncertain, afraid that in facing the bad

parts of those they love they will lose touch with the good parts. The bad will contaminate the good, giving rise to a persecuting world. This is why, for example, lovers frequently idealize one another, why popular culture creates movie star idols, and why people need enemies to create and sustain their heroes. Like taboos and superstitions, these idealizations protect us from our own 'demons', from the bad objects of our internal world that make living painful.

(Hirschhorn 1988: 178–9)

A further demonstration of organisational splitting is provided in a very tangible form in current evidence of rising exclusion rates of learners with emotional/behavioural difficulties and the lack of adequate provision for this group (e.g. Audit Commission/HMI 1992). Below are some other examples of splitting.

Example: A headteacher's comments on links with a local college of further education

I refer here to a meeting which I had with a headteacher, in which my role involved working with both the head's school and a local college, and facilitating links between them. During our meeting the headteacher suggested that the difficulties in the links between the school and the college were all located in the college. Given that at that time I was new in post, and perhaps perceived to be unaware of all the pertinent facts, the situation was potentially ripe for splitting to occur, and my unconscious collusion in the operating dynamic. However, given also what I had briefly seen of the college, I wondered if there was possibly some splitting taking place, and in order to be perceived as not colluding with this, I made reference to the responsibilities of all the organisations involved in the links programme. This intervention seemed to create the necessary boundary, and on that occasion the headteacher did not continue to pursue the 'splitting' line of argument.

Example: A review of education support services

This example relates to a local education authority review of an educational support service. During the period described, I was a teacher in the support service. This example took place against the background of planning for the introduction of the local management of schools and of the threat of rate-capping of the council concerned, factors which created a sense of vulnerability in support service staff. At this time of possible cut-backs, staff in the service felt very anxious about the impending review of support provision. The review was to be conducted by managers within the local education authority and was co-ordinated by a senior manager, whom staff in the support service had known over a period of years. Even though the support service staff respected this manager's work, a number of staff in the service began to think and to articulate thoughts such as, 'Our service is really important, and the senior manager doesn't understand what it's all about.' In the minds of staff it was as if this manager became all-destructive, and unable to retain the sense of good regard in which the support services were viewed. In the fantasies of the support service staff, splitting took place in order to help retain a sense of our own goodness at a time of threat. In a sense the manager 'carried' the badness for the support teachers. Where fantasies such as these take hold, this inhibits team members' capacities for thinking, reflection and collaborative work. This example also serves as an illustration of the dynamic of distortion, discussed below.

Example: The academic and pastoral divide

Another form of splitting which commonly occurs in secondary schools is the separation of the academic and pastoral systems. The pastoral system deals with difficulties arising out of troublesome behaviour. In many schools, the special educational needs co-ordinator is given a role within the academic system, but little formal relationship with the pastoral system. In this way, the school attempts to keep those learning difficulties which are perceived to relate to emotional/behavioural factors apart from other forms of learning difficulties which the SEN co-ordinator supports. The hidden assumption here seems to be that emotional/behavioural issues are best dealt with through the structures for 'discipline' and that those pupils showing such difficulties do not also have needs which require support to gain access to the curriculum. Keeping academic and pastoral systems as separate organisations within the school may, at one level, be an attempt to minimise the production of anxieties in staff, but, since it achieves this through splitting, it also avoids a more holistic and proactive approach which might seek to develop the role of all staff in understanding and supporting the learning of such pupils. The holistic approach may potentially be more difficult or painful for staff, and social defences may operate to deny such pain.

Example: The National Curriculum and the whole child

I mentioned in the introduction to the last chapter some anecdotal evidence from my work as an advisory teacher about the perceptions of teachers in the primary phase in relation to the National Curriculum. Primary school teachers have traditionally shown particular concern for the development of the whole child. However, it seems to be the perception of teachers in this phase that it is becoming increasingly difficult to keep the whole child in mind, whilst also being under pressure to deliver an increased curriculum content load, and good test results for the school. This situation is ripe for splitting. Indeed, some teachers have suggested that, from their own point of view, they *either* work to deliver the National Curriculum *or* remain concerned with children's individual needs. When under pressure the splitting mechanism operates in people's perceptions, and this inhibits the potential for development. In this case the task is to work to *integrate* good practice in terms of concern for the whole child, and in delivering the National Curriculum.

Denial

Menzies Lyth's (1970) examination of anxiety experienced by nurses in the National Health Service provides a classic example of a social defence system. She found that organisational practices had grown which enabled nurses to minimise their interactions with patients, and therefore feelings of attachment which might grow whilst the nurses were carrying out their primary tasks could be denied. Rather than a system of patient care which acknowledged and sought to meet the patients' emotional needs, to minimise their worry and stress, a system had developed which denied the emotional elements of the work.

Systems theory can also be used to examine the educational issue concerning the integration or segregation of students with special needs. The urge to split off and deny the potentially painful conflicts involved in trying to meet the social and emotional needs of such students leads to the generation of social defences. These might manifest, for example, in arguments for short lessons rather than block timetabling, withdrawal groups, and segregation.

Example: A high school headteacher and a pupil with special educational needs

A somewhat traditional school had gone some way towards introducing mixed attainment teaching (a notion preferable to 'mixed ability' teaching). In an informal discussion about a student who had a Statement under the 1981 act and who was said to have a reading well below his chronological age, the headteacher said to me in explanation of why he did not really want this student in his school, and in a very dismissive tone of voice, 'It's all right for the middle schools, they can do a bit of mixed ability teaching, but we've got other pressures.' The attitudes underlying such comments seem to advocate splitting off the perceived problem, rather than facing and enduring the difficulties of 'other pressures' and the genuinely demanding emotional and practical tasks of creating and sustaining classrooms which meet a range of individual needs. The sense of difficulty was acknowledged by the headteacher, but he denied the need to work on the difficulties.

Distortion

In order to avoid painful or anxiety-provoking situations, and through the use of social defences, staff may retreat from their roles and tasks, and from the organisational boundaries. Where staff make use of social defences to avoid emotional conflict, relationships at work become depersonalised. Where this process becomes entrenched, the capacity of a group or team of people to accomplish its primary task becomes distorted. Social defences frequently create a distorted relationship between the group and its wider environment, including its clients and competitors. These systematic distortions serve to relieve the group of part of its anxiety, but inhibit the resolution of the emotional and interpersonal difficulties present in the situation. There was an element of distortion in the above example about the review of an education support service.

Distortion mechanisms which staff might employ specifically in relation to children with emotional and behavioural difficulties include, for example, unwitting collusion by the staff with the idea that certain children are uncontainable. In such circumstances staff may maintain a magical notion of there being a better provision for certain children which can somehow find the answers to complex issues. These assumptions might be

MANAGING THE ORGANISATION

a defence against the pain aroused in the staff rather than a consideration of the reality of better care. The contrary urge to think that 'we can do it all', without the need for other agencies, might also be a defence. Such omnipotent, 'doing-something-about-it' and driven urges are the opposite of emotional holding (see Chapter Four).

Hirschhorn (1988) uses the concept of the 'subjective boundary' to explain the dynamics of distortion. Although the official boundary of the organisation may correspond to its task, budget, or location, people create and sustain psychological boundaries that become as powerful and real as pragmatic boundaries based on task, money, or location. When people face uncertainty and feel at risk, they set up psychological boundaries that violate the pragmatic ones relating to the organisation's tasks, simply to reduce anxiety. Relations between groups within an organisation are a fertile breeding ground for such phenomena. Higgin and Bridger (1965) and Adair (1986) acknowledge the significance of inter-group rivalry and that myths about the 'other' group may emerge even where there is evidence that the myth is false. Adair (1986) reports that people's hostility towards another subgroup in an organisation can lead to the formation of negative stereotypes about that other subgroup, the slackening of inter-action and a decrease in communication, which can lead to interpretations made upon presuppositions and prejudices, and the distortion of communication.

Hirschhorn (1988) suggests that the anxiety chain underlying such dynamics consists of several interconnnected processes. First, he maintains, anxiety about work can lead people to step out of their work roles and turn away from work realities by creating a surreal world in which challenges are met by increased dependence, defensive denial or fantasies of omnipotence. Second, according to Hirschhorn, when people depend on one another to do effective work, when they must collaborate, one person's anxiety may trigger an *anxiety chain* through which people become enmeshed in collective fantasies. Third, these fantasies may generate violent feelings, as people both punish themselves for their own failings and imagine that others are their persecutors. Fourth, Hirschhorn argues, as people step out of role, they also step away from one another. They experience other people as having the characteristics of fantasy figures, especially fragmented or caricatured figures who are either all good and beautiful or all bad and evil. Some roles in organisations may be particularly susceptible to the dynamics of distortion. I now consider the potential for distortion and the role of special educational needs co-ordinators in schools.

Example: The role of the special educational needs co-ordinator

A school's special educational needs co-ordinator has the task of working on behalf of children who have difficulties of one kind or another. Any sort of difficulty is a potential snag around which communications may go wrong. The title of Moore and Morrison's (1988) book, *Someone Else's Problem?*, illustrates the issue, by suggesting that staff in schools may often perceive or wish that children with difficulties could be just that – someone else's problem. Staff may wittingly or unwittingly try to shift responsibility to the SEN co-ordinator for dealing with those issues with which they would rather not deal. Not only may the SEN co-ordinator be overtly asked to take on work which may not be part of the formal role, but his/her post may also serve to attract 'flak' which does not really belong to him/her. It can be as if there is a 'subjective boundary' around the role of the SEN co-ordinator, the interpretation of which staff may seek to manipulate to serve their own ends.

Below is a list which indicates aspects of the role which a group of inner city primary school special educational needs co-ordinators felt they fulfilled. Given the complexity of the role, and the amount of work it involves at the interface of various boundaries, these functions may become so distorted that the SEN co-ordinator is pushed into taking on roles and responsibilities which are more appropriately deployed amongst other staff members:

- recognising and identifying any special educational needs amongst the entire school population;
- being able to talk with parents in the face of their defences;
- engaging with other staff in planning curricular activities to meet children's special educational needs;
- liaising with all members of staff about the needs of children and ongoing work with their parents;
- liaising with outside agencies in relation to particular children;
- recording information about children's progress in a way which is helpful to all staff involved with each child;
- dealing with difficult children throughout the school, and supporting other staff in this task;
- working with the staff on how the responsibility for special educational needs can be shared;
- being a 'referee' between children and staff, particularly ancillary staff;
- overcoming the 'labelling' of children by other staff;
- training other staff about special educational needs;
- supporting teachers, e.g. helping them to keep their patience in the face of difficulties in relationships with children;
- keeping a SEN perspective alive in the school in the face of many pressures;
- supporting the entire range of special educational needs;
- relating to governing bodies;
- working collaboratively with other staff;
- running meetings.

The danger of distortion is exacerbated by the complexity of the role, and the need for the SEN co-ordinator to work across a number of organisational boundaries. S/he may often be the recipient of the unconscious anxiety experienced by other staff members. The person in this role has to face the challenge of providing a container for the worries of staff when they become 'infected' with anxieties. Just as the children's difficulties require emotional containment and holding (see Chapter Four), if staff have a 'good enough' experience of being emotionally contained, the 'container' becomes internalised, taken in, and they become better able to provide their own container. This, in turn, facilitates a greater capacity for thought, reflection, and toleration of difficult feelings by the staff, and reduces their dependency upon social and personal defence mechanisms.

Exercise: Recognising social defences

*/**

1 What examples of splitting, denial or distortion can you think of from your own organisation?
2 What sorts of pressure draw staff out of role to collude with 'anti-task' urges?
3 How does the behaviour of staff in groups or teams reinforce social defence mechanisms?

PROVIDING AN EFFECTIVE ORGANISATIONAL BASE

Given the various factors which can impede development within organisations, and the particular anxieties generated in work with children experiencing emotional and behavioural difficulties, the issue of clarity in roles, relationships and communications becomes particularly pertinent. The organisation itself is effective when, in relation to the emotional development of its 'clients', it functions to encourage the provision of emotional holding and ego strengthening through its organisational practices. 'Good managment is itself therapeutic for children, since it affects the models that staff present to children for identification' (Menzies Lyth, in Dockar-Drysdale 1990: xii). Elsewhere she elaborates the point:

> A very important characteristic of good management seems . . . to be a developed capacity to . . . struggle with task definition, to get it as precise and realistic as possible and to sustain the values that go with it, to protect the institution and its staff from undue pressures across the boundaries, to mitigate anti-task phenomena such as in socially structured defence mehanisms or subcultures, to effect such institutional changes as are desirable for task effectiveness, and to reconcile the needs of the task and the psychosocial needs of the members of the institution, both staff and clients.
>
> (Menzies Lyth 1988: 235)

These issues are explored below in relation to the themes of values, reparation, the whole task and whole-organisation policy; flexibility and the capacity for organisational change; role, task and authority issues; the use of consultation and joint problem-solving (Hanko 1990); and work at the boundaries of the organisation. Throughout this book there has been a concern with what was described in the introductory chapter as 'process' thinking. Just as we might view every single task in relation to an individual or a group of children as part of a process, so 'every single task throughout an organization must be viewed as a process' (Oakland 1989: 9). The notion of total quality management focuses on the process of ensuring that the inputs to the system are capable of meeting the requirements of the system.

Relating to the whole organisation

Although people often rely on social defences to contain their anxieties, thereby making scapegoats of clients, co-workers or people relating to the organisation from the wider environment, the paradoxical urge to restore one's experience of psychological wholeness and to repair the real or imagined psychological damage one has done in devaluing others is also often present: this desire to offer reparation helps to limit the level of social irrationality in group settings and provides a basis for group development (Hirschhorn 1988). The desire to offer reparation is enhanced when the staff of an organisation feel that they relate to the whole task of the organisation rather than just their own part in it. A school which wishes to generate a reparative culture may do so by enabling its staff to relate positively to the school's aims and ethos in the way in which staff conduct their day-to-day business. Recent developments in organisational management focus on the need to link the organisation's aims to objectives for individual staff members, through the identification of necessary competencies, support mechanisms, and the setting of targets, by means of line management coaching and appraisal. Enabling staff to relate purposefully not just to the organisation's aims, but to the value an organisation creates for clients, helps the staff to link their efforts to the shared purposes of the organisation. When this happens, staff members focus on the work itself, and people are less afraid to scrutinise their working relationships and are therefore less likely to distort them with projections and introjections which limit their capacity to observe and learn (Hirschhorn 1988).

Hirschhorn suggests that a reparative culture might have three particular dimensions:

1 Managers and employees experience their organisation as an instrument for accomplishing valued purposes.
2 Managers and employees are keenly aware of the primary tasks of the organisation. Organisations with a reparative culture value the quality of the product or service highly and develop group norms which support staff pride in their work.
3 The organisation develops relatively 'non-narcissistic' processes in which

good and bad aspects of organisational life are acknowledged and psychological splitting is limited. For example, staff acknowledge that the evaluation of their performance is in the best interests of the 'clients', themselves and the organisation. Where 'the organization acknowledges the good and the bad in its process and does not deny the pain and injury of working with others, people feel relatively whole and contain their propensity to scapegoat co-workers or clients' (Hirschhorn 1988: 229).

Work on social defence systems suggests that *whole-school policies* provide a very significant vehicle for staff to relate to a holistic vision of ethos and educational practice in their school, thus, in psychodynamic terms, stimulating the desire to offer reparation, and serving to reduce the potential development of social defence systems. Watkins (1989) suggests that no part of a school can claim a monopoly on caring, and that the caring functions of a school are whole-school functions. There is now widespread acknowledgement of the importance of developing whole-school policies to meet special educational needs (e.g. Ramasut 1989, Thomas and Feiler 1988). A whole-school policy for SEN supports the attitudes and practices consistent with the school ethos. The whole-school policy is a way of setting down the philosophy and principles of the school, and how these are implemented in terms of appropriate organisation, curriculum delivery and the recording and monitoring of pupil progress. It is widely acknowledged that whole-school policies are most effective where the staff are most involved and consulted, so that the policy has the commitment of the entire school community (e.g. London Borough of Merton 1991).

Whole-school agreement about roles, responsibilities and procedures may serve to provide a necessary chain of emotional holding for the staff, who are then enabled to provide such holding for the children. For example, the times most often identified by staff for the manifestation of emotional and behavioural difficulties are breaktimes and lunchtimes, periods when children move around the school, and the beginnings and ends of sessions, days and terms. These are all times when pupils are most vulnerable and most readily suffer when emotional containment is inadequate. Schools might therefore benefit from the use of the concepts of emotional containment and ego strengthening to help develop effective management policies and practices. Questions which schools might ask of themselves in this respect include:

- Is there school-wide agreement on setting and maintaining expectations and boundaries for pupils, and does any such agreement provide containment through the way in which it is implemented?
- Do staff, professional and ancillary, themselves feel contained so that they can in turn offer emotional containment for the children?
- Is there what might be called a 'chain of holding situations' to facilitate

emotional containment through the school? A chain of holding situations exists where senior staff are themselves contained, and are therefore able to offer containment to other staff, who are then able to offer emotional holding to the children.

- Are there regular meetings to offer a forum for teachers to air concerns and develop responses to children with special needs?

Exercise: Whole-school policy and emotional/behavioural issues

*/**/***

Shown below are a number of points to consider in formulating whole-school policy on behavioural issues. I suggest two ways in which this list can be used as a training exercise. The first is a relatively simple format: rank these as a list of priorities for your school/institution. Where a group is to undertake this exercise, it can be helpful to print each item from the list on a separate card, and for group members to rank them within a pyramid or diamond shape – which gives scope for equal rankings.

The more complex version of this exercise is explained after the list.

Ethos

- Does the school have a positive atmosphere in which there is a sense of shared purpose and values – a sense of community?
- In what ways does the school encourage mutual respect, social responsibility and self-discipline?
- In what ways does the school encourage children/young people to take responsibility for their behaviour and that of others?
- In what ways does the school ensure that care and control are not dichotomised?
- Are there whole-school approaches to talking about feelings as part of everyday school experience?
- Is there consistent communication of a sense of belief in the children?
- Are there whole-school guidelines on teacher responses to difficult behaviour – confronting where necessary whilst avoiding judgement or emotional threat?
- Are there whole-school approaches to building self-esteem, e.g. circle-time, achievement boards?
- In what ways are the whole child and the whole school kept in mind?
- Does the school adopt a proactive approach to behaviour? Is there a positive emphasis on achievement and praise?

- Are expectations high and boundaries about unacceptable behaviour clear?
- Is there a school-wide agreement on expectations and boundaries, and how these are communicated to learners and parents?
- Are expectations communicated consistently across the school?
- Is the policy perceived to be the responsibility of all staff, and known by all staff and pupils?
- Are there whole-school approaches to the emotional preparation for ends of days/terms/years, and for the loss of significant staff/peers?

Curriculum

- Do classroom management practices support the school's behaviour policy?
- Does curriculum planning practice take account of emotional factors in learning, e.g. anxiety–risk ratio, structuring for success?
- Are pupils enabled to build self-esteem and to experience themselves as valued members of groups?
- In what ways does the school encourage learners to be involved in their own formative appraisal/Record of Achievement?
- Is the success of learners positively reinforced in tangible ways?
- What sorts of attitude towards learning do the pupils show?
- Are there whole-school approaches to providing opportunities for exploring emotional issues symbolically through imaginative work?
- Are there whole-school approaches to positive reinforcement of social as well as academic developments?
- How does the school plan for continuity in work across changes of teachers/educational years?
- Are there whole-school approaches to training children in social skills, e.g. negotiating and working in groups?

Procedures

- Are the roles and responsibilities of staff clear in relation to behaviour policy?
- Are the 'routes' for following up behaviour issues clear?
- Is there a known and consistent recording mechanism for behavioural issues? Are the records monitored?
- Is there an integrated approach to the work of pastoral and academic systems?
- Does the school have guidelines for supporting bullies and victims?

Support

- Are there opportunities for the staff to share what they feel confident or pleased about in their work?
- Is there a 'chain of holding situations' to enable staff to feel contained so they can in turn provide emotional containment for the children?
- Is there a means for staff to work together to share questions, ideas, solutions in a problem-solving framework?
- Are there regular joint problem-solving/early warning meetings to air concerns and develop responses?
- Are ancillary staff involved in policy-making, training and review?
- Is there a clearly understood system of access to support agencies?
- Are there agreed ways of fostering mutual support amongst the staff?

Working with parents

- How does the school help parents to become more aware of how they can contribute to their child's learning?
- How does the school support regular contact with parents to set goals and develop supportive strategies?

You may wish to add your own points to the list.

***

A list like the one above can be used to help staff develop whole-school policy on behaviour. Ask the staff to work in groups, and each group to work on one of the above sets of questions. The groups should be given a specific task in relation to these questions, e.g. develop a list of objectives and possible strategies to achieve those objectives, using these questions as prompts to your discussion. The subgroups flip-chart their work and feed back to the whole group. The whole group is then asked to prioritise the suggestions made by the subgroups in terms of the developments which are most necessary in the school. One way of doing this is to allocate each member of staff a specific small number of votes (depending on the group size), and to take a vote of priorities on each of the lists of objectives and strategies devised by the subgroups. This is a speedy mechanism for devising the outline of a policy (in terms of objectives and strategies to be used) and getting a sense of the perceptions of the staff on the issues to be prioritised for developmental work.

Flexibility and the capacity for organisational change

The first part of this chapter highlighted ways in which organisations defend against changes and development. In a climate of rapid change, staff need opportunities to reappraise the organisation's values and their means of effective participation in the changing organisation. The systems approach to organisations reveals that organisational change is an essential part of a continuous process, through which the organisation maintains its equilibrium and effectiveness. Opposition and resistance to change can be understood by seeing them as the fear which people have of relinquishing established social systems that have helped to defend them against anxiety in the past.

> Since all variables in the system are interlinked, a rigidity in one will also affect the others, and the loss of flexibility will spread through the system . . . The flexibility of a system depends on how many of its variables are kept fluctuating within their tolerance limits: the more dynamic the state of the organism, the greater its flexibility. . . . Loss of flexibility means loss of health.
>
> (Capra 1982: 294–5, 354)

The need for members of an organisation to participate in the development of change is now widely recognised. 'Unless people have the opportunity to participate in the changes they will not be able to influence the formation of new social systems and the result will be an increase in suspicion, hostility and aggression' (De Board 1978: 143). Mongan and Hart (1989) suggest seven lessons for individuals concerned with managing processes of change within a school:

- Explore the resources and constraints of the circumstances in which change is to be introduced, and plan any initiative to use resources to maximum effect.
- Seek the active involvement and collaboration of at least one other person, rather than trying to go it alone.
- Seek institutional support and sanction for any initiatives.
- Work initially with a self-selected group of colleagues.
- Expect, and understand the reasons for, resistance, responding sensitively.
- Consult fully with colleagues not immediately involved.
- Enlist the involvement and co-operation of pupils, and ensure that they, as well as staff, receive support throughout the process.

Any change elicits emotional reactions, since it implies the loss of an old, known situation. Marris (1986) argues that loss is usually threatening, since the structure upon which learning has depended is undermined, stimulating a sense of anxiety and disorientation of purpose. Change may be experienced as catastrophic, even when rationally recognised for the

273

better, as it threatens the established and familiar order and requires new attitudes and behaviours, changes in relationships and a comparatively unknown future.

> Everyone in the organisation has come to understand his or her job – the purposes it satisfied, its give and take, the loyalties and rivalries it implies – as a familiar pattern of relationships on which they rely to interpret the events of the working day. This definition of their occupational identity represents the accumulated wisdom of how to handle the job, derived from their own experience and the experience of all who have had the job before, or share it with them. Change threatens to invalidate this experience, robbing them of the skills they have learned and confusing their purposes, upsetting the subtle rationalisations and compensations by which they reconciled the different aspects of their situation. . . . If innovation is imposed upon them, without a chance to assimilate it to their experience, to argue it out, adapt it to their own interpretation of their working lives, they will do their best to fend it off. . . . Like in mourning, a conflict dramatises a transition. . . . The working out of grief is projected as negotiation, through which everyone will come to reformulate their own sense of the meaning of their situation.
>
> (Marris 1986: 156–60)

Given the significance of such issues in organisational effectiveness and development, Marris suggests three principles for the management of change. First, change should expect and even encourage conflict, since people need the opportunity to react, to consider their ambivalent feelings and work out their own sense of the change. Second, the process of change implementation should respect subjective experiences of the change. Third, there needs to be time and patience to accommodate diverse interests and for grief to be worked through, as a crisis of reintegration, which can neither be escaped, nor resolved by anyone on behalf of another, nor hurried (Marris 1986).

In relation to the development of values and effective staff participation, what is important 'is not so much what *is* as what is *believed* to be [so that] an important managerial quality . . . is the imagination to see the world through the eyes of others, and to be able to identify the costs that *others* will carry' (Watson 1986: 104). Staff members involved in organisational change need to be helped to explore 'a series of emerging constructions of reality, including revision of the past, to correspond to the requisites of new players and new demands' (Moss Kantor 1983: 287). This corresponds to Marris's (1986) indication that for an innovation to be assimilated its meaning must be considered and shared. Greenfield (1989: 87) also argues that 'organisational change requires more than structural change; it requires changes in the meanings and purposes that individuals learn within

274

their society'. To this end he argues that there are three tasks: to map the versions of reality which people see around themselves; to discover stresses and disjunctures that threaten these definitions of reality; and to develop the commitment of people to new social goals and the means they consider effective for achieving them. 'Organizations do not always behave in a logical, predictable, manner. Acknowledging this reality, the non rational model attempts to turn it to the advantage of those in the system' (Patterson *et al.* 1986: 27).

Change is a process and 'it is *individuals* who have to develop new meaning' (Fullan 1991: 92). Developing meaning involves evaluating one's own values against the proposed change, considering losses incurred by change and new opportunities presented by it, reflecting upon skills and experiences which can be taken forward and made use of in the new situation, and gaining clarity about new roles and structures. 'The most beneficial approach consists in our being able to understand the process of change, locate our place in it, and act by influencing those factors that are changeable and by minimizing the power of those that are not' (Fullan 1991: 103). How 'subjective realities are addressed or ignored is crucial for whether potential changes become meaningful at the level of individual use and effectiveness' (Fullan 1991: 43).

Fullan (1991) suggests that themes in the implementation process prior to developmental change are vision-building, evolutionary planning, and monitoring/problem-coping. The building of vision involves the 'dismantling of dysfunctional old truths' (Peters 1990: 388), which benefits from the capacity, in Moss Kantor's words, 'to create and use myths and stories' (1983: 288). A process of formulating the value system is necessary, based on a few basic values and designed to unleash excitement (Peters and Waterman 1982). This requires the strengthening of shared vision and commitment. Staff need to be enabled to work through various 'levels of concern' (Hall and Hord 1987): what is their awareness of the reasons for change? What information do they have/need? How will proposed developments be managed? What will be the consequences of implementation? What opportunities for collaboration will there be? Planned change also involves work on structures, practices, beliefs and understanding.

The degree of flexibility and capacity for change will also depend upon the organisation's culture. Handy (1985) suggests a four-fold typology of organisational cultures: club (based on power), role (based on role functions), task (job- or project-oriented) and person (in which the individual is the central point). Weightman (1992: 58) points out that understanding the cultural nature of a particular school (or other organisation) is important for understanding the means of influence within it, giving the example that 'presenting the case for reform to a role culture by chatting in the staff room might not be as effective as preparing a well-argued document, whereas the reverse might hold true in a task culture'.

Buckley and Styan (1988) argue that management structures with shallow hierarchies are more responsive to changes than autocratic or bureaucratic ones with steep hierarchies and tight role definitions. Shallower hierarchies are also more effective where teachers fulfil multiple roles. Shipman comments that the Education Reform Act:

> increases the amount [of information] available, and directs much of it outside as well as around the school. That circulation of information is more typical of modern, information-based organisations than of traditional top-down hierarchies. Management will have to be alert to the possibility that the Act will alter the structure of schools.
>
> (Shipman 1990: 115)

Shipman argues that empowering staff to take decisions is the only real solution to the shift away from 'top-down' information circulation to the increasing amount of information produced and circulated at all levels within schools and colleges, and that management should spread leadership functions, rather than just delegating. The more teachers are empowered to deploy their own authority the more they are able to respond flexibly and creatively to the diverse needs of learners, and the more they are likely to cater for individual needs. An organisational climate which facilitates such work is dependent upon a sense of shared purpose and authority among staff. Schools create structures and define roles to create boundaries for individuals not only through the hierarchy structure but also through decision-making structures and lines of authority and responsibility. It is now necessary to explore more fully the significance of the concepts of role, task and authority.

Role, task and authority

The clarity of purpose required for any effective work also demands clarity about role functions within the organisation and the primary tasks expected of the role. 'Role is the idea or conception in the mind through which a person manages himself and his behaviour in relation to the system of which he is a member, so as to further its aim or its purpose' (Grubb Institute 1991: 5). Taking up a role implies making judgements about one's position in the organisation in relation to its aims. It involves being aware of and alert to:

> all the external and internal forces which put pressure on the system, making one's own judgements about how to respond to those forces at the time, so as to further the aim. . . . Taking up a role is not a mechanistic idea, but the result of the interaction between the person and circumstances in performance of a task.
>
> (Grubb Institute 1991: 5, 10)

Making judgements about role function and the performance of task within the dynamic context of the school (or other organisation) implies making use of one's 'observing ego' from the perspective of one's role.

> To take up a role implies being able to formulate or discover, however intuitively, a regulating principle inside oneself which enables one, as a person, to manage what one does in relation to the requirements of the situation one is in, as a member of this organisation or group.
>
> (Grubb Institute 1991: 4)

The Grubb Institute assert that taking up a role has a knock-on effect, with role behaviour creating opportunities and space for colleagues to take up their respective roles themselves:

> In taking a role, because the attitude of the role-taker is focussed on the task, he/she will be more interested in expecting and encouraging colleagues to focus on the task. That is, they will establish their own specific role relations with the task instead of having to rely on personal relations.
>
> (Grubb Institute 1991: 11)

Exercise: Your job description and your role

*/**

Consider your job description, and the above definition of role.

1 In which aspects of your job description are you most comfortably in role?
2 How do you take up your role in relation to various aspects of your job description?
3 In what ways are you drawn out of role?
4 What helps and what hinders you in taking up your role?

Achievement in role-related tasks is related to authority and power. These are the means by which the people in an organisation are linked to its purpose.

> Anyone contemplating, or involved in, a process of influence needs to reflect upon his source of power, and thence the range of influence that it suggests. In particular he needs to remember that the source of power, and the method of influence, will depend as much on the individual recipient and his perceptions as on the person applying the influence. The perception of the individual will be very largely coloured by the nature of his psychological contract with that group.
>
> (Handy 1985: 136)

Figure 31 shows the four main types of power which have been identified. As shown in the table, these four main types are given different names by Handy (1985) and the Grubb Institute (1991). Whilst their definitions of most of these categories are similar, Handy's notion of personal power relates to personal attributes, such as charisma, whereas the Grubb Institute conceives personality characteristics as projected power, or attributions given to one by others.

Authority is an attribute related to roles within a system. 'To exercise authority is to relate to what one does and the powers one has, so as to further the aim of the system or sub-system to which one has been appointed' (Grubb Institute 1991: 20). Power can be conceived of as an attribute relating to skill (personal power), what one controls or owns (instrumental power), title (official power) and attributions given to one by others (projected power) (Grubb Institute 1991).

> Where authority is dominant a person will neither seek to control others nor avoid being controlled by them. He will rather be concerned with management of the process in which he and those he works with are engaged in seeking to achieve the aims of their system. In so doing, by exercising authority on behalf of the system via his role, he creates the opportunity (the space) for others within the system to be free to take authority in their roles to join with him in working to the system's aims and objectives.
>
> (Grubb Institute 1991: 21)

The Grubb Institute argues that the tasks of management are accomplished more effectively if the manager exercises authority instead of relying on power:

After Handy 1985	After Grubb Institute 1991	
Expert power	Personal power	Relating to skill and expertise
Resource power	Instrumental power	Relating to what one owns or controls
Position power	Official power	Relating to title – power as a result of position in organisation
Personal power	Projected power	Personal attributes/Attributions given to one by others

Figure 31 Types of power

so long as the manager can keep the *aim of the system* centrally in mind, and take the trouble and time to brief others about the system, its aim and its tasks, he will be drawing upon his personal power, but others will be experiencing his *role* as a competent manager, not as a person concerned for himself and his own or sectional interests. If the manager is then able to monitor or manage his behaviour *in role*, i.e. concentrating on the system, then the other managers and staff working with him will experience him as *exercising authority* not power.

(Grubb Institute 1991: 25)

Exercise: Authority and power

*/**

1 What are the sources of your power within your school (or other organisation)?
2 In what ways do you exercise authority in the deployment of your role?

There are a number of problems about taking up a role. Handy and Aitken (1986) identify the potential areas of difficulty, shown in Figure 32.

Role theory offers a tool to help in understanding how people perceive other people in organisations. Our interactions with people are affected to a significant extent by the way we perceive them. Handy argues that:

roles are important to interactions since they provide *categories* into which we can fit data about people and make some assumptions. In seeking for role clarification we often rely on inadequate information, reject conflicting evidence, and are biased by early impressions.

(Handy 1985: 89–90)

Role ambiguity	It is unclear what one is meant to do or be in a certain role.
Role conflict	Arises when one of the roles we hold is in conflict with another of our roles.
Role overload	Too many responsibilities and not enough hours in the day.
Role underload	Underutilisation of one's skills, knowledge or experience.

Figure 32 Problems in taking up a role
(Handy and Aitken 1986)

279

This can lead to role confusion, or misperceptions about individuals in role. 'When interacting with individuals, separately or in groups, we continually seek for *role clarification*, since lack of congruence between the role perceptions of the interacting parties will lead to misinterpretations' (Handy 1985: 90). Many of the problems in organisations arise from misperceptions about role, or bad communications because of false role expectations.

The environment within which schools operate has become more turbulent, less predictable, and shaped by a growing number of outside factors. In such a context, because of the emotional difficulties surrounding change (see above), the irrational aspects of staff groups are more likely to become important factors. In these circumstances, clarity about their roles on the part of staff is dependent not just upon clear descriptions of the responsibilities of roles, but upon the capacity to maintain clear perceptions and awareness of feelings about their experiences of fulfilling complex roles in a rapidly changing environment. In schools, as in other organisations, there are also increasing expectations for people to work collaboratively as team members, a development which offers much potential, but which also has its dangers. 'When tasks are not clear, we lack a context for taking our roles . . . Paradoxically we depersonalize others when we step out of role. By implication we personalize our relationships when we take our role' (Hirschhorn 1988: 49, 55).

When one has a clear idea of one's role, one has access to a particular ego standpoint as a reference point from which to review one's performance in role and the meaning of related anxieties. When faced with anxiety, one can use one's role to mediate the immediate affect of a situation, and to help evaluate the location of the anxiety by considering its relationship to the role, as well as to the individual within the role. By knowing what one feels, one knows what the situation means, and then one knows, in the light of one's intentions, how to act. However, it is not often that teachers have structured and valued opportunities to undertake these sort of considerations to help in the fulfilment of their roles and primary tasks.

> The challenge is to help create a climate in which it is not just acceptable but *normal* for teachers to talk openly about their feelings, their perceptions, their misgivings . . . The only possible form that climate can take is one which acknowledges as legitimate and appropriate expressions of doubt, uncertainty, confusion and anxiety. . . . If you have to be *sure* before you open your mouth, most people are going to stay quiet. This type of open learning environment is after all standard for social workers and counsellors, and there is no reason why it should not be equally standard for teachers.
>
> (Claxton 1989: 72–3)

In working to marshal conscious thoughts, people may also 'revisit' their unconscious relationship to the issues under discussion. Just as projections from pupils might help to explain something of their feelings (see Chapter Three), so understanding feelings about issues to do with one's role and task in a work setting helps to identify the dynamics which impinge upon, hinder or facilitate the enactment of that role and the performance of primary tasks.

Where the work context is a potential source of anxiety because of both the emotional/behavioural issues of the learners, and also the rapidly changing environment within which schools operate, then the management task involves enabling people to remain clear, and to be empowered in relation to their roles. It is achieved, organisationally, not only through clear line management and supervision arrangements, but, crucially, through the practices of joint problem-solving (Hanko 1990) and consultation. Effective strategies for organisation development are aided by collaborative and interactive models which emphasise problem-solving, because of their focus on growth and development (Aubrey 1990).

Consultation and joint problem-solving

Ainscow (1991) argues that the two key strategies in making schools more effective for all learners are for schools to become better problem-solving institutions, and for teachers to strengthen their role as 'reflective practitioners'. He asserts that 'problems that occur in schools can be seen as opportunities for learning. . . . A successful school is one in which the relationships and interactions are facilitated and co-ordinated in order that the people involved can achieve their common mission' (Ainscow 1991: 8–9). He argues that traditional teacher education, particularly in the SEN field, has been seen as the search for solutions to solve a technical task, but that, given recent views of special educational needs as a function of learning contexts, teachers become more effective where they reflect upon and analyse classroom practice and organisational policy. Of particular significance is the teacher's reflection upon particular children as they interact with particular tasks and processes (Ainscow 1991). Given processes of projection (see Chapter Two), the dynamics involved in working with emotional/behavioural issues can become confusing, and the perspective derived from consulting with another person can be of significant benefit. The value of consultation for those seeking to facilitate emotional development and learning is becoming increasingly recognised (e.g. Hanko 1990). In mainstream school settings, it is also becoming recognised that it is useful for the SEN co-ordinator or those in support roles to use joint problem-solving and consultation approaches to help other teachers mobilise their strengths in working with children with special educational needs. Bowers makes the argument in very strong terms, stating that it is:

281

vitally important that those in support roles should develop levels of awareness and skills which, until now, have not been strongly in evidence in the teaching of children with special educational needs. Dedication, commitment, a capacity to care and faith in others' pronouncements and prescriptions are not enough. . . . As changes occur in our education system, then competencies which have previously not been expected become vital in those charged with support for the less advantaged pupils in our schools.

(Bowers 1989: 53)

Joint problem-solving brings together the various people involved in an issue and, within a process-oriented framework, aims to facilitate communication between them, to clarify differences in perception of the problem by focusing on *how* it occurs rather than *why*, to negotiate commonly agreed goals, and to explore specific steps towards change (Dowling 1985). The advantage of joint problem-solving is that it pools the experience and expertise of staff at the point where it is felt to be most needed. Consultation is the process whereby someone facilitates the problem-solving of another person or group. The general principles of these approaches are articulated in Figure 33.

Schein suggested three main types of consultancy: purchase of expertise, doctor–patient, and process consultation. Of these, process consultation best suits situations where the issues relate to the dynamics of interaction. 'Within this model the consultant ensures that the client *retains responsibility* for whatever problems there are and *continues to take responsibility* throughout the time of the involvement. . . . Effective process consultation involves assisting others to solve their own problems' (Bowers 1989: 38–9). This principle mirrors similar principles which are part of the counselling process, and which were discussed in Chapter Six.

Consultation may take a variety of styles, the appropriateness of each style being a function of the particular task in hand. The continuum of possible styles is described in Figure 34.

Interaction analysis:	Identifying interactions with a view to moving staff to self-sufficiency in problem-solving
Empirical approach:	Focuses on data provided by client
Reference to the unique:	Reference to the uniqueness of a situation rather than using a general solution

Figure 33 Principles of consultation and joint problem-solving
(adapted from Schein 1969)

Prescriptive–Informative–Catalytic–Supportive

Prescriptive mode:	'Try this . . .'
Informative mode:	'Have you seen . . .?' 'Why don't you ask . . .?'
Catalytic mode:	Reflecting, listening, joint problem-solving
Supportive mode:	Approving, confirming, helping the consultees to find their own solutions

Figure 34 Continuum of consultation styles
(adapted from Heron 1976)

The catalytic and supportive styles of consultation have many advantages in trying to strengthen teachers' capacities and clarity about their roles in relation to complex issues of facilitating emotional development and learning. These modes can be used proactively, to prevent worrying situations from escalating into further difficulties. This work enables teachers to explore and understand the situation in interactional terms, and to become more aware of their own role in its dynamics. The processes of work require consultees to feel under no pressure to have predetermined answers and, if there are anxieties, to have them contained and their meanings explored. To these ends, whether as consultant or as participant in a joint problem-solving activity, the effectiveness of the consultation is enhanced when the following principles and processes are taken into account.

Dowling and Osborne (1985) suggest a five-stage framework in consultation work. The first stage of the process is decribed as *joining manoeuvres*. This is the stage in which participants get the feel of the situation, and the consultant has the task of finding out how the problem is viewed by the various parties, leaving his/her own value system aside as much as possible (Bowers 1989). Bowers makes the point that a consultant (who may be external or internal, such as a support teacher) should take account of ways in which his/her own team's culture relates to the culture of the consultee team:

> Placing children with special needs first, and assuming that children's learning failures stem from inappropriate teaching, come naturally to many support team members. For many ordinary school teachers, on the other hand, these may be alien values. An effective support consultant will need to remain aware of the norms and expectations of the culture from which he or she stems, while acknowledging that they are not universally held outside that culture.
>
> (Bowers 1989: 40)

The consultant's task at this stage is to appreciate the setting in which the work takes place and to convey this appreciation, and also to demonstrate the ability to set and maintain boundaries, including time boundaries and the boundary of what one will and will not address from one's role. The consultant should also be clear about expectations and purpose, and so set the stage for reflection. This defining of the contract for the work, whether formal or informal, is a vital part of the initial stage of engagement. Bowers (1989) lists the elements of the contract as: the boundaries of the consultant's involvement; the purpose of his/her involvement; the kind of information the consultant needs; his/her role and what s/he will deliver; the support and involvement s/he needs from the client(s); the time schedule; and ground rules about confidentiality. He suggests (Bowers 1989) that consultants need, at this stage, the abilities to ask direct questions about the client's expectations of the consultant; tease out the client's position in relation to other members of the client system; state clearly what the consultant is prepared to offer and how s/he is prepared to work; and, where necessary, discuss with the client just why the contracting meeting is not going well.

The second stage (Dowling and Osborne 1985) is termed *defining the problem*. The consultant's task at this stage is to enable those involved to trust him/her sufficiently to provide the relevant information. This involves being able to probe unthreateningly the underlying aspects of the client's problem. This needs great care, since the client's sense of competence may be threatened by such discussion, and it is important that the consultant quickly develops a climate of trust. Clients might reveal that the actual problem is different from the problem initially presented. The consultant's use of open questions and statements invites exploration and collaboration. Closed questions and statements minimise such possibilities. Open questions are answerable, insight-generating, non-threatening, non-rivalrous and non-defensive (Hanko 1991). Formulating questions by beginning, 'Don't you think . . .' or 'I think . . .' is likely to produce a yes/no answer. In contrast, questions which lead to joint exploration are more likely to begin with, '*Could* it be that . . .?', '*What* would happen if . . .?', '*How* . . .?' (Hall and Hall 1988, Hanko 1990, 1991). In using such approaches, the consultant also avoids colluding with being given the role of the 'sole expert' (Hanko 1990). Where the consultant is successful in avoiding this collusion, de-skilling of staff is also avoided, and the professional autonomy of school staff is maintained and reinforced.

Where the consultant is able to appreciate how those involved feel about the situation, s/he is better able to contain anxieties aroused in the consultee(s). The consultee(s) may project some of their concerns onto the consultant, who, in the transference (see Chapter Two), may be made to feel anxieties similar to those experienced by the consultee(s). In this way the dynamic of the consultation may mirror the conflict faced by the consultee(s).

Dowling and Osborne (1985) refer to the third stage of the consultation process as *formulating the problem in interactional terms*. This requires the consultant to appreciate how the feelings of those involved relate to their capacities to find and use effective strategies. The consultant, whilst respecting the feelings of others (e.g. their feeling threatened by change), should not collude with any splits or defences employed by the consultees, and should avoid judgemental attitudes towards others. The consultant's capacities for this work are enhanced to the extent that s/he is aware of aspects of her/his own personality which affect the way s/he relates to the work under discussion. This requires the capacity to avoid 'jumping in with one's own stuff'. Where it is appropriate to acknowledge feelings in pursuit of the task, they are best acknowledged – both by consultant and consultees – within a framework of ownership of subjective experience by making 'I' statements about what one feels. An experienced consultant may make use, when appropriate, of his/her feelings and experiences in the consultation to acknowledge that the dynamics in the consultation might mirror the dilemmas or questions faced by the consultee in the issue which is being discussed.

The fourth stage of the consultation process (Dowling and Osborne 1985) is *reframing*. Reframing refers to helping the client to see the issue from the perspective of a new frame of meaning. To reframe means:

> to change the conceptual and/or emotional setting or viewpoint in relation to which a situation is experienced and to place it in another frame which fits the 'facts' of the same situation equally well or even better, and thereby changes its entire meaning. . . . What turns out to be changed as a result of reframing is the meaning attributed to a situation, and therefore its consequences, but not its concrete facts – or as the philosopher Epictetus expressed it as early as the first century AD: 'It is not things themselves that trouble us, but the opinions we have about these things.'
>
> (Watzlawick *et al.* 1974: 95)

Reframing can be a powerful tool for changing staff perceptions in a manner which strengthens people to work with an issue which, in the previous frame, seemed immensely difficult. The idea of reframing is illustrated by the difference between an optimist and a pessimist, the one saying that a glass is half full, the other saying that the same glass is half empty. Cox and Theilgaard (1987) claim that the essence of creativity lies in the capacity to change frames of reference rapidly, illustrated by an example from the Zen Buddhist tradition. Zen master Tai-Hui showed his monks a stick and said, 'If you call this stick a stick you affirm; if you call it not a stick, you negate. Beyond affirmation and negation what would you call it?' This is philosophically the same principle as that used in Hegelian dialectics, with its emphasis on a process that moves from an oscillation between thesis and antithesis to the synthesis transcending dichotomy (Watzlawick *et al.* 1974).

Example: Reframing

Dowling gives a useful example of a reframing statement:

A mother defined the school her child attended in particular, and the educational system in general, as conspiring to prevent her very bright daughter from developing her full potential. The school staff in turn regarded this mother as difficult and obstructive and their attempts to change her behaviour achieved very little. The situation escalated to such a pitch that the mother was banned from the school. From an interventive point of view, to put pressure on this mother to see the good points of the school or to try to put the school's case to her would only exacerbate her need to prove that she was right and 'they' were wrong.

A reframing statement about her being a caring parent who knew her daughter well and was aware of her needs may have lowered her defences and enabled her to accept that perhaps there was an alternative way of putting her feelings across. The situation ceased to be defined as 'her being wrong, the school being right and the expert forcing that view on her'. Instead she was defined as a good, caring parent who might not have found a way of conveying her views to the school successfully.

(Dowling 1985: 25)

The reframing process enables the consultee to consider the issue under discussion with a different perspective and different attitudes, thus facilitating a shift in the interactive dynamic. With a change of attitudes and approach, the possibility of different interventions becomes clearer.

The fifth stage of the process of consultation and joint problem-solving is termed, by Dowling and Osborne (1985), *task-setting*. In this phase the consultant continues to work from and extend the strengths of staff, tapping latent, sometimes unrecognised, skills and supplementing teacher expertise, by enabling consultees to come to their own resolutions about what further action they might take.

Exercise: Self-assessment of consultation and joint problem-solving skills

*

This profile is not meant to contain an exhaustive list of skills, but to serve as a tool for reflection. Complete the self-assessment profile to rate your current skill level on a scale of high/medium/low.

To be aware of one's own feelings	H M L
Not to get 'caught up' in other people's negative feelings	H M L
To respond thoughtfully, rather than react unconsciously, to the behaviour of others	H M L
To listen openly rather than selectively	H M L
To be aware of one's own body language	H M L
To be aware of the body language of others	H M L
To be aware of others' feelings	H M L

To empathise with others' feelings	H	M	L
To be able to appreciate and respect colleagues' concerns and anxieties	H	M	L
To listen affirmatively	H	M	L
To confront others non-threateningly	H	M	L
To respect the point of view of others, even if different from one's own	H	M	L
To communicate directly and clearly	H	M	L
To establish expectations with the agreement of others	H	M	L
To allow and enable others to initiate ideas	H	M	L
To ask people to say how they are feeling	H	M	L
To be able to hold back without needing always to contribute	H	M	L
To respect, silently but attentively, the contributions of others	H	M	L
To be able to weigh up arguments without 'sticking an oar in'	H	M	L
To be able to think diagnostically whilst continuing to listen attentively	H	M	L
To be able to consider unconscious aspects of interactive processes	H	M	L
To be flexible in responses	H	M	L
To show trust in other people	H	M	L
To be able to work from and build on the strengths of others, thus empowering others, without needing to be the sole expert who provides the answers	H	M	L
To keep material confidential when appropriate	H	M	L
To decide which material should or should not be kept confidential	H	M	L
To use an appropriate style of consultation depending on the needs of the situation	H	M	L
To be able to convey one's understanding and appreciation of the work of others	H	M	L
To be able to ascertain information by asking open-ended questions	H	M	L
To be able to recognise interactive dynamics underlying the situation, e.g. using one's experience of projection within the consultation to inform one's understanding of the issues involved for the consultee	H	M	L
To be able to perceive issues from different points of view, and to reframe in a way which helps consultees	H	M	L
To enable others to come to their own solutions or goals, without the impulsive need to present solutions oneself	H	M	L

Exercise: Consultation

***

This exercise needs a small group. Before the exercise begins, the group should agree the boundaries of confidentiality and time. One person provides an issue or problem for consultation. This might be any work situation which the consultee would like some help in thinking about, or in which s/he feels 'stuck'. A small number of people act as consultants. A further person might act as observer. At the end of the exercise the observer gives the group feedback on the processes of the consultation.

Exercise: Developing joint problem-solving skills – a role-play

***

This exercise is a group role-play. Before the role-play starts, the situational information is given to all participants, and the role-related information is given only to those playing the relevant role. The information given for this exercise is adaptable to suit a variety of circumstances.

Information given to all participants: the context

The role-play is to consider a review meeting of the progress of a boy called Michael, aged 10. Michael has been referred for educational support because of disruptive behaviour. He has had one term of support. It has been agreed to hold a review meeting after this term, because of the degree of concern about him. The meeting is held in school. The timing of the meeting was arranged between the headteacher and the support teacher; it was the latter who informed the mother about the meeting. Michael lives with both parents and an older sister who goes to the local college.

Class teacher

You are pleased to have the support of the additional teacher, and to see Michael's parent. It is the first time you have seen the parent since Michael started working with the support teacher. You are concerned about:

- Michael's poor level of reading;
- Michael's outbursts of temper, which you often manage by sending

---

him out of the class, despite being discouraged from doing so by senior managers;

- his difficulty in settling in after breaks.

Michael can be difficult to handle, and sometimes you do not know how to do this effectively. You quite like Michael, but wish he would let you get closer to him.

You feel the headteacher should be more supportive in terms of helping staff in the school to collaborate through the review and improved implementation of whole-school policy.

Headteacher

Your concerns at this time are these:

- Michael seems to be sent out of the classroom more than you would like.
- Michael's behaviour in the playground.
- You do not want to be openly disloyal to your class teacher, but you are not sure about the effectiveness of his/her classroom management skills.

Support teacher

During the last term you have been involved in supporting Michael's educational development and he has responded to you without any major difficulties. He has tended to be rather compliant with you. He has appeared to be not very involved, at an emotional level, in the relationship. He superficially gets on with the other children in support lessons when the topics are emotionally safe, but when feelings are being discussed, he tends to withdraw.

There has not been any marked change in Michael's educational attainments during the term. His reading continues to be poor for his age.

Parent

You have seen some improvement at home in the last term with Michael, though he still tends to be sullen and moody, but rarely angry. You know Michael's reading is poor, and are worried about it, but find it difficult to read with him at home.

The relationship with your spouse is very poor at the moment – you are having quite a few rows. Your spouse is often out of the house. You suspect the influence of this on Michael, but have not talked to him about it. You have more or less convinced yourself that Michael's older sister does not seem to be negatively affected by the situation between you and your spouse. Any opportunities to locate current problems with Michael as the fault of the school make you feel relieved.

Observer 1

Observe the ways in which the interventions of the support teacher get both taken up and supported, and the ways in which they get blocked.

Observer 2

Observe the extent to which the stages of consultation are reflected in the meeting, i.e.:

• joining manoeuvres;
• defining the problem;
• formulating the problem in interactional terms;
• reframing – giving the problem a new frame;
• task setting.

Observer 3

Observe ways in which emotional containing/holding and ego strengthening are facilitated.

Observer 4

Observe the strengths in the support teacher's interventions.

Work at the boundaries of the organisation

The rapidly changing social context in which we live is reflected in the amount of change recently and currently experienced in educational establishments. In the past, not only schools but organisations in general were able to give their almost undivided attention to what was happening inside their organisation. Today, the general social and political environment impinges much more than previously upon the work of schools. As a result of recent legislative changes, the roles of central government, local industry, Training and Enterprise Councils, parents, and governing bodies all have a much more direct impact on what happens in schools. Schools are also more autonomous: more decision-making power about relationships across the boundaries is located in the school itself. In terms of systems theory, schools used to be much more akin to closed systems, whereas today they are much more open. 'The open-system concept highlights the vulnerability and interdependence of organizations and their environments. . . . environment is important because it affects the internal structures and processes of organizations' (Hoy and Miskel 1989: 29). Today schools are open systems to the extent that judgements about management issues are based on what school managers consider to be the perceptions of a range of external stakeholders, whose actions are influenced by the market. There is a changing culture which demands that schools (and indeed a range of other organisations) need to spend time, energy and money managing their affairs in relation to their external environments. The demands and requirements of the external environment necessitate that schools become involved in increasingly complex mediation work (Bridger 1991). Whereas in the past the work beyond the boundary of the school organisation was simply divided between the headteacher and one or two other members of staff, today many staff are involved in work at the interface of the school and other organisations. This has necessitated a huge change in activities at the boundaries of schools as organisations.

Today the boundary of the school's work as an organisation is complex. It is even difficult to determine whether some groups of stakeholders should be regarded as external or internal to the institution (Glatter 1989). Stewart (1989: 37) suggests that with the new agenda, 'the school territory is jointly owned, the boundaries are permeable with regular flow across and control is again a joint affair'. Where managers take account of the impact of the external environment upon a school, the significance of uncertainty is highlighted. Boundaries help define relationships, and the relationships which staff have with even simple boundaries can create anxiety. The increasing complexity of work at the boundaries of schools provides additional potential for staff anxiety to be generated.

> A boundary can create anxiety in three ways. First, when inappropriately drawn, it creates destabilizing dependencies so that people are unable to accomplish their tasks. Second, when appropriately drawn, the boundary may highlight the risks people face in trying to accomplish their tasks. . . . Third, when appropriately drawn, the boundary may stimulate the feared consequences of one's own aggression or aggression from others.
>
> (Hirschhorn 1988: 37)

As the boundaries between the internal and external environments of schools and other organisations are much more complex today than a decade ago, the staff roles are also much more complicated and interdependent. These changes potentially create greater pressures, due to the greater complexity of teachers' roles and tasks, and also because they

require individua
practices, which are all areas of potential resistance and conflict.

The boundaries around physical systems are more clearly defined than those around social systems. The elements of a so-called open system are continually in contact with their environment. The boundary is of particular significance in an open system, since exchanges take place at the boundary, enabling the system to maintain its dynamic equilibrium. An individual may be seen as an open system, and so may an organisation.

> When open systems theory is applied to groups and organisations . . . the organisation is then seen as a living system, open to and in contact with its environment, where the essential need is for work to be done at the boundaries, so that appropriate exchanges can be made across the boundary, thereby maintaining the organisation in a state of dynamic equilibrium with its environment. . . . the work of continually monitoring and reacting with the environment, and maintaining an appropriate internal organisation, is an energy-consuming task that can create intense anxieties. . . . The withdrawal of energy from engagement with reality moves the organization into a closed system, which by definition can do no work.
>
> (De Board 1978: 141)

Watkins (1989) argues that, in relation to personal and social education, the overlapping influences of home, school and neighbourhood in students' 'life spaces' should be taken account of in enabling young people to gain perspective on their lives, and that schools will not be able to achieve this if they play a highly boundaried role: 'there need to be permeable boundaries, where the realities of home and of neighbourhood are brought into the school experience' (Watkins 1989: 52).

Teachers' work with parents is an example of work at the boundaries of schools, and 'when teachers take the pastoral aspect of their role seriously they have to face outwards from the school' (Watkins 1989: 63–4). It is with parents of pupils 'that schools have invested most heavily in establishing communication networks' (Williams 1989: 16) across the boundaries of the organisation. If exchanges at the boundary of an organisation enable it to maintain its dynamic equilibrium, then it follows that the teacher's work with parents has implications for the health of the school as an organisation.

> If we adopt a participatory, rather than a compensatory, model of parental involvement (e.g. Widlake 1986), founded upon the assumption that most parents will want to help their children, given the right opportunities, information and encouragement, then our responsibility is to create the conditions which will foster maximum involvement.
>
> (Mongan and Hart 1989: 88)

The so-called 'Warnock Report' (DES 1978) highlighted the significance of partnership with parents, and there is now a substantial literature in this field (e.g. Sardow *et al.* 1987, Wolfendale 1983) which shows that partnerships between schools and parents have much potential for helping children's learning. Mitchell (1989: 93) points out that it 'is now received wisdom that "improvement" in home–school links has been instrumental in improving the academic attainment of many children in primary and secondary schools'. Williams (1989: 18) argues that 'relationships between schools and their communities are dependent on the degree of mutual trust and confidence which exists through a genuine understanding of their interdependence and recognition of differentiated roles and functions'.

Such trust and differentiated interaction require careful management. Relationships with parents is also an area full of possibilities for the development of defences and splitting, with schools and parents potentially blaming each other for difficult situations which might develop, thereby inhibiting the capacity for joint work on problem resolution. This is particularly the case with the parents of children experiencing emotional and behavioural difficulties, who are likely to have more than average anxieties about their children. Hence, given the discussion above about the development of social defences, work at the boundaries of schools with this group of parents is of particular significance.

The 'emotionally holding school' manages its boundaries with parents in such a way as to work effectively with the actual or potential anxieties which might manifest in working in partnership with them. The parents of troubled children may themselves feel frustrated and confused. They may, in some way, feel themselves to be failures as parents. Such parents, in their anxiety state, may face themselves with questions like, 'What did I do wrong?' Such questions reinforce the possibilities for them to feel guilt or blame, and in so doing, inhibit their capacity to think about their child's needs, perhaps reinforcing an already difficult dynamic. Questions from parents about what they *should* have done are often better dealt with in terms of what collaborative approaches the school and parents might take thenceforth. School and community relationships need to be 'consciously developed through co-operative collaborative enterprise' (Williams 1989: 29). The skills which teachers develop in providing emotional holding and ego strengthening for children, and in joint problem-solving with other staff, may be redeployed in engaging and working effectively with anxious parents or parents of children experiencing emotional and behavioural difficulty.

Example: Work with a parent

In the months since Simon had been attending tutorial class he had made noteworthy progress with his reading. One day he arrived for his session accompanied not just by his escort but also by his father. He said he had asked his father to come because he wanted him to hear him read. So whilst I worked with the other children in the group, Simon sat to one side and read to his father. Listening to what followed was, for me, a painful experience, since this father gave his son no encouragement, and instead repeatedly articulated negative comments about Simon's reading. It seemed to me that, rather than any purposeful maliciousness being involved, this father was unaware of the processes of creating a 'facilitating environment' for his son's reading. Furthermore, as a precursor to any information-giving on my part about how this father might help Simon with his reading, it seemed necessary to affirm this father's parenting role. Simon's invitation to his father to come to the session to hear him read gave me an opportunity to point out to the father the importance Simon attached to his father's support.

This example of work with an individual parent serves to demonstrate important underlying principles of work with parents as a collective group. With regard to more general work with parents, the following questions may be pertinent to school staffs wishing to build collaborative relationships with parents of troubled children:

- What initiatives are taken to introduce the school to parents?
- What is done to give parents an understanding of what the school is trying to do, and of their part in it?
- What does the school do to help parents become more aware of, and interested in, the way they might contribute to the learning of their child?
- How are parents informed about the expectations of the school, and how is this information reinforced? For example, are the communications about expectations made both verbally and in writing?
- What expectations are set about when and how often teachers and parents meet?
- How is a mainstream school's policy for SEN discussed with parents?
- Can the school's brochure for parents be improved?
- Are parents clear that the school recognises and values the experience and knowledge they have of their children?
- How are parents encouraged to offer this knowledge? Are opportunities provided regularly, as well as when something particular has occurred?
- How does the mainstream school plan for continuity in work with parents of children with SEN through changes of teachers and educational years?
- Are there opportunities for parents to be supported through a series of joint problem-solving meetings with teachers?

This last question poses a series of further questions (with acknowledgement to ILEA 1982 for aspects of these):

- What arrangements are there for parents to discuss their child's developments and progress with the teachers, and other professionals, both informally and in connection with statutory requirements for review and assessment?

- What are the various kinds of meeting held for parents? What proportion of parents come to each kind? How does the school get in touch with those who do not attend?

- In what circumstances would the school invite parents to participate in a non-statutory review leading to mutually agreed goals? Watkins and Wagner (1987) argue that such meetings might be most useful when the child's behaviour varies little across the various aspects of school life, when there does not seem to be any discernible pay-off for the behaviour in the immediate situation, and when it is known that parental involvement has been important in the past for similar sorts of difficulty in school.

- How are interviews with parents best conducted?

- How can the school use its contacts to relate to parents in a non-threatening and non-judgemental way, building empathy and trust, whilst working to contain parental anxieties, demonstrate the importance of the parents for their children, build on those interventions the parents are able to make which are positive, avoid exploring the child's difficulties in causal terms, but formulate co-operation in terms of how school and parents might move forward together from the current position? How can the school also work to provide expectations of parents which elicit realistic and appropriate parental responsibility, undertake joint goal setting with parents to encourage children's active participation in learning, and maintain communication between home and school (e.g. through the use of a home–school diary)?

- How are complaints and difficulties dealt with? Do parents feel their views are listened to?

- Is the school able to offer any experiences which provide good role-models for those struggling with parenting?

Exercise: Work with parents

*/**/***

How might considerations of the above series of questions about work with parents contribute to developmental work in your organisation?

Exercise: Joint problem-solving and policy development

***

This is a group role-play exercise, in which some participants are asked to form a working group, and others are observers. Roles may be allocated at random (by, for example, inviting participants to choose task cards). The roles, the observation tasks and the role-play task are adaptable to suit a variety of circumstances, according to the size and composition of the training group.

The task cards assign roles for both members of the role-play group and observers. Examples are given below.

Role-play group

- Headteacher.
- Deputy headteacher (you have been asked to chair the meeting).
- Special educational needs co-ordinator.
- Classroom teacher.
- Ancillary member of staff.
- Governor.
- Parent.

Observers

- Collect evidence of the ways in which any 'flak' or difficulties are passed from one part of the organisation to another.
- Collect evidence of the ways in which difficulties or anxieties are avoided. These may include splitting, denial, or the distortion of experience.
- Collect evidence of the ways in which people get caught up in the drive to 'do' something, at the expense of working reflectively.
- Collect evidence of the ways in which people are reminded of:

  - the need to relate to the 'whole child';
  - the need for each staff member to be able to relate to the whole task of the school.

- Collect evidence of the ways in which the group works towards:

  - *all* staff being able to participate in the development of changes;
  - staff being given opportunities to work on the new meanings which changes might bring to their sense of occupational identity.

- Collect evidence of the ways in which the group tries to ensure clarity of role and task for members of staff.
- Collect evidence of the concerns expressed for what happens at the 'boundaries' of the school as an organisation – i.e. between the school, and other agencies/parents/governors.

A scenario and a task are given by the facilitator, e.g.: there is concern about children with emotional and behavioural difficulties in your school. You have done some training and development work in this area, but there is a general feeling that the school is still working reactively rather than proactively on 'emotional/behavioural difficulty' (ebd) issues. This meeting is the first to work on whole-school policy as it relates to children experiencing emotional/behavioural difficulties.

This exercise is best facilitated by giving observers an opportunity to clarify their briefs, and a few moments for role-play members to prepare. The facilitator sets an appropriate amount of time for the role-play, and manages the time boundary.

Debriefing

At the end of the role-play the potential of this exercise is realised through several stages of debriefing:

1 Members of the role-play group are invited to say how they feel, given their experiences in participating in the role-play task, from the point of view of their role.
2 Members of the role-play group are then invited to de-role (for example, by saying their own name).
3 There is feedback from the observers.
4 Members of the role-play group have an opportunity to comment on the fairness of the feedback.
5 There is a general discussion of the issues raised.

NB The debriefing for this exercise requires much more time than the role-play itself.

Exercise: Developing policy from the perspective of various interest groups

***

This exercise is adaptable to a variety of circumstances. The training group is asked to imagine the following scenario: a school recognises it has some issues to face about students with emotional/behavioural difficulties. A situation has developed whereby the school has agreed to set up a forum to work on these issues, which will represent the interests of pupils, teachers, school senior management and parent-governors. The forum is to meet three times.

Members of a training group are divided into four groups, each of which represents the interests and perspectives of one of the four groups given above. One person in the training group is randomly assigned the role of chairing the forum meetings. (During the subgroup meetings this person is able to visit and observe the subgroups.) The facilitator(s) leading this exercise act as consultants, particularly in subgroup meetings.

Subgroup meeting – current experiences

Each of the subgroups works separately. Subgroup task: describe your current experiences from the point of view of the group whose interests you represent. Identify the underlying problems which are getting in the way of progress.

Forum meeting – current experiences

The four groups come together for the forum meeting. It is chaired by the person who has been assigned this role. Task of meeting: to share definitions of the problem from the perspectives of the four groups whose interests are represented, and to develop a shared understanding of the factors reinforcing current problems.

How can things be improved?

Should the trainer(s) wish to make an input, this is an appropriate point to do so.

Subgroup meetings

Subgroups work separately. Task: to consider how the situation might be improved from the perspective of the group you represent, and to make recommendations to take to the final forum meeting.

Forum meeting

Task: develop an action plan agreed by all parties, and agree the responsibilities each of the subgroups would have in implementing the plan.

Debriefing

Participants are asked to reflect upon the implications of what they have experienced and learned during this exercise for their own work roles.

SUMMARY

- Effective schools depend on processes which facilitate the dynamics of interaction within the organisation.
- The capacity for effective participation in an organisation, and for its change, is affected by subjective perceptions and affective experiences. Work with troubling children increases the anxiety levels of staff, thus rendering the subjective realms of work within the organisation pertinent and potentially powerful.
- Organisations function as systems which develop social defences against difficult feelings aroused in the organisation's operation. Social defences manifest in various forms, such as splitting, denial and distortion.
- Providing an effective organisational base to facilitate emotional growth and learning involves working with the desire to offer reparation and the need to relate to the whole task of the school or other organisation. This highlights the significance of working on whole-school policy for the health of the organisation as a system.
- In facilitating flexibility and the capacity for organisational change, given the inhibiting effect of defences – for example against change – the capacity of managers to help staff to develop positive subjective perceptions of working within an organisation is of particular significance.
- Clarity about role and task helps to further the institution's aims, to mitigate anti-task phenomena, and for staff to work with an 'observing ego'. When staff take up their roles effectively, task-focused work is enhanced. Where staff work in role, in furtherance of the organisation's aims, others experience the exercise of authority.
- Joint problem-solving and consultative approaches help the school to be an effectively learning organisation in which staff are empowered to find their own solutions to problems. The process involves enabling staff to reflect upon the meaning of their experience of interaction, defining problems in terms of the interaction surrounding them, and developing new perceptions, attitudes and interventions.
- Exchanges which take place at the boundary of the organisation enable the system to maintain its dynamic equilibrium. Managing the boundaries of schools has in recent years become more complex, but effective management of the boundary is an important component in defining task and purpose, and so providing an effective organisational base.

AFTERWORD

During the writing of this book, the media have increasingly highlighted a number of related issues – bullying, juvenile crime and the rising rate of school exclusions of pupils with behaviour difficulties. Whilst there are no easy answers to these problems, the general principles of this book are pertinent to considering them. We become available for learning and development only when we have the inner experience of emotional containment or holding. We live at a time when some troubled children are expressing in very graphic, public and disturbing ways their lack of a sense of emotional containment, and their search for limits and for meaning. The effectiveness of our provision of the necessary emotional containment for troubled and troubling children depends upon the extent to which we relate to the issues at hand, in what I have described as a 'process'-related manner. Where we can learn to consider each of our interventions (at macro and micro levels) as a series of processes which contribute to the processes of emotional growth, then it is more likely that the potential of individuals for growth and learning will be released. The chapters in the second part of this book outline the processes involved in facilitating emotional growth and learning. Rather than being prescriptive in nature, I have sought to explore the psychological nature of the processes, in the hope that readers will be able to imagine how they might apply such thinking in a range of contexts, settings and organisations.

In Britain the culture of public service organisations is changing in adaptation to their market contexts. With the customer supposedly paramount, services are increasingly seeking to become more 'client'-related. But the market is an inadequate barometer of the needs of public service clients. It may pander to unconscious drives, rather than help us reflect upon and meet needs arising from individual and societal ills. The health of our collective psyche depends upon us finding meanings which nourish our lives. At this time of rapid change, the structures which have provided meaning for us are no longer reliable. It seems more and more apparent that each individual is faced with the struggle for meaning – meaning in relation to our social and economic environment, meaning in relation to the individual's potential. Inevitably, children bring these dilemmas and conflicts into our educational and social service institutions. The values and the structures of these services are also undergoing rapid change. At a time of rapid social flux, when we cannot depend upon old solutions which were previously appropriate, there seem few stable structures of meaning to which we can look for solutions.

In times such as these, it becomes increasingly important to be clear about the affective impact of our work, helping children to develop meaning in the wider world. This means that we need to be clear about the emotional processes in which we are engaging, to understand the affective experience of others, and to use this understanding to help us to become clearer about the sorts of response which are likely to be effective. In educational and social service provisions, the way in which we perform our daily tasks expresses what we as individuals and services have made of these underlying meanings. The more we can be attuned to young people's needs from a 'process' perspective, the better placed we will be to help them find personal and shared meanings, and to foster emotional growth and learning.

APPENDIX 1
THE TUTORIAL CLASS SERVICE

Tutorial classes in inner London specialise in work with children whose learning is impeded by a range of emotional and behavioural factors. The first class was established in 1947 in Stepney, to cater for returned evacuees whose emotional difficulties inhibited their educational development. From its inception until a reorganisation in 1988, the tutorial class service was the responsibility of ILEA's Schools Psychological Service.

The service aims to enable children to use the educational and social opportunities offered within mainstream education; to foster children's learning and growth by working through emotional difficulties which have inhibited their educational development; actively to support children to remain integrated within mainstream education; and to provide when necessary ongoing observation and assessment to help clarify children's special educational needs.

Referral to tutorial class takes place at Warnock Assessment Stage 4, i.e. when there is continued school concern about a child after the school has attempted to meet the child's needs through active consultation with parents, supportive school-based provision, and clarifying and improving management strategies. Another condition for referral is the clear expectation that tutorial class intervention will enable the child positively to remain in and use the mainstream school, with the aim of complete, full-time reintegration.

Placement in tutorial class is always part-time, usually about two sessions a week. This enables children to have continuity of experience with the mainstream classroom for most of their timetable. The work takes place in a small-group setting, where fewer relationships provide intense opportunities for working on the capacity for relationship. The service works through the curriculum to promote emotional and social growth, and to improve access to learning. Part of the work is to improve literacy and numeracy skills, to give children confidence in their ability to learn and their desire to do so. Creative arts and play are used to help foster emotional

growth, and the children are encouraged to work on their feelings, relationships and behaviour. Working on personal and social development in
this way helps reduce anxiety and promotes the child's access to learning
and the curriculum. The average length of stay is eighteen months, and at
the end of placement 80 per cent of children are successfully reintegrated
full-time in their mainstream schools, with a minority being referred to
special schools.

The tutorial class service also works consultatively with schools and
parents to support the learning of referred children, and contributes to
in-service training on special educational needs related to emotional and
behavioural difficulty.

From its inception in the late 1940s the service expanded, and by the late
1970s there were fifty-five classes throughout inner London, working at any
one time with about a thousand troubled children of ages between 5 and
16, attending on part-time placements. An example of one borough gives
an impression of the extent of service at borough level. In the London
Borough of Hackney, with a teaching staff of six teachers-in-charge serving
a potential catchment including seventy-two primary schools, six classes
worked at any one time with a total of about a hundred pupils on roll.
Despite the cost-effective nature of the service, with the break-up of the
ILEA, and the Education Reform Act's requirements for LEAs to delegate
budgets, tutorial classes in the various boroughs have in recent times met
various fates.

APPENDIX 2
SANDPLAY

Margaret Lowenfeld first used sandplay in 1928 at the Institute of Child Psychology, London. She used it mainly as a technique for studying non-verbal communication in children, and developed a graphing approach for statistical purposes. It was Dora Kalff, a Jungian analyst working in Switzerland, who developed the therapeutic aspects of sandplay and the interpretation of meaning.

A sandtray is used, its size corresponding to what the eye can encompass. The sandtray provides a context within which the child experiences a free and protected space. The sandbox and sand suggest a neutral starting-point, and provide the opportunity for a relaxed space, within which images may flow. In making a sandworld the individual sculpts the sand and adds his/her choice of miniature objects. The construction of a sandworld takes place free of the will of others. There should be a wide range of miniatures available, from which the person making a sandworld can choose those which are subjectively appealing or meaningful. In order to provide the necessary emotional container for this work, sandplay should take place in an emotionally contained environment in which the process is respected and honoured.

Sandplay is a means by which one can express oneself non-verbally and experience oneself. The sandworld corresponds to an inner situation or drama, in a way which is comparable to a dream experience. Sandplay thus serves as bridge between inner and outer worlds. The therapeutic value comes through the process of making imaginative connections, rather than through interpretations from another person. The person grows emotionally through giving expression to the inner drama, creating a metaphor which allows it to move, symbolically. Any image freed by a construction of it in turn frees the image for movement. In play the ego is in submission to the creative imagination. The experience of sandplay thus widens the possibilities for growth.

References: Dundas 1978; Jung Institute San Francisco 1981; Kalff 1980; Reed 1975; Ryce-Menuhin 1991; Weinrib 1983.

GLOSSARY

Acting-out

The behavioural expression of disturbing feelings.

Affect

Feeling, emotion.

Archetypes

The concept developed by Jung to refer to those organisers of experience which are strong and potentially overwhelming energies within the collective unconscious and which structure our behaviour and lay down patterns for our thinking, beliefs and action.

Behaviourism

Founded on the work of John B. Watson, and sometimes referred to as social learning theory. Based on the assumption that most human behaviour is completely determined by the environment. Reality is considered to be external, quantifiable, and objectively perceptible. This school of thought considers that we learn through recognisable processes of reinforcement, and therefore that behaviour can be modified.

Collective unconscious

A shared and underlying aspect of the unconscious which serves as a repository of 'symbolic memory', available to individuals across cultures and time, whose existence was established by Jung.

Defences

Used in this book to refer to psychological barriers to growth or relationship which function to protect the personality from the fear of attack or anxieties, and to keep the conflicts which they mask out of conscious awareness.

Denial

A form of defence which is used to block unwanted aspects of experience. It involves an avoidance of the acceptance of painful feelings, often at an unconscious level.

Depressive position/experience

A concept developed by Klein. The depressive position refers to the psychological state in which a person is able to perceive him/herself and other people as whole, separate persons, and in which one can acknowledge ambivalences, that good and bad emanate from the same people, and that one can have a range of feelings (e.g. love and hate) for the same person.

Differentiation

The term given to the process of planning and delivering the curriculum – teaching methods, learning activities, assessment methods and resources – to cater for the needs of individual pupils.

Distortion

A form of psychological defence in which an individual unconsciously distorts his/her experience to fit in with his/her subjective perception of reality.

Ego

The conscious part of the personality which mediates and relates to inner and outer realities.

Ego-provision

Refers to the provision of an auxiliary ego, i.e. the adult uses his/her ego on behalf of the child to provide structured help for the child to contain disturbing feelings. This is particularly important for unintegrated children. Dockar-Drysdale makes the distinction between ego-provision and ego-support.

Ego strength

Refers to the strength of functioning of the ego part of the personality.

Ego-support

Refers to planning and provision to support the development of poorly functioning aspects of the ego. This aspect of provision is particularly important in reinforcing the independence of those children whom Dockar-Drysdale describes as newly or relatively integrated. Dockar-Drysdale makes the distinction between ego-provision and ego-support.

Emotional holding or containing

Similar concepts – emotional holding is Winnicott's and emotional containment is Bion's. They refer to the process of holding or containing disturbing feelings, to show that such feelings can be tolerated, managed, thought about and understood as having meaning, so that one might develop a different relationship with them.

Facilitating environment

A concept developed by Winnicott. The facilitating environment is an environment which subtly adapts to meet a child's needs as they change in relation to maturational processes. Initially the environment is essential to the child in order to meet dependency needs, and gradually it becomes less essential as the child grows towards independence.

Formative assessment

The ongoing assessment of a pupil's achievements so that appropriate next steps in learning may be planned by pupil and teacher.

Identification

A concept of Freud's which refers to one person having emotional ties with another person (or object), and experiencing aspects of the other person as part of him/herself.

Individuation

A concept developed by Jung which refers to a person becoming him/herself, whole, and distinct from, yet in relationship with, other people.

Integrated/unintegrated

Distinction made by Dockar-Drysdale to refer to the relative development of ego functioning. An unintegrated person has very little ego availability, and is characterised by internal chaos and disorganisation which may manifest, for example, in helplessness, insecurity, panic or disruption. An integrated person has achieved psychological separation and is able, at least to some extent, to relate to the notion of being responsible for one's own actions.

Internalisation

The process by which all experiences or attributes of others are 'taken in' and established within the psyche of an individual.

Introjection

Notion developed by Freud. It refers to the process in which the individual takes attributes of other people (or objects) into him/herself and installs them as part of his/her own inner world (Reed and Palmer 1972). This is an important mechanism for growth, since it is through the introjection of 'good objects' such as loving relationships that one develops the sense of being a lovable and loving person. Introjection may also be a mechanism for defence, by the individual setting up inside him/herself an image of someone else which can be the subject of internal control.

Life space

A concept developed by Lewin which refers to the frame of reference, or formulation of reality, which an individual makes because of his/her sub-jective perceptions and experiences of the world.

Maladjustment

Notion prevalent in British education circles from the Second World War until the Warnock Report of 1978 (DES 1978). It was based on a medical model which tended to focus on individual 'illness'.

Neurosis/neurotic experience

Anxiety states in which the capacity for insight remains available (in con-trast to psychotic experience), and which are only quantitatively different from 'normal' experience.

Object relations theory

A theory, derived from psychoanalysis, which explains psychological activity in terms of humans relating to 'objects' or entities which attract attention or satisfy a need (Samuels *et al.* 1986).

Observing ego

Refers to an individual's capacity to observe him/herself and use the observations to make judgements about him/herself and to manage him/herself in relation to other people or a task.

Omnipotence

Refers to wilfulness and having to have things one's own way. Psychoanalytic theory suggests that omnipotence is related to the fear that getting one's own way is the only way of preserving the experience of things being good. Omnipotence is a characteristic of what Klein refers to as the 'paranoid-schizoid' state.

Paranoid-schizoid state

Notion developed by Klein to refer to a state in which the individual wishes to remain in control of experience. In this state the individual lacks the capacity to tolerate negative feelings – these are split off and experienced as belonging to someone else. The individual is then able to experience him/herself as being totally good.

Personal constructs

A notion developed by Kelly to describe the interpretations and personal systems of meaning which people make of the world from the point of view of subjective reality.

Pleasure principle

A notion of Freud's which refers to unconscious desires or impulses derived from the physical instincts which relate to drives toward wish fulfilment. Freud contrasts this principle with the reality principle.

Potential space

A notion developed by Winnicott: a space in which the worlds of fantasy and play and shared reality overlap and contribute to self-realisation.

Projection

A notion of Freud's which relates to the unconscious process by which a person pushes out unwanted feelings (through actions or comments) in the attempt to lodge them in other people or things. It is a defence mechanism through which the projecting individual controls problematic feelings and obtains a temporary sense of release, and genuinely believes that the person/object onto whom the feeling is projected is the source of that feeling.

Projective identification

A process whereby individuals and groups expel parts of themselves (into another person or object) and unconsciously identify with the projected material seen in others. The person or object is then experienced as if it were the projected content.

Psyche

The totality of psychological processes, conscious and unconscious.

Psychosis/psychotic experience

An experience in which uncontrollable fantasy breaks loose in the psyche and insight is unavailable to the person involved. Psychotic experiences may arise from both affective and organic conditions.

Reality principle

Developed by Freud, who believed that what he referred to as 'pre-conscious' material, which contains all the ideas and memories capable of becoming conscious, operates in a more disciplined way than the unconscious, takes into account the demands of reality and tolerates delays of satisfaction. Freud contrasts the reality principle with the pleasure principle.

Repression

A defence mechanism by which emotions or ideas which are unacceptable to the ego are rendered unconscious.

Self

A term of which many psychological writers have developed different concepts. In this book it is used to refer to the dynamic centre of the psyche which experiences the unity of the personality as a whole (after Jung), which is also similar to Winnicott's notion of the self as a 'totality based on the operation of the maturational process' (Winnicott 1970).

Special educational needs

Notion developed by the Warnock Report (DES 1978) as relating to individual needs rather than developmental deficits. The 1981 Education Act defines a child as needing special educational provision if s/he has a disability which interferes with his/her education, or if s/he has a significantly greater difficulty in learning than the majority of children of his/her age. It has since become increasingly recognised that special educational needs often arise as a result of interaction between the child and the environment. School and classroom organisation play a part in causing and alleviating special educational needs.

Splitting

A concept central to Klein's theories, which describes the defence mechanism in which 'bad' experiences are split off, cutting out negative feelings, but producing a situation in which feelings and relations are cut off from one another.

Social defences

Defences against anxieties evoked by institutional membership, which are adopted by groups and which become established in social systems such as organisations. Work on social defence systems was pioneered by Jaques, a Kleinian psychoanalyst.

Super-ego

A notion of Freud's which relates to unconscious self-judgement. Super-ego mechanisms are mobilised when uncertainty in a situation evokes memories of having been a 'bad' child, of having failed in the eyes of parents. The perceived external threat is linked with a feeling of worthlessness, as though good people would or should never face such a threat (Hirschhorn 1988).

Transference

An unconscious process in which emotions related to a significant relationship are transferred onto another relationship, thus promoting the transfer of feelings held about one person onto another person.

Transitional objects/experience

Concept developed by Winnicott. A transitional object is one to which a young child can relate as a 'not me' object, and which thus acts as a bridge between the states of being psychologically merged in another person and being separate from and in relationship with another person. The transitional object, such as a soft toy, stands *for* a relationship to a key adult, and *between* the child and the key adult. The child projects onto the transitional object the good relationship s/he has with a key adult and so feels protected by the transitional object in the absence of the key adult. This gradually helps the child to develop the ability to hold in mind those images and feelings associated with the key adult, and so to feel confident to extend his/her independence.

BIBLIOGRAPHY

Achenbach, T.M. and Edelbrock, C. (1983) *Manual for the Child Behaviour Checklist and Revised Child Behaviour Profile*, Vermont: University of Vermont.

Adair, J. (1986) *Effective Teambuilding*, London: Pan.

Adams, T. (1986) 'Holding and the Shadow – Holding On', unpublished paper given at a conference organised by the ILEA Schools Psychological Service, London.

Adamson, E. (1984) *Art as Healing*, London: Coventure.

Ainscow, M. (1989) 'How Should We Respond to Individual Needs?', in Ainscow, M. and Florek, A. (eds), *Special Educational Needs: Towards a Whole-School Approach*, London: Fulton.

Ainscow, M. (1991) 'Effective Schools for All: An Alternative Approach to Special Needs', in Ainscow, M. (ed.), *Effective Schools for All*, London: Fulton.

Ainscow, M. and Florek, A. (1989) 'A Whole School Approach', in Ainscow, M. and Florek, A. (eds), *Special Educational Needs: Towards a Whole-School Approach*, London: Fulton.

Ainsworth, M.D.S. (1967) *Infancy in Uganda: Infant Care and the Growth of Attachment*, Baltimore: Johns Hopkins University Press.

Allan, J. (1988) *Inscapes of the Child's World: Jungian Counselling in Schools and Clinics*, Dallas: Spring.

Anderson, J. (1988) *Thinking, Changing, Re-arranging: Improving Self-Esteem in Young People*, Portland, Oregon: Metamorphous.

Appignanesi, R. (1979) *Freud for Beginners*, London: Writers and Readers.

Argyris, C. (1985) 'Defensive Routines', in Pugh, D.S. (ed.) *Organization Theory*, Harmondsworth: Penguin.

Ashton-Warner, S. (1980) *Teacher*, London: Virago.

Association of Educational Psychologists (1992) Press release, 21 January.

Aubrey, C. (1990) 'An Overview of Consultation', in Aubrey, C. (ed.) *Consultancy in the UK: Its Role and Contribution to Educational Change*, Basingstoke: Falmer Press.

Audit Commission/HMI (1992) *Getting in on the Act*, London: HMSO.

Avens, R. (1984) *The New Gnosis*, Dallas: Spring.

Axline, V. (1971) *Dibs, In Search of Self*, Harmondsworth: Penguin.

Axline, V. (1989) *Play Therapy*, Edinburgh: Churchill Livingstone.

Bachelard, G. (1969) *The Poetics of Space*, Boston: Beacon.

Bachelard, G. (1971) *The Poetics of Reverie: Childhood, Language and the Cosmos*, Boston: Beacon.

Bachelard, G. (1987) *The Psychoanalysis of Fire*, London: Quartet.

Baldwin, J. and Wells, H. (1979) *Active Tutorial Work, Books 1–5*, Oxford: Blackwell.

Bales, R.F. (1950) *Personality and Interpersonal Behaviour*, New York: Holt, Rinehart and Winston.

Ball, S. (1990) *Politics and Policy Making in Education and Explorations in Policy Sociology*, London: Routledge and Kegan Paul.

Ballard, J. (1982) *Circlebook*, New York: Irvington.

Barrett, M. and Trevitt, J. (1991) *Attachment Behaviour and the Schoolchild: An Introduction to Educational Therapy*, London: Routledge.

Baumann, D. (1989) 'The Soul of the Giant', lecture to the Analytical Psychology Club of London.

Becker, H.S. (1963) *Outsiders*, New York: Free Press.

Bennathan, M. (1992) 'The Care and Education of Troubled Children', *Therapeutic Care and Education*, 10, 1: 37–49.

Berger, M.L. and Berger, P.J. (eds) (1972) *Group Training Techniques*, Aldershot: Gower Press.

Bettelheim, B. (1978) *The Uses of Enchantment: The Meaning and Importance of Fairy Tales*, Harmondsworth: Penguin.

Bion, W.R. (1989) *Experiences in Groups and Other Papers*, London: Routledge.

Blackham, H.J. (1978) 'The Concept of Autonomy', in Blackham, H.J. (ed.), *Education for Personal Autonomy: An Enquiry into the School's Resources for Furthering the Personal Development of Pupils*, London: Bedford Square Press.

Blanchard, P. (1946), 'Psychoanalytic Contributions to the Problems of Reading Disabilities', *Psychoanalytic Study of the Child*, 2: 163–87.

Blishen, E. (1969) *The School that I'd Like*, Harmondsworth: Penguin.

Booth, T. and Coulby, D. (eds) (1987) *Producing and Reducing Disaffection*, Milton Keynes: Open University Press.

Bowers, T. (1989) 'From Support to Consultancy', in Bowers, T. (ed.) *Managing Special Needs*, Milton Keynes: Open University Press.

Bowlby, J. (1980) *Attachment and Loss*, London: Hogarth.

Bowlby, J. (1988) *A Secure Base: Clinical Applications of Attachment Theory*, London: Routledge.

Box, S. (1978) 'Teacher–Child Inter-action as a Basis for Understanding Disturbances of Children at School', in Blackham, H.J. (ed.), *Education for Personal Autonomy: An Enquiry into the School's Resources for Furthering the Personal Development of Pupils*, London: Bedford Square Press.

Bridger, H. (1991) 'Consultation', presentation to the Advanced Course in Consultation to Individuals, Groups and Organisations, Tavistock Centre for Human Relations, London.

Brockbank, J.P. (1971) '"Pericles" and the Dream of Immortality', in Muir, K. (ed.), *Shakespeare Survey, Vol. 24*, Cambridge: Cambridge University Press.

Bruce, T. (1983) 'The Management of Anxiety', lecture to the ILEA Schools Psychological Service Counselling Course, Dartford.

Brunner, J.S. (1980) 'Possible Castles', paper delivered at the Gordon Mills Lecture, Austin, University of Texas.

Buckley, J. and Styan, D. (1988) *Managing for Learning*, London: Macmillan.

Button, L. (1974) *Developmental Group Work with Adolescents*, London: University of London Press.

Button, L. (1981) *Group Tutoring for the Form Tutor, Book 1*, London: Hodder and Stoughton.

Button, L. (1982) *Group Tutoring for the Form Tutor, Book 2*, London: Hodder and Stoughton.

Campbell, J. (1968) *The Hero with a Thousand Faces*, Princeton: Princeton University Press.

Campbell, J. (1969) *The Flight of the Wild Gander: Explorations in the Mythological Dimension*, Chicago: Gateway.

Campbell, J. (1974) *The Mythic Image*, Princeton and Guildford: Princeton University Press.

Canfield, J. and Wells, H.L. (1976) *100 Ways to enhance Self-concept in the Classroom*, Englewood Cliffs: Prentice-Hall.

Capra, F. (1982) *The Turning Point: Science, Society and the Rising Culture*, London: Fontana.

Cartledge, G. and Milburn, J.F. (eds) (1986) *Teaching Social Skills to Children: Innovative Approaches*, Oxford: Pergamon.

Case, C. and Dalley, T. (eds) (1990) *Working with Children in Art Therapy*, London: Tavistock/Routledge.

Casement, P. (1990) *Further Learning from the Patient: The Analytic Space and Process*, London: Tavistock/Routledge.

Caspari, I. (1976) *Troublesome Children in Class*, London: Routledge and Kegan Paul.

Caspari, I. (1980) 'Play and Learning', *Therapeutic Education*, 8, 1, 12–19.

Chilsholm, B., Kearney, D., Knight, G., Little, H., Morris, S. and Tweedle, D. (1986) *Preventative Approaches to Disruption: Developing Teaching Skills*, London: Macmillan.

Chodorow, J. (1991) *Dance Therapy and Depth Psychology: The Moving Imagination*, London and New York: Routledge.

Claxton, G. (1989) *Being a Teacher*, London: Cassell.

Cline, T. (1990) 'Developments in the Identification and Assessment of SEN: A Review', paper given at the International Special Education Congress, Cardiff.

Coch, L. and French, J.R.P. (1948) 'Overcoming Resistance to Change', *Human Relations*, 1, 512–32.

Colman, A.D. (1992) 'Depth Consultation', in Stein, M. and Hollwitz, J. (eds), *Psyche at Work: Applications of Jungian Analytical Psychology*, Wilmette, Illinois: Chiron.

Conoley, J.C. (1981) 'The Process of Change: The Agent of Change', in Conoley, J.C. (ed.), *Consultation in Schools: Theory, Research, Procedures*, New York and London: Academic.

Cooper, J.C. (1978) *An Illustrated Encyclopaedia of Traditional Symbols*, London: Thames and Hudson.

Coulby, D. and Harper, T. (1985) *Preventing Classroom Disruption*, London: Croom Helm.

Cox, M. (1990) 'The Group as Poetic Playground: From Metaphor to Metamorphosis', Foulkes Lecture to the Group Analytic Society, London.

Cox, M. and Theilgaard, A. (1987) *Mutative Metaphors in Psychotherapy – The Aeolian Mode*, London and New York: Tavistock.

Croll, P. and Moses, D. (1985) *One in Five: The Assessment and Incidence of Special Educational Needs*, London: Routledge and Kegan Paul.

Currie, H. (1990) 'Making Texts more Readable', *British Journal of Special Education*, 17, 4: 137–9.

Daniels, H. (1992) 'Differentiation', presentation to the Merton, Sutton and Kingston SENIOS Course, London.

Davies, M. and Wallbridge, D. (1990) *Boundary and Space: An Introduction to the Work of D.W. Winnicott*, London: Karnac; New York: Brunner/Mazel.

Day, C., Johnston, D. and Whitaker, P. (1985) *Managing Primary Schools*, London: Harper and Row.

De Board, R. (1978) *The Psychoanalysis of Organisations: A Psychoanalytic Approach to Behaviour in Groups and Organisations*, London and New York: Tavistock/Routledge.

De Board, R. (1983) *Counselling Skills*, Aldershot: Wildwood House.

Dennison, B. and Kirk, R. (1990) *Do, Review, Learn, Apply: A Simple Guide to Experiental Learning*, Oxford: Blackwell.

Department of Health (1991) *Children in the Public Care. A Review of Residential Child Care*, London: HMSO.

DES (Department of Education and Science) (1978) *Special Educational Needs (The Warnock Report)*, London: HMSO.

DES (Department of Education and Science) (1985a) *Better Schools*, London: HMSO.

DES (Department of Education and Science) (1985b) *The Curriculum 5 to 16*, London: HMSO.

DES (Department of Education and Science) (1989a) *A Report by HM Inspectors on a Survey of Provision for Pupils with Emotional/Behavioural Difficulties in Maintained and Special Schools and Units*, London: DES.

DES (Department of Education and Science) (1989b) *A Survey of Pupils with Special Educational Needs in Ordinary Schools, 1988–89: A* Report by HMI, London: DES.

DES (Department of Education and Science) (1989c) *Discipline in Schools (The Elton Report)*, London: HMSO.

DES (Department of Education and Science) (1989d) *National Curriculum, From Policy to Practice*, Stanmore: DES.

DES (Department of Education and Science) (1989e) *Personal and Social Education 5–16, Curriculum Matters 14, An HMI Series*, London: HMSO.

DES (Department of Education and Science) (1990) *Special Needs Issues: A Survey by HMI*, London: HMSO.

DES (Department of Education and Science) (1992) *The Education of Very Able Children in Maintained Schools: A Review by HMI*, London: HMSO.

DES (Department of Education and Science) and the Welsh Office (1987) *National Curriculum Test Group on Assessment and Testing, A Report*, London: DES.

DFE (Department for Education)/Welsh Office (1992) *Choice and Diversity*, London: HMSO.

Dockar-Drysdale, B. (1990) *The Provision of Primary Experience: Winnicottian Work with Children and Adolescents*, London: Free Assocation.

Donnington, R. (1963) *Wagner's 'Ring' and its Symbols*, London: Faber and Faber.

Douglas, T. (1978) *Basic Groupwork*, London: Routledge.

Dowling, E. (1985) 'Theoretical Framework: A Joint Systems Approach to Educational Problems with Children', in Dowling, E. and Osborne, E. (eds), *The Family and the School: A Joint Systems Approach to Problems with Children*, London: Routledge and Kegan Paul.

Dowling, E. and Osborne, E. (eds) (1985) *The Family and the School: A Joint Systems Approach to Problems with Children*, London: Routledge and Kegan Paul.

Dreifuss, G. (1988) 'Empathy', in Spiegelman, J.M. (ed.), *Jungian Analysts: Their Visions and Vulnerabilities*, Phoenix, Arizona: Falcon.

Dundas, E. (1978) *Symbols Come Alive in the Sand*, Aptos, California: Aptos Press.

Dunne, E. and Bennett, N. (1990) *Talking and Learning in Groups*, London: Routledge.

Dyke, S. (n.d.) 'Endings', unpublished paper given at a conference organised by the ILEA Schools Psychological Service, London.

Edinger, E.F. (1973) *Ego and Archetype*, Harmondsworth, New York and Ringwood: Penguin.

Edmunds, F. (1979) *Rudolf Steiner Education: The Waldorf Schools*, London: Rudolf Steiner Press.

Egan, K. (1992) *Imagination in Teaching and Learning*, London: Routledge.

Ellis, A. (1962) *Reason and Emotion in Psychotherapy*, New York: Lyle Stuart.

Eraut, M., Nash, C., Fielding, D. and Attard, P. (n.d.) *Flexible Learning in Schools*, London: Employment Department.

Erikson, E. (1977) *Childhood and Society*, London: Paladin.

Estrada, P., Arsenio, W.F., Hess, R.D. and Holloway, S.D. (1987) 'Affective Quality of the Mother–Child Relationship: Longitudinal Consequences for the Children's School-relevant Cognitive Functioning', in *Developmental Psychology*, 23, 2: 210–15.

Everard, B. and Morris, G. (1990) *Effective School Management*, London: Paul Chapman.

Feiler, A. and Thomas, G. (1992) 'Special Educational Needs, Past, Present and Future', in Thomas, G. and Feiler, A. (eds), *Planning for Special Needs: A Whole-School Approach*, Hemel Hempstead: Simon and Schuster.

Ferenczi, S. (1916) *Contributions to Psychoanalysis*, Boston: Richard Badger.

Ferguson, M. (1982) *The Aquarian Conspiracy*, London: Paladin.

FEU/Training Agency/Skill (1989) *Learning Support*, Oxford: Opus.

Fordham, M. (1969) *Children as Individuals*, New York: G.P. Putnam's Sons.

Foukes, S.H. and Anthony, E.J. (1984) *Group Psychotherapy, the Psychoanalytical Approach*, London: Karnac.

Fraiberg, S. (1968) *The Magic Years*, London: Methuen.

Freud, A. (1968) *The Ego and Mechanisms of Defence*, London: Hogarth.

Freud, S. (1933) *New Introductory Lectures on Psychoanalysis*, Standard Edition, Vol. 22. London: Hogarth Press and Institute of Psychoanalysis.

Frude, N. and Gault, H. (1984) *Disruptive Behaviour in Schools*, Chichester: John Wiley.

Fullan, M. (1985) 'Change Processes and Strategies at the Local Level', *The Elementary School Journal*, 85, 3: 391–421.

Fullan, M. (1988) 'Change Processes in Secondary Schools: Towards a More Fundamental Agenda', mimeo, University of Toronto.

Fullan, M. (1991) *The New Meaning of Educational Change*, London: Cassell.

Galloway, D. (1981) *Teaching and Counselling: Pastoral Care in Primary and Secondary Schools*, London: Longman.

Galloway, D. (1990) 'Elton and School Support', presentation to an INSET series organised by Hackney LEA School Support Service, London.

Galloway, D. and Goodwin, C. (1987) *The Education of Disturbing Children*, London: Longman.

Galton, M. and Williamson, J. (1992) *Groupwork in the Primary Classroom*, London: Routledge.

Gardiner, J. (1991) 'More than Happy to go to the Wall', *Times Educational Supplement*, 11 January.

Gendlin, E.T. (1981) *Focussing*, New York: Bantam.

George, D. (1991) 'NACE Conference Keynote Lecture: Overview of the Conference and Future Challenges', presentation to the conference of NACE, University of East Anglia.

Ginott, H. (1961) *Group Psychotherapy with Children: The Theory and Practice of Play Therapy*, New York: McGraw-Hill.

Glatter, R. (1989) 'Introduction: Coping with a New Climate', in Glatter, R. (ed.) *Educational Institutions and their Environments: Managing the Boundaries*, Milton Keynes: Open University Press.

Gleeson, D. (ed.) (1987) *TVEI and Secondary Education: A Critical Appraisal*, Milton Keynes: Open University Press.

Gordon, T. (1974) *TET: Teacher Effectiveness Training*, New York: Widen.

Graham, P. and Rutter, M. (1970) 'Identification of Children with Psychiatric Disorder', in Rutter, M., Tizard, J. and Whitmore, K. (eds) *Education, Health and Behaviour*, London: Longman.

Gray, J. and Richer, J. (1988) *Classroom Responses to Disruptive Behaviour*, London: Macmillan.

Green, H. (1964) *I Never Promised You a Rose Garden*, London: Pan.

Greenfield, T.B. (1989) 'Organisations as Social Interventions', in Bush, T. (ed.), *Managing Education: Theory and Practice*, Milton Keynes: Open University Press.

Greenhalgh, P. (1987) 'The Holding/Letting Go Dialectic as a Factor in the Recovery of Learning', *Maladjustment and Therapeutic Education*, 5, 3: 37–43.

Greenhalgh, P. (1988) 'The Discovery of Learning Through Involvement with the Imaginal', *Journal of Educational Therapy*, 2, 2: 45–58.

Greenhalgh, P. (1991a) 'Working with Groups: The Functions of the Group in Work with Children Experiencing Emotional and Behavioural Difficulties', *Maladjustment and Therapeutic Education*, 9, 1: 28–32.

Greenhalgh, P. (1991b) 'The Creative Tension of Separation and Integration: Processes in Support Provision for Children with Emotional and Behavioural Difficulties', *European Journal of Special Needs Education*, 6, 3: 177–84.

Griffiths, M. (1993) 'Records of Achievement: Empowerment and the Transition', paper given at the conference, 'Valuing Continuing Achievement', South East Records of Achievement, Sutton, Surrey.

Grubb Institute (1991) *Professional Management*, London: Grubb Institute.

Hall, E. and Hall, C. (1988) *Human Relations in Education*, London: Routledge.

Hall, E.F. (1992) 'Assessment for Differentiation', *British Journal of Special Education*, 19, 1: 20–3.

Hall, G. and Hord, S. (1987) *Change in Schools*, New York: State University.

Hamacheck, D.E. (1978) *Encounters with the Self*, New York: Holt, Rinehart and Winston.

Handy, C. (1985) *Understanding Organisations*, London: Penguin.

Handy, C. (1989) *The Age of Unreason*, London: Arrow.

Handy, C. and Aitken, R. (1986) *Understanding Schools as Organisations*, London: Penguin.

Hanko, G. (1990) *Special Needs in Ordinary Classrooms*, 2nd edn, Oxford: Blackwell.

Hanko, G. (1991) 'Breaking Down Professional Barriers', *Maladjustment and Therapeutic Education*, 9, 1: 3–15.

Hannah, B. (1981) *Encounters with the Soul: Active Imagination as Developed by C.G. Jung*, Santa Monica: Sigo.

Hardy, B. (1975) *Tellers and Listeners: The Narrative of Imagination*, London: Athlone.

Hargreaves, D., Hestor, S.K. and Mellor, F.J. (1975) *Deviance in Classrooms*, London: Routledge and Kegan Paul.

Hargreaves, D.H. (1982) *The Challenge of the Comprehensive School: Culture, Curriculum and Community*, London: Routledge and Kegan Paul.

Hargreaves, D.J. (1989) *Children and the Arts*, Milton Keynes: Open University Press.

Harland, J. (1987) 'The TVEI Experience', in Gleeson, D. (ed.), *TVEI and Secondary Education: A Critical Appraisal*, Milton Keynes: Open University Press.

Hart, S. (1992) 'Differentiation – Way Forward or Retreat?', *British Journal of Special Education*, 19, 1: 10–12.

Heap, K. (1965) 'The Scapegoat Role in Youth Groups', *Case Conference*, 12: 215–21.

Hendrick, D. (1989) 'Endings', presentation to conference of ILEA Tutorial Class Service, Aylesford.

Heron, J. (1976) 'A Six Category Intervention Analysis', *British Journal of Guidance and Counselling*, 2, 14, 3–155.

Hersh, R.H., Paolitto, D.P. and Reiner, J. (1979) *Promoting Moral Growth – From Piaget to Kohlberg*, London: Longman.

Higgin, H. and Bridger, H. (1965) *The Psychodynamics of an Inter-Group Experience*, Tavistock Pamphlet No. 10, London: Tavistock.

Higgins, R. (1990) 'Emotional and Behavioural Difficulties (EBD): Some General

Points', in Varma, V.P. (ed.), *The Management of Children with Emotional and Behavioural Difficulties*, London: Routledge.

Hillman, J. (1967) *Insearch: Psychology and Religion*, Dallas: Spring.

Hillman, J. (1979) *The Dream and the Underworld*, New York: Harper and Row.

Hillman, J. (1985) *Anima, An Anatomy of a Personified Notion*, Dallas: Spring.

Hinson, M. (1991) 'Aspects of Coping with Change', in Hinson, M. (ed.), *Teachers and Special Educational Needs: Coping with Change*, Harlow: Longman in association with NARE.

Hirschhorn, L. (1988) *The Workplace Within: Psychodynamics of Organizational Life*, Cambridge, Massachusetts, and London: MIT Press.

Hitchcock, G. (1988) *Education and Training 14–18: A Summary of Major Initiatives*, London: Longman.

Hobson, R.F. (1985) *Forms of Feeling*, London: Tavistock.

Holt, J. (1965) *Why Children Fail*, Harmondsworth: Penguin.

Hopkins, D. (1991) 'Changing School Culture through Development Planning', in Riddell, S. and Brown, S. (eds), *School Effectiveness Research: Its Messages for School Improvement*, Edinburgh: HMSO.

Hornby, G. (1990) 'A Modular Approach to Training', *British Journal of Special Education*, 17, 4: 156–61.

Horney, K. (1949) *Our Inner Conflicts*, London: Routledge and Kegan Paul.

Horney, K. (1951) *Neurosis and Human Growth*, London: Routledge and Kegan Paul.

Horwitz, L. (1981) 'Projective Identification in Dyads and Groups', in Colman, A.D. and Bexton W.H. (eds), *Group Relations Reader, Vol. 2*, Sausalito, California: A.K. Rice Institute.

Hoy, W.K. and Miskel, C.G. (1989) 'Schools and their External Environments', in Glatter, R. (ed.), *Educational Institutions and their Environments: Managing the Boundaries*, Milton Keynes: Open University Press.

Hunt, J. and Hitchin, P. (1985) *Projects*, Lancaster: Framework.

ILEA (Inner London Education Authority) (1982) *Keeping the School under Review: Special Schools*, London: ILEA.

ILEA (Inner London Educational Authority) (1984) *Improving Secondary Schools (The Hargreaves Report)*, London: ILEA.

ILEA (Inner London Education Authority) (1985) *Educational Opportunities for All? A Report of the Committee Reviewing Provision to Meet Special Educational Needs*, London: ILEA.

ILEA (Inner London Education Authority) (1989) *The National Curriculum: A Planning Guide for Primary Schools*, London: ILEA.

Jacobs, M. (1982) *Still Small Voice: An Introduction to Pastoral Counselling*, London: SPCK.

Jacoby, M. (1990) *Individuation and Narcissism: The Psychology of Self in Jung and Kohut*, London and New York: Routledge.

Jaques, E. (1951) *The Changing Culture of a Factory*, London: Tavistock.

Jaques, E. (1955) 'Social Systems as a Defense against Persecutory and Depressive Anxiety', in Klein, M., Heimann, P. and Money-Kyrle, R. (eds), *New Directions in Psychoanalysis*, London: Tavistock.

Jenkin, F. (1989) *Making Small Groups Work*, Oxford: Pergamon.

Johnson, J., Rasburg, W. and Siegel L. (1986) *Approaches to Child Treatment: Introduction to Theory, Research and Practice*, Oxford: Pergamon.

Jones, K. (1987) *The Consultant Teacher – Special Educational Needs*, Stratford upon Avon: National Council for Special Education.

Jordan, J. (1974) 'The Organisation of Perspectives in Teacher–Pupil Relations: An Interactionist Approach', unpublished M.Ed. Thesis, University of Manchester.

Jung, C.G. (ed.) (1964) *Man and His Symbols*, London: Aldus.

Jung, C.G. (1966) *The Practice of Psychotherapy*, Collected Works, Vol. 16, London: Routledge and Kegan Paul.

Jung, C.G. (1970) *Mysterium Coniunctionis*, Collected Works, Vol. 14, London: Routledge and Kegan Paul.

Jung, C.G. (1971) *Psychological Types*, Collected Works, Vol. 6, London: Routledge and Kegan Paul.

Jung, C.G. (1973a) *Experimental Researches*, Collected Works, Vol. 2, London: Routledge and Kegan Paul.

Jung, C.G. (1973b) *Letters I (1906-1950)*, London: Routledge and Kegan Paul.

Jung, C.G. (1977) *Memories, Dreams, Reflections*, Glasgow: Collins.

Jung Institute San Francisco (1981) *Sandplay Studies: Origins, Theory and Practice*, San Francisco: C.G. Jung Institute of San Francisco.

Kakabadse, A., Ludlow, R. and Vinnicombe, S. (1988) *Working in Organisations*, Harmondsworth: Penguin.

Kalff, D.M. (1980) *Sandplay: A Psychotherapeutic Approach to Psyche*, Santa Monica: Sigo.

Kelly, A.V. (1989) *The Curriculum: Theory and Practice*, London: Paul Chapman.

Kelly, G.A. (1955) *The Psychology of Personal Constructs*, New York: Norton.

Khaleelee, O. and Miller, E. (1985) 'Beyond the Small Group: Society as an Intelligible Field of Study', in Pines, M. (ed.), *Bion and Group Psychotherapy*, London: Routledge.

Killeen, J. (1993) 'Linking Pastoral and SEN Systems', paper given to the Merton LEA course, 'Management and Consultancy Skills to Meet Special Educational Needs', Merton, 3 March.

Klein, M. (1946) 'Notes on Some Psychoid Mechanisms', *International Journal of Psychoanalysis*, 27: 99–110.

Kohlberg, L. (1976) 'Moral Stages in Moralisation: The Cognitive Developmental Approach', in Lickona, T. (ed.), *Moral Development and Behaviour: Theory, Research and Social Issues*, New York: Holt, Rinehart and Winston.

Kolb, D.A. (1984) *Experiential Learning – Experience as the Source of Learning and Development*, Englewood Cliffs, New Jersey: Prentice Hall.

Kounin, J.S., Friesen, W.V. and Norton, E. (1966) 'Managing Emotionally Disturbed Children in Regular Classrooms', *Journal of Educational Psychology*, 57: 1–13.

Kutnick, P.J. (1988) *Relationships in the Primary Classroom*, London: Paul Chapman.

Kyriacou, C. (1991) *Essential Teaching Skills*, Oxford: Blackwell.

Langham, M. and Parker, V. (1988) *Counselling Skills for Teachers*, Lancaster: Framework.

Laslett, R. (1982) *Maladjusted Children in the Ordinary School*, Stratford upon Avon: National Council for Special Education.

Laslett, R. (1983) *Changing Perceptions of Maladjusted Children 1945–1981*, Association of Workers for Maladjusted Children.

Lee, H. (1963) *To Kill a Mockingbird*, Harmondsworth and Ringwood: Penguin.

Leech, N. and Wooster, A.D. (1986) *Personal and Social Skills, A Practical Approach for the Classroom*, Exeter: RMEP.

Lewin, K. (1948) 'Experiments in Social Space', in Lewin, G.W. (ed.), *Resolving Social Conflict*, New York: Harper and Bros.

Liebmann, M. (1986) *Art Therapy for Groups: A Handbook of Themes, Games and Exercises*, London: Routledge and Brook Line.

London Borough of Merton (1991) *L.E.A. Guidelines on the Formulation and Review of Whole School Policy for Special Educational Needs*, London: London Borough of Merton.

McCaslin, N. (ed.) (1975) *Children and Drama*, London: David McKay.

McConkey, R. (1985) *Working with Parents: A Practical Guide for Teachers and Therapists*, London: Croom Helm.

Maggs, P. (1987) 'Working with Behaviour Problems: Growth through Work', unpublished paper given at a conference for staff working in ILEA boarding schools for children with emotional and behavioural difficulties, London, May.

Maggs, P. (1989a) 'The Seeds of Discontent', unpublished paper given at the Caldecott Community, Ashford, November.

Maggs, P. (1989b) 'D&T', unpublished paper given at Tutorial Class Teachers' Annual Residential Conference, Maidstone, October.

Marc, O. (1977) *Psychology of the House*, London: Thames and Hudson.

Marris, P. (1986) *Loss and Change*, London: Routledge and Kegan Paul.

Maslow, A.H. (1943) 'A Theory of Human Motivation', *Psychological Review*, 50: 370–96.

Maslow, A.H. (1954) *Motivation and Personality*, New York: Harper and Row.

Matte Blanco, I. (1975) *The Unconscious as Infinite Sets: An Essay in Bi-logic*, London: Duckworth.

Menzies Lyth, I.E.P. (1970) *The Functioning of Social Systems as a Defence Against Anxiety*, London: Centre for Applied Social Research and Tavistock.

Menzies Lyth, I.E.P. (1988) *Containing Anxiety in Institutions*, London: Free Association.

Menzies Lyth, I.E.P. (1989) *The Dynamics of the Social*, London: Free Association.

Merton, R. (1968) *Social Theory and Social Structure*, London: Collier and Macmillan.

Miles, M. (1990) 'Art as a Pathless Land', in Usher Gallery and Radcliffe Press (eds) *The Journey*, Lincoln: Lincolnshire County Council Recreation Services.

Miller, A. (1985) *Thou Shalt Not be Aware: Society's Betrayal of the Child*, London and Sydney: Pluto.

Miller, E.J. and Rice, A.K. (1967) *Systems of Organisation*, London: Tavistock.

Milner, M. (1971) *On Not Being Able to Paint*, Oxford: Heinemann.

Mitchell, G. (1989) 'Community Education and the School: A Commentary', in Glatter, R. (ed.), *Education Institutions and their Environments: Managing the Boundaries*, Milton Keynes: Open University Press.

Mongan, D. and Hart, S. (1989) *Improving Classroom Behaviour: New Directions for Teachers and Pupils*, London: Cassell.

Montgomery, D. and Rawlings, A. (1987) *Classroom Management*, Leamington Spa: Scholastic.

Moore, J. and Morrison, N. (1988) *Someone Else's Problem? Teacher Development to Meet Special Educational Needs*, London: Falmer Press.

Morrison, K. and Ridley, K. (1989) 'Ideological Contexts and Curriculum Planning', in Preedy, M. (ed.), *Approaches to Curriculum Management*, Milton Keynes: Open University Press.

Mortimore, P., Sammons, P., Stoll, L., Lewis, D. and Ecob, R. (1988) *School Matters: The Junior Years*, Wells: Open Books.

Moss Kantor, R. (1983) *The Change Masters*, London: Unwin Hyman.

Murgatroyd, S. and Reynolds, D. (1984), 'Leadership and the Teacher', in Harling, P. (ed.), *New Directions in Educational Leadership*, Lewes: Falmer Press.

Nash, R. (1973) *Classrooms Observed*, London: Routledge and Kegan Paul.

National Curriculum Council (1989a) *Curriculum Guidance 2 – Curriculum for All: Special Educational Needs in the National Curriculum*, York: NCC.

National Curriculum Council (1989b) *Circular No. 5*, York: NCC.

NUT (National Union of Teachers) (1990a) *Special Educational Needs and the National Curriculum*, London: NUT.

NUT (National Union of Teachers) (1990b) *Your School, Local Management of Schools and Special Educational Needs*, London: NUT.

Nelson-Jones, R. (1988) *Practical Counselling and Helping Skills*, London: Cassell.

Neumann, E. (1959) *Art and the Creative Unconscious*, Princeton: Princeton University Press.

Neumann, E. (1973) *The Child, Structure and Dynamics of the Nascent Personality*, London: Karnac.

Nisbet, R.A. (1969) *Social Change and History, Aspects of the Western Theory of Developments*, Oxford: Oxford University Press.

North, R.F.J. (1988) 'Restricted Choice in the Management of Change', *Educational Management and Administration*, 16, 163–71.

Norwich, B. (1990) *Reappraising Special Needs Education*, London: Cassell.

Oakland, J.S. (1989) *Total Quality Management*, Oxford: Butterworth-Heinemann.

Oaklander, V. (1978) *Windows to Our Children – A Gestalt Therapy Approach to Children and Adolescents*, Moab, Utah: Real People Press.

Parkes, C.M. and Stevenson-Hinde, J. (eds) (1982) *The Place of Attainment in Human Behaviour*, London: Tavistock.

Patterson, J., Purkey, S. and Parker, J. (1986) *Productive School Systems for a Nonrational World*, Alexandria, Virginia: Association for Supervision and Curriculum Development.

Perlman, M.S. (1992) 'Toward a Theory of Self in the Group', in Stein, M. and Hollwitz, J. (eds), *Psyche at Work: Workplace Applications of Jungian Analytical Psychology*, Wilmette, Illinois: Chiron.

Peters, T. (1990) *Thriving on Chaos: A Handbook for Management Revolution*, London: Pan.

Peters, T. and Waterman, R. (1982) *In Search of Excellence*, London: Harper and Row.

Piaget, J. and Inhelder, B. (1969) *The Psychology of the Child*, London: Routledge and Kegan Paul.

Pollard, A. (1985) *The Social World of the Primary School*, New York: Holt, Rinehart and Winston.

Postlethwaite, K. and Hackney, A. (1988) *Organising a School's Response: Special Needs in Mainstream Schools*, London: Macmillan.

Preedy, M. (1988) *Managing Schools: Managing Curricular and Pastoral Processes*, Block 3 E325, Milton Keynes: Open University Press.

Quinton, D. (1987) 'The Consequences of Care: Adult Outcomes from Institutional Rearing', *Maladjustment and Therapeutic Education*, 5, 2: 12–17.

Ramasut, A. (1989) *Whole School Approaches to Special Needs*, Lewes: Falmer Press.

Reardon, R.C., Hersen, M., Bellack, A.S. and Folley, J.M. (1979) 'Measuring Social Skill in Grade School Boys', *Journal of Behavioural Assessment*, 1: 87–105.

Redfearn, J. (1985) *My Self – My Many Selves*, London: Academic Press.

Redl, F. (1956) 'The Phenomenon of Contagion and "Shock Effect"', in Eissler, K. (ed.), *Searchlights on Delinquency*, New York: International Universities Press.

Reed, B. and Palmer, B. (1972) *An Introduction to Organisational Behaviour*, Lectures 1, 2 and 3, London: Grubb Institute.

Reed, J.P. (1975) *Sand Magic – Experience in Miniature: A Non-verbal Therapy for Children*, Albuquerque: JPR.

Reinert, H.R. (1976) *Children in Conflict*, New York: C.V. Mosby.

Reynolds, D. (1985) *The Effective School*, Lewes: Falmer Press.

Richardson, E. (1975) 'Selections from "The Environment of Learning"', in Colman, A.D. and Bexton, W.H. (eds), *Group Relations Reader*, Sausalito, California: A.K. Rice Institute.

Rimmer, A. (1992) 'Death of a School', *Therapeutic Care and Education*, 10, 1: 55–9.

Robinson, E. (1991) *The Power of Art*, Guild Lecture No. 236, London: Guild of Pastoral Psychology.

Rogers, C.R. (1942) *Counselling and Psychotherapy*, Boston, Massachusetts: Houghton Mifflin; London: Constable.

Rogers, C.R. (1951) *Client-centred Therapy*, London: Constable.

Rogers, C.R. (1961) *On Becoming a Person*, London: Constable.

Rogers, C.R. (1978) *Carl Rogers on Personal Power*, London: Constable.

Rogers, C.R. (1983) *Freedom to Learn for the 80's*, New York: Charles E. Merrill.

Rollinson, R. (1992) 'Myths We Work by', *Therapeutic Care and Education*, 10, 1: 3–22.

Roose-Evans, J. (1987) *Inner Journey, Outer Journey*, London: Rider.

Rosenthal, R. and Jacobson, L. (1968) *Pygmalion in the Classroom*, New York: Holt, Rinehart and Winston.

Rothenberg, A. (1979) *The Emerging Goddess*, Chicago: Chicago University Press.

Rustin, M. and Rustin, M. (1987) *Narratives of Love and Loss: Studies in Modern Children's Fiction*, London: Verso.

Rutter, M., Maughan, B., Mortimore, P. and Ouston, J. (1979) *Fifteen Thousand Hours*, London: Open Books.

Ryce-Menuhin, J. (1987) 'The Gifted Child', paper given at the Conference of the Guild of Pastoral Psychology, 3 September.

Ryce-Menuhin, J. (1988) *The Self in Early Childhood*, London: Free Association.

Ryce-Menuhin, J. (1991) *Jungian Sandplay; The Wonderful Therapy*, London and New York: Routledge.

Salmon, P. (1988) *Psychology for Teachers: An Alternative Approach*, London: Hutchinson.

Salmon, P. and Clare, H. (1984) *Classroom Collaboration*, London: Routledge and Kegan Paul.

Salzberger-Wittenberg, I., Henry, G. and Osborne, E. (1983) *The Emotional Experience of Learning and Teaching*, London: Routledge and Kegan Paul.

Sambrooks, J.E. (1990) 'Behavioural Approaches to the Management of Children with Emotional and Behavioural Difficulties', in Varma, V.P. (ed.), *The Management of Children with Emotional and Behavioural Difficulties*, London: Routledge.

Samuels, A. (1985a) 'Symbolic Dimensions of Eros in Transference–Countertransference: Some Clinical uses of Jung's Alchemical Metaphor', *International Review of Psychoanalysis*, 12: 199–214.

Samuels, A. (ed.) (1985b) *The Father, Contemporary Jungian Perspectives*, London: Free Association.

Samuels, A., Shorter, B. and Plaut, F. (1986) *A Critical Dictionary of Jungian Analysis*, London: Routledge and Kegan Paul.

Sardow, S., Stafford, D. and Stafford, P. (1987) *An Agreed Understanding*, Windsor: NFER/Nelson.

Schaffer, R. (1977) *Mothering*, Glasgow: Fontana.

Schein, E.H. (1969) *Process Consultation*, Reading, Massachusetts: Addison-Wesley.

Sen, G. (1988) 'Space: Concept and Meaning', *Mirmar*, 27, 60–3.

Shaw, A. and Evans, M. (n.d.) *Working with Groups*, London: HEC/TACADE.

Shipman, M. (1990) *In Search of Learning: A New Approach to School Management*, Oxford: Blackwell.

Shorter, B. (1987) *An Image Darkly Forming*, London: Routledge and Kegan Paul.

Sikes, P. and Taylor, M. (1987) 'Some Problems in Defining, Interpreting and Communicating Vocational Education', in Gleeson, D. (ed.), *TVEI and Secondary Education, A Critical Appraisal*, Milton Keynes: Open University Press.

Skinner, B.F. (1973) *Beyond Freedom and Dignity*, Harmondsworth: Penguin.

Spillman, J. (1991) 'Decoding Differentiation', *Special Children*, 44: 7–10.

Steiner, R. (1965) *The Education of the Child*, London: Rudolf Steiner Press.

Stevens, A. (1986) *Withymead, a Jungian Community for the Healing Arts*, London: Coventure.

Stevens, W. (1952) *Collected Poems*, New York: Alfred A. Knopf; London: Faber and Faber.

Stewart, N. (1989) 'Curriculum Experience and Structured Partnership', in Sayer, J. and Williams V. (eds), *Schools and External Relations*, London: Cassell.

Stott, D.H. and Marston, N.C. (1971) *Bristol Social Adjustment Guides*, Sevenoaks: Hodder and Stoughton.

Storr, A. (1989) *Solitude*, London: Fontana.

Stradling, R. and Saunders, L. (1991) *Differentiation in Action*, London: HMSO.

Strubel, R. (1983) 'Individuation and the Group', in Beebe, J. (ed.), *Money, Food, Drink and Fashion and Analytical Training: Depth Dimensions of Physical Existence. The Proceedings of the 80th International Congress for Analytical Psychology*, Dallas: Spring.

Thomas, G. and Feiler, A. (1988) *Planning for Special Needs: A Whole-school Approach*, Oxford: Blackwell.

Thomas, G.V. and Silk, A.M.J. (1990) *An Introduction to the Psychology of Children's Drawings*, Hemel Hempstead: Harvester Wheatsheaf.

Thompson, D. and Barton, L. (1992) 'The Wider Context: A Free Market', *British Journal of Special Education*, 19, 1: 13–15.

Tomlinson, P. and Kilner, S. (n.d.) *The Flexible Learning Framework and Current Educational Theory*, Sheffield: Employment Department.

Tourquet, P.M. (1974) 'Leadership: The Individual and the Group', in Gibbard, G.S., Mann, R.D. and Hartman, J.J. (eds), *Analysis of Groups*, London: Jossey-Bass.

Training Agency/FEU/Skill (1989) *Learning Support: A Staff Development Resource Pack for Those Working with Learners who have Special Needs*, Sheffield: Training Agency.

Trowell, J. (1990) 'The Development Perspective', presentation to the Advanced Course in Consultation to Individuals, Groups and Organisations, The Tavistock Clinic, October.

Tuby, M. (1988) 'Groups – Kinship and Consciousness', *Telarius*, 1, 2.

Tuckman, B.W. (1965) 'Developmental Sequence in Small Groups', *Psychological Bulletin*, 63: 384–99.

Turner, V. (1974) *Dramas, Fields and Metaphors: Symbolic Action in Human Society*, London: Cornell University Press.

Ullman, L. and Krasner, K. (1965) *Case Studies in Behaviour Modification*, London: Holt, Rinehart and Winston.

Underwood Report (1955) *Report on the Committee of Maladjusted Children*, London: HMSO.

University of Keele (1992a) *Education Management: Managing Teaching and Learning*, Keele: University of Keele, Inservice Education and Management Unit.

University of Keele (1992b) *Managing Change and Conflict*, Keele: University of Keele, Inservice Education and Management Unit.

University of Nottingham, School of Education (1991) 'Course details: Master of Education, Human Relations', Nottingham: University of Nottingham.

Upton, G. and Cooper, P. (1990) 'The Ecosystemic Approach', *Maladjustment and Therapeutic Education*, 8, 1: 3–18.

von Franz, M.L. (1980) *Alchemy – An Introduction to the Symbolism and the Psychology*, Toronto: Inner City Books.

von Franz, M.L. (1982) *Interpretation of Fairy Tales*, Dallas: Spring.

Warnock, M. (1977) *Schools of Thought*, London: Faber and Faber.

Watkins, C. (1989) 'The Caring Functions', in Sayer, J. and Williams, V. (eds), *Schools and External Relations*, London: Cassell.

Watkins, C. and Wagner, P. (1987) *School Discipline: A Whole School Approach*, Oxford: Blackwell.

Watson, L. (1986) 'The Loser and the Management of Change', *School Organization*, 6, 1: 101–6.

Watzlawick, P., Weakland, J. and Fisch, R. (1974) *Change: Principles of Problem Formulation and Problem Resolution*, New York and London: W.W. Norton and Co.

Weick, K. (1976) 'Educational Organizations as Loosely-coupled Systems', *Administrative Science Quarterly*, 21: 1–19.

Weightman, J. (1992) 'Effecting Change in Schools: Working in the Organisation', in Thomas, G. and Feiler, A. (eds), *Planning for Special Needs: A Whole School Approach*, Hemel Hempstead: Simon and Schuster.

Weiner, G. (ed.) (1985) *Just a Bunch of Girls*, Milton Keynes: Open University Press.

Weinrib, E.L. (1983) *Images of the Self: The Sandplay Therapy Process*, Santa Monica: Sigo.

Wells, L. (1981) 'The Group-as-a-whole Perspective and its Theoretical Roots', in Colman, A.D. and Bexton, W.H. (eds), *Group Relations Reader, Vol. 2*, Sausalito, California: A.K. Rice Institute.

Weston, P. (1992) 'A Decade for Differentiation', *British Journal of Special Education*, 19, 1: 6–9.

Whileshire, B. (1982) *Role-playing and Identity: The Limits of Metaphor*, Bloomington: Indiana University Press.

Whitaker, D.S. (1985) *Using Groups to Help People*, London and New York: Tavistock/Routledge.

White, M. (1989) 'Magic Circle', *Times Educational Supplement*, 30 June.

Wickes, F.C. (1977) *The Inner World of Childhood*, London: Coventure.

Widlake, P. (1986) *Reducing Educational Disadvantage*, Milton Keynes: Open University Press.

Williams, A. (1991) *Forbidden Agendas: Strategic Action in Groups*, London and New York: Tavistock/Routledge.

Williams, V. (1989) 'Schools and their Communities: Issues in External Relations', in Sayer, J. and Williams, V. (eds), *Schools and External Relations*, London: Cassell.

Wilson, M. (1983) *Stories for Disturbed Children*, Stratford upon Avon: National Council for Special Education.

Winnicott, D.W. (1964) *The Child, the Family and the Outside World*, London and Harmondsworth: Penguin.

Winnicott, D.W. (1965) *The Family and Individual Development*, London: Tavistock; New York: Basic Books.

Winnicott, D.W. (1970) 'Basis for Self in Body', in Winnicott, D.W. (ed.), *Psychoanalytic Explorations*, London: Karnac.

Winnicott, D.W. (1974) *Playing and Reality*, London: Pelican.

Winnicott, D.M. (1975) *Collected Papers: Through Pediatrics to Psychoanalysis*, London: Hogarth.

Winnicott, D.W. (1984) *The Maturational Processes and the Facilitating Environment*, London: Hogarth.

Witty, G. and Menter, I. (1991) 'The Progress of Restructuring', in Coulby, D. and Bash, L. (eds), *Contradiction and Conflict: The 1988 Act in Action*, London: Cassell.

Wolfendale, S. (1983) *Parental Participation in Children's Development and Education*, New York: Gordon and Breach.

Woods, P. (ed.) (1980) *Pupil Strategies: Explorations in the Sociology of the School*, London: Croom Helm.

Wright, K.J.T. (1976) 'Metaphor and Symptom: A Study of Integration and its Failure', *International Review of Psychoanalysis*, 3: 97–109.

Yardley, A. (1970) *Senses and Sensitivity*, London: Evans.

Zinkin, L. (1991) 'The Klein Connection in the London School: The Search for Origins', *Journal of Analytical Psychology*, 36: 37–61.

Zukav, G. (1979) *The Dancing Wu Li Masters: An Overview of the New Physics*, London: Fontana.

INDEX

abuse 10, 59, 66–72, 75–6, 82, 84, 147, 162
acting out 49, 52, 54, 81, 108, 112, 126, 130, 136, 187, 192, 305
action-planning 234–5, 238–9
adolescence 29, 111, 134, 246
anxiety–risk ratio 231, 233, 239
archetypes 152, 154, 305
assessment: of child–family interaction 101–4; of child–peer interaction 99–103; of child–school interaction 101, 103; of child's subjective experiences 104–6; of child–teacher interaction 97–9, 102–3; curriculum-based 232–5; diagnostic models 96–7; examples of 55, 57–9, 68, 69, 73, 144, 147–8, 149, 158–63, 164
attachment 33–7, 43, 49, 71, 72, 126–8; anxious avoidant 36; anxious resistant 36; secure attachment 34–6
authority (within school/organisation) 277–81
auxiliary ego 109, 134, 167

basic assumption groups 202–5
beginnings 123–6, 209
behaviourism 3, 9, 243, 305
boundaries: and defences 50, 54; for emotional containment and stability 110–16, 120, 123, 137, 176–9, 207; group boundary control 215–16; and limits 52, 73, 99, 111–14, 123, 186; of the organisation 290–3, 299; personal boundaries 86, 173, 176–9, 188

Bowlby: and abuse 59, 75; and abused parents 72; and attachment 33–7, 49–50, 127; loss, anxiety and anger 126; potential pathways 10; secure base 108–9; and super-ego 76–7
bullying 55, 69, 81, 271

case examples of work with children: Alan 92–3; Carol 153, 192; Carrie 69–70; Darren 57–9; Dave 157–62; George 165, 194; Ishret 144; Jason 164–5; Jenny 162–3; John 55, 68–9, 95, 119, 120, 153, 192; Joshua 60–1; Kelvin 39–42; Mary 73–4, 149–50; Matthew 169–70; Melissa 146–7; Peter 147–9, 169–70; Richard 52–3, 146, 194; Simon 293–4; Sonya 145; Terry 112, 193, 194; Thomas 184–5; Tyron 116
circle-time 171
classroom management 56, 138, 216, 224–6, 249–51
collective unconscious 149–50, 305
communication blocks 45–9, 51, 77, 179; see also defences; social defences
confidentiality 174, 176, 178–9, 187, 215
consultation 281–90
contagion in groups 201
co-operative learning 196, 229, 235–6
counselling 172–88
countertransference 90
culture: and endings 127; and ethos 101; reparative 268–70; school effectiveness and change 255, 275–6